DARK TROPHIES

Dark Trophies

Hunting and the Enemy Body in Modern War

Simon Harrison

berghahn
NEW YORK · OXFORD
www.berghahnbooks.com

Published in 2012 by

Berghahn Books
www.berghahnbooks.com

©2012, 2014 Simon Harrison
First paperback edition published in 2014

All rights reserved. Except for the quotation of short passages for the purposes of criticism and review, no part of this book may be reproduced in any form or by any means, electronic or mechanical, including photocopying, recording, or any information storage and retrieval system now known or to be invented, without written permission of the publisher.

Library of Congress Cataloging-in-Publication Data

Harrison, Simon, 1952–
  Dark trophies : hunting and the enemy body in modern war / Simon Harrison.
    p. cm.
  Includes bibliographical references and index.
  ISBN 978-0-85745-498-0 (hardback : alk. paper) – ISBN 978-1-78238-520-2 (paperback : alk. paper) – ISBN 978-0-85745-499-7 (ebook)
  1. Military trophies–History. 2. Military history, Modern. I. Title.
  D214.H36 2012
  355.02074–dc23

                                              2011044384

British Library Cataloguing in Publication Data

A catalogue record for this book is available from the British Library.
Printed in the United States on acid-free paper.

ISBN:978-1-78238-520-2 paperback
ISBN: 978-0-85745-499-7 ebook

To my wife Ayfer

When their enemies fall [the Gauls] cut off their heads ... and these first-fruits of battle they fasten by nails upon their houses, just as men do, in certain kinds of hunting, with the heads of wild beasts they have mastered.
(Diodorus of Sicily, Book V. Trans. C.H. Oldfather)

[I]f Culture is the Subject's nature, then *Nature is the form of the Other as body*, that is, as the object for a subject. Culture takes the self-referential form of the pronoun 'I'; nature is the form of the non-person or the object, indicated by the impersonal pronoun 'it'.
(Viveiros de Castro 1998: 478)

Contents

Acknowledgements		ix
Introduction:	Dark Trophies of Enlightened War	1
Chapter 1	Schemas and Metaphors	11
Chapter 2	Hunting and War: The European History of a Metaphor	21
Chapter 3	Bodies and Class in the Age of Revolution	31
Chapter 4	The European Enlightenment and the Origins of Scalping	39
Chapter 5	Skulls and Science	49
Chapter 6	The Collecting Expedition as a Magical Quest	59
Chapter 7	Skulls and Scientific Collecting in the Victorian Military	69
Chapter 8	From Hero to Specimen: Phrenology, Craniology and the American Indian Skull	83
Chapter 9	Ethnology, Race and Trophy-hunting in the American Civil War	93
Chapter 10	Museums and Lynchings: Bodies and the Exhibition of Order	107
Chapter 11	Savages on the Frontiers of Europe	117
Chapter 12	Skull Trophies of the Pacific War	129
Chapter 13	Transgressive Objects of Remembrance	141
Chapter 14	The Colonial Manhunt and the Body Parts of Bandits: Hunting Schemas in British Counter-insurgency	155

Chapter 15	Kinship and the Enemy Body in the Vietnam War	165
Chapter 16	Returning Memories	177
Conclusion		187
Bibliography		197
Index		229

Acknowledgements

I thank the Economic and Social Research Council for the award of a grant (RES-062-23-0567) which allowed me a three-year period of full-time research in which to prepare this book. Early versions of some of the chapters were presented as seminars to social anthropologists at the following universities: Brunel, Cambridge, Edinburgh, Oxford, St Andrews, Queens University Belfast, University College London and the Australian National University. I thank the members of those seminars for their useful comments.

I am grateful to the publishers of *Comparative Studies in Society and History*, *Journal of Material Culture* and *Journal of the Royal Anthropological Institute* for allowing this book to include materials which appeared originally in a number of earlier articles (Harrison 2006, 2008a, 2010).

Many individuals have assisted with the preparation this book either by commenting on drafts of chapters, by guiding me through often unfamiliar research literatures or by providing ethnographic and historical information. Two anonymous readers for Berghahn Books saved the book from many errors. I would also like particularly to thank the following: Ramazan Altintas, Robert Balcomb, Chris Ballard, Ronnie Gamble, Harrell Gill-King, Ken Gillings, John Harries, Robin Hide, Arnold Howard, Ron Locke, Erik Lyman, Dereyk Patterson, Keiko Tamura, Emiko Ohnuki-Tierney, Danielle Trussoni, Barbara Wavell, Mark Wells, Geoffrey White and Carl Zipperer.

Introduction

Dark Trophies of Enlightened War

Combat Stress and the Enemy Dead

Ever since the emergence of professional standing armies in early modern Europe, military personnel have been expected to treat the bodies of the enemy dead honourably. Of course, such courtesies have at times been extended almost exclusively to enemies of high rank. Nevertheless, there are standards of civilized behaviour in war which forbid the soldier to maltreat the dead body of an enemy. To mutilate or desecrate corpses on the battlefield, or to collect and keep body parts, as some indigenous societies practised in the form of scalping or headhunting, would seem thoroughly malicious and reprehensible to military personnel and civilians alike. These sorts of behaviour, together with other stereotypically primitive practices such as cannibalism and human sacrifice, comprise the stock Western image of savagery.

When international humanitarian law began to develop in the second half of the nineteenth century, it formalized these norms and made the maltreatment of enemy remains illegal. The Geneva Conventions of 1949 directed that the war dead be identified and buried in marked and properly maintained graves so as to permit their repatriation after hostilities have ended. The Conventions also defined looting or despoiling of dead bodies as war crimes and required that steps be taken to ensure that the personal effects of the dead return to their next of kin. Military authorities view maltreatment of the dead on the part of their personnel in the same way as other violations of the laws of war, such as torture or the killing of prisoners. That is, they regard them as not only wrong but counterproductive in almost all circumstances, because they undermine support for the war effort at home, strengthen the determination of the enemy, and put their own side at risk of reprisals.

To the extent to which the causes of this type of misconduct have been investigated at all, the maltreatment of enemy remains is generally considered a type of deviance, or a symptom of a transient psychological disorder, brought about by the stresses of battle. When these stresses are prolonged and intense they can lead individuals to make abnormal decisions, or to engage in acts which appear aberrant in peacetime. Service personnel who refer in their memoirs to having witnessed or carried out such misconduct often account for it in this way in retrospect, as a symptom of the extreme psychological pressures experienced by soldiers in warfare, on account of traumatic events such as the death of comrades (see, for instance, Sledge 1981).

In the United States Army, maltreatment of enemy dead is currently viewed, in a similar way, largely within the framework of abnormal psychology. Military psychologists have developed a classification in which the behavioural symptoms of combat stress fall into two main types. On the one hand, stress in battle can give rise to positive or adaptive reactions such as acts of heroism and self-sacrifice, heightened loyalty to comrades and tolerance of hardship. These can contribute to a soldier's successful performance of his role. There are also negative or maladaptive reactions to combat stress. These dysfunctional reactions comprise, first, a group of behavioural disorders called battle fatigue, which includes depression, anxiety and exhaustion, among other symptoms. The maladaptive responses also include a second group of reactions called misconduct stress behaviours. These range from forms of indiscipline such as self-injury, alcohol and drug abuse, and fraternization between ranks, to serious criminal offences such as murdering prisoners or non-combatants, torture, rape, looting, and murdering one's superiors (Ritchie et al. 2008; United States Department of the Army 2003).

The *U.S. Army Combat Stress Control Handbook* outlines fifteen or so offences as examples of misconduct stress behaviours. One of them is the mutilation of enemy dead, which it describes as follows:

> **4-6. The Misconduct Stress Behavior of Mutilating Enemy Dead**
> a. This practice has been prohibited by civilized nations as a violation of the Law of Land Warfare but may still be approved in some regions of the world. Collecting scalps, ears, gold teeth, and so forth as trophies can still become common practice (as in the island battles of the Pacific in WWII) as signs of racial hatred and dehumanization against a stubborn and merciless enemy.
> b. Leaving deliberately mutilated bodies (especially with facial and genital mutilation) for the enemy to find is less common, but also occurs as bitterness increases. Despoiling or pillaging the dead is, of course, a war crime and is punishable by court-martial.
>
> **Note**
> Mutilating the dead must be prohibited, since it dehumanizes both those who do it and those who condone it. It tends to provoke reprisals, alienate world and home front opinion, and contribute to guilt and post-traumatic stress symptoms when the soldier returns home (United States Department of the Army 2003: 60; see also United States Department of the Army 1994).

According to army psychiatric doctrine, stress reactions need to be rapidly identified, and preventative measures taken, on the grounds that they can become the psychiatric syndrome known as post-traumatic stress disorder if they are left untreated (United States Department of the Army 2003: 91–102). A study of veterans of the Vietnam War has offered support for this view, finding an association between participation in acts such as mutilation of the dead and the later development of this disorder (Hiley-Young et al. 1995).

Of course, military psychiatry and military law recognize that misconduct is not always caused by combat stress, and that war crimes can be committed by soldiers who have never been exposed to such stresses and simply possess 'antisocial norms' or deviant personality characteristics. In military law, combat stress is therefore not a defence in criminal cases, but evidence of extreme stress can be an extenuating factor when setting punishments (United States Department of the Army 2003: 63).

Mutilation of dead bodies seems, then, to be recognized in the military as a recurrent type of misconduct, but a common consensus among military psychiatrists, soldiers and civilians is that it is in most cases a temporary behavioural disorder related to stress in battle. Such assumptions have led some authors to suggest that these practices can occur in any society in times of violent conflict, and in this sense are universal, although they have been socially permissible only in some societies and periods of history (see, for instance, Chacon and Dye 2008).

Aims and Methodology

As we saw, the *U.S. Army Combat Stress Control Handbook* identifies two motives for the ill-treatment of the dead. In some cases, soldiers have disfigured bodies and left them for the enemy to find, with the aim of terrorizing or demoralizing the enemy. More commonly, the *Handbook* states, the dead have been mutilated for 'trophies'. In this book, I explore the history and meaning of this latter practice, an aberrant form of collecting which I will call military trophy-taking.

Most of the material on which I draw relates to Britain, France, Germany, South Africa, Australia and the United States, and specifically to their colonial histories. Very little is known of the prevalence of trophy-taking in the armed forces of these or other states in wartime, nor of the meaning it might have to those who engage in it. It is certain, however, that behaviour of this sort has occurred among a small minority of soldiers over the past century or two in European and North American armed forces, just as have other violations of wartime norms, despite the regulations forbidding them and the condemnation of the majority of service personnel (Bourke 1999; Bryant 1979: 298-303).

I focus in this way on trophy-taking partly because this enables me to supplement soldiers' accounts of such behaviour with other kinds of supporting evidence. War veterans sometimes refer in their memoirs to having witnessed or perpetrated such acts, and much of the material I discuss in this book comes from sources such as these. However, there are certain methodological problems associated with the use of veterans' memories of war experiences. In many cases, events are described many years after they occurred, and it is often impossible independently to corroborate these recollections, as A. Young (1995) observed in his study of veterans of the Vietnam War undergoing treatment for post-traumatic stress disorder.

However, independent evidence of the occurrence of trophy-taking in the armed forces comes from a number of sources, including museology and forensic anthropology. A subfield of forensic anthropology deals specifically with the identification and analysis of human remains, usually skulls or crania, brought home illegally by military personnel mostly from the Pacific War and Vietnam War (Bass 1983; Gill-King 1992; Maples and Browning 1995: 27–29; Sledzik and Ousley 1991; Taylor, Roh and Goldman

1984; Valentin and Miller 2004; Willey and Leach 2003). These publications contain photographs and illustrations of such remains, which it would be gratuitous to reproduce here. This book refers to a number of photographic images of this sort, all but one of which are in the public domain, and their sources are clearly indicated for the benefit of readers who wish to view them. Some human remains appropriated as war mementos have also found their way into museum collections. In recent years, archaeology and museology have faced demands by indigenous peoples for the return of ancestral remains some of which are known to have originated as battlefield souvenirs collected by nineteenth-century colonial soldiers (Harrison 2008a; Riding In 1992a, 1992b; Thomas 2000).

In short, military trophy-taking is an activity which generates material objects, and some of these have continued to circulate, and to be used for a variety of different purposes, long after the end of the conflicts in which they originated. Some of these objects have had long and complex post-war social lives, to borrow Appadurai's (1986) term, quite independent of their military origins, and their peacetime careers are in some respects their most important and significant attributes. Such objects not only constitute forensic evidence of trophy-taking, but the many uses to which they may be put after they are taken from the enemy dead also call for examining.

Trophy-taking and Race

A further reason I restrict my subject matter specifically to military trophy-taking is so that I may take advantage of some of the methods and perspectives developed in anthropological studies of indigenous warfare. There is, of course, a substantial ethnographic literature concerned with societies in which the taking of heads or other body parts as trophies was a normal and socially acceptable accompaniment of warfare. In some societies it was a central element of warfare, and enemy body parts had an important ritual value and could be carefully preserved, treasured and exchanged. Anthropologists have interpreted such practices by relating them to their social and cultural context; for instance, to indigenous understandings of masculinity, fertility or power (Harrison 1993; Hoskins 1996a). Unfortunately, the types of warfare fought by the professional militaries of modern states have tended implicitly to appear by contrast as technical, impersonal and instrumentally rational activities moderated by law. I hope this book will show such dichotomies to be misleading. An adequate understanding of military trophy-taking requires exploring the ways in which it is embedded in the wider milieus in which it occurs. As we will see, important keys to its explanation are to be found in anthropological studies of the cultural symbolism of warfare in indigenous societies.

In the chapters that follow, it will become evident that the history of this practice has been linked inseparably with the history of racism since the emergence of concepts of race in the second half of the eighteenth century. A striking feature of military trophy-taking from that period onwards is that it has been carried out, at least among European and North American military personnel, almost exclusively against enemies whom they have represented as belonging to 'races' other than their own. Among these personnel, it has almost always occurred as a specifically racialized form of violence, and could arguably be considered a type of racially motivated hate crime specific to military personnel in wartime. Despite its illegality, it is nevertheless an expression of ideologies which have enjoyed wide acceptance and legitimacy over much of the past two centuries.

This, then, appears to be an unusual and distinctive type of war crime, in that military personnel almost never commit it against enemies they perceive as belonging to their own 'race'. Soldiers who have perpetrated this offence appear to have drawn a marked distinction between two categories of enemy: those they perceive as belonging to their own race, and those perceived as belonging to another, with the key difference between them lying in the ways their bodies could be treated after death.

In the cultural backgrounds of soldiers who commit these offences, there appear to be strongly internalized prohibitions against maltreating the remains of racially close enemies. These learned inhibitions appear powerfully effective in themselves, so much so that they do not require policing or external sanctions even in the most stressful and bitter conflicts. Military trophy-taking therefore seems to be evidence of an important, but perhaps insufficiently recognized, feature of ideologies of race: namely, that they intuitively structure attitudes and behaviour towards the dead body. It would be surprising if they did not, because they are, after all, ideologies which naturalize social inequalities by misrepresenting them as founded in the physical body and in human biology. The bodies of those whom one accepts as members of one's own 'race' therefore appear in certain key respects sacrosanct, even when they are one's enemies in war. These co-racial enemies may certainly be fought and killed in battle, but after death it seems their bodies become inviolable.

Expeditionary Trophy-taking and the Metaphor of the Hunt

In this respect, military trophy-taking has a number of striking similarities with a pattern of trophy-taking described by anthropologists in some indigenous Amazonian, Southeast Asian and Melanesian societies. This pattern, which I will call expeditionary trophy-taking, has as its key feature a sharply defined distinction between close and distant enemies, in which people regard only their close enemies as fully human or akin in nature to themselves. McKinley (1976) provides an insightful and succinct account of what I call expeditionary trophy-taking, though he does not employ this term. In this pattern, it is perfectly permissible to kill close enemies, but it is forbidden to take the heads of people so close to home. Heads or other body parts are taken only from enemies who are socially (and perhaps also geographically) remote and classified as semi-human or subhuman, or as denizens of the wild. The Iban of Borneo, for instance, practised headhunting against distant strangers whom they called by a term translatable as 'not-people' (McKinley 1976: 108). In New Guinea, the Marind-Anim, who called themselves *anim-ha*, or real humans, took heads only from non-Marind, the *ikom-anim*, or strangers, whom the Marind seem to have regarded as subhuman, existing only to serve as victims for their annual headhunting expeditions (Van Baal 1966: 676–96). Among the Jivaro of Ecuador, too, the people from whom heads were taken were 'generally total strangers. One immutable rule of head-hunting is that its victims must be Jivaros, but Jivaros of a different tribe with whom no known links of kinship exist, who speak a different dialect and whose patronyms are unknown' (Descola 1996: 275).

This, then, is a pattern in which trophies are taken only from members of a culturally defined category of strangers or foreigners, on territory away from home. Often, the expedition is represented as a sacred, ritualized journey or quest. In this respect, it has features in common with pilgrimage, and even with certain forms of tourism (cf. Graburn 1989, 2000; Nash 1989; Pannell 1992). As we will see, it has significant commonalities in particular with what has come to be known as 'dark tourism' or thanatourism, involving journeys to sites of death (Lennon and Foley 2004; Sharpley and Stone 2009). As a personal mission to bring relics home to family and kin as symbols of achievement and success, a trophy-taking expedition often has the character of a rite of passage into manhood (see McKinley 1976).

Raiding of this sort is also often equated with the hunting of animals, though metaphors of fishing or harvesting are sometimes employed as well, perhaps together with tropes of hunting (Davison and Sutlive 1991; Harner 1972: 186, 189; Hoskins 1996b: 23). Expeditionary trophy-taking seems to occur only in societies in which men, or most men, hunt and hunting is understood as an iconically male pursuit. In effect, cultural models of predation or, more broadly, of consumption, are extended into the domain of warfare, and used as models on which violence towards members of a socially constructed category of remote enemies can be patterned.

In short, this is a form of warfare in which certain categories of enemies are strongly dehumanized or depersonalized, and represented as animal quarry, not merely to be killed but also, in some sense, consumed. In the mythology of the Asmat people of western New Guinea, the ancestors instituted the practice of headhunting as a replacement for the hunting of wild pigs, so that human game became a substitute for animal game (Zubrinich 1999). Similar conceptions seem to have been held by the Mundurucu in Brazil, who carried out headhunting raids of up to a thousand miles against outsiders whom they looked upon as game animals to be hunted for sport (Murphy 1957: 1026).

Competing Representations

Expeditionary trophy-taking is connected, then, with social classifications in which a group of people represent certain other groups as subhuman or animal-like, belonging perhaps to the realm of nature, or to the wild. But to view it simply as a reflection of these categorizations would be a misinterpretation. Rather, the warmaking is a key part of a system of social practices by which such classifications are sustained and reproduced. When men in these societies take trophies from distant enemies, they do not do so because they classify these enemies literally as animals, any more than those indigenous peoples who metaphorize trophy-taking as fishing or harvesting think their enemies are fish or vegetables. Expeditionary trophy-taking is a cultural practice, distinctive to some kinds of societies in which men hunt animals, in which the humanness of some chosen category of people is masked or denied.

In some societies which practised this type of warfare, such as the Melanesian community of Avatip (see Harrison 1993), it was rare in practice for fighters to take the heads of strangers. Much more commonly, the attackers and the victims were all too closely connected by clanship and kinship, and the assailants' purpose was, as it were, to make their victims distant, to generate estrangement and produce a category of people as enemies with whom to fight. At Avatip, an essential part of the preparation for headhunting raids was the performance of special rituals and magic by the hereditary war-magicians. These symbolic acts temporarily suspended the fighters' normal identities, and placed them in a dangerous state of ritual potency in which the fighters were said to have become the hunting dogs of their war-magicians. In this transformed condition, they were unaccountable and potentially homicidal to anyone else, not only to their victims but even to their own wives and children.

These ritual practices suspended and denied the fighters' normal relations with their victims, and replaced them with predatory violence. In this way social actors created group boundaries, at least for a certain period, and thus, in a sense, brought the groups themselves into provisional existence. In war, they attributed to themselves and their opponents a less than fully human status – the role of hunter and his dogs on the one hand, and of quarry on the other. But this was predicated on an underlying assumption of their natural mutual kinship and relatedness, an assumption which required special ritual acts to suspend it. It could not be suspended permanently, because normal ties of sociability were always in the end regenerated. Ritualized warfare and headhunting in societies such as Avatip, then, did not simply express a particular scheme of social classifications, but involved the contextual activation of some schemes and the temporary abrogation of other, contrary ones. These forms of violence involved acts of social reclassification or counter-classification in conflict with models of sociality characteristic of non-ritual contexts. Powerful cultural metaphors equated warfare with hunting, but these were also at odds with other understandings of sociality, and together these formed an arena of competing representations (Harrison 1985, 1989, 1993, 2005).

Colonial Metaphors of Hunting and War

I argue in this book that the misconduct stress behaviour of mutilating enemy dead for trophies and the practices of ritualized warmaking I have just outlined are in a certain sense the same phenomenon under different names. They are outward expressions of powerful and compelling underlying metaphors in which war is represented as similar to the hunting of animals, metaphors which play in both cases a role in creating and maintaining fundamental social boundaries.

Although military trophy-taking might seem a rare and obscure form of deviance, it is significant for social theory because it offers important evidence of the power of metaphor in structuring and motivating human behaviour. A theory associated with the cognitive linguist George Lakoff proposes that metaphor is a powerful influence on thought and action, and that human reasoning takes place largely in terms of cognitive or conceptual metaphors. These are analogies which enable the mind to build up representations of complex domains of knowledge by using as scaffolding other domains that have a simpler, more familiar or more easily grasped conceptual structure. Drawing on these ideas, I discuss in the following chapter what I call metaphors of social practice. These are conceptual metaphors in which one form of social behaviour is understood and experienced partly in terms of another, or one domain of social existence is made to lend meaning and coherence to a second. I argue that representations of war as a hunt are a widespread social practice metaphor in which cultural models connected with the hunting of animals are projected or transferred into the context of warfare and shape behaviour there.

Chapter Two then traces the history of this metaphor in European military cultures from the Middle Ages up to the colonial period. In European societies, hunting was long considered an essential part of military training and education, and for centuries the military retained a strong tradition of hunting as a recreation, certainly among its higher-ranking personnel. In the cultures of early modern Europe a dichotomy also emerged between civilized war, which aspired to be both rational and humane, and primitive war, which was characterized by dark, irrational practices such as cannibalism and headhunting. Such savage customs were often compared to the instinctual behaviour of predatory animals such as wolves or bears. Savages were therefore peoples who could be understood as doubly animal-like: first, because of the natural ferocity they were understood to manifest and, second, because they were - in the eyes of some colonial soldiers - legitimate objects of trophy-hunting and similar forms of savagery themselves. This second sort of savage violence, or counter-violence, could be justified as reprisal for the first.

In Chapters Three and Four, I discuss relations between eighteenth-century Europeans and American Indians in this light, showing how both groups drew upon the domain of human violence towards animals for their cultural models of human violence. I explore some of the ways in which this underlying commonality between them influenced the frontier conflicts in North America at the time. In particular, I argue that it led to settler militia groups developing forms of reprisal and atrocity derived partly from Indian practice, and partly from the collecting practices of Enlightenment natural science.

I said earlier that military trophy-taking has been closely connected with the emergence of concepts of race. The particular forms taken by this misconduct seem in fact to have changed over time in accordance with changing understandings of race. In Chapters Five and Six I focus on the second quarter of the nineteenth century, when evidence began to appear of the collection and use of human skulls as war mementos in the Euro-American militaries. I show how this was closely connected with developments in Victorian medicine, psychology and anthropology in which the collection, measurement and classification of skulls became central to scientific understandings of human difference.

One of the key rituals of conquest and domination in the culture of nineteenth and early twentieth-century colonialism was the hunting of native game animals for trophies. Many colonial soldiers, particularly officers, were predisposed to view war as a sort of blood sport or game hunt, equating their indigenous enemies with animals (Cartmill 1993; Ritvo 1987). Chapter Seven discusses the use of human skulls as war mementos and trophies by nineteenth-century British soldiers in Africa. At one level, such treatment of the enemy dead was of course repugnant to most Victorians, evoking images of primitive headhunting. However, I argue that these practices of trophy-taking emerged through an appropriation of developments in science in which significant human differences – between the deviant and normal, between the criminal and the law-abiding, and between races – were increasingly assumed to be expressed in the skull, in variations in its shape and supposed degree of development. Aberrant and atavistic though these colonial military practices appeared to many contemporaries, they were local expressions of the growing transnational authority and prestige of scientific rationality.

I explore these topics further in Chapter Eight, in relation to the collection and study of American Indian crania by nineteenth-century phrenologists and craniologists in the United States. In Chapter Nine I discuss the collection and use of enemy skulls and other bones as trophies by soldiers and their supporters in the American Civil War. Although this practice was condemned by many at the time as the behaviour of 'savages', I argue that it was, again, a local symptom of the shifts taking place after the Enlightenment in the ways in which human diversity was conceptualized.

In the next two chapters, I discuss the internalization of colonial hunting imagery: that is, the use of such imagery in representing racial divisions within the colonial nation itself. First, Chapter Ten examines the role of hunting imagery in racial spectacle lynchings in the southern United States in the late nineteenth and early twentieth centuries. Chapter Eleven focuses on the symbolism of racial boundaries in the European theatres of the two world wars. It discusses the controversial employment of non-white soldiers by France and Britain in their wars with Germany, and also shows how some of the atrocities of Nazi racial science drew upon collecting practices long established on the colonial frontiers, applying them to the establishment of racial boundaries at home.

The remaining chapters of the book discuss the conditions under which enemy body parts are treated as war trophies, and the uses to which these objects may be put after the war, focussing on the Pacific War, the British counter-insurgency wars in Malaya and Kenya, and the Vietnam War. In all of these conflicts, military trophy-taking was related to highly racialized perceptions of the enemy, and the pervasiveness of hunting imagery in the ways these wars were represented and experienced.

Powerful and compelling cultural schemas associating masculinity, war and hunting have thus motivated some servicemen, under certain conditions, to treat enemy remains as trophies. These later chapters also seek to answer a further question such behaviour raises: namely, why the behaviour seems to disappear rapidly from public recollections and commemorations of war, even when it appears to have occurred relatively widely and many service personnel have brought human trophy objects home, or sent them home, to their families as gifts and war mementos. I argue that these memorial objects appear to transgress cultural distinctions between persons and things in such a way as to resist assimilation into the social relations of their collectors and, ultimately, into collective memory.

Between the eighteenth and twentieth centuries, military trophy-taking occurred most often in frontier warfare, and especially in contexts such as jungle warfare, where conditions were such that military operations lent themselves particularly readily to being experienced as a sort of hunting expedition or safari, with the enemy figuring as more like an animal than a human opponent. The history of this form of misconduct is entwined with the history of colonial warfare, against non-European others who could often be viewed as at or beyond the margins of the human.

The practices of soldiers serving in colonial wars thereby sometimes came to resemble those of indigenous peoples for whom expeditionary trophy-taking was a normal and accepted part of war. The use of enemy body parts as war trophies, whether it happens to be defined culturally as an honourable achievement, a stress-related behavioural disorder, a war crime, or in some other way, seems to be motivated by very similar symbolic associations between war and hunting, and between enemies and quarry. It can in principle occur in any conflicts in which such imagery of human predation upon animals plays an important ideological role.

Trophy-taking is therefore neither a hallmark of 'primitive' war, nor a private stress reaction to which fighters everywhere are susceptible in battle. Rather, it is a symbolic practice in which the cognized boundaries between humans and animals, expressed in the activity of hunting, are shifted into the domain of human relations, and made to serve there as a model for violence between social groups. These conceptual transpositions are perhaps most likely to be made by men for whom hunting represents an important component of their social identity. Whether they hunt for subsistence or for recreation does not seem to make much difference. More important is that they conceptualize war and hunting in such a way that they can experience war as a kind of game hunt and also, perhaps, that hunting can appear to them a type of warfare carried out against animals. That is, they understand both activities as violent and deadly contests of power. Incidents of trophy-taking in war may therefore occur among men from such backgrounds whether these practices are socially acceptable or not. Where these acts are unacceptable, as in the armed forces of contemporary nation states, they may appear to be a type of behavioural disorder or misconduct, but they nevertheless originate in the same metaphorical concepts in both cases.

Chapter 1

Schemas and Metaphors

Conceptual Metaphor

Metaphor is more than just a rhetorical ornament of language, or a poetic device. It has often played a vital role in the development of scientific theory. Metaphors of animal and plant breeding, for instance, were crucial to Darwin's understanding of the processes of evolution by natural selection. Evidence from cognitive science suggests that much of human thinking – from routine practical reasoning in daily life to the most abstract forms of mathematical problem solving – may be metaphorical or analogical in nature, rooted in a capacity to perceive correspondences, similar patterns in apparently diverse phenomena (Barnes, Bloor and Henry 1996; Fauconnier and Turner 2002; Gruber and Bödeker 2005; Pramling 2009; Stepan 1993).

Lakoff and Johnson (1980), for instance, argue that the metaphors which pervade everyday speech – idioms such as 'spending' time or 'paying' someone a visit – are surface expressions of conceptual metaphors, deep-rooted analogies with which we structure experience. A pattern of meaning is extended or projected – 'mapped' in Lakoff and Johnson's terminology – from one topic or idea (the metaphor's source domain) to another (the target domain). Typically, the source domain is a relatively concrete, clear, simple or familiar concept. In many cases it corresponds to some aspect of bodily experience, such as movement, direction, containment, force or weight. The target domain, on the other hand, is usually a more abstract, complex, unfamiliar or specialized region of knowledge. Similar metaphors tend to recur in many different languages, because they are ultimately grounded in the universal human experience of embodiment (Lakoff and Johnson 1980; Lakoff 1989, 1993).

To Lakoff and Johnson, then, the way we apprehend experience and reason about it is embedded in metaphor, and metaphor is in turn based in primordial bodily experience (see also Fauconnier and Turner 2002). Of course, this does not imply that all conceptual metaphors have their immediate source in the body. Many of the metaphors which underlie the way people reason and act are mappings between different domains of social action, or different regions of social experience. The conceptual metaphor *argument is war* – manifested in expressions such as 'shooting down' an argument, 'defending' a claim and 'attacking' a point (Lakoff and Johnson 1980: 4) – draws entirely on the world of social relations. Anthropologists would tend to use the term 'cultural metaphors' for concepts such as these, to emphasize that these are not just phenomena of individual psychology but are socially shared and transmitted by cultural learning. They may reflect culturally specific values and beliefs and have their most powerful expression in the symbolism of ritual (Fernandez 1977).

Almost universally we find cultural metaphors which draw upon a small number of core domains – broadly those to do with human reproduction, subsistence and kinship – whose imagery is mapped onto fields of social action such as politics, religion or cosmology (see, for instance, M. Douglas 1966, 1996; Hertz 1960; V. Turner 1967). These fundamental source domains are among the earliest a person usually acquires in his or her psychosocial development. Their conceptual structure is simple and general enough to be applied metaphorically to a wide variety of other domains acquired in later life.

Certain domains may be natural mutual attractors of this sort, with an intrinsic similarity of structure, an inner isomorphism, that draws them towards each other almost inexorably. Sex and eating are perhaps two such domains, with a similar internal structure to do with the gratification of organic drives. The cultural metaphors to which their similarities give rise seem motivated strongly by human neurophysiology and many are probably intelligible universally (Lakoff and Johnson 1980; Leach 2001). In many agrarian societies, complex patterns of cultural symbolism link cultivation with human procreation and child rearing. Children and plants, wombs and fields, sowing and impregnating, are all conceptually equated with each other in certain respects (Fox 1971; Goody 1973; Harrison 1982). This book explores the connections between two cultural domains which are often coupled with each other and resonate in this way, wherever they both occur: namely, hunting and warfare, two forms of armed, organized bloodshed with strong experiential similarities.

Many conceptual metaphors have, then, as their source domain, a social practice, or context of social behaviour, and a second such social domain as their target. So, hunting can serve in this way as a model for warfare, or parenthood as a pattern for government. In cases such as these, one social context is made to stand for another, or a social practice is structured conceptually in terms of another. When social practices are connected in this manner, the roles of source and target may be reversible, and contextual rather than absolute. In other words, such metaphors often work in both directions. Signification flows both ways and the two domains 'interanimate' each other (Stockwell 1999: 129–31).

I will call a mapping of this sort between one form of social behaviour and another a metaphor of social practice. Such metaphors seem to have a close affinity to what social practice theorists such as Bourdieu and Giddens call schemas. According to practice theory, social life consists of recurring situations or contexts which have their own models or patterns of behaviour. Social actors use these schemas, sometimes also called scripts, to recognize, understand and predict the social behaviour of others in a given scenario, and also to generate such situationally appropriate behaviour themselves (Bourdieu 1977; Giddens 1979; Schank and Abelson 1977; Sewell 2005). Schemas are organized hierarchically, containing other, lower-level schemas together with rules regarding the circumstances under which they can be appropriately activated. A schema can thus form part of a larger, higher-level or parent schema.

A person can be imagined as having a sort of portfolio, an organized repertoire, of these models – some relatively specialized and context-specific, others more general and abstract – which guide his or her behaviour without necessarily determining it in detail. To be socially competent is to know schemas to apply appropriately in given situations – including novel and unfamiliar situations – and to switch from one schema to another according to the context, in much the same way that a fluent speaker can shift between different speech registers according to the social setting.

Schemas do not simply guide or constrain social behaviour. More importantly, they enable it in the first place. They permit this productivity because no matter how specific they may be, they can be applied in a range of settings and are not bound exclusively to one, narrowly defined context of use. Giddens, who calls them 'rules', describes them as generalizable procedures (see Sewell 1992). They are formulas for generating action in many different settings. Bourdieu characterizes schemas as 'transposable', a property that gives them a vital role in the performative competence he calls habitus. They allow a social actor to translate a consistent, enduring pattern of sensibilities and dispositions into practice in a wide range of different contexts.

The Limits of Metaphor

I am suggesting that actors, in their models of social action, tend to perceive certain domains of social life as instantiating schemas of social behaviour in exemplary ways. These domains represent reference points, standards to which others more or less closely approximate. So, for instance, competition in the world of politics or business is often described in imagery drawn from the domain of competitive sports such as professional football (Gannon 2001; R.W. Gibbs 1994: 140–42; Howe 1988; Koller 2004; Wakefield 1997). The family may be understood as the epitome of the sorts of social cohesion that should characterize a nation or a workplace (Crawley 2004; Holliday and Letherby 1993; Lakoff 2002; Mandell 2002). In Balinese society, political and status rivalries among men seem to have their purest and most concentrated expression in the sport of cockfighting (Geertz 1973).

These sorts of reference points can help people to improvise appropriate behaviour in complex, fluid, unfamiliar and poorly understood contexts. They do so by allowing people in one situation to act partly as if they were in another situation with a simpler and more clearly defined conceptual structure. For example, a soldier might attempt to deal with the intense stress and confusion of combat by assimilating it conceptually to the simpler, more familiar and more easily comprehended activity of hunting. A person may thus engage in one type of activity while drawing upon the meaning of another. These are metaphors, then, which are not just spoken or thought about but performed and lived.

A social actor's competence must furthermore involve an understanding not only of the generative potential of such metaphors, but also of their limitations and diminishing appropriateness in certain contexts. This is evident from Lakoff and Johnson's discussion of the metaphorical concepts in terms of which sexual desire is understood in U.S. culture. The cognitive domains on which these concepts draw include those of hunger, animality, physical force and war. When Lakoff and Johnson analysed a collection of interviews with men who were attempting to justify rape, they were dismayed and disturbed to find that these rationalizations employed precisely the same set of conceptual metaphors. The basic ideas and folk categories that underlie conventional reasoning about sexual desire, concepts shared by all normal people, women and men alike, in U.S. society, can also lend coherence and reasonableness to behaviour which they themselves would deem highly deviant and abhorrent (Lakoff and Johnson 1980; Lakoff 1989: 412–14).

Clearly, the same cultural metaphors can generate both normal and abnormal behaviour, or have normal and pathological expressions. Or, to put this the other way around, many transgressive forms of behaviour are shaped and motivated by the same cultural metaphors as normal behaviour. They result from socially conventional 'generalizable procedures' (in Giddens' terminology) having been overgeneralized. They are the behavioural manifestations of transposable schemas, as Bourdieu calls them, overextended or transposed beyond their normally accepted scope.

We therefore need to explain why, if much social behaviour can be understood as an outward expression or actualization of shared metaphorical concepts, some of these actualizations are classified as permissible and some are not. In other words, we have to understand how the boundaries of conceptual metaphors are defined in the minds of social actors. A person's competence, or performative fluency, must involve a grasp not only of the generative capacities of the schemas in terms of which he or she acts, but also of the limits of their applicability – if only so that he or she may circumvent these constraints all the more effectively.

Metaphors and Taboos

Metaphors reflect cognitive processes in which two domains of experience are brought together in such a way that one serves as a template with which to comprehend the other. This model of metaphor seems to be in some respects a curious mirror image of a theory in social anthropology concerned with special types of ritual prohibitions and avoidances usually called taboos (M. Douglas 1966). Taboos are prohibitions whose violation provokes reactions of fear, revulsion or disgust, and places the transgressor in a state of impurity or defilement. Just as with conceptual metaphors, the surface expressions of taboos can be linguistic; in this case, they take the form of verbal avoidances and self-censorship. But, again like metaphor, taboo is not exclusively, or indeed primarily, a phenomenon of language but rather of cognition.

According to this view, taboos reflect a special mode of thinking based on a binary, Aristotelian logic. This is a mode of categorization in which class membership depends on the absolute presence or absence of some diacritical feature, and does not allow ambiguity or degree. In effect, taboos are attempts to censor aspects of experience which fail to conform to a scheme of classifications whose logic seeks rigidly to obey the law of the excluded middle. Just as many conceptual metaphors connect domains of social behaviour or interaction, using one as a model for another, many taboos seem intended to do the reverse and keep domains apart. Hence they are especially prevalent in systems of ritual classifications, which tend to be ideologically highly simplified and idealized representations of the ordering of society (Bloch 1989). Such systems may dichotomize people and rank them by value and status, as male or female, insider or outsider, living or dead, human or non-human, ruler or subject, native or foreigner, believer or unbeliever, and so forth, with nothing in between. The innumerable hybrids, marginal cases, third terms and other anomalies to which such schemes give rise are relegated to some residual category of the unclean, unmentionable or conceptually invisible. For this reason, it is more useful to view the role of taboos positively rather than negatively. A system of taboos implies, and supports, a certain way of categorizing experience – in particular social experience – and of ranking things in some hierarchy of social value.

In this respect, both metaphors and taboos seem to be devices for reducing the complexity of experience. The dilemma which experience presents is that it overloads us with information. It requires us to select some of this and bring it to the fore, and to treat the rest as residual or relegate it to the background. Metaphor and taboo seem to represent two complementary strategies for condensing experience or reducing its disorder and complexity. Metaphors simplify by reducing the apprehension of differences, while taboos do so by diminishing the apprehension of similarities.

Let us take as an example the metaphor which occurs in *Proverbs 12:4*, in which a virtuous wife is said to be a crown to her husband. We understand this to mean that a virtuous wife is a credit to her husband and enhances his social standing, as a crown enhances a king. At least, we guess that this is the particular shared attribute the proverb is seeking to make salient and, in doing so, we temporarily set aside all the ways in which we know that wives and crowns are unlike each other. A wife is not made of metal or jewels, is not circular in shape, is not worn on her husband's head, and so forth (cf. Stockwell 1999: 137). We ignore, marginalize or suppress all the obvious and innumerable differences between wives and crowns while we attend to a certain similarity of function which the metaphor seems to be imputing to these two otherwise quite disparate entities. The metaphor, then, brings wives and crowns together in a conceptual relationship in which a single common feature is highlighted, and a large region of difference is set aside (see Figure 1.1).

Taboos, on the other hand, simplify in the opposite way, by suppressing the apprehension of some of the similarities between things and accentuating the differences. Let us take the prohibition of incest, which (in contrast to the metaphor of wives and crowns) establishes from a man's point of view a sort of anti-metaphoric relation between wives and sisters: it defines them as a pair of entities, or rather a pair of social relationships, which must not be thought of in the same way. It defines a wife and a sister as mutually incomparable in a certain respect – namely, that the sister is a first-degree blood relation and the wife is not – and brings this difference conceptually to the fore. But the many important respects in which a wife and sister are alike – that they are both female in their reproductive functions, so that a man could potentially mate and beget children with either or both – are marginalized or suppressed cognitively. So effective is this censorship of likeness that such possibilities usually do not even occur to most normal, properly socialized men. A taboo, then, simplifies the relationships between two regions of experience by filtering out their resemblances or commonalities and highlighting or emphasizing their contrasts and differences. A metaphor draws our attention to correspondences between two ideas, while a taboo attempts to deny or suppress them.

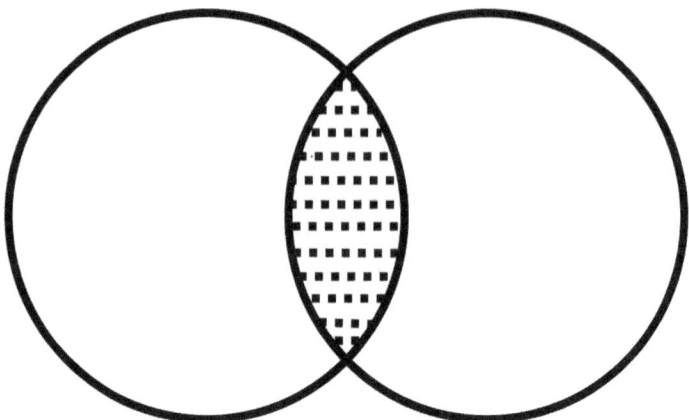

Figure 1.1a Taboo: wife and sister

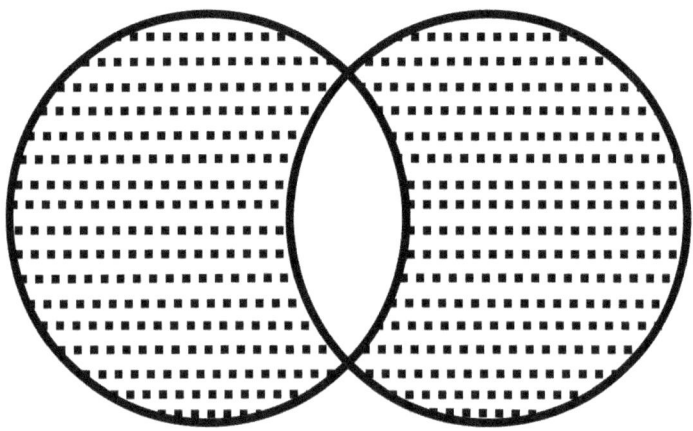

Figure 1.1b Metaphor: wife and crown

The key property that a metaphor and a taboo have in common is that they both relate together two ideas or topics that are apprehended as having an incomplete similarity, a semantic overlap. A metaphor brings the shared attributes to the foreground and pronounces them marked. The differences become mere noise; they represent what Lakoff and Johnson (1980) call the 'unused portion' of the metaphor. In the case of taboo, on the other hand, figure and ground are reversed. The salient features, the focus of attention, are the regions of dissimilarity, while similarities are suppressed or relegated to the background.

Clearly, relations neither of metaphor nor of taboo are likely to form between cognitive domains that lack any semantic common ground. In the Western cultural tradition, and perhaps in many others too, there seems to have been little elaboration of conceptual relationships between cooking and navigation, or dance and law enforcement, or fishing and child rearing. At least part of the probable reason is that these domains tend not to be internally structured in most cultures in ways that make them mutually comparable or facilitate the transposition of schemas from one to the other.

In short, metaphor and taboo are conceptual relationships that emerge only between domains cognized as having certain partial similarities. The central difference between metaphor and taboo lies in the ends to which they put these resemblances. Metaphor utilizes them to connect domains (as source and target, or as prototype and derivative) and taboo uses them to partition and separate them. A metaphor highlights a perceived correspondence between two domains. A taboo attempts to deny a correspondence and make it inexpressible.

In other words, two regions of social experience connected by a conceptual metaphor could just as meaningfully or intelligibly be separated by a taboo, and vice versa. Indeed, the most fundamental and widespread taboos, such as those which disallow incest or the consumption of human flesh, seem to be attempts to prevent the recognition of isomorphisms between certain social practices, or rather between the conceptual schemas which underlie and motivate them. There is a very real homology between the adult brother-sister relationship and adult opposite-sex relations in general, in that they are all potentially sexually reproductive. But this an homology which the incest taboo seems specifically intended to deny. Cultural prohibitions of cannibalism deny, in a similar way, the very obvious fact that human flesh has the same potential dietary uses as animal flesh. Such taboos define regions of social practice which must not even be thought of as alike: the treatment of a dead animal and a dead person, the bond between a brother and sister and between a husband and wife, and so forth. Their effect is to declare certain conceptual metaphors out of bounds, or to keep them from emerging.

A practice normal in one cultural milieu may therefore exist only as a prohibition in another, and one social group's conceptual metaphor may be another's taboo, because they have both arisen from an apprehension of the same underlying resemblances. This may be, in part, the key to our ability to understand the social practices of other cultures no matter how different from our own. Their practices may build upon mappings we ourselves may not utilize, or may forbid, but which are nevertheless recognizable and potentially available to us (Boon 1982). They hold up a sort of mirror to our transgressions, in which we may recognize our own forms of deviance.

Interstitial Practices

Taboos often seem to serve, then, to circumscribe the culturally acceptable limits of metaphors. They restrict the range of practices such metaphors can generate, or inhibit the formation of metaphors in the first place, by defining domain boundaries across which conceptual schemas cannot be transposed, or can be transposed only in some limited ways.

It is as though social practices were arranged in the minds of social actors in a matrix, along one axis of which the boundaries between neighbouring domains are relatively permeable, schemas can be freely transposed or extended, and conceptual metaphors can readily form. Along the other axis, cultural taboos maintain strong boundaries

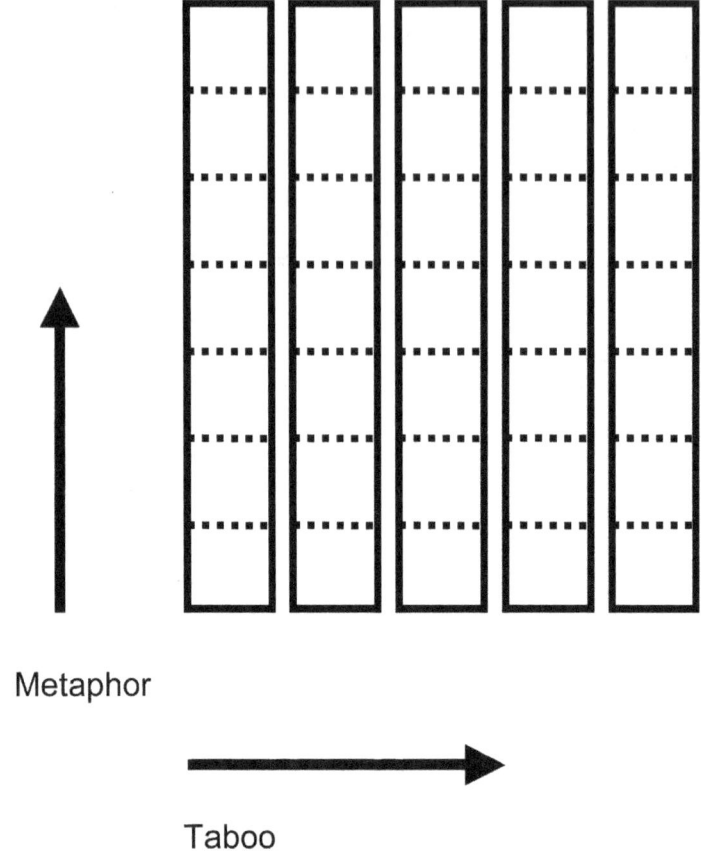

Figure 1.2 Metaphoric and taboo relationships between social practices

between domains, keeping them strictly compartmentalized and distinct (see Figure 1.2). Many unused pathways for mapping social practices onto one another are therefore potentially available to the social actor. A culture at a given point in time represents a selection from a much larger reservoir of possible transpositions.

Of course, social actors do sometimes activate unconventional or forbidden connections between domains. Incest and cannibalism sometimes occur in societies where they are proscribed. I shall call these forms of transgressive behaviour *interstitial practices*. An interstitial practice is a pattern of transgressive activity that arises at the margins, or intersections, of two or more contexts of social action, when interactional schemas or scripts belonging to one of these settings are applied, or rather misapplied, in another neighbouring setting. That is, a schema whose use is normal in one domain is transposed into another where the practices that enact it conflict with a cultural prohibition. Interstitial practices are expressions of censored cultural metaphors, or of cultural metaphors extended beyond their accepted limits.

One characteristic of interstitial practices is a degree of social invisibility. It is not only that such practices tend to be clandestine. There may also be strong public resistance to acknowledging their occurrence, as was the case in Europe historically with incest and with the sexual abuse of children, both of which involve extensions of schemas of sexuality in unacceptable contexts. Interstitial practices are systematically undercognized or 'muted' (Ardener 1975) regions of social behaviour, the dark interstices of institutional domains.

Practices of this sort emerge, then, when schemas proper to a particular social context are used to pattern behaviour in another, and thereby breach some cultural prohibition. This is a type of transgressive behaviour which is not so much abnormal in itself, but arises when schemas perhaps entirely appropriate in one setting are activated in a second setting where they are out of place. Interstitial practices combine different social contexts in ways that seem to subvert their proper boundaries, boundaries which may reflect some fundamental categorical distinctions, such as those between human beings and animals, between permitted and forbidden sexual partners, or between persons and things.

These transgressive behaviours are not mere errors on the part of social actors, due to some individual pathology or failure of socialization. The misapplications of conceptual schemas from which they arise, the activations of these schemas out of context, do not occur randomly but are systematic and provide important clues to the way cultural knowledge is structured and stored in the minds of social actors. Specifically, they are a function of the way that such knowledge is organized in underlying patterns of conceptual metaphors and prohibitions, and are evidence of the key role these patterns play in shaping social behaviour.

Chapter 2

Hunting and War: The European History of a Metaphor

Medieval Europe

The chapters that follow are an attempt to recover the outlines of a history of certain interstitial forms of collecting in Western cultures. These are practices in which schemas concerned with the hunting of animals and with the consumption or use of their remains have been transposed into military contexts. These transpositions, and the practices they generated, form part of a symbolic association between hunting and war with deep roots in European history.

I begin with a short historical overview of this cultural metaphor, taking as my starting point the Middle Ages, a period when hunting and war were closely and very overtly related. They were the two activities most central to the social status of the nobility, and were fundamental to medieval notions of kingship. In England, the stag hunt *par force* – on horseback with hounds – was an essential part of the training and preparation of nobles for war, and a peacetime surrogate for battle. When the king toured the country with his court, he came equipped to hunt on his subjects' lands – estates which they held as his vassals – and his retinue included hundreds of hunting dogs and scores of dog-handlers. The royal itinerary was a display of his military and political power over his subjects, expressed symbolically as a display of the king's prowess as a hunter (Almond 2003; Griffin 2007: 29–31; Marvin 2006: 6–7; Thiébaux 1967).

In war, the nobility distinguished closer and more distant enemies, and different rules of war applied to each. Their close enemies were fellow Christian knights. A knight who killed another in battle had to treat his enemy's body with the honour due to a person of high status. So, for instance, after the Battle of Hastings in 1066, William punished one of his retainers who had hacked at the dead body of Harold with his sword (Stacey 1984: 30). The principle aim of knightly warfare, however, was not to kill one's enemy but to capture him and hold him for ransom. Enemy knights were worth far more alive than dead. A knight defeated in battle, if he surrendered to someone of equal status, would probably be spared and become the honoured, if involuntary, guest of his captor until he could buy his release.

In this respect, the Anglo-Normans saw themselves as very different from the Celtic peoples of the British Isles, whose usual aim in war was to enslave their enemies or kill and mutilate them (Contamine 1980: 291; Gillingham 1999). The Irish, Scots and Welsh collected and displayed enemy heads as trophies well into the twelfth century (Strickland 1996: 307). They seem particularly to have sought the heads of renowned and high status enemies, because, for them, possession of the head of a distinguished person itself conferred status and renown.

Gillingham argues that the development of notions of battlefield chivalry in France, and in England after the Norman invasion, were connected with changes in the economy which underwrote the institution of ransom. In particular, the knights' control of castles and fortified towns provided them with collateral with which they could buy their safety if they were defeated in battle.

> [T]he proliferation of the towns and castles of the new landscape meant a proliferation of strong-points from which men of high status could control territory, and hence a proliferation of assets which they could, in the event of defeat, use as bargaining counters in exchange for a promise to spare their lives and/or limbs. In societies where there were few such strongpoints – as in the less wealthy peripheries of the British Isles in the twelfth century – there was less to be gained from showing mercy; there was correspondingly more to be gained from directly targeting the persons of enemies, killing, mutilating or imprisoning them, or taking hostages from among them. (Gillingham 1999: 114–15)

The Celtic peoples were enemies beyond both the rules of chivalry and the economic relations that supported these rules. Their manner of making war appeared more like the hunting of animals, and they in turn could therefore be fought in the same way. In the wars between the English and Welsh from the eleventh to the thirteenth centuries, both sides took heads in battle. But, as Suppe (1989) shows, they understood beheading in fundamentally different ways. To the Welsh, taking the head of an enemy was an acknowledgement of the victim's status and therefore, almost, a perverse compliment or means of honouring him. To the English, on the other hand, decapitation had a strongly judicial character, whether carried out in battle or afterwards upon prisoners (Strickland 1996: 309–10). Beheadings and public displays of severed heads were a degradation which defined the victims as criminals. They were the punishment for treason or rebellion. In short, both sides practised decapitation, but each regarded the other's beheading practices as shameful and disgusting, and reacted with retaliatory head-taking of their own. The English nobility found it insulting that the Welsh should try to kill them in battle, as if they were commoners, rather than hold them for ransom as befitted their rank. For their part, the Welsh found it offensive and distressing that the English should treat the heads of famous fighters who died honourably in battle as if they were those of felons (Suppe 1989).

Welsh heads taken by the English were sent to the king, and then put on public display, a practice which seems to have echoed the treatment of the heads of animals killed in the hunt. The normal practice of a successful hunting party was to return home in a triumphal procession, accompanied by music of trumpets and pipes. The hunters would carry the animal's head home in front, and present it to the lord of the hunt, the owner of the lands on which the hunt had taken place (Griffin 2007: 31; Marvin 2006:

76–77; Yamamoto 2000: 111–12). If the stag had a particularly fine set of antlers – 'if he were a great Deare of heade' – these would be nailed to the lord's walls as a trophy (Marvin 2006: 126–28).

An important turning point in medieval English attitudes to the enemy body is marked by the death of Simon de Montfort, leader of the Barons' Revolt against Henry III, at the battle of Evesham in 1265. After he was killed – probably by his chief enemy Roger Mortimer - his body was mutilated, and his head carried off the battlefield on a spear (Labordier, Maddicott and Carpenter 2000: 405; Maddicott 1996: 342). His head, hands and genitalia were sent to Mortimer's castle and presented to his wife. Mortimer's men held a feast that night in the Great Hall, with the head displayed on the lance (Costain 1951: 322). At the time, such degrading treatment of a noble's body was unprecedented, and was viewed as shameful even by some of the supporters of the king (Gillingham 1999: 131–32; Maddicott 1996: 342).

There is every evidence that de Montfort's killing and mutilation had been planned, and did not simply happen spontaneously in the heat of battle. Normally, a man of his rank would have been allowed to surrender. But the problem faced by the king and his supporters was that there was no precedent at the time for the trial and execution of a rebel of his rank. It would have been morally impossible to execute him judicially, so the king's party had made the decision that he should, in effect, be executed during the battle itself (Gillingham 1999: 131–32; Labordier, Maddicott and Carpenter 2000: 403).

What is particularly noteworthy about the manner of the mutilation of his body is the way it seems to have re-enacted the butchering of a stag after a royal hunt. A common convention at the time was that the stag's right forefoot, testicles and head were reserved for the lord of the hunt. These, and the other parts of the animal, were then brought to the lord in procession, with the animal's head at the front and the testicles and certain other delicacies carried behind on a forked stick (Marvin 2006: 138 39; Thiébaux 1967: 271–74).

Besides echoing the treatment of the carcass of a stag killed in the hunt, the treatment of de Montfort's body also foreshadowed the practice of drawing and quartering, which later became formalized under Edward I as the standard punishment for treason (Prestwich 1988). Initially Edward employed this punishment in his military campaigns against the Scots and Welsh. Later, both he and his successors employed it also against their own nobles. The death of de Montfort therefore marks a point after which the bodies of the nobility were no longer considered truly sacrosanct (Gillingham 1999).

We can see this, for example, in the execution of Hugh Despenser the Younger in 1326. He had been the chamberlain of Edward II, and, according to their enemies, also his lover. He was led to his execution through the streets of Hereford preceded by one of his vassals, who carried a lance with the Despenser banner attached to it in reverse as a sign of ignominy. According to one source, the vassal also carried his own intestines on the end of the lance. Despenser was hanged until semi-conscious; then he was disembowelled, his heart was cut out, and he was castrated, beheaded and quartered. His viscera were burnt in front of him, and his severed head sent to London, where it was taken through the streets in a public procession accompanied by horns and trumpets and set on a pole on London Bridge. His quarters were sent to different parts of England for display on city walls or gates (Westerhof 2007).

The standard punishment for treason in English law from Edward I onwards, then, bore resemblances to the 'unmaking' of a stag – the complex ritual of butchering which came at the end of a successful medieval hunt. And when the severed heads of traitors were taken in procession, accompanied by fanfares, either to the Tower of London or to London Bridge, to be put on display, it echoed the way the head of a stag or boar was borne triumphantly home after a hunt (Westerhof 2007: 105). Like game killed in the royal hunt, such ritual proclaimed that the dead bodies of the king's enemies belonged to him as a sort of tribute from his loyal subjects and were thereafter his to dispose of as he wished. A variety of methods were use to preserve the heads of executed traitors: they were dipped in pitch, or parboiled with cumin to deter birds (Jezernik 2001: 22). After a certain time, perhaps many years, the king would usually release the remains to the families for burial (Westerhof 2007: 105).

Kings, however, could not always control the public meanings of these objects. To the king's critics and political opponents, the remains of an executed traitor could become objects of devotion, holy relics like those of a martyred saint. So, for example, Edward II found himself having to combat an unauthorized and seditious cult when the gibbeted remains of rebels he had executed were attributed by his enemies with miraculous powers, and became a focus for pilgrimages (Webb 2000: 169–70). The imagery of hunting and butchery of animal carcasses could be challenged with alternative representations of martyrdom and sainthood.

An imagery of hunting seems, then, to have informed medieval English warfare against the Celtic peoples of the British Isles, and also the punishment of rebels and traitors, two contexts which in practice often overlapped. This imagery could also be given free rein in warfare against enemies outside the Christian faith. During the Crusades both Franks and Muslims took heads, ears and noses in battle (Meller 1924: 210; Strickland 1996: 303, 307). At the same time, the nobility on both sides shared similar conventions of chivalry and, it seems, sometimes had to resist the force of these conventions in order to maintain appropriate attitudes of aggression. When Richard I was criticized for appearing to have become too close to Saladin's brother Al-Adil during the Third Crusade, he countered these accusations of fraternization by raiding the Turks and returning with heads hanging from his horse's bridle (Strickland 1996: 101). Even cannibalism against infidels was not always disapproved of. One group of participants in the First Crusade were a people called Tafurs, impoverished remnants of the disastrous Peasants' Crusade. Unable to afford swords and lances, they went into battle armed with sticks and other home-made weapons. They had a reputation as ferocious fanatics and were said to cook and eat the flesh of the Turkish dead. When the Emir of Antioch protested about the Tafurs' cannibalism of his soldiers' bodies during the siege of his city, the leaders of the Crusade apologized but professed themselves unable to control this group (Cohn 1970: 65–67; Contamine 1980: 61). The Franks understood such behaviour as a sign, not of savagery but of extreme religious devotion, when it was carried out against heretics or infidels.

Savagery and the Body

Between the eleventh and the thirteenth centuries, then, Frankish culture distinguished a range of types of warmaking. The most fully socialized forms of conflict were the tournament-like contests between fellow Christian nobles. At the other, least socialized extreme were wars against infidels, which the Franks tended to view as quite proper and justified wars of extermination. But there seems to have been little conception that there could be whole peoples whose essential character it was to wage civilized wars, and other lesser peoples who embodied the savage aspects of war in their nature. The Irish, it is true, were sometimes said to be cannibals, who would cut out a dead enemy's heart and take it away to devour (Strickland 1996: 309). But trophy-taking and even perhaps cannibalism were understood as practices in which anyone, including Christians irrespective of nationality or rank, could in principle engage, in an appropriate context. Such practices were viewed as distinguishing different kinds of situations or relationships, rather than different kinds of people.

When recognizably modern standing armies began emerging in Europe in the second half of the seventeenth century, these organizations began also to formulate codes of conduct, which expressed a kind of professional comradeship between soldiers regardless of nationality. In much the same way, other professions such as physicians, lawyers or scholars had come to develop a sense of shared identity across national boundaries through the formalization of shared codes of behaviour. By the eighteenth century, European national armies had developed among themselves conceptions, originating in medieval chivalry, of a specially limited form of warfare governed by a set of mutual understandings called the laws and customs of war. These were intended to give certain protections to non-combatants and military personnel in wartime. So, for instance, soldiers who surrendered could expect to be treated as prisoners of war, rather than simply executed or otherwise harmed. Officers could expect that the enemy would dispose of their remains with respect if they were killed in battle. Civilians could expect not to be harmed so long as they remained uninvolved in the fighting. At first, such conventions had no legal force but consisted simply in informal norms of military honour and decency. But they later came to form the basis of international humanitarian law and were formalized in the Geneva Conventions. The fundamental feature of this theory of limited and humane warfare was that it defined combatants as legal equals, with specific rights and obligations distinct from those of civilians or non-combatants (M.J. Howard, Andreopoulos and Shulman 1984; S.C. Neff 2005).

The laws and customs of war emerged at a time when European powers had begun to acquire colonial empires, and in many respects these conventions were formulated in contrast to European perceptions of the warfare of uncivilized peoples whom they were seeking to colonize. This dichotomy focussed particularly upon the treatment of the body. The differences between civilized people and savages in warfare were understood to be especially apparent in their behaviour towards the enemy dead. Savages were attributed with an excessive brutality towards their enemies, manifested in customs such as cannibalism and the taking of body parts as trophies (see, for example, S. Marks 1970: 246). Humanity and self-restraint in war, shown above all by honour shown to the dead bodies of defeated enemies, became, as they had been for the Greeks and Romans, a part of a claim to civilized superiority over barbarian peoples (Visser 1982). This assumed superiority, symbolized in the respectful treatment of the enemy body, itself became part of the justification for colonial conquest (Hoskins 1996b).

So, for example, the English in Elizabethan times portrayed the Irish as 'Cannibals who do hunt one another [i.e. for food]' (Canny 1973: 587). In the seventeenth century, American Indian warmaking sometimes seemed to Europeans, in a very similar way, less like war than like the hunting and killing of other people as if they were game.

> Opportunity to organize concerted tribal wars existed briefly during the summer months when the bands congregated at tribal centers and had some leisure. Wars could then be organized, but they were sporadic, individualistic affairs. A Jesuit observer condemned both the Indians' motives and scale of operations with a succinct phrase – 'their war is nothing but a manhunt' – and narrated how a war party of thirty men dwindled to fifteen who returned home satisfied after they had taken the scalps of three unoffending members of a friendly tribe. In Europe such waylaying would have been called brigandage rather than war. (Jennings 1975: 155, footnotes omitted; see also Slotkin 1985)

Together with cannibalism (Arens 1979) and human sacrifice (Obeyesekere 2005), practices such as scalping and headhunting came to be viewed as hallmarks of the primitive. They are still widely assumed by many theorists of human conflict to be features of premodern or 'primitive' warfare, epitomizing its savagery and irrationality and sharply distinguishing it from modern war (see, for instance, Keeley 1997: 100; Harvey 2002).

The common attribute of these savage practices, as portrayed by Europeans, was the treatment of human beings as if they were animals for consumption. By implication, a civilized people was assumed to distinguish humans from animals. A defining characteristic of savages, on the other hand, was the failure or inability properly to recognize this distinction. They hunted, killed and ate other humans to gratify their own appetites as if their victims were animals, and in this respect they acted as if they were predatory animals themselves. The implication was that savages were men who had yet to develop a full awareness both of their own humanness, and of the humanness of others, and had not yet mastered their own animal nature. In short, savagery was a state in which humanity was as yet unable to differentiate itself fully from the animal world.

It has often been noted how social groups tend to project onto outsiders behaviour which these groups themselves prohibit, attributing to other groups practices which invert their own moral standards (see, for instance, Kuper 1988). The long-standing Western preoccupation with practices such as headhunting and cannibalism as markers of savagery perhaps has its roots in this sort of projection. Ever since the Middle Ages, hunting had been understood in European military culture as an essential preparation for war, and an enthusiasm for the chase had been regarded as a mark of a true soldier. These two forms of organized violence, though closely related, were nevertheless distinct in a very fundamental way: one was directed against humans and the other against animals. Savages, on the other hand, were imagined as transgressing such constraints. They not only hunted animals, but also hunted and killed one another, not having learned fully to distinguish themselves and other humans from animals nor having gained control of their own animal appetites and impulses.

These stereotypes of the primitive warrior as an indiscriminate predator, a hunter who preys on humans and animals alike, seem implicitly to emphasize and reaffirm an important symbolic boundary between two strongly interconnected domains of European culture. The savage warrior was imagined to inhabit a region forbidden to the civilized soldier, intermediate between hunting and war. In that transgressive realm the normal conceptual distinctions between hunting and war were absent, permitting behaviour that combined or conflated these two distinct forms of violence.

The restraint and regulation of violence, which Elias (1969) saw as key ingredients of the development of civilization, certainly came to form an important part of Europeans' conceptions of themselves as a civilized people. But they probably had more to do with ideology than with practice. In medieval society, the manner in which people fought wars depended on whom they were fighting and on their relationship with their enemies. But from the Enlightenment onwards, the conduct of war was increasingly understood to reflect differences in the nature of peoples and to be a marker of ethnic or racial identity. The figure of the headhunter or cannibal emerged as a specific type of exotic and primitive human, evocative of extreme remoteness from Europe in time, space or both (J. Fabian 2002; Hoskins 1996a; Lindenbaum 2004). This notion of the 'savage' as a type of human being, and a concept of savagery as an attribute of persons rather than of relationships, emerged with European colonialism. And the form in which this savagery was imagined was largely a reflection of the long-standing relationship between hunting and war in European culture itself.

Contractual Humanity in War

By the eighteenth century, then, Europeans had developed a view of themselves as conducting civilized and humane wars by virtue of their character as a civilized people. European perceptions of the warfare of uncivilized peoples are illustrated by the observations of Eldred Pottinger, a British officer present in the city of Herat in Afghanistan in 1837, when it was under siege by the Persian army. Each day, Afghan soldiers would sortie out to try to destroy the Persian trenches and fortifications. They would return with prisoners, and with enemy heads. The ruler of the city, the Wuzeer, paid them rewards for these heads, which would then be brandished at the Persians from the city walls. Pottinger recorded his reactions in his private journal:

> I have not thought it necessary to recount the number of heads that were brought in daily, nor indeed do I know. I never could speak of this barbarous, disgusting, and inhuman conduct with any temper. The number, however, in these sorties was always insignificant, and the collecting them invariably broke the vigour of the pursuit, and prevented the destruction of the [enemy's] trenches. There is no doubt great terror was inspired by the mutilation of the bodies amongst their comrades. But there must have been, at least, equal indignation - and that a correspondent exaltation was felt by the victors at the sight of these barbarous trophies, and the spoils brought in. (Kaye 1857: 229)

On one occasion, an Afghan soldier returned from a sortie and brought to the Wuzeer the head of one of his own dead comrades, another brought this unfortunate comrade's ears, and the pair tried to pass these off as enemy remains and claim a reward. To Pottinger, this was a style of warfare that was not just repulsive, but fundamentally irrational and self-defeating. It seemed, just as American Indian warfare had seemed to the seventeenth-century Jesuit to be merely unregulated violence, much of it purposeless and misdirected, the combatants having no aims other than to gratify their own desires.

But the obedience of European armies to civilized conventions of war was far from absolute. Nor was it, of course, inherent in the European character. In practice, it was highly contractual and conditional. The legal parity of opponents, on which the laws of war were based, reflected the contingent historical reality that early modern European armies were approximately equally matched in power. As long as one party to a conflict respected the customs of war, so would the other. States reserved the right to carry out reprisals if their opponents did not abide by these conventions. If, for instance, one side mistreated its prisoners of war, the other could quite properly and legitimately retaliate with equivalent transgressions of its own, to punish its opponents and compel them to change their behaviour (S.C. Neff 2005).

One context in which it was often difficult to apply the laws and customs of war was that of conflicts with opponents who were not European, regular soldiers. Such opponents included rebels, insurrectionists and partisan or resistance fighters such as the Spanish guerrilla forces which fought Napoleon's army in the Peninsular War of 1807–14. Typically such combatants did not fight according to the standard conventions but employed tactics which the regular military condemned as dishonourable and underhand, such as sabotage and sniping. Nor did they wear uniforms to identify themselves openly as combatants but dressed as civilians. Soldiers faced with such opponents viewed them as illegitimate combatants with no entitlement to participate in the fighting. They were simply civilians who had forfeited any legal protections and turned criminal by taking up arms, and could be punished accordingly – for instance, by summary execution.

In other words, the laws and customs of war also gave rise, perversely, to a residual category of opponents to whom these conventions did not apply. Such enemies were not protected by the laws and customs of war because they behaved neither as soldiers nor as civilian non-combatants, and could therefore only be classified as a type of outlaw or bandit. The use of military force against such opponents was understood not as war, because war was a relation between legal equals, but as a type of criminal prosecution or law enforcement.

The same situation also arose in colonial wars, when European armies fought indigenous, non-European peoples who did not fight by the conventions of civilized war, or were not expected to do so. In effect, a civilized army fought such groups from a permanent stance of reprisal. The later chapters of this book will illustrate how ideology and practice were therefore often markedly at variance. Civilized behaviour towards one's opponents in war was usually feasible only when they were themselves other national armies of the same type as one's own, or gave indications that they would obey the same conventions. In practice, war continued to take different forms, and to follow different rules, depending on the type of relationship the opponents had, or sought to have, with one another – much as it had done in the Middle Ages or, indeed, in indigenous societies such as the Mundurucu.

Furthermore, from the dichotomy between savagery and civilization, an ideology also emerged according to which it was allowable or even necessary, when fighting 'savage' enemies, to adopt their methods, to some extent imitating the savagery imputed to them and reciprocating it (Canny 1973; Roque 2010: 33; Scheck 2005; Slotkin 1979; Taussig 1987: 122–26). Such behaviour followed logically from the right of reprisal. A well known example I discuss in Chapter Four was the rapid and widespread adoption of the practice of scalping by European colonists in North America (Axtell 1981; Slotkin 1973: 183). Colonial warfare could therefore give rise to strange cultural hybrids, such as a victory march through Boston in 1725, in which British officers paraded in wigs made from human scalps (Axtell 1981: 232). Savage enemies were categorized, on the one hand, as wild, animal-like and fundamentally unlike civilized opponents. But, for the same reason, they could be exemplars of uninhibited aggression, to be copied and internalized. The civilized soldier might sometimes justifiably step into the territory of the savage, the prohibited borderland between war and hunting where the two activities merged. There, he became a soldier-hunter, whose enemies seemed closer to predatory animals in their behaviour than to human opponents.

Of course, to imitate such enemies in this way was potentially to dissolve the very differences on which the imitation was predicated. If civilized soldiers sometimes reciprocated their opponents' savagery, and so in their own eyes came to resemble them, they also had to be able to disown or deny these resemblances, when they stepped back out of the savage's world and returned to their own.

Chapter 3
Bodies and Class in the Age of Revolution

The French Revolution and the Terror

In his history of the French Revolution, Thomas Carlyle reminds his readers of the shocking allegations, widely believed at the time, concerning the Reign of Terror. After aristocrats were guillotined their bodies were taken, so it was claimed, to a tannery at Meudon, near Paris, where they were skinned, and the skins made into leather. Such leather was said to have been used to bind copies of the constitution, the works of Rousseau and other revolutionary publications. Hence the remark attributed to Carlyle, that the French aristocrats who scoffed at Rousseau's writings ended up with their skins covering the second edition of his works.

Other products, too, Carlyle alleged, were made from such skin, including those politically fraught articles of clothing: the culottes, or knee-breeches, worn by gentlemen. Urban working men, the *sans-culottes*, could dress after the revolution in breeches made from the skins of the elite, and so become grotesque travesties of their superiors. Such imagery of savage usurpation and imposture appears also in Carlyle's other main atrocity story, concerning blond perukes. These, he tells us,

> are made from the Heads of Guillotined women! The locks of a Duchess, in this way, may come to cover the scalp of a Cordwainer; her blonde German Frankism his black Gaelic poll, if it be bald .... History looking back over Cannibalism ... will perhaps find no terrestrial Cannibalism of a sort on the whole so detestable .... Alas then, is man's civilization only a wrappage, through which the savage nature of him can still burst, infernal as ever? (1837: 341–42)

His depiction of a shoemaker masquerading in the blond tresses of a beheaded duchess suggests a hideous commingling of the sexes, and of the classes. The bodily conjunction of a swarthy Gael with a fair-haired, fair-skinned Teuton transgresses even the racial distinctions of the time. This image would have evoked in Carlyle's readers the same horror – and would have done so for the same reasons – as contemporary accounts of 'wild Indians' in North America carrying off as trophies the blond hair of innocent white women (see Namias 1993: 117–44).

For Carlyle, then, the image of the Paris mob disporting itself in the skin and hair of murdered aristocrats was a graphic reminder of the way the savagery of human nature cloaks itself in a veneer of civilization. Whether such atrocities really did occur is perhaps impossible to determine now and, in a sense, is relatively unimportant. A more interesting and useful question is why it seemed so self-evident to Carlyle and his contemporaries that 'savagery' was a condition whose principal expressions were violent appropriations of body parts such as skin and hair.

Throughout his work, Carlyle repeatedly depicts the revolution as a cannibal, a monster that eventually consumed its own children as the revolutionaries turned their ferocity inward upon themselves, and started sending one another to the guillotine (Easson 1993: 102; Vanden Bossche 1991: 85–86). Earlier, Edmund Burke had portrayed the revolutionaries in similar terms in his political speeches and writings. Like Carlyle, he used the term 'cannibalism' to suggest not only the literal consumption of human flesh but more generally the desecration or dishonouring of the bodies of the dead, acts that he felt would make those who perpetrate them grow increasingly brutal and savage. To all the other accusations against the Jacobins, he writes,

> let us join the practice of cannibalism …. By cannibalism I mean their devouring as a nutriment of their ferocity, some part of the bodies of those they have murdered …. By cannibalism I mean also to signify all their nameless, unmanly and abominable insults on the bodies of those they slaughter. (Quoted in Gibbons 2003: 38; see also Malchow 1996: 63)

So, for instance, when he describes the women's march on Versailles in October 1789, which brought the royal family in captivity back to Paris in a chaotic triumphal parade, he compares it to an Iroquois war party bringing home captives to be ritually tortured and killed. The spectacle resembled

> a procession of American savages, entering into Onondaga, after some of their murders called victories, and leading into hovels hung round with scalps, their captives, overpowered with the scoffs and buffets of women as ferocious as themselves. (Burke 2001 [1790]: 226)

Conservatives such as Burke and Carlyle were alarmed at the threat of radicalism spreading to Britain and Ireland, and their evocation of Indian savagery to demonize the revolutionaries was, of course, only rhetoric. But I want to suggest that the comparison they drew here actually contains an important element of truth, and points to some important similarities between the class conflicts in Europe at the time and frontier conflicts in North America. In fact, these were more than just similarities; they were actual connections, and they hinged, just as Carlyle and Burke suggest, on the treatment of the dead bodies of enemies.

Dissection and the Law in Europe

Their portrayals of the revolutionaries as savage cannibal figures are slightly puzzling in one respect. The gruesome atrocities of which the Jacobins were accused were not, in fact, very different from the conventional legal punishments meted out on felons in

Britain and elsewhere in Europe at the time. Between 1752 and 1832, judges in Britain could order that a murderer not only be hanged, but that the body be given afterwards to the surgeons for dissection. This was the only legal source of cadavers for medical research and training, at a time when the medical profession was growing rapidly. One of the ways in which hospitals and medical schools could supplement their incomes was by manufacturing and selling souvenir items from the remains of these dissections. The demand for such mementos on the part of the public was partly connected with long-standing beliefs in Europe that the bodies of executed felons, and artefacts associated with their death, had medicinal powers or could bring good luck (McLynn 1989: 271; Potter 1993: 162–63). But, perhaps more importantly, justice was understood as collective and participatory. Those who attended and witnessed an execution were, in effect, actors in it and could reaffirm and commemorate their involvement in this collective deed by keeping mementos of it afterwards.

A public demand for such mementos was not new. In the case of executions of major political figures, the meaning of these objects had often been deeply contested. At the execution of Charles I in 1649, the spectators took souvenirs of his hair and the blood-soaked sand. They dipped their handkerchiefs in his blood and took away pieces of the block (Clymer 1999). Similar scenes occurred at the execution of Louis XVI (R.J. Evans 1996: 98).

According to the Royalist army officer and historian Sir Roger Manley, soldiers had tried to disperse the crowd immediately after Charles' beheading, but despite their efforts the spectators

> were inhumanely barbarous to his dead corpse. His hair and his blood were sold by parcels. Their hands and sticks were tinged by his blood and the block, now cut into chips, as also the sand sprinkled with his sacred gore, were exposed for sale. Which were greedily bought, but for different ends, by some as trophies of their slain enemy, and by others as precious reliques of their beloved prince. (Quoted in Fumerton 1991: 9)

Some took these objects to venerate them, much as the devotees of saints martyred in the Inquisition would retrieve their remains from the fire, and keep them as holy relics (Given 1997: 77). An enduring cult of 'Charles the Martyr' emerged after his death, and his relics were believed to have magical powers. Lockets and rings were made, supposedly containing pieces of his hair, blood-stained grains of sand or pieces of linen stained with his blood. Other relics included books whose bindings were said to be stained by the king's blood or to contain a strand of his hair (Fumerton 1991: 9). The keeping of such relics was highly ambiguous, and indeed an important part of the political utility of these practices was that they were open to diametrically opposed interpretations. Both loyalty and dissent, the vilification and the veneration of an executed enemy of the state, could be displayed through almost identical outward behaviour towards his bodily remains.

In 1661, following the restoration of the monarchy, Cromwell and two other deceased signatories to the king's death warrant were posthumously convicted of high treason. Their bodies were exhumed, hanged and decapitated at Tyburn, and their heads set on spikes over Westminster Hall. The body of one of them, John Bradshaw, president of the tribunal that had convicted the king, was unwrapped from its shroud and, according to one eyewitness, apprentices took the opportunity to cut off the fingers and toes and sell them to the spectators for souvenirs (Clymer 1999; McMains 2000: 144, 154, 156, 204).

Similar treatment was meted out on the body of David Tyrie, a naval clerk executed in Plymouth in 1782 for spying for the French.

> With no well-placed or influential friends to plead on his behalf for public or Royal sympathy, Tyrie was hanged, decapitated and quartered for his treason, as the law required. The execution, before a huge crowd, was extremely gory and provoked a distasteful and brutish public response, his dismembered body was fought over, and his limbs and fingers torn off for souvenirs. No-one emerged with much credit or decorum from the death of Tyrie; indeed the scenes beneath the scaffold reflected so poorly on the solemnity of the occasion that he became the last treason convict ever to be quartered. (Poole 2000: 76)

According to a local newspaper report at the time, his remains were buried immediately after the execution and 'no sooner had the officers retired, but the sailors dug up the coffin, took out the body, and cut it in a thousand pieces, every one carrying away a piece of his body to shew their messmates on board' (Hampshire Chronicle 1782).

Like kings, notorious traitors and murderers were public celebrities, though of a perverse sort, their lives and deaths commemorated in ballads, broadsides and other forms of popular culture. The merchandising of their body parts, and artefacts connected with their crimes and punishments, was an intrinsic part of late eighteenth and early nineteenth-century celebrity culture, especially in Britain. Attending public dissections had been a fashionable leisure activity since at least the seventeenth century (Gatrell 1996; Nunn 2005). Pieces of rope from an execution could sell for a guinea an inch, and pieces of a murderer's skin could fetch even higher prices. Such objects could become wealthy collectors' items, intended for the cabinets of curiosities, or private museums, of cultured men, an important element in the fashion for collecting at the time.

One of the best known cases of this sort was one of the last: the execution of the notorious Edinburgh body-snatcher William Burke, hanged in front of a large crowd in 1829. The body was dissected and then put on public view, still on the slab in the anatomy theatre, as if it were 'lying in state', while an estimated thirty thousand people filed past to view it. His skin was later removed, tanned and sold in strips, and some of the purchasers of the larger pieces had them made into wallets, pocketbooks and similar items. The porter at the Anatomy Rooms of the University, who had joined the establishment around the time of Burke's execution, carried a tobacco pouch of Burke's skin until his death in 1860, to commemorate the date of his arrival (Roughead 1921; W. Turner 1868: 163).

Burke's skeleton was articulated and exhibited in the museum. At the time, there was much public hostility to medical schools because of their association with body-snatching, an activity in which Burke was implicated. The public display and merchandising of Burke's remains by the Edinburgh medical school may perhaps have been not only an attempt to capitalize on the public fascination with executions, but also a community relations exercise aimed at winning favour with the lay population.

William Roughead, a Scottish lawyer born in 1870, who published the definitive study of the case of Burke and his accomplice, Hare, in 1921, describes how he inherited from his grandfather a piece (so his grandfather told him) of Burke's skin, which resembled in colour and texture a piece of an old brown belt (1921: 66). Roughead recalls how, when he was a child, his grandfather would often show him the skin and relate to him the story of Burke and Hare. His grandfather had apparently bought the skin for a shilling as a young man, and he kept it inside an old snuff box, wrapped in a piece of paper on which he had written: 'Piece of Skin, tan'd from the Body of Burke the Murderer' (1941: 120).

The publishers of an account of Burke's trial also seem to have bought a large piece, probably with the intention of producing a special copy of the book bound in Burke's skin as a collector's item. Following some other murder trials, the court proceedings were bound in the murderer's skin. This had been done in 1828 with the body of William Corder, a Suffolk farmer's son, whose scalp, with one ear still attached, was also tanned and displayed in a leatherwork shop on Oxford Street in London (Gatrell 1996: 258). Books bound partly or wholly in human skin were rare collectors' items, exotica usually found only in the libraries of wealthy bibliophiles and literati with a penchant for the Gothic (Blumenthal 1955: 76–93).

Given the prevalence of such medico-judicial practices in Britain at the time, the indignation of writers such as Carlyle and Burke towards the alleged savagery of the French revolutionaries' treatment of the bodies of their class enemies seems a little disingenuous. At the same time, it is conceivable that some leather goods were, just as Carlyle alleged, occasionally made from the bodies of people killed during the revolution. Masson (2004) discusses a controversy which arose in 2003 over a display, in the Museum of Nantes, of a flayed human skin described by the museum's records as that of a soldier killed in 1793, during the unsuccessful siege of the city by royalist forces.[1] I know of no cases of items of clothing being manufactured from the skins of executed murderers in Britain. But the *Encyclopédie* of 1791 mentions a late eighteenth-century Paris surgeon, M. Sue, presenting a pair of slippers, made from human skin, to the French royal family's private museum (L.S. Thompson 1946: 94). There were scandals in the Paris police force as recently as the 1890s when some senior officers were accused of obtaining skin from the autopsies of executed murderers, and having it tanned and made into commemorative card-cases and other items (L.S. Thompson 1946: 99). Old attitudes to crime and punishment seem to have died much harder than imagined by Foucault (1995), and may have persisted in covert and submerged forms well into the modern era.

In Britain and Ireland, public opinion started to turn in the late eighteenth century against practices such as gibbeting – the public display of the bodies of executed felons – and the display of traitors' heads on city gates (McLynn 1989: 274; Potter 1993: 73). Along with public executions, and the carnival atmosphere which often attended them, such practices came increasingly to be seen during the nineteenth century as among those 'nutriments of ferocity' of which Burke wrote: brutal practices which nourished further brutality in those who took part in them. The spread of more modern and humane sensibilities eventually led to the abolition of public executions and similar events. The Anatomy Act of 1832 ended the dissection of murderers, and the souvenir industries which had grown up around this practice gradually disappeared.

Class, Collecting and the Law

Curiosities and collectibles had occasionally been made from the skins of dissected criminals in Europe since the Renaissance (Egmond and Zwijnenberg 2003; Park 1994: 26). In Britain, such practices only became regular occurrences during the period of the so-called Bloody Code, a ramshackle collection of laws which evolved between the late seventeenth and early nineteenth centuries, motivated largely by fear of the mob on the part of the property-owning classes. During this period, more than two hundred offences, mostly against property, became capital crimes, although the death penalty seems in practice to have been applied highly inconsistently. The purpose of law at the time was not to ensure justice, but to maintain proper relations of deference between social classes and instil in the lower classes a combination of fear and gratitude (Hay et al. 1975; McLynn 1989: xvi). It was during this period that the Murder Act of 1752 was passed, allowing judges to add anatomization to the death penalty for murder, thereby creating a context in which surgeons and other functionaries connected with executions could subject the bodies of murderers to indignities such as having their skins tanned and made into souvenir pocketbooks, purses and so forth.

After 1752, versions of the Murder Act were soon adopted by the American states, and judges in British North America also had the option of sentencing murderers to dissection. In the United States, dissections were carried out well into the nineteenth century, but such sentences seem to have been imposed less often than in Britain, and when they were, it was more often upon blacks than whites convicted of murder (Banner 2002: 76–80, 234), a point to which I return in a later chapter. As in Britain, anatomizations could generate private mementos, as well as scientific specimens. Nat Turner, a slave executed for leading a revolt in 1831 in Virginia was, like William Burke in Edinburgh, anatomized and skinned, and a purse or wallet was made from his skin (French 2004: 279; Greenberg 2003).

All the available evidence indicates that dissection and its aftermath were feared as a punishment far more than execution itself (Banner 2002: 81–83; Sappol 2002: 104). Many people in Britain and North America, including African slaves, understood the doctrine of the resurrection of the body very literally, and believed that their prospects of an afterlife depended on their being given Christian burial with the body intact, so that the body could be reunited with the soul on Judgement Day (Egerton 2003: 153–54; Linebaugh 1975; McLynn 1989: 271–72; Richardson 1987).

In short, a fundamental part of the way class relations were expressed during this period in Europe, and in European settler society in North America, was through honour and dishonour shown towards the body, living and dead. This was also very apparent, for example, in the institution of the army. The bodies of officers killed in action were buried with honours, according to their rank. Those of common soldiers were buried with little or no ceremony in mass graves, or even left where they lay (see, for instance, Ariès 1977: 547; Cox 2004: 163–98). At times, their remains seem to have been regarded as a sort of industrial by-product or waste. The bones of the men and horses left on the battlefield at Waterloo were collected by English contractors, who had them ground down into fertilizer and sold to farmers in the north of England (Ignatieff 1998: 113; Sappol 2002: 184). The best quality dentures in England at the time, affordable only by the affluent, were made from what were called 'Waterloo teeth', collected from the battlefield remains of soldiers, most of whom were young men with healthy dentition (T. Anderson, O'Connor and Ogden 2004; Richardson 1987: 67; Whittaker 1993). In short, the sanctity of the human body, in particular the dead body, was not absolute at that time, but graded explicitly and purposefully according to social class.

In effect, class distinctions were modelled in some respects on the conceptual boundary between human beings and animals – specifically, upon the human use of animals for food, clothing and other materials. This was conspicuously so in the case of criminals, whose relation with the state was implicitly a class distinction. Part of the punishment of the felon was an extreme and public reduction to a status similar to that of an animal carcass, during or after execution (Obeyesekere 2005: 243–47). The ultimate degradation a person could undergo was to be dismembered in this way, and to have their body parts taken and used as commodities, as an industrial raw material, bought and sold like the remains of livestock.

The most graphic form these penalties took were the punishments for treason, which included burning or dismemberment alive and the display of severed heads and other body parts on public buildings. Historically, the powers to impose such punishments belonged to the king. To keep and display the body parts of one's enemies was something that could only be done by kings, or in their name.

As public sensibilities began to turn against these practices in the late eighteenth century, dissection and its aftermath seem to have offered a way of continuing them in a more moderated, medically sanitized and publicly acceptable form (Banner 2002: 76) and, also, in a kind of privatized or devolved form. Anyone with the resources to establish a private museum or collection could, in effect, arrogate to himself a role which seemed to reflect, in miniature, a king's power to punish crime and treason. Kings, of course, did not traffic in the body parts of public enemies, but a private collector could. In the process of becoming privatized and devolved, these objects also became commoditized.

A catalogue of a private collection, or 'cabinet of curiosities', which was put up for sale in Ripon, Yorkshire, in 1867, lists among its contents a part of the tongue of a woman hanged for murder at York in 1809, along with a piece of the skin of Ann Barber, who had murdered her husband and been hanged, also at York, in 1821 (Dennis 1867). Other items include 'Nine Indian arrows' and 'Swathing clothes, of curious workmanship, belonging to the ancestors of the Earl of Wakefield'. Of the fourteen items listed in the 'Miscellaneous' section of the catalogue, three are described as body parts of executed murderers, and another is the coat-sleeve and cap allegedly worn by a murderer when he committed his crime. The catalogue is typical of such private collections at the time. Pearce (1995: 127–28) mentions one which included the arm of the Marquis of Montrose, executed for treason in Edinburgh around 1650.

In Bristol in 1821 an eighteen-year-old youth called John Horwood was executed for killing a woman who rejected his advances. Afterwards, his body was dissected by Richard Smith, the senior surgeon at Bristol Royal Infirmary and a prominent member of Bristol's social elite. Smith had established an anatomy museum at the infirmary, and put Horwood's skeleton on display there in a case, alongside the skeletons of two women who had been hanged for infanticide a few years earlier. Smith had taken an intense interest in Horwood's murder case, and had amassed a large collection of documents relating to his trial and punishment. He had these bound in Horwood's tanned skin, and put this volume on display alongside the murderer's skeleton (Fissell 2002: 168; 'F.S.' of Churchdown 1856). For Smith, this museum was clearly more than merely an assemblage of anatomical and pathological specimens. It was a personal trophy room meant to showcase his history of contributions to justice and righteousness, and his personal commitment to upholding order.

Clearly, he viewed himself and his museum as having more than just a narrowly defined medical or scientific role, but moral and even juridical functions as well. Medical science served ends higher than just its own; it was one of the channels through which the retributive power of the law or state expressed itself. Post-mortem punishments meted out on the bodies of murderers at the time were therefore not understood as acts of savagery – or were viewed as a necessary, tolerable sort of savagery – so long as they served the purpose of deterrence and contributed to the security of the propertied classes.

Jacobins and American Indians, on the other hand, appeared wholly individualistic, politically egalitarian and republican in their treatment of the body parts of their enemies. Any man sufficiently ferocious, irrespective of birth or class, could acquire and keep such objects and use them for his own personal ostentation. To writers such as Carlyle and Burke, then, the revolutionary and the Indian cannibal were similar, not because they both dismembered their enemies and displayed or consumed their body parts, but, more importantly, because they did not do so in ways which upheld the rightful order of society, but flouted or even reversed it.

In short, the cannibal was a thinly disguised metaphor for the lower classes (Malchow 1996: 41–123). As writers such as Carlyle and Burke applied the term to the French Revolution, cannibalism meant the vengeful consumption of the body of a superior person by an inferior. It was a metaphor for the destruction of the natural hierarchy of society by those ranked lowest within it. The savage practices of American Indians and Jacobins – resentful subordinates who dishonoured and desecrated the bodies of their superiors – were a nightmarish inversion of the proper relations between classes.

Note

1. A Scottish museum possesses what it describes as the skin of a French officer who died during the capture of the Dutch town of Breda in 1793 (see Royal College of Surgeons of Edinburgh 2007).

Chapter 4

The European Enlightenment and the Origins of Scalping

Hunting and War in the Eastern Woodlands

Among the Eastern Woodland Indians of North America, as in Europe, the killing and consumption of animals seem to have provided important conceptual metaphors for certain kinds of social relationships, and vice versa. Indigenous warfare, for instance, was modelled in many respects on hunting. Among the Iroquois, hunting and war were the two principal occupations of men, and both boys and adult men practised them regularly with the use of weapons (Benn 1998: 70; Graymont 1972: 17). Training for hunting was also training for war because indigenous warmaking employed much the same weaponry, techniques and skills as the hunting and stalking of deer and other game, and this remained the case after the introduction of firearms (P.M. Malone 2000; Starkey 1998: 27; cf. Keener 1999).

At the same time, many of the Eastern Woodland peoples regarded their relationship to the game they hunted as a social relationship, rather than as a merely instrumental or utilitarian one in some narrow sense. In other words, they categorized the animals in important respects as persons, with whom they were connected by strong mutual obligations and dependencies (Hallowell 1960; Tanner 1979).

Similar conceptions seem to have been reflected also in the ways in which they related to their enemies in war. One important goal of warfare among the Huron and Iroquois, for instance, especially after their populations began to decline in the eighteenth century, was to take captives, adopting them as relatives and incorporating them into their kin groups as replacements for dead members whose loss they were mourning. Some of these adopted captives were selected to be tortured to death in public sacrificial spectacles in which they were expected to display their bravery and powers of endurance. Afterwards, the victims' flesh or organs were consumed to acquire their strength and courage (Brandao 2000: 39–41; Richter 1983; Trigger 1990). Nevertheless, the aim in both these cases was clearly similar. It was not so much to destroy the enemy but, through processes either of nurture or consumption, to assimilate them as social persons into the victor's kin group and so contribute to the group's continuation.

Scalping and the Frontier

Despite the claims of some modern-day American Indians that the British invented scalping and brought it to North America, there is ample evidence not only of scalping in American Indian warfare in pre-Columbian times, but of the collection and use of heads, hands and a wide range of other body parts as trophies (Axtell 1981; Chacon and Dye 2008; Jennings 1975: 166). Again, such practices seem to have been closely connected with the fundamental role of men as hunters of game. Human body parts brought home from raids not only were used in status rivalry and self-aggrandizing display, but also played an important role as gifts, as prestige goods exchanged between local groups as symbols of friendship or alliance. English colonists were, from the beginning, actively involved in such transactions, but understood such gifts as tribute. In fact, they enforced such a view, demanding heads and scalps from their Indian allies as acts of homage and submission (Coleman 2003; Lipman 2008).

Setting aside their other obvious differences, many European and Indian cultures at the time did share at least one fundamental characteristic: their conceptual models of violent power relations between people drew partly upon cultural domains to do with the killing, butchering and consumption of animals. Nor were the forms of violence they derived from this extended metaphor themselves especially dissimilar on the surface. It was rather that acts similar to those directed against the enemy body in kin-based American Indian tribal and clan politics were, in Europe, a part of the violence of class politics. In this chapter, I explore the ways in which these two systems of cultural symbolism came to interact and shape one another during the eighteenth and early nineteenth centuries.

Although the British did not introduce scalping to North America they certainly did promote it there, and commercialized it by offering bounties to their Indian allies for the scalps of hostile Indians. At the same time, and in much the same way, indigenous practices of hunting and trapping became commercialized, even industrialized, in the fur trade. Scalp bounties drew upon the historical precedent in England of offering rewards for the heads or scalps of wolves, and so equated Indians with ferocious local wildlife (Coleman 2003). Eventually, rewards for Indian scalps were offered to anyone, not just Indians. Some colonists found that scalp hunting was more rewarding financially than farming, and adopted it as a full-time occupation.

The authorities usually burned or buried redeemed scalps to prevent fraudulent attempts to use the same scalp twice. But they sometimes kept them for display, as they did in the courthouse at Salem, whose walls were decorated with redeemed scalps until the demolition of the building in 1785 (Axtell 1981: 218). Such practices, evoking the scalp-bedecked 'hovels' of Onondaga, as Burke had put it, and the displays of traitors' heads on city gates in England, seem to have drawn on both English and Indian traditions.

Although whites who scalped Indians did so principally for the bounty, some of them also seem to have acquired and kept them for status and display as personal trophies (see, for example, Benn 1998: 84–85). By the middle of the eighteenth century, scalping had become completely assimilated into European colonial culture in North America (Axtell 1981: 232; Ward 2003: 200). Or rather, it belonged to a creolized frontier culture common to many groups, whether identified by themselves or others as European settlers, Indians, 'mixed blood', or in some other way (R. White 1991). They dressed alike, in mixtures of Indian and European clothing, farmed and hunted in much the same ways, and depended on the same material culture. As Calloway points out, eighteenth-century Indian and European settlements in the eastern United States are often impossible to distinguish archaeologically, and what often brought groups into conflict was not that they were alien to each other. It was their similarities that caused conflict, because they were competing for the same resources (1997: 56; see also Richter 2001).

Second Skins: Soldiers and Race in the Eighteenth Century

The French and British soldiers who came to North America to serve in the Seven Years' War were trained in sieges and formal set-piece battles on open ground, the conventional forms of European warfare. Indians, on the other hand, more often employed tactics such as ambushes, sniping, or shooting from cover, rooted in the techniques of hunting deer and other game animals in woodland. European soldiers viewed these 'skulking' (P.M. Malone 2000) methods of fighting as dishonourable and underhand, though they eventually adopted similar techniques themselves (Calloway 1997: 102–103) or formed special units who adopted them.

An example was a military force called Rangers, which the British in North America employed specifically to hunt and fight Indians allied to the French in the Seven Years' War. This was a militia made up of local settlers and frontiersmen, who employed many of the warfare practices and tactics of the Woodland Indians whom they fought. In particular, they specialized in a pattern of long-distance, mobile raiding rather than conventional, pitched battles. The British measured the effectiveness of the Rangers' raids by the numbers of scalps they brought back (Grenier 2005: 130). Although they proved indispensable in helping eventually to defeat the French, British officers and regular soldiers tended to look down upon them as insubordinate semi-savages, little better than Indians themselves, because they did not fight according to the European conventions.

The 'savagery' of Indians seemed self-evident in practices such as torturing prisoners of war to death, or mutilating the bodies of those killed in battle and taking away parts of the body as proof of the killing. A lieutenant in a Scottish highland regiment expressed shock after his first sight of bodies treated in this way: 'I dare say no human creature but an Indian or Canadian would be guilty of such inhumanity as to insult a dead body' (quoted in Calloway 2008: 100). To Europeans, it must have seemed that Indian warriors were less like professional soldiers of the time, with their codes of honour and propriety, and much more akin to executioners, an ignoble and defiled trade whose task was to reduce human bodies to the level of animal carcasses (see Stuart 1999).

Nevertheless, some British and French soldiers certainly did scalp Indians, primarily because the bounties offered were sometimes substantial (Way 1999). British soldiers in the Seven Years' War received £5, sometimes 5 guineas, for an Indian scalp, a sum representing about five months' wages for an ordinary private (Brumwell 2002: 184–85). Similar bounties of five months' pay for a private soldier were offered in the American forces for the scalps of Indians allied with the British in the War of 1812 (Benn 1998: 85).

Soldiers in the French, British and American revolutionary armies sometimes dressed as Indians or wore mixtures of European and Indian dress when on campaign; and by choosing particular mixtures of costume they made assertions about their identity and their intentions (Calloway 1997: 63). All the North American colonial conflicts involving France and Britain were full of incidents in which captured 'Indians' were said to have been exposed as 'Whites' after their warpaint was removed. Many of the supposedly 'Indian' units who fought for the French in the Seven Years' War included Métis – part-French backwoodsmen whom the British called Canads or Canadians, and who lived, dressed and fought as Indians. Soldiers would also dress as Indians to commit atrocities (Mann 2005: 9–10, 115), not only to disguise themselves and deflect blame but also, perhaps, because this cross-dressing was felt to free the wearer inwardly from some of the formalities and constraints of conventional European war. Any man dressed as an Indian appeared to proclaim an intention not to abide by civilized rules of conduct, and could therefore be expected to be treated accordingly if he fell into enemy hands. Hence Wolfe's famous but curiously worded order to his men in July 1759 during the siege of Quebec: 'The general strictly forbids the inhuman practice of scalping, except when the enemy are Indians, or Canadians dressed like Indians' (Wright 1864: 531).

These chameleon-like transformations of identity through choice of dress and body decoration were facilitated by Enlightenment understandings of race. In the eighteenth century, it was assumed that racial differences consisted largely in differences in skin colour and hair type, and that these came from external causes such as diet and climate (Eden 2001; Finch 2001). For instance, it was assumed that Africans brought to England would become white after a certain number of generations, due to exposure to English food and weather. Likewise, it was expected that a population of Europeans living in Africa would naturally become black after a certain time had passed (Wheeler 2000). So while skin colour was an important marker of difference, it signified the accidents, rather than the essence, of human physical nature. Human beings had the same capacities regardless of their type of skin or hair; these superficial features were envisaged as rather like a costume, covering a nature essentially identical in all peoples.

In North America at the time, medical experiments had been carried out on blacks to discover whether they could lose their pigmentation, for instance by being caused to sweat profusely, and there were a number of celebrated cases of spontaneous transracial metamorphosis in which a black person or an Indian had supposedly begun turning into a white person for no apparent reason. The French naturalist Buffon thought that it was the American climate that had caused Indians to become red-skinned and savage, implying that any people who lived there long enough might undergo the same transformation (Melish 2001; Sweet 2003: 271–311).

Racial identities were unstable and mutable and racial boundaries crossable, in ways that would become inconceivable in the nineteenth century. Then, European concepts of race would change radically, with a shift from 'surface' to 'structure' in conceptualizations of human physical variation (Wheeler 2000: 31–33). In the Victorian period, European soldiers serving in Africa, or United States soldiers on the American frontier, were much less likely to adopt African or American Indian costume because, by then, human types were no longer viewed as a matter simply of costumes and surfaces, but as essential, immutable difference embedded in the interior of the body. The conceptual boundaries of race would harden and become uncrossable.

Scalping and Cultural Hybridization

It was partly these conceptualizations of racial differences that made skin and hair particularly appropriate parts of the American Indian body for eighteenth-century soldiers and settlers to collect as battle trophies. They were the surface features of the body in which racial distinctions were understood to have their locus (Shoemaker 2001). They were the parts, indeed perhaps the only parts, that could be made to signify categorical differences between Europeans and Indians, who were in other respects all too alike.

There is evidence that some European colonists developed their own variations, embellishments and elaborations of scalping during the second half of the eighteenth century. Pieces of skin were sometimes said to have been taken from dead Indians, tanned and made into leather items. In 1760, an English visitor wrote that some settlers carried tobacco pouches made from the skin of Indians (Axtell 1981: 312–13). After an attack by a militia force on an Indian community in Ohio in 1782, razor strops purportedly made from strips of the victims' skin were sold as souvenirs in the Pittsburgh area (Mann 2005: 165). Similar events were reported during the War of Independence, most notably during the punitive expedition of 1779 led by Major General John Sullivan against the four nations of the Iroquois League that had allied themselves with the British. The only battle during this expedition took place at Newtown on 29 August 1779.

> Lieutenant William Barton recorded in his journal the day after Newtown that, at 'the request of Maj. [Daniel] Platt,' he had 'sent out a small party to look for some of the dead Indians,' but that the squad 'returned without finding them.' Going out again around noon, they finally came across their prize and 'skinned two of them from their hips down for boot legs; one pair for the Major and the other for myself.' ... Lieutenant Rudolphus Hovenburgh also dispatched a squad, noting that of the nineteen it found dead on the ground, 'Sm Skn. By our S. fr. Bts,' that is, 'Some skinned by our soldiers for boots.' ... On 31 August [a Sergeant Thomas Roberts, himself a shoemaker by trade] reported on yet another skinning party sent out in the morning which 'found 2 Indians and Skin thear Legs and Drest them for leggins'. (Mann 2005: 86)

Again, such acts – if they did indeed occur – seem to have drawn on both European and Indian practices. On the one hand, the wearing of items made of Indians' skin, in much the same way as Indians themselves wore scalplocks, can be understood as adaptations or extensions of scalping. On the other, it also recalled the English practices of using the tanned skin of executed murderers to make commemorative pocketbooks, court proceedings bound in human leather and similar collectibles.

Settlers sometimes attributed to Indians similar acts. The Chippewas, for example, were accused of making a tobacco pouch from the skin of the arm of a British officer in Pontiac's War (Nester 2000: 77; Peckham 1947: 136). On another occasion, a settler killed an Indian who was using an old leather glove as a tobacco pouch, the settler claiming that it had been made from the skin of a white child (Kelsay 1986: 18).

Events similar to those following the Battle of Newtown were also reported to have taken place after the Battle of Horseshoe Bend in March 1814, the final battle of the Creek War. A nineteenth-century historian was told that the Tennessean troops partially skinned the bodies of dead Indians after the battle to make reins for their horses:

> They began at the lower part of the leg near the heel, and, with a knife, made two parallel incisions through the skin, about three inches or more apart, running these incisions up the leg and along the side of the back and down the other leg to the heel. The strip between these incisions was then skinned out, and the soldier then had a long strap of human skin, which he used as a bridle rein. (Quoted in Kanon 1999: 14; see also Remini 2001: 78)

In the War of 1812, a Shawnee chief called Tecumseh led an Indian confederacy which allied itself with the British in Canada, against the United States. He was killed at the Battle of the Thames in October 1813. The next day, soldiers found his body and took his clothing as souvenirs, and Kentuckian troops arriving later claimed to have scalped him and taken skin from his back and thigh, with so many of them wanting a part of his body that many ended up with small pieces 'the size of a cent piece' (Sugden 1985: 180). One soldier exhibited what he claimed was a strip of Tecumseh's skin in Washington the following winter. As an old man nearly fifty years later, in 1862, another of these soldiers wrote to President Lincoln asking for the release of his grandsons, who had become prisoners of war while serving in the Confederate States Army. In his letter he wrote proudly that he had served his country as a young man by helping to kill and skin Tecumseh: 'I hope [helped] Kill Tecumseh and hope Skin him and brot Two pieces of his yellow hide home with me to My Mother & Sweet Hart' (Townsend 1955: 337). Some veterans of the War of 1812 seem to have kept such mementos for the rest of their lives: one of them produced what he said was a piece of Tecumseh's skin when he was interviewed in 1886 (Sugden 1985: 180–81; Sugden 1997: 378–80).

Comparisons

According to a nineteenth-century Wyandot historian who interviewed Indians who had fought in this battle, the dead Indian whose body was mutilated was not Tecumseh but another whom the soldiers had mistaken for him. Moreover, he wrote, many soldiers boasted of having personally killed Tecumseh and taken parts of his body as trophies, including soldiers who could not possibly have done so.

> 'I killed Tecumseh; I have some of his beard' one would say; 'I killed Tecumseh,' another would clamour; 'I have a piece of his skin to make me a razor strop!' none of these bragadocias were in the last battle, in which the brave Chief received his mortal wound. (P.D. Clarke 1870: 115)

If Clarke's account is accurate, many of the soldiers clearly viewed such trophy-taking as not merely acceptable but admirable. Clarke himself seems to have had no doubt that they had mutilated a dead Indian for trophies, though he denies that the victim was Tecumseh. But it is certainly possible, as he suggests, that soldiers' claims to possess memorabilia of the death of Tecumseh were often quite fraudulent, and that many of the objects they purported to be the dead chief's bodily relics were nothing of the sort.

Furthermore, all of these claims or reports of trophy-taking need to be understood in their historical context. In York in England, five years before the death of Tecumseh, a fortune teller called Mary Bateman was sentenced to hang for the murder of some of her clients, with the judge ordering that her body be anatomized. After she was hanged, her corpse was put on display at Leeds General Infirmary, which charged the public 3d a head to view it. Two and a half thousand people came, netting the hospital some £30. The surgeons dissected her body, sent her skin to a tannery, and distributed it in small pieces for souvenirs, in accordance with what a contemporary writer described as 'a custom in Yorkshire' (Rede 1831: 56). Items described as pieces of her skin were still being offered for sale as good luck charms in the Yorkshire town of Ilkely in the 1890s (Potter 1993: 163). The part of a human tongue I mentioned in the last chapter, listed in 1867 as part of a private collection of curiosities, was hers according to the collection's catalogue.

What is particularly distinctive about settler culture in North America in the late eighteenth and early nineteenth centuries is the way that collecting practices such as these, concerned with commemorating crime and punishment, were recontextualized within the cycles of atrocity and mutual reprisal in border warfare. It was as if these practices of retributive justice were taken out of the anatomy rooms of hospitals and medical schools and out of the libraries and cabinets of private collectors, and re-imagined as acts of war, a context in which they could serve as a reply to real or imagined atrocities of Indians. In this form they acquired new dimensions of meaning which their European precursors largely lacked. Besides being militarized, they also became strongly racialized and, in a certain sense, democratized.

These new features were evident in the reported treatment of the body of Tecumseh. This was not a typical act of scalping, in which the trophy is credited to one person. Rather, a large group of men claimed to have shared out small pieces of skin among themselves. In this respect, it resembled the treatment in Britain of the bodies of executed murderers such as William Burke or Mary Bateman. It expressed a collective agency. And, according to those who claimed to have carried out this act, they treated only Tecumseh's body in this way. It was his specific identity as a notable and celebrated person that had made pieces of his skin valuable to them. The Kentucky militiamen who boasted of having scalped and mutilated him, and taken pieces of his 'yellow hide' home to their mothers and girlfriends, would therefore have been able to portray this behaviour in two alternative ways. On the one hand, the act they described was sufficiently similar to the practices of the Indians, including Tecumseh's own men, that it could be made to seem an act of revenge, an indulgence in the Indians' own savagery, as if the perpetrators were simply members of one tribe fighting another on equal terms. At the same time, it was similar enough to the conventional treatment of the body of a heinous murderer during and after anatomization in Britain and North America at the time as to appear a mere variation upon normal Euro-American judicial practices. In other words, the militiamen could just as reasonably have represented their actions as the execution of justice upon a criminal, with themselves as the state's representatives or instruments: that is, as the effect of the power of the state, or of the law, acting through them.

Perhaps only the first of these views was available to the surviving members of Tecumseh's confederacy. The Iroquois, for instance, certainly retaliated when they found their dead mutilated. On one occasion during the War of 1812, British officers remonstrated with some of their Indian allies for having mutilated the corpse of an American soldier. The Indians replied that they were simply reciprocating what was being done to them. As one of them put it: 'If the Big Knives when they kill people of our color leave them without hacking them to pieces ... we will follow their example' (Benn 1998: 85).

The Vendée

So far, I have viewed Europe as a source of influences on frontier North America, but it is quite conceivable that the influences may not have been entirely one way. A possible example of an effect in the opposite direction occurred at the height of the Terror, when a royalist revolt broke out among the peasants in La Vendée, a département in western France. From 1793 to 1796 an exceptionally violent and brutal civil war was fought in this region with many well documented atrocities committed by both sides (D.A. Bell 2007: 179). One I want to focus on occurred in Angers around 1794, when on a number of occasions skin was said to have been removed from the bodies of dead peasants, and used to make officers' riding breeches (Secher 1986: 134–35). A shepherd who claimed to have witnessed this recalled that the bodies 'were skinned to the middle of the body because they cut the skin below the belt, then along each thigh down to the ankles, so that after it was removed the breeches were partially formed; all that remained was to tan and sew' (quoted in Secher 1986: 134). Fourteen years after soldiers in the American revolutionary army reportedly flayed the legs of dead Iroquois to make officers' riding boots and leggings, the same practice was reported among officers in the French republican army suppressing an insurgency in their own homeland. This is surely a noteworthy coincidence. To my knowledge, neither European nor North American military personnel have committed, or been accused of committing, this particular atrocity in any other conflict.

Nor was this the only similarity between the Vendée and Sullivan's expedition against the Iroquois. The Committee for Public Safety, in ordering 'the destruction of farms, forests and villages' in the Vendée (Sutherland 2003: 222), closely echoed George Washington's orders to Sullivan to achieve 'the total destruction and devastation of their settlements' (Mann 2005: 56). Both campaigns were aimed at the removal of the native population and the destruction of their homes and food stocks, and both have been interpreted by some historians as early modern instances of genocide. There were even similarities in the animal terminology used to refer to the Indians and the peasants, who were labelled 'wolves', or their children 'wolf-cubs' (Beckett 2001: 26; Stannard 1992: 119).

One possible explanation of these coincidences is that some French officers knew of Sullivan's punitive expedition against the Iroquois and used it as a model. French servicemen, including infantry soldiers, had served in the War of Independence, though not, it seems, in Sullivan's expedition and, of course, the American Revolution was viewed as a model by French radicals.

A factor that may have facilitated a transfer of North American frontier tactics to France was the underlying similarity between the practices of war in North America and European practices, not of war – for these were indeed very different from their American counterparts – but of criminal justice. It was European penal systems which bore similarities to North American frontier warfare. If French officers did in fact carry out acts such as wearing the skin of peasant rebels, perhaps they conceptualized their actions not so much as those of war, but – like the Tennessee militiamen with the body of Tecumseh – more like the execution of the judgement of the law upon felons and brigands.

In the campaign against the Vendéeans, then, methods which had just emerged in North American border warfare may have been brought back to metropolitan France. The escalating cycles of atrocity that led eventually to men conceiving – and perhaps committing - acts such as the wearing of boots and leggings made from Indians' skin may have shifted the boundaries between war and law enforcement not only on the colonial frontiers but at home as well.

Conclusion

In the previous chapter, we saw how a set of practices to do with the retributive treatment of the human body emerged in Europe in the middle of the eighteenth century at the intersection of medical science and criminal justice. At the same time, reports of similar practices among settler militiamen emerged in North America in the context of frontier warfare. They also disappear or subside at around the same time, during the nineteenth century. The Sand Creek Massacre of 1864, discussed in Chapter Eight, was perhaps the last large-scale case in which such acts were perpetrated against North American Indians.

The emergence of these reported practices in both Europe and North America, involving the making and collecting of commemorative objects of human skin, is best understood not as a coincidentally similar pair of historical processes, but as a single, interrelated set of changes happening simultaneously and being expressed in two different contexts. Not only were European societies already by that time so closely interconnected politically and economically with American Indian and other indigenous societies that their identities were all being shaped in relation to each other (Kidd 2004; Morgan 1999; Richter 2001), but more basically, there were domains of cultural symbolism in which eighteenth-century Indians and Europeans had strong mutual affinities in the first place. In creating their conceptual metaphors or models of violent power relationships, they all drew upon their conceptions of the relationship between humans and the animals which they used as a source of food and raw materials. As a consequence, when they offered violence to one another they were strongly predisposed not only to model it on the killing and consumption of animals, as they understood these activities, but also to project such behaviour onto one another. The significant differences were that American Indians derived these understandings from the context of intertribal conflicts, and Europeans derived them from the context of class conflicts, while the colonial frontier violence that connected them in North America came to combine features of both.

It was because of this that American Indian societies could seem to Europeans such as Burke and Carlyle to mirror some of the more disturbing realities of their own society's violent class politics. The macabre crimes which they and other conservatives imputed to the French Revolution – the human tanneries, the manufacture of leg-wear of human skin, and the wigs made from the severed heads of women – were, perhaps, nothing more than propagandist fictions. But whether they were fantasies of savagery or actualities, they and the contemporaneous atrocities of frontier warfare in North America seem to have formed part of the same, shared universe of cultural symbolism.

Chapter 5
Skulls and Science

The Mythic Structure of Body-snatching

In a widely recurring theme in folk tales and mythology, a hero undertakes a dangerous journey, a magical or sacred quest. He undergoes a variety of tests and trials in the course of his travels, and overcomes many obstacles. Eventually he wins a magical object or treasure. With this prize, he returns home to a triumphal welcome.

Many observers have noted some significant parallels between these narratives and rites of passage such as rituals of initiation into adulthood. A narrative of an heroic quest has three episodes: the arduous outward journey, the gaining of the treasured object, and the victorious return. A rite of passage too, as first described by the anthropologist van Gennep (1909), has a similarly tripartite structure. The initial phase separates the novices from the community and detaches them from their current social roles. In the second, transitional or 'liminal' phase, the novices are set apart from the community in a specially sacred or polluting state. In the third and final stage, they return to the community, and are reincorporated into it in their new status. In other words, a rite of passage enacts the outlines of a story of a sacred, heroic quest. Like the heroes of these stories, novices undergoing initiation may be subjected to ordeals in which they must prove themselves. To put it the other way around, myths and folk tales concerning magical quests seem to be narrative representations of rites of passage, with the winning of the magical prize or treasure signifying the hero's attainment of adulthood or of some other valued status in society (Eliade 1958; Gilet 1998; Propp 1958).

From the late eighteenth century, men engaged in science and medicine often seem to have drawn implicitly upon very similar themes in giving accounts of their status in society and, in particular, in mythologizing their involvement in procuring cadavers for medical training. The eminent Bristol surgeon Richard Smith, whose anatomical museum I mentioned in Chapter Three, recalled in his memoirs how he had often stolen bodies and body parts for his anatomy lessons during his student days. Far from being ashamed of his adolescent body-snatching, he remembered it proudly (Fissell 2002: 141).

> [U]se makes mastery, and we had reduced this to so regular a system that we practiced it two years without suspicion – we procured a key to the dead house and provided ourselves

> with screws – hammers – wrenching iron – nails, and everything likely to be wanted …[;] whilst the family were at dinner we stole into the Dead House – removed the Extremities, Head, or anything else we wanted, even the whole corps, and then made all fast, and in the same order as before. (Quoted in Fissell 2002: 142)

We will see more examples of these attitudes in later chapters. British physicians such as Smith, trained before the Anatomy Act of 1832, all experienced many difficulties as students in obtaining cadavers for their surgical training. They often had to procure them from body-snatchers or, like Smith, resort to body-snatching themselves. After funerals, the relatives of the deceased sometimes posted armed guards in the cemetery for several days to protect the body from theft. From the public's point of view, physicians and their students habitually desecrated the bodies of the dead in a manner they associated with the punishment of the most heinous criminals. From the late eighteenth century, there were riots against the surgeons and medical schools, both in Britain and North America (Linebaugh 1975; Sappol 2002: 108–109).

In 1761 the son of a coal miner was brought to the infirmary at Bristol, England, with a head injury and died shortly afterwards.

> The boy's father stormed up to the home of the hospital surgeon, John Castelman, in the middle of the night. He had opened the coffin containing his son's body, and found the head was missing. The collier threatened to 'pull the Furnary down about thy ears!' if Castelman did not return the son's head immediately. Kingswood colliers were a notoriously riotous lot, and Castelman hurried to the hospital, returning with the head in a sack. (Fissell 2002: 142)

Patients who died in the infirmary were routinely anatomized. In 1806, the hospital received an anonymous letter complaining,

> there is scarcely an unfortunate fellow creature who has died in the Infirmary for a considerable time past, whose remains have not been most Shockingly Mutilated by a Mr. Lawrence, Pupil to the Surgeons. Head, Arms, Legs in short all parts have been taken away from the Dead by him. Some of the nurses through bribery leaving the coffin unclosed. (Quoted in Fissell 2002: 142–43)

Although it was illegal and hazardous, stealing cadavers and body parts became an intrinsic part of the medical student's life. Despite the risks, or indeed because of them, body-snatching could take on something of the character of an exciting rite of passage. Sappol has described the highly masculine and exclusive culture of the nineteenth-century U.S. medical schools; as a rite of initiation into this world, a new student might be expected to take part in a body-snatching, to prove he was worthy of entering it (Sappol 2002: 80–89). An activity which the public regarded as disgusting and sacrilegious and made medical students widely detested became, for them, a matter of pride, a daring adventure and initiatory ordeal in which students proved themselves worthy of elevation into the medical profession.

The prize of an exploit such as this was a cadaver or body part. The difficulties and obstacles that apprentice surgeons had to overcome on their journey to professional recognition were those posed by their own society's norms of decency and morality.

For these men, the successful theft of a cadaver or body part, profoundly transgressive as it was, signified the victory of knowledge over ignorance, of reason over emotion and superstition. It was an achievement that proved the higher man had mastered the lower within the aspiring physician's own character (Fissell 2002: 141; Sappol 2002: 74–89).

The New Paradigm of Biological Variation

In the 1820s and 1830s, a special form of body-snatching or grave robbery became common. Its purpose was not necessarily to obtain the entire body, but specifically the head or skull. At this time, human skulls had come to acquire a central place in scientific investigations of individual and racial differences and, as a result, they became valuable commodities.

One major form taken by this new interest in the skull was the science – as its followers considered it – of phrenology, which claimed that moral, temperamental and intellectual propensities were reflected in the form of the skull, and could be identified through an examination of its shape. The principles of phrenology were first formulated by Franz Gall in Germany in the late eighteenth century, and elaborated and publicly promoted by his student Johann Spurzheim, and by George Combe in Scotland. Phrenology postulated the existence of some thirty faculties (the exact number varied), with names such as philoprogenitiveness (reproductive desire), constructiveness (mechanical skill), combativeness, benevolence and veneration, localized in different regions on the cortex of the brain. The relative development of each of these faculties in the individual could be ascertained by examining the shape of the head (van Wyhe 2004). Although phrenology ceased to be taken seriously by scientists by the 1850s it became, particularly in the United States, a commercially highly successful popular science and philosophy of self-help, and by the middle and later decades of the nineteenth century many lay Americans considered it 'a scientific achievement on par with the invention of telegraphy or daguerreotypy' (Hanlon 2003: 284).

Phrenologists had a particular interest in the heads and skulls of men, living or dead, whom they deemed to be of superior intellect or artistic genius. In the early decades of the nineteenth century, the tombs of many such men were robbed after their deaths and their heads or skulls taken as phrenological specimens (Dickey 2009; Henschen 1966).

One of them was the composer Haydn. After he died in 1809, two adherents of phrenology – a friend of Haydn's called Rosenbaum and another, Peter, the director of a local prison – bribed the gravedigger to remove the composer's head and bring it to them. They cleaned the skull, and kept it on a white silk cushion trimmed with black, inside a specially made black wooden box with glass windows and a golden lyre on the top. In 1820, when Haydn's patron Prince Esterházy had his body exhumed to give him a more fitting tomb, the officials who opened the coffin were shocked to discover that the head was missing. Their enquiries led them to Rosenbaum, but when the police searched his house, his wife hid the skull in her mattress and lay on it, pretending to be indisposed. Later, following the Prince's offer of a large bribe, Rosenbaum handed over the skull of someone else, pretending it was Haydn's, and this was buried with the composer's remains. When Rosenbaum was dying, he bequeathed Haydn's skull to Peter, asking him to bequeath it in turn to the museum of the Gesellschaft der

Musikfreunde in Vienna, which had a large collection of Haydn memorabilia. The skull remained there from 1895 until 1954, when it was finally reunited with the rest of Haydn's remains (Geiringer 1982: 191–92).

In the case of Beethoven, too, many people sought to obtain parts of his body as soon as it became apparent that he was dying. In the days before his death in 1826, and for several days afterwards, numerous visitors came to his house and took clippings of his hair. The day after he died, his body was autopsied, the top of the skull was sawn off and the temporal bones were removed and taken away for study. Reportedly, they ended up in the possession of a mortuary orderly who sold them to a foreign physician, and are now lost. A few days after the funeral, Beethoven's friends received word from the sexton that he had been offered 1,000 florins for Beethoven's skull. There was such concern over this that his friends engaged watchmen to guard the grave every night for some time after the funeral (Meredith 2005).

In 1863 the Gesellschaft der Musikfreunde had the remains of Beethoven and Schubert exhumed in order to provide them with more fitting resting places. They discovered that a substantial layer of bricks had been built over Beethoven's coffin after its burial specifically to protect the head from grave robbers. The main goal of the exhumations was to examine the two composers' skulls phrenologically, because a striking difference in head shape had often been noted between the two composers. As one of Beethoven's friends observed, 'The walls of Beethoven's skull exhibit strong density and thickness, whereas Schubert's bones show feminine delicateness' (quoted in Meredith 2005: 4). It had long been felt that these differences in skull form corresponded to differences in the character of their musical works – Beethoven's music being forceful, masculine and heroic, and Schubert's having more delicate and feminine qualities. The committee considered whether these

> two precious relics, having been taken from the soil, should be kept permanently in proper surroundings and a worthy place that would closely reflect the grand activity of the spirits that lived in these bony dwellings. Nothing could seem more appropriate for this purpose than the first musical organization of Vienna and of the Austrian empire that had already existed in the days of both composers and that would possess within a few years a new facility that would be worthy to keep the two remains. (Quoted in Meredith 2005: 4)

In the end, however, the committee decided to re-inter the skulls, along with the other bones of both composers, in the newly prepared vaults. But they kept pieces of the original coffins and some of the nails, as well as fragments of clothing and clippings of hair, apparently as personal keepsakes. In addition, Professor Romeo Seligmann, a member of a prominent family of Vienna physicians, was allowed to take photographs and make drawings, measurements and plaster casts of the skulls. During this process, an unknown person secretly retained some ten fragments of Beethoven's skull and gave them to Professor Seligmann, for his skull collection. Seligmann had a small metal box specially made to store them in, a reliquary carefully shaped to fit the bone fragments, and inscribed the lid with the word 'Beethoven'. The box and skull fragments have remained until recent times in his family (Meredith 2005).

Hagner (1999, 2003) has observed how the skulls of men regarded as geniuses became at this time objects both of scientific interest and of reverence, with these two attitudes, the scientific and the hagiographic, inextricably intertwined. In many ways, the preoccupation of phrenology with the skulls of superior men echoed earlier practices of venerating saints' relics. In an age of science, the skull of the genius was the successor to the holy relic of the saint during the age of religion. These priceless objects continued to be surrounded by much the same outward symbolism of veneration, such as the use of special reliquaries in which to house them. And, just as with the remains of medieval saints (Geary 1986), there was often intense competition for the possession of the most prestigious relics.

Although the keeping, and in some cases theft, of the skulls of exemplary men were therefore not entirely new, phrenology gave these practices a new impetus and significance. So, when Descartes died in Stockholm in 1650 he was buried there, until his remains were exhumed in 1666 in order to be repatriated to France. While the French ambassador removed the first joint of the right index finger as a personal keepsake, it appears that a captain in the Swedish guards also surreptitiously took the philosopher's skull and replaced it with another. The skull was then resold a number of times, and came to be inscribed with the name of Descartes and those of its successive owners. It eventually came into the possession of the Swedish chemist Berzelius, who offered it to the French naturalist Cuvier in 1821 to make amends for his countryman's theft of the skull. The skull now rests in the Musée de l'Homme in Paris (Aron 1996; Gaukroger 1995: 417).

Criminal Skulls

Phrenologists were also interested in the heads of convicts for the insights these might yield into the causes of criminality. The skulls of executed murderers and traitors and plaster casts of their heads were kept in this way because it was assumed that the study of their shape and structure by suitably qualified experts could yield clues to the causes of homicide, treason, political extremism, religious fanaticism and other evils. An early example from France is the skull of Solayman al-Halabi, a Syrian student who in 1800 assassinated General Kleber, the commander of the French forces in Egypt at the time. After Al-Halabi was publicly executed in Cairo by impalement, his skull and skeleton were sent to the Museum of Anatomy in Paris, as phrenological specimens of murder and fanaticism, and this museum came to house many other similar specimens (Al-Shetawi 1987: 45–47; Gorton 1851: 440).

In Britain the earliest organization of phrenologists was the Phrenological Society of Edinburgh, established by George Combe in 1820. It built up a collection of 'national skulls' from various parts of the empire, and many of its members also had private collections of their own. Some of the skulls were those of convicts, obtained from jails and executions in Britain and overseas. The Society acquired skulls of convicts from Australia and had the skulls of those hanged during the 1822 insurrection in Ceylon. It also possessed seven skulls originating in a mass execution of Indian thugs in 1833, sent by the Bengal Medical Service on the orders of the Chief Secretary to the Government of India, an admirer of phrenology. Because many of the skulls coming from the colonies originated in executions or the deaths of convicts in prison, they could provide material for the study of racial and national characteristics, as well as of criminality, and racial difference and criminal deviancy could easily become conflated (C. Anderson 2004: 183–85).

If the study of the skulls of geniuses was the secular, scientific successor to the worship of saints' relics, museum displays of the skulls of notorious murderers and traitors seem in many respects to have inherited some of the functions of earlier practices such as gibbeting and the public exposure of the bodies or body parts of executed felons. Indeed, in Britain at least, phrenology emerged into public consciousness precisely at the time that legal reforms were abolishing practices such as the anatomization of murderers and the public display of executed bodies. The museum therefore seems to have taken over some of these punitive functions, allowing these to continue in a publicly acceptable form. The criminal heads and skulls displayed in phrenological collections were objects of scientific interest and of public dishonour at the same time.

Later in the nineteenth century, Cesare Lombroso developed his school of criminal anthropology, which had much in common with phrenology though Lombroso himself sought to repudiate such connections. The criminal, like the genius, emerged as a distinct anthropometric 'type' (even a biological type) of human, distinguishable by outward signs such as the shape of the ears, or the toes, as well as the skull. To Lombroso, criminals were a sort of quasi-race, a biologically inferior or degenerate class of human, a reversion to the savage. Their criminality was assumed to be passed on by heredity (Horn 2003).

Inevitably, anatomical and anthropometric analyses of the skulls of notorious or celebrated persons were interwoven with moral, aesthetic and political judgements, as happened with the skull of Charlotte Corday.

> Although uncertainty surrounds how it was first acquired, the cranium of Marat's murderer passed through several hands until around 1840 it served as a grim table-decoration, terrifying select dinner guests at the house of [the collector of revolutionary memorabilia] Corbeau de Saint-Albin. It then probably passed to education minister Victor Duruy, then Prince Roland Bonaparte, before turning up in the anthropological section of [the] 1889 Universal Exhibition. Probably purchased from the executioner in 1793, whoever first acquired the skull appeared to have bribed others into silence by handing out her front teeth as gifts. (Stammers 2008: 306)

During the scientific congresses which took place as part of the Universal Exhibition in Paris in 1889, commemorating the centenary of the French Revolution, the interpretation of Corday's skull became the subject of a celebrated dispute between Lombroso and the French anthropologist Topinard. While Topinard considered Corday's cranium to exhibit typical feminine beauty, curvaceousness and delicacy, Lombroso detected upon it a special feature he called the occipital fossa, which he believed to be a mark of irredeemable criminality and degeneracy (Dick 1993).

One of the last acquisitions of this sort by the Museum of Anatomy in Paris seems to have been the head of the Dutch exotic dancer and courtesan known as Mata Hari, who was executed by the French for espionage during the First World War. As no relatives came forward to claim her body, it was used for dissection by medical students. Her head was embalmed, and kept in the museum as part of its collection of heads of celebrated criminals. In 2000 it was discovered to be missing, and is presumed to have been stolen (T.M. Proctor 2003: 177).

Skulls and Racial Science

In the United States, a scientific interest in the human skull specifically as evidence of racial variation was represented by the work of craniologists such as Samuel Morton, who published his landmark *Crania Americana* in 1839. Morton's principal interest lay in distinguishing races on the basis of differences in cranial capacity and brain size. He had amassed a large personal collection of skulls from many parts of the world, and on the basis of his measurements of their capacity he claimed that a natural hierarchy of races existed, with Africans having the smallest brains and whites the largest (S.J. Gould 1996).

Although phrenology was a theory of individual psychology, not of race, it nevertheless had implications for the definition of races, and had a significant influence on Morton's own ideas. Phrenological understandings of racial types were essentially characterological. So, for example, to the U.S. phrenologist Orson Fowler, who ran a large phrenological business empire from his headquarters in New York, an American Indian was an Indian by virtue of his essential quality of independence and wildness; what made a Jew a Jew was his inherited acquisitiveness. Africans, he believed, were characterized by qualities such as fondness for children, politeness and excellence as waiters (1852: 132–40).

But both phrenology and racial craniometry had several important features in common. First, though the particular characteristics by which they distinguished races tended to differ, they were both based on the assumption that the characteristics were innate, hereditary and largely immutable; second, they ordered people in natural relationships of superiority and inferiority; and third, they were objectively discoverable through examination of the shape and size of the skull.

This interest in the skull as the key diacritic of racial hierarchy, which lasted throughout the nineteenth century and beyond, represented a marked departure from Enlightenment understandings of race. In the eighteenth century, as we saw earlier, races had tended to be viewed as variations of skin colour, hair and facial features brought about by climate and historical chance. They were understood as superficial differences resting on the foundation of a shared and universal human nature (Bieder 2000: 32; B. Douglas 2008). But in the early part of the nineteenth century, racial differences began to be portrayed as much deeper, more radically biological and historically immutable.

> The races of men, like those of the canines and other animals, though modified by climates, are never transformed into each other. The white man, the negro, the Jew, the greyhound, the foxhound, the pointer, preserve their types and instincts in all climates. (Nott 1866: 117)

Collecting

The special significance which this new paradigm gave to the skull resulted in a demand for specimens for craniological and phrenological study by physicians and other scientists. Phrenologists and craniologists were particularly keen to acquire skulls they understood as exceptional and rare. On the one hand, they wanted the skulls of those they placed above the average, such as creative geniuses and superior intellects. On the other hand, they also sought skulls of those they ranked lower than the average man: the outlaw, the insane, the pathological and the racially foreign.

Such specimens were highly sought after, and scholars circulated and exchanged them internationally as if they were precious valuables (Luyendijk-Elshout 1997). Their aim was to discover the upper and lower boundaries of the normal by means of the measurement of differences in skull form. They assumed that the categories of people which these boundaries defined were distinct, biologically defined 'types' and formed a hierarchy. At the top was the artistic or scientific genius. Below the genius was the average man of European stock. Below the average European man were criminals, the insane and members of other races – and, arguably, women (Stepan 1993). Below these lower forms of humans were animals. The natural world was thus arranged as if on the rungs of a vast ladder, a scala naturae, a great chain of being (K. Anderson and Perrin 2009).

The anatomical museums and phrenological collections in which these taxonomies were displayed were popular among the nineteenth-century public (Sappol 2002, 2004). A mid nineteenth-century U.S. visitor to Europe recorded her impressions of the famous Museum of Anatomy in Paris, with its displays of skulls arranged in order of their level of moral and intellectual development:

> This collection is far superior to all others of the kind in the world, being formed under the superintendence of the illustrious Cuvier and Buffon. Here are skeletons of all animals, of entire whales, and skulls of all races of men. The celebrated Dr. Gall, the founder of Phrenology, left his great collection of skulls to this Museum. The skulls are arranged in regular sequence, from the idiotic skull of the Caffre or Hottentot – and scarcely human creature of African islands – up to the great and noble type of the Anglo-Saxon. There are also skeletons of all nations .... There is the skeleton of the celebrated dwarf, 'Bebe' [and] a great many skeletons of Negroes, Chinese, Calmucks, Cossacks, that of the assassin of Gen. Kleber, and there are Egyptian mummies; in short, the whole tremendous premises of Comparative Anatomy are here exposed. (Washington 1860: 683)

A collection of this sort was, conceptually at least, a pyramid of skulls, with one, or a few, pre-eminent specimens – such as the skull of Descartes – at the top, and increasing numbers on each descending level. At the apex, there was rarity and quality; at the bottom, mass and quantity.

Thus while the skulls of famous poets and composers were sought after just as much as those of the Maori or American Indians, and their graves were just as likely to be violated, those who stole the skulls of celebrated artists or philosophers tended to represent the theft, as we have seen, as a selfless and even heroic act of homage or devotion. But collectors often treated the remains of colonized peoples and lower races as examples simply of natural history, in much the same category as animal specimens. In 1898 a correspondent wrote to Charles de Vos, the Director of the Queensland Museum in Australia.

> How are you off for Tasmanian Tigers[?] If you would like one or two I may be able to send you a good example and I think later on I may be able to send you a skull of a tasmanian [sic] aboriginal which you may possibly not have in your museum. We have not got a skull of a Queensland Native considering the large number I have collected in the

Torres Strait. I often wish I had a few of them. However, anything you can make up will be greatfully [*sic*] received. (Robins 1996: 14; see also Turnbull 2001, 2007)

Another correspondent wrote to de Vos the same year:

Dear Sir, I have forwarded from here a shipment to Brisbane 1 case containing

1 skeleton of Maori

a lot of Moa bones, all I have been able to get

1 skeleton of a Huia

1 skeleton of a Blue duck. (Robins 1996: 14)

Many of these early collectors were medical doctors, and had internalized the ethos of professional triumphalism which pervaded the nineteenth century medical schools in regard to the human body. A particularly notorious case concerned the death of William Lanney, in the town of Hobart in the British colony of Tasmania in 1869. The local scientific community at the time considered Lanney to be the last aboriginal Tasmanian man, the only surviving male of a dying race. His remains were as a consequence coveted by two competing scientific factions. One was represented by William Crowther, an honorary medical officer at the local hospital, who had undertaken to send Lanney's skeleton to the Hunterian Museum of the Royal College of Surgeons in London. The main figure in the rival faction was George Stokell, the hospital's resident surgeon. He had been instructed by the local Royal Society to acquire the body for the Society's own 'national' museum. Crowther, fearing the Tasmanian authorities were favouring his rivals, stole into the hospital together with his son and an apprentice shortly after Lanney died, and secretly removed Lanney's skull. He replaced it with that of a white schoolmaster, Thomas Ross, a recently deceased patient. When Stokell discovered the theft, he reported it to the Royal Society, and was instructed to immediately remove Lanney's hands and feet to prevent Crowther from obtaining a complete skeleton. Lanney's remains were then buried, but shortly afterwards, Stokell dispatched body-snatchers to disinter his remains and return them to the hospital where he removed the remaining bones. The discovery of the mutilation of Lanney and Ross's bodies sparked a major scandal in the colony, and led to the introduction of an Anatomy Bill modelled on the British Anatomy Act of 1832, legalizing the use of unclaimed bodies for dissection (MacDonald 2005, 2006).

Stokell also took some of Lanney's skin and had a purse made from it as a gift for a friend, as if Lanney had been an executed felon (MacDonald 2006: 185). If this object was a trophy of sorts, it was a memento of Stokell's triumph, not over Lanney of course, but over his medical rivals. Nevertheless, in perpetrating on Lanney's body an act usually carried out only on the bodies of anatomized murderers, Stokell expressed an implicit equation between criminals and the lower races, two human types assumed to be in a similar structural relation with the European norm.

Chapter 6

The Collecting Expedition as a Magical Quest

Scientific Collecting and the Metaphor of the Hunt

We have seen that the collection of cadavers and human body parts for medical and scientific study in the early nineteenth century was sometimes represented in imagery of an initiatory ordeal or quest. Such a quest for rational knowledge could also be described metaphorically as a hunt, one in which the prizes sought by the hunter were human remains rather than those of animals.

The robbing of graves for osteological collections, for instance, like the practice of body-snatching from which it had developed (see Highet 2005), was a secret, illicit, often dangerous and typically nocturnal, predatory adventure. The anthropologist A.C. Haddon recalls one night in Ireland in the 1890s when he and a companion went by boat to an old rural church and burgled it for skulls.

> When the coast was clear we put our spoils in the sack and cautiously made our way back to the road. Then it did not matter who saw us. The sailors wanted to take the sack when we got back to the boat but Dixon would not give it up and when asked what was in it said 'Potheen' [illicit spirit]. So without any further trouble we got the skulls aboard and then we packed them in Dixon's portmanteau and locked it and no one except our two selves had any idea there are a dozen human skulls on board and they shan't know either. (Quiggin 1942: 70)

As Urry observes, Haddon's account of this exploit reads more like an adventure story 'from the *Boy's Own Journal* than a report from a Fellow of the Royal Society' (1989: 13). Victorian accounts of the activities of collectors – their own accounts, and those of their admirers - are full of references of this sort to their daring escapades, their courage, perseverance and dedication, and the difficulties, hardships and dangers they overcame for the sake of science (see, for instance, A. Fabian 2003).

Between 1877 and 1889, the Austrian explorer, naturalist and collector Andreas Reischek collected Maori artefacts and human remains, often under conditions of secrecy and considerable personal risk. A contemporary New Zealand newspaper praised him as 'brave, enduring, self-sacrificing and indomitable .... [T]aking him all in all, as an example of enthusiasm and unselfishness in scientific pursuit, I know of none to compare with him in New Zealand' (quoted in Kolig 1986: 55).

Similar laudatory language was used to describe the robbing of Aboriginal graves in Australia (Turnbull 1999: 220). A French newspaper of 1831 describes the Verreaux brothers in similar terms. They were naturalists and taxidermists who, most notoriously, removed the corpse of a bushman from a grave, preserved it, and brought it to Paris as a natural history specimen (see Parsons and Segobye 2002).

> Two young people, Messieurs the Verreaux brothers, have recently arrived from a voyage to the ends of Africa, to the land of the Cape of Good-Hope. One of these interesting naturalists is barely eighteen years old, but he has already spent twenty months in the wild country north of the land of the Hottentots, between the latitudes of Natal and the top of St Helena Bay. How can one possibly imagine what deprivations he had to endure? Our young compatriots had to face the dangers of living in the midst of the natives of this zone of Africa, who are ferocious as well as black, as well as the fawn-coloured wild animals among which they live, about which we do not need to tell. We want to speak only about the triumphs of their collecting, and do not know which to admire more, their intrepidity or their perseverance. Humans, quadrupeds, birds, fish, plants, minerals, shells – all of these they have studied. Their hunting has given them tigers, lions, hyenas ....But their greatest curiosity is an individual of the nation of the Betjouanas. This man is preserved by the means by which naturalists prepare their specimens and reconstitute their form and, so to speak, their inert life. He is of small stature, black of skin, his head covered by short woolly and curly hair, armed with arrows and a lance, clothes in antelope skin, made of bush-pig, full of small glass-beads, seeds, and of small bones. Another thing that we are rather embarrassed to find a suitable term to characterise, is the very special accessory of modest clothing worn by the Betjouanas, which we find most striking.
>
> Messieurs Verreaux have deposited their scientific riches at the stores of Monsieur Delessert, rue Saint-France, n.3. There they are generously put on display for the public, without charge. It would be well if the Jardin des Plantes took this opportunity to extend its collections, already so beautiful, to become even more desirable – and to use the skills which they do not already possess of Messieurs Verreaux with the time, the talent, and the energy necessary to go out to Africa to catch nature in the ace. (Quoted in Molina 2002: 34)

The colonies were a vital source of specimens for anthropologists, anatomists and others interested scientists. In southern Africa early in the nineteenth century, the naturalist Ludwig Krebs sent to German museums consignments including items he described as a 'Hottentot in brine', a 'Kaffer's skull in spirits', and a 'complete Bushman in brine in a barrel' (Ffolliot and Liversidge 1971: 70, 172, 230). As late as the 1890s, the naturalist Jameson brought a preserved African head to London (Franey 2001: 230). Travellers to the colonies – explorers, naturalists, physicians, anthropologists, missionaries and so forth – were urged to collect skulls in particular. They obtained them from graves, hospitals, execution sites and battlefields (Franey 2001: 222; Luyendijk-Elshout 1997; Roque 2010; Stern 1971: 59).

Pannell (1992) has described the close parallels between the accounts of Victorian natural science collecting expeditions, and narratives of headhunting raids in some indigenous societies. The people of Amaya in the Moluccas, for instance, represented their headhunting forays in imagery of a journey to another world, where foreign heads were appropriated as sources of power. The late nineteenth-century natural scientist

Wallace and, later, the Scottish naturalist Forbes, who both collected in the region of the Amaya, represented their own collecting ventures in strikingly similar terms. Besides obtaining many specimens of the local fauna and flora, Wallace collected head measurements from the Amaya and Forbes collected actual human skulls from them, and both described themselves, very much as did the Amaya, as having journeyed to another world in search of such trophies, in this case a world of the exotic and primitive past (see also Hoskins 1996b: 15–17).

Although Pannell suggests no explanation of the similarities between these narratives of travel to distant worlds, the answer perhaps lies in the way the world of nineteenth-century museum collecting, as Griffiths (1996: 12, 19, 21) observes, was pervaded by metaphors of 'prey', 'quarry', 'trophies' and 'prizes': in other words, by the language of the hunt or chase. This was the golden age of trophy-hunting, when hunting and museum collecting were inextricably linked, and there was often little or no meaningful distinction between a mounted trophy head and a natural history specimen (Pearce 1995: 184–85; Mackenzie 1987: 180). Moreover, the distinction between civilized and savage peoples was often equated with the distinction between domestic and wild animals, thereby casting savages in the role of game or quarry (Ritvo 1987: 16; cf. Landau 1996).

Sometimes such conceptions were acted out very literally. During a series of punitive raids by local settlers in Queensland, Australia, in 1865, Korah H. Wills, a farmer and future local mayor, dissected the corpse of an aboriginal man and exhibited the remains during a fundraising event for charity.

> On one of those occasions, I took it in my head to get a few specimens of certain limbs and head of a Black fellow, which was not a very delicate operation, I can tell you. I shall never forget the time when I first found the subject that I intended to anatomise, when my friends were looking on, and I commenced operations dissecting. I went to work business-like to take off the head first, and then the arms and then the legs, gathered them together and put them into my pack saddle.
>
> Well, I took my trophies home to the Station that morning, and in the afternoon my friends were all going down to the Lagoon to fish and Bathe and I took some of my limbs to the Lagoon also to divest of its flesh as much as I could and I got pretty well [on] with it until it became dark and I had to give up the unholy job, and we went back to the Station for supper and yarns, and pipes, and nightcaps of whisky before turning in .... I exhibited my Skull (pardon... my blackfellow's), arms and legs, to the disgust of many. I remember I had to cover them up with a flag, the Union Jack. (Quoted in Monaghan 1991: 33; see also Turnbull 1997: 37–38)

The Curator of the Australian Museum wrote to the Director of the Colonial Museum in New Zealand in 1882:

> With respect to the skulls I shall be glad to have authentic 'Moriori' [indigenous people of the Chatham Islands] and can send a few Australian [in] exchange. The shooting season is over in Queensland and the 'Black Game' is protected now by more humane laws than formerly. So it is impossible to obtain reliable skulls and skeletons. (Quoted in Turnbull 1991: 9)

The Exotic: Heads as Trade Goods

Early in the nineteenth century, Europeans developed a particular interest in some indigenous peoples who seemed, like themselves, to attribute a special value and significance to human heads or skulls, and appeared to possess collecting practices of their own regarding these objects. The Maori people of New Zealand, for instance, sometimes preserved the elaborately tattooed heads of their enemies and those of their own forebears, and these objects, called *mokomokai*, became highly sought after as curios among European collectors early in the nineteenth century. European trade with Maoris for mokomokai peaked between 1820 and 1830, coinciding with the high point in the popularity of phrenology internationally. As it happened, firearms had started to be introduced to the Maori at this time, and rival tribes competed to acquire these new weapons and use them against each other, resulting in the series of devastating intertribal conflicts known as the Musket Wars. The international demand for *mokomokai* as collectibles seems to have been an integral contributory factor in these conflicts. Maori traded heads for weapons and ammunition with which to obtain further heads, in a spiral of escalating violence which came to an end only once all the tribes had acquired firearms and these weapons no longer conferred a competitive advantage (Henare 2005; Obeyesekere 2005: 43–45, 117–38; Robley 1896).

Exoticism, the representation of other cultures and their products as desirable objects of consumption (Huggan 2001), is often understood to rest upon representations of difference and otherness. But the attraction of the foreign may derive rather from perceptions of its disturbing resemblances and connections with the culturally familiar. The appeal of the exotic may lie, in other words, not just in difference but in the recognition of elements of oneself in the remote other. In particular, other cultures may be attractively 'exotic' to the extent that they seem to realize and fulfil behaviour deemed transgressive at home.

Much of the fascination which 'headhunting' held for many Victorians as an icon of the primitive was perhaps due to it appearing to resonate with their own collecting practices in ways that could seem both exciting and uncomfortable. That is, in being readily intelligible to the Victorians as a modality of hunting, a form of predation upon human quarry, headhunting seemed to expose truths about their own collecting practices, and reflected their anxieties concerning these medical and scientific uses of the body. Headhunting was not simply a strange custom, then, but a strangely familiar one. The preserved heads kept by peoples such as the Maori were desirable exotic objects to Europeans, not because they were entirely alien but, quite the opposite, because they evoked the existence of commonalities beneath the surface differences between the civilized man and the savage.

A situation comparable to that of the early nineteenth-century Maori seems to have arisen later in the century in Ecuador, among the Jivaro people, more properly called the Shuar. The Shuar became notorious internationally at this time for their practices of raiding their neighbours for heads, from which they prepared ritual objects called *tsantsa*, usually referred to in English as shrunken heads. Again, these objects became highly valuable exotic curios, and a growing demand for them in the international market in ethnographic curiosities resulted in an escalation in local warfare. In the late nineteenth and early twentieth centuries there was a marked intensification of Shuar warmaking, and this seems to have been a result of increasing contact and trade with European outsiders. The Shuar began to raid neighbouring peoples specifically to obtain heads and exchange *tsantsa* for European manufactured goods, including firearms. As with the Maori earlier, Shuar warfare at this time was fuelled by the demand for *tsantsa* in the global curio market (Bennett Ross 1984; Rubenstein 2004, 2007; Steel 1999).

In the case of the Shuar and Maori then, an exchange relationship formed in which indigenous peoples were induced to offer material evidence of savagery for Western consumption, in return for manufactured goods. This trade fed back into local patterns of warfare and intensified them, further confirming outsiders' perceptions of these peoples as warlike primitives. The European image of the primitive headhunter seems to have developed, then, at the same time as close interconnections developed between the collecting practices of colonizer and colonized, a synergy in which each stimulated or intensified the collecting activities of the other.

The Schweinfurth Expedition

These connections between the complex cultural preoccupations of nineteenth-century Europeans with the human skull and head and their stereotypes of exotic savagery are graphically illustrated by Georg Schweinfurth's expedition to central Africa from 1868 to 1871. Schweinfurth – a botanist, explorer and ethnologist sponsored by a German scientific institute – had two particular aims in addition to exploration and ethnological collecting: he wished to collect human skulls for German museums, and to find proof of cannibalism among the natives of unexplored central Africa (Schweinfurth 1874). To this end, he determined on reaching the kingdom of Monbuttoo (Mangbetu, in the modern-day Democratic Republic of Congo) where, so he had been told, the people were particularly ferocious cannibals who raided their enemies specifically to eat them.

Schweinfurth's two aims of collecting skulls and discovering cannibalism meshed with each other perfectly. Having reached the Monbuttoo, he decided that the easiest way to gather skulls was to buy up the remains of their cannibal feasts.

> 'Bring your weapons,' I would say; 'bring your weapons, and the produce of your handicraft, your ornaments and tools, and I will give you beautiful things in return; bring the fruits of your forests, and the leaves of the trees on which they grow: bring the skins and skulls of animals; but above all bring the human skulls that remain over from your meals: they are of no use to you – bring them, and I will give you copper in exchange'. (Schweinfurth 1874: 54)

Word spread that he was someone who would trade valuable copper rings in return for skulls. The people responded by bringing him large amounts of human skeletal material. Some of it was still wet and appeared freshly boiled, and he supposed it must have come straight from their platters. Most of the material was so damaged and incomplete it was of no use to him. But he found some usable specimens and purchased them. In one stroke, he obtains his osteological specimens, and confirmation of the people's savagery.

> I had rarely occasion to repeat my request, but almost before my wish was uttered there was opened a regular curiosity mart; goods were bartered, and a flourishing trade was done.
>
> The stock of bones that was thus brought to me in one day was quite astonishing, and could not do otherwise than remove any lingering hesitation I might have in believing the cannibal propensities of the people. There were piles of every kind – fragments of skulls, and lower jaw-bones from which the teeth had been extracted to serve as ornaments for the neck. The belief seemed to be that I had no intention of dealing otherwise than wholesale. Proofs enough were before me; sufficient, I should suppose, to silence even the most stubborn scepticism. It cost me some trouble to convince the people that my requirements only extended to such skulls as were perfectly uninjured, and that for such only could I be content to pay. For a perfect skull I promised an armlet of copper, but I found that nearly all that were brought to me had been smashed for the purpose of extracting the brains. Out of the two hundred skulls that were produced, I was able to select no more than forty, each of which I carefully labelled for consignment to Europe. (Schweinfurth 1874: 54)

Schweinfurth had travelled to the Monbuttoo from Khartoum with a party of ivory merchants and their armed escort. These traders had regular and longstanding commercial relations with the Monbuttoo, and Schweinfurth travelled under their protection. It is likely that the Monbuttoo identified him with the traders, albeit a trader in human bones rather than elephant ivory. Indeed, he may have appeared to them to be offering them bounties for human skulls, in much the same way that the ivory traders accompanying him offered them material inducements to hunt elephants.

Some of the Africans thought that he planned to eat the bones, or make poison from them. As Jahoda puts it, his avidity for skulls led the Africans he encountered to 'suspect that it was the explorer who had a predilection for cannibalistic practices' (1999: 121). In an attempt to allay these rumours, he tried to explain the principles of phrenology.

> To those who brought the skulls, I thought it expedient to explain that we wanted them, so that in our far-off country we could learn all about the people who dwelt here, and that we were able, from the mere shape of the head, to tell all about people's tempers and dispositions, their good qualities and their bad; and that for this purpose we gathered skulls together from every quarter of the globe. When the Khartoomers [ivory traders accompanying his party] saw that the collection was now going on for a second year, they were only the more confirmed in their belief that I submitted them to a certain process by which I obtained a subtle poison. From the more dense and stupid natives, the idea could not be eradicated that I wanted all the bones for my food. To save the honour of Europe, and in love for the science of which I was the representative, I lavished on these errors an incense unbefitting the doctrines of Gall's phrenology. (Schweinfurth 1874: 55)

Later, he and his party were attacked a number of times by communities through which they passed. On one of these occasions, the leader of the ivory traders was wounded and, in revenge, some of his retainers decapitated the bodies of those they killed and brought the heads back to camp. 'As no value appeared in any quarter to be attached to the heads I appropriated them to myself, and was thus able to add to the variety of my collection of skulls' (Schweinfurth 1874: 174). He boiled the heads in his tent with a sense of grim satisfaction, likening himself to Nemesis, bringer of justice and retribution:

> Probably with their own eyes these heads had watched the stewing of other human heads, but now they had to simmer on in my caldron. Although I was quite aware that the [Moslem]

> Nubians reckoned the bones of all heathens and unbelievers as entitled to no more respect than the bones of brute beasts, yet for decency's sake I preferred performing the operation in the seclusion of my tent. Notwithstanding that my dogs had not had any animal food for several days, they could not be induced to eat a morsel of the boiled human flesh. (Schweinfurth 1874: 178)

Once his party had been attacked, his collecting activities and the preparation of specimens began to take on a punitive significance for him. When he boiled the Africans' heads, the procedure seemed to him so much like the cannibal practices he attributed to these men that it turned into a fantasy of revenge. In this respect, his attitudes were in stark contrast with those of many of the other members of his party. 'All the negroes attached to our caravan had a superstitious horror of the practice of decapitating the dead, and the Nubians would have deemed themselves defiled by touching the corpse of a heathen' (Schweinfurth 1874: 174). The fact that many of the Africans he encountered seemed repelled by the practice of taking the heads of enemies, and regarded the dead bodies of those they killed as defiling, was clearly very puzzling to Schweinfurth, and required special explanation. He resolved it by supposing that Africans were either headhunters and cannibals or, if they were not, they were prevented from being so by their religious prejudices and superstitions. Either way, their primitiveness was confirmed.

On a later occasion, after another fight, local Africans brought him skulls to trade for copper.

> The skulls in the Anatomical Museum of Berlin that are numbered 36, 37, and 38 might be supposed capable of unfolding a deplorable tale of these depredations. Some natives brought them to me fresh boiled, only a few days after the raid had been perpetrated; they had heard from the Monbuttoo that I was accustomed to give rings of copper in exchange for skulls, and as I was not able to bring the poor fellows to life again I saw no reason why I should not purchase their remains in the interests of science. (Schweinfurth 1874: 222-23)

Schweinfurth's expedition was, in a sense, a self-fulfilling prophecy. He intended to find evidence of cannibalism and headhunting, and his own actions – especially the collecting practices he employed – were virtually guaranteed to elicit the very evidence he sought. First, he offered trade goods in return for evidence of such savagery. These were exchanges in which he paid, or otherwise solicited, the peoples he encountered to produce signs of their savage nature, or to enact his own European fantasies of primitiveness. Second, his journey through central Africa, accompanied by a large armed escort and acquiring skulls along the way by a combination of violence and trade, was itself a sort of headhunting expedition. It may have seemed so to some of the local communities through which he passed. Certainly, it was almost bound sometimes to elicit reprisals in kind. Though apparently quite unaware that he was doing so, he was himself reproducing the very behaviour he was looking for in those whom he encountered, and inducing them to reproduce the same behaviour in reply.

The Wollaston Expedition

The more elaborate and extended a collecting expedition, the more it could come unwittingly to assume the form of a military raid – or indeed to resemble European conceptions of a headhunting foray. The expedition of 1912–13 to Dutch New Guinea organized by A.F.R. Wollaston seems a case in point. Wollaston was a British doctor, naturalist and explorer, and was accompanied on this expedition by a Dutch officer and military escort and a large number of porters. His main purpose was to make the first ascent of the peaks of the Central Range, but he also collected ethnological and natural history specimens on this expedition, including a series of human skulls. Although Wollaston in his accounts of the expedition provides no information on how he acquired these skulls, they appear to have originated in a tragic series of events brought about by his expedition's arrival (see Ballard 2001).

Travelling upriver from the coast, Wollaston encountered the Amungme, a highland people for whom this was their first encounter with Europeans. They had a long history of millenarian religious movements even before European contact, and welcomed Wollaston's party as spirits having come to lead them to paradise. Many of the Amungme, travelling in whole families, came down from the highlands to visit the expedition's base camps in the lowlands. Amungme interviewed by Ballard in the 1990s remember it as a catastrophe. Large numbers of people started dying mysteriously, and the contemporary Amungme say the mass deaths were caused by spirits associated with the lowlands. Wollaston's own account confirms the deaths. On returning from the central mountains, retracing their steps, he and his companions were shocked to find the bodies of thirty or forty people along the track, with no apparent cause of death. Their guides suggested that they had died of hunger. The Amungme themselves say that many more people died, and that when their relatives came to retrieve their bodies after Wollaston's party had left, they discovered that a number of them had been beheaded and their heads taken away, an occurrence that they found baffling. As Wollaston was a trained medical doctor this is most likely to have been carried out by Wollaston himself, or under his supervision, while the expedition were dismantling their camp and preparing to leave. In other words, he may have decided to avail himself of an opportunity for scientific collecting offered by what appears to have been an epidemic of some sort, caused by his own arrival (Ballard 2001).

Curiously, Wollaston's behaviour, in reaching the Amungme from the coast with a large party of armed men and departing with severed heads, seems to have unwittingly re-enacted the behaviour of the near neighbours of the Amungme, the Asmat, a people of the coastal lowlands who raided widely for heads in pre-contact times. It is possible that the Amungme, or other groups through whose territory Wollaston passed and who also had no traditions of headhunting themselves, may have sought to make sense of Wollaston's arrival in this way, by assimilating it into their own cultural categories as a raid by a party of coastal headhunters.

White Headhunters

Such parallels between headhunting and the collection of osteological specimens on the colonial frontiers were often quite apparent to contemporary observers. Between 1871 and 1872 the British mounted a punitive expedition against the Lushai, a hill people of northeast India, in response to their raids into the lowlands. An officer who took part commented ironically on the mutual interest in collecting one another's skulls shown by the Lushai and the military physicians who accompanied the force. The medical personnel were

> quite eager for Lushai skulls as any Lushai could have been for theirs, though, in the interests of civilisation, the Lushai's head would have reposed in glass cases on velvet cushions probably, while those of our friends would have been elevated on poles exposed to the wind and the rain. (Woodthorpe 1873: 268–69, quoted in Zou 2005: 96)

As Zou points out, these shared preoccupations with human skulls were quite evident to the indigenous peoples of northeast India themselves. Around 1936–37, the anthropologist Fürer-Haimendorf was

> collecting specimens of four heads from the head-tree of the Konyak Naga hills, and packing the gruesome booty into a carrying basket on his back, 'much to the amusement of the Nagas and the slightly shocked surprise of the sepoys' who accompanied him (Fürer-Haimendorf 1939: 165). On the same occasion, [he] managed to laboriously write down one complete song sung by the Konyak Nagas, thinking that he had 'captured on paper another part of the old headhunting ritual'. But, to his amused surprise, Fürer-Haimendorf learned, with the help of his interpreter's word-for-word translation into Assamese, that the song was composed in his honour as the *white headhunter*. (Zou 2005: 96)

The Nagas seem to have drawn strong parallels between headhunting and the hunting of animals. Among the Sema Nagas, for example, headhunting was called 'touching meat' and involved many of the same taboos and ritual observances that men had to follow when hunting tigers and leopards (Hutton 1921: 173, 179). After a successful hunt, the carcasses were beheaded and divided up in much the same way 'as in the case of the killing of a human enemy, tiger and leopard being reckoned for many purposes as practically equivalent to men' (Hutton 1921: 76).

In other words, the resemblances the hill tribesmen perceived between their headhunting practices and the ethnological field researcher's activities were by no means superficial. Their own headhunting raids and the collecting practices of their colonial visitors were both informed by conceptual schemas whose roots lay in the lived or imagined experience of hunting animals. Both parties gave significance to the collection of human body parts; and though their respective practices were of course quite dissimilar in many respects, they nonetheless drew much of their meaning from underlying metaphors of hunting. On encountering one another, each side sought to make sense of the other's exotic collecting interests in these same shared terms as well.

Chapter 7

Skulls and Scientific Collecting in the Victorian Military

Skulls as Trophies of Hunting and War

Many nineteenth-century British soldiers serving in the colonies were enthusiastic collectors. Sometimes, after successful military actions, they took weapons and other items from the enemy dead as battle trophies, perhaps from people whom they had personally killed. A popular souvenir of this sort among soldiers in the Eighth Frontier War (1851–53) against the Xhosa in the Eastern Cape were the ivory amulets worn by Xhosa men. When Xhosa were fatally wounded they would smash their ornaments to deny the whites these highly prized trophies (Mostert 1992: 1251; see also Peires 1989: 50).

The acquisitiveness of soldiers sometimes extended to the taking of enemy body parts. This tended to occur during the looting of possessions from the battlefield dead, as exemplified by the circumstances of the death of Hintsa, a chief of the Xhosa in the Sixth Frontier War (1834–36). He was shot and killed by a settler militiaman named Southey while allegedly escaping from the custody of the British military commander.

> Southey was first beside the body and quickly took Hintsa's brass ornaments for himself. As the others gathered around, they grabbed for what was left of Hintsa's beads and bracelets. George Southey or his brother William cut off one of Hintsa's ears and someone else took the other ear. Assistant Surgeon Ford of the 72nd Highlanders was seen trying to extract some of the Chief's teeth. (Mostert 1992: 725–26)

The commander himself took Hintsa's spear and some of his bracelets and sent them to his wife as souvenirs. According to some contemporary reports, someone cut out 'the emblems of [Hintsa's] manhood' (quoted in Mkhize 2009: 214) and his ears were later offered for sale on the streets of Grahamstown (Lehmann 1977: 178, 196; for other similar cases, see Peires 1989: 398; Ritvo 1987: 271).

Other body parts, particularly skulls, were also taken as souvenirs. In 1847 an ensign serving in the Seventh Frontier War wrote to his parents in England that he had seen 'a Kaffir's head' for sale in Cape Town, but had decided not to buy it because he was sure he could get one of his own once he had begun duties on the frontier (Morris 1996: 75).[1]

A photograph taken in 1879 shows an officer of the 80th Regiment at the entrance to his tent during the Anglo-Zulu War (Locke and Quantrill 2002: 119). He poses among a collection of personal possessions: rugs, leopard skins, weapons and an oriental musical instrument, possibly a souvenir of some earlier posting. A British flag is draped over a folding table on which there are framed photographs of women in bustles. Just visible behind these is a human skull, its discreet placement perhaps suggesting some ambivalence about the display of such an object. The previous year the officer's regiment had served in the Ninth Frontier War (1877–78), and the skull was probably a memento of that campaign (Locke 2004).

British soldiers in the Cape Frontier Wars often equated fighting the Xhosa with killing animals and, in particular, with hunting (Peires 1989: 50, 306). One of Victorian Britain's central rituals of imperial conquest, in Africa, India and other colonial possessions, was the recreational hunting of indigenous game animals and the preservation and display of their remains: heads, skulls, horns, skins and so forth (Mackenzie 1988; Ritvo 1987).

In many respects, hunting prowess was as central to middle- and upper-class Victorian and Edwardian notions of masculinity as it was for indigenous peoples such as the Ilongot (Collier and Rosaldo 1981), and this was especially so among military officers. For them, hunting was an essential part of the preparation of men for war. The ritual of 'blooding', for example, in which the novice hunter is daubed with the blood of his first kill, was regarded as an essential mark of entry into full adult masculinity for young imperial officers (MacKenzie 1987: 188; Mangan and McKenzie 2003, 2009). And it was through devotion to the sport of hunting that a man demonstrated those sterling qualities of self-mastery needed to rule over others. The British, in their own view, had gained an overseas empire because they were a virile race, and this was demonstrated above all by the evident fact that they were keen hunters. Some other European peoples never acquired colonial empires or, like the Belgians and Portuguese, soon lost them because of their innate weakness and effeminacy, shown by their lack of interest in big game hunting. In British opinion, they dissipated themselves uselessly with 'native' women instead of channelling their manly vigour into hunting the native animals (MacKenzie 1987: 178–79). In short, to the nineteenth-century British colonial officer class, hunting, masculinity and empire building were inextricably connected (Cartmill 1993: 135; Ritvo 1987: 254–55).

Hunting was therefore an important leisure pursuit in the Victorian military, and many colonial officers were keen sportsmen, who hunted the local wildlife, accumulated animal trophies, and brought these home at the end of their service. These demonstrations of violent power and mastery over the local wildlife symbolized mastery over land and people. To take human trophies as if their colonial subjects were native fauna was an extreme but entirely coherent extension of this metaphor.

In 1891 the Belgians sent an expedition to take control of the Katanga region of Congo for King Leopold, under the leadership of a Canadian explorer and soldier, Captain Stairs. One of Stairs's officers killed the local king, Msiri, took his head back to camp and announced: 'I have killed a tiger! Vive le roi!'. The expedition returned to the coast the following year, bringing the king's skull with them in a kerosene tin, as if it was the trophy of a hunting expedition (Crawford 1912: 308–10; Gordon 2001: 320; Stairs and MacLaren 1997: 386).

The appropriation and display of such human trophies are illustrated by the treatment of the body of Luka Jantje, a Tswana chief killed in battle against the British in 1896. Shortly after the chief's burial, one of the officers present declared that he would 'like that fellow's skull' (Chilvers 1933: 132) and bribed one of his men five pounds to exhume the body, take the head, and boil it to remove the flesh. When reports of this event appeared in the press, an acrimonious dispute ensued among the Cape's political elite, amidst which the officer was forced to resign his commission. But he kept the skull; later in life, working as a shift foreman on an East Rand mine, he still had it on display on the wall of his room, in much the same way that a game hunter would display the trophy head of an animal (Chilvers 1933: 133; Shillington 1985: 239–40).

Another African leader whose remains met with such treatment was Bambata, a chief killed leading the last Zulu revolt against the British in 1906 (S. Marks 1970, 1986). He was killed at the bottom of a steep ravine, and a decision was made that it was too difficult to retrieve his body and that his head should be removed. The head was placed in a tent under armed guard and his followers were brought into the tent to view the head, to persuade them to surrender. The official reports state that the head was treated with dignity and that afterwards, the head and body were given burial together. However, it appears that somebody obtained Bambata's skull and kept it. For in 1925, a photograph of a human skull appeared in *The Nongqai*, the monthly magazine of the South African Armed Forces. The following text accompanied the photograph (see Gillings 1989, 2002): 'The bottom photograph shows the actual skull of the rebel leader, Chief Bambata, who was slain at the Mome Gorge, and decapitated for identification purposes. His skull is the only relic of a Rebellion which cost the Government 740 000 pounds to suppress'.

The skull is mounted on a shield-shaped plaque, exactly as the trophy skull or horns of a game animal might be. The plaque also bears a small metal nameplate just below the skull. This is a common feature on hunting trophies and, though no writing is legible in this case, it would typically be engraved with the date and place of the animal's death, the name of the species and perhaps the name of the hunter who killed it. There is obvious damage to the skull around the orbit of the left eye. Bambata was shot in the back of the head, with the bullet exiting through his left eye, and this trophy object seemed intended to commemorate not just Bambata's death but also the manner of his death.

Some colonial officers brought relics of this sort home to Britain after the end of their period of service. While serving in the Ninth Frontier War, Lieutenant (later Major-General Sir) Frederick Carrington obtained a skull which he believed to be that of the Xhosa leader Sandile, who was killed in 1878 in that war (Hummel 1989: 163–67; Gon 1984: 122–23). Carrington had not taken part in the fighting in which Sandile died, and how he obtained the skull is not known. But he returned to England with it, and for many years kept it on the mantelpiece in his Gloucestershire country estate. When he married, late in life, his wife announced that she would not stay in the house 'if that thing stayed in the dining room' and demanded that it be given burial (Hummel 1989: 164). Carrington interred it on his estate in 1905, under a headstone which read: 'Here lies the head of Sandilli [sic] chief of the Gaika nation killed in action in the Peri bush

King William's Town 1878'. All the available evidence, carefully reviewed by Hummel, is that Sandile's body was not decapitated, and the skull was probably a fraud sold to Carrington by some 'peddler of war relics' (Hummel 1989: 164). If this was the case, it suggests that the commoditization of such trophies was not uncommon at the time.[2]

Some relics of Bambata appear also to have found their way to England, as was discovered in 2002 by historical researchers examining the personal effects of a Colonel Alexander, an army engineer who served in South Africa at the time of the Bambata Rebellion (Gillings 2002). His army records state that he was born in Dublin, was fluent in French and Zulu, and married an American. He was decorated twice in the First World War and, in 1919, was Deputy Controller of the Baghdad railway system. In the Second World War, he and his wife managed Ashorne Hill, the residence of staff of the British Iron and Steel Confederation after their evacuation from London. It was here, among the animal trophy heads, spears and other Africana that appear to date from Alexander's period at the house, that an envelope was discovered among his effects. It carried the name 'Bambata' spelt backwards, and contained a typed report of Bambata's death and a clipping of African hair. The likeliest explanation of this discovery is that cuttings of Bambata's hair were taken from his body as souvenirs by military personnel. If so, it was not the first time this had happened to the body of an African leader killed in action against the British. Thirty years earlier, it had been done to the body of Sandile (Gon 1984: 122; Mostert 1992: 1252).

There seems to be little evidence of British military personnel in the Victorian era, or later, taking body parts as trophies from enemies who were white or European, or trafficking in their remains as war memorabilia. So, for example, we do not seem to find accounts of nineteenth-century servicemen perpetrating such acts in the Napoleonic wars, or the Crimean War, or against Dutch settlers in the Boer Wars. The looting of personal effects from the dead was certainly common, but soldiers seem to have drawn a moral boundary preventing them from using as souvenirs the body parts of opponents with whom they understood themselves as sharing racial identity or kinship (Harrison 2006). That is, they seem to have drawn a distinction between two categories of enemy, one closely related and the other distant, codifying this dichotomy in the permissibility or impermissibility of taking their body parts as trophies. In effect, they acknowledged close enemies as human, while equating distant ones with game animals or quarry.

Outsavaging the Savages

Some African societies also seem to have had ritual practices involving the taking and use of enemy body parts. British soldiers were sometimes victims of such acts. So, for example, in the First Ashanti War in 1824, the head of the British Governor Sir Charles McCarthy was taken and his skull made into a ceremonial drinking bowl for the Ashanti king (McCaskie 2003: 424). In southern Africa, the Xhosa and Zulu sometimes mutilated the bodies of British soldiers, taking heads, skulls or other body parts, in most cases for use in war magic. British civilians and soldiers expressed horror at such acts (see, for instance, Locke and Quantrill 2002: 84, 228; Peires 1989: 48–49, 52, 105; S. Marks 1970: 245–46).

It is possible that some soldiers who took enemy skulls were attempting to copy and reciprocate their enemies' behaviour. The British and Xhosa certainly reciprocated other sorts of brutality, such as the torture of prisoners, as they came increasingly to dehumanize each other in the course of the Frontier Wars (Mostert 1992: 1117; Peires 1989: 48–49, 52).

A probable example of this sort of reactive or retaliatory trophy-taking is the treatment of the remains of the Mahdi, the religious leader who led an insurrection in the Sudan in the 1880s. In 1885, his forces destroyed the British-led garrison at Khartoum, killed the commander, General Gordon, decapitated his body and put the head on display. When the Anglo-Egyptian army defeated the Mahdists at the Battle of Omdurman in 1898, its general, Kitchener, who had idolized Gordon, ordered the Mahdi's tomb to be blown up.

> [T]he body of the Mahdi himself was dug up and flung into the Nile – not, however, until the head was severed, and this was purloined by Kitchener as a trophy of war. He appears to have had a notion that he might have used the skull for an inkstand or a drinking cup, or alternatively that it might have been forwarded as a curiosity to the Royal College of Surgeons in London. (Moorehead 1971: 335)

The skull was placed in an empty kerosene drum 'for future disposal', an official expression meaning, according to Churchill, that it would be 'passed from hand to hand till it reached Cairo, where it would be treated as "an interesting trophy"' (Churchill 1899: 212; see also Manchester 1983: 281). Churchill's comment suggests that he was quite familiar with such behaviour.[3] It is difficult to avoid the conclusion that Kitchener's treatment of the Mahdi's remains was a post-mortem settling of scores over the death of Gordon and the mutilation of his body, thirteen years earlier.

On the rare occasions when these colonial practices came to public attention in metropolitan Britain, they caused public scandal and considerable official embarrassment.[4] There was, for instance, an outcry over the treatment of the remains of the Mahdi

> when it became known to the public, and not even the General's popularity in England (where he was idolized after Omdurman) was able to protect him from it. Queen Victoria was deeply shocked – she thought the whole affair 'savoured too much of the Middle Ages' – and Kitchener was obliged to write her a mollifying letter. [The British Consul-General] in Cairo meanwhile quietly possessed himself of the skull, and sent it up to the Moslem cemetery at Wadi Halfa, where it was secretly buried by night. (Moorehead 1971: 335–36)

Victorian civilians and soldiers alike agreed that such behaviour had no place in civilized war. But their conceptions of civilized war seem sometimes to have been subtly at variance. Civilians tended to assume that civilized soldiers fought civilized wars by definition, no matter whom they were fighting. For such soldiers to mutilate enemy dead or take body parts as trophies was absolutely anomalous, even inconceivable.

But some members of the military appear to have had a more complex and nuanced view, in which civilized warfare was one of two varieties of warfare in which a civilized soldier might engage, depending on whom he was fighting. From this perspective, civilized soldiers fight civilized wars when they fight other civilized soldiers. But against savages they may fight savage wars. The difference, accordingly, between a civilized and savage combatant is that a savage is only able to fight savage wars, while a civilized soldier can choose to wage either type of war. To put this differently, the civilized soldier imagined that within himself a second, savage, soldier was encompassed and subsumed. This encapsulated savage could be released in appropriate contexts, above all when fighting other savages. A sergeant in a Highland Scots regiment recalls going into battle against the Xhosa:

> Nervousness gives place to excitement, excitement to anger; and anger may be supplanted by barbarism as an infuriated soldiery rush on, heedless of their doom. Their only thought is of victory; and when victory is gained, it requires a masterly general to restrain the men from deeds which cannot be named. (Quoted in Peires 1989: 49)

Victorian soldiers and civilians took for granted a fundamental divide between savage and civilized people, with the former distinguished from the latter by primitive customs such as headhunting. They also agreed that the dead bodies of civilized enemies were owed respectful treatment, and that savages did not understand such rules.

But some colonial soldiers went further, considering it acceptable to treat the remains of savage enemies in the same way that such peoples themselves treated (or were assumed or expected to treat) their own enemies' remains. These soldiers thereby expressed a sense of possessing natural and self-evident rights over the bodies of lesser races, including the right to appropriate the brutal practices of such races and retaliate in kind against those who desecrated British dead.

They seem, in other words, implicitly to have conceived of war as an inherently relational or reciprocal activity, in which enemies negotiate the kind of war they are waging, communicating with one another, in particular, through their behaviour towards each other's dead. That is, engaging or not engaging in acts such as trophy-taking represents part of a dialogue in which the two sides are trying to construct a relationship and rules of conduct towards each other, a negotiated culture of combat. From this point of view, 'savage' and 'civilized' denote not so much contrasting categories of enemies as contrasting modes of interaction to which encounters between enemies can give rise.

In some situations, colonial officers might therefore treat enemy remains in a manner suggestive of primitive trophy-hunting. But they would not consider themselves to have thereby become savages because, crucially, they refrained from using the remains of civilized enemies in this way and, in their own view, thereby showed that they respected higher values and were fully capable of moral discrimination.

Furthermore, although the collection of enemy skulls could evoke images of primitive 'headhunting', a long-standing icon of savagery in the Western imagination, the emergence of such practices among nineteenth-century British soldiers in Africa was connected with the developments in Victorian science in which the collection, measurement and classification of skulls became central to scientific understandings of human difference, especially moral and intellectual inequality (Bank 1996; van Wyhe 2004). That is, these practices of military trophy-taking, primitive and atavistic though they seemed to contemporary observers, actually arose in connection with the growth in authority and prestige of scientific naturalism and rationality. The use specifically of

Africans' skulls as war trophies allowed soldiers who saw the transgression of civilized norms as a defining characteristic of savages to maintain distinctions between themselves and savages and yet transgress these same norms themselves.

Of course, from another point of view, their appropriations of African people's skulls and other body parts could appear to realize some dark fantasies of human nature. Such behaviour could be interpreted, for instance, as a perverse victory for the colonized who, by allowing or encouraging brutality towards themselves, had managed to tempt into savagery those who had come to rule and civilize them, as Conrad imagined with the figure of Kurtz.

Thus while trophy-taking in the Victorian military originated in ideologies of racial superiority, it could be valorized either negatively or positively within these same ideologies' terms. Those who carried out such acts and those who deplored them both tended to do so in the name of a moral distinction between 'savage' and 'civilized' whose truth they jointly upheld.

Skulls of Chiefs and Kings

Alfred Grenfell, later Field Marshall Lord Grenfell, fought in the battle of Ulundi, at which the Zulu state was finally defeated. In his memoirs, he recalls revisiting the old battlefield in 1881, two years after the Zulu defeat:

> I made a long ride with Buller and Donald Browne into Zululand to see our old fighting ground at Ulundi. When we arrived, we found the old track across the Umfolozi River where our square had stood. I stood at the place, which was still marked by cartridges, at the corner of the square where the Zulus had made their last attack. I told Buller that I had seen a Zulu Induna shot in the head by Owen's machine-guns, of which there were two at this corner. He was leading his men on and got as close as eighteen yards from the square, for I had measured it after the action. I again paced the eighteen yards and came to my old friend, a splendid skeleton, his bones perfectly white, his flesh eaten off by the white ants. I felt I could not part with him, so I put his skull into my forage bag, and brought it home with me. It now adorns a case in my collection of curiosities. (Grenfell 1925: 65–66)

In its use of approbatory terms such as 'splendid' in reference to the remains of a dead enemy, this passage resonates with some enduring themes in Western ideologies of hunting.[5] One is that a 'true' hunter feels affection and respect towards the animals he kills and pays homage or tribute to them by keeping parts of them as trophies. Another, related theme, rooted in the aristocratic hunting traditions of medieval Europe, is that hunters and their quarry alike are ranked by degrees of inherent quality or nobility, with the noblest game reserved for a hunting elite (Cartmill 1993; Herman 2001). When Grenfell took the induna's skull from the battlefield at Ulundi, he could justifiably have considered himself similar in rank in the British Army to an induna in the Zulu army. In the induna's impressive remains (the 'old friend' he 'could not part with') he acknowledged the presence of someone with whom he shared relative equality (within, of course, their quite separate social worlds), much like a medieval king acknowledged in the nobility of the stag he hunted the equivalent, in the animal realm, of his own royal status in the human realm.

Similarly, it would have been egregious for someone of the rank of Kitchener to have valued the skull of an anonymous Mahdist foot soldier as a war memento, and it would have been equally inappropriate for the skull of the Mahdi to have ended up as a souvenir in the hands of an ordinary British trooper. On this both Kitchener and the Mahdi would probably have agreed. Between the hunter and prey, the soldier and the skull, the collector and the collected, propriety required a parity of status.

The Ashanti king acknowledged this when he kept Sir Charles McCarthy's skull as a ceremonial drinking bowl. So did Sir Frederick Carrington in keeping the skull of someone he referred to as 'Sandilli, chief of the Gaika nation' on the mantelpiece in his dining room. In nineteenth-century British military culture, and in some African societies with which the British fought, the taking of enemy remains in war was structured by principles of rank and hierarchy, and by a mutual recognition of the existence of these principles in one another.

For this reason, the taking of African heads and skulls by the British military seems to have been carried out predominantly, though not exclusively, by members of the officer class, and their victims tended to be similarly high-ranking Africans. But the perception that their own commitment to principles of rank and hierarchy was often mirrored by the African peoples whom the British fought could at times make it seem that they and their opponents were uncomfortably alike: not so much colonizers and colonized, rulers and ruled, but partners joined together in violent exchanges of killings, of body parts for body parts, mutilations for mutilations, moderated only by a shared commitment to distinctions of rank and status.

These similarities between some African peoples' practices and their own, or those of their own society's recent past, were not lost on contemporary European observers. At the time of the Anglo-Zulu War, for example, only a century had passed since the judicial practice of displaying human heads in public had come to an end in England (McLynn 1989: 274). Hence when the explorer Burton, travelling through an African chiefdom in 1859, saw skulls of the chief's enemies displayed on stakes, the spectacle reminded him of the Temple Bar, the London city gate on which heads of traitors were displayed until the previous century (Franey 2001: 225–26).

When a high-ranking colonial officer such as Kitchener took the head or skull of an enemy leader, his actions, too, must have evoked these sorts of historical resonances, perhaps echoing the events of 1746, when the leaders of the Jacobite rebellion were executed and their heads displayed on the Temple Bar, where they remained until 1778. Kitchener's revenge on the Mahdi's remains has even closer parallels with the post-mortem punishment meted out in 1661 on the exhumed corpse of Oliver Cromwell and his associates under Charles II after the Restoration, discussed in Chapter Three.

A Victorian military officer fighting 'savages' in the colonies could do something impermissible when fighting civilized enemies: namely, indulge in a form of cultural nostalgia, resurrecting some of the more grisly military and judicial practices of his own society's recent history and performing these as exemplary political symbolism. In doing so, he was reaching back into a less civilized past to retrieve for himself some of the former functions of a king. In this retrospective appropriation of royal power by the individual colonial officer, the anatomical or ethnological museum – or the private connoisseur's cabinet of curiosities – replaced the Temple Bar as a site for the exemplary display of body parts of enemies of the state.

In some cases, the officer's African colonial subjects, too, may have viewed him as behaving like a chief or king. In fact, if he took the skull of a chief or king, they could have understood him as making a claim to the succession. One apparent case of this sort concerns the death of Mkwawa, chief of the Wahehe people in German East Africa (Baer and Schröter 2001; Winans 1994). In 1891, his army defeated a German expeditionary force sent into his territory, and killed its commanding officer. Mkwawa was then hunted relentlessly for a number of years by a German force under a British-born officer called Tom Prince (later, von Prince). Finally cornered in 1898, Mkwawa killed himself. His head was removed and brought to Prince's headquarters, where it was boiled to remove the flesh. Prince and his wife kept the skull in their house, treating it as what one visitor to the household described as a 'family trophy' (Baer and Schröter 2001: 187–88). There is evidence that Prince eventually had the skull sent to a museum in Germany (Baer and Schröter 2001; Winans 1994).

After Mkwawa's death, the German authorities rewarded Prince for his services, awarding him the hereditary title 'von' among other honours. But they also required him to move to a distant part of their East African colonial territory, concerned that his personal influence over the Wahehe was becoming too great. Some of the Wahehe seem to have begun to regard him as their new leader – no longer Mkwawa's adversary but his replacement or successor. Prince's superiors certainly suspected this was the case: that the Wahehe were transferring their loyalties to von Prince in person, instead of to the German state, and that he was behaving in ways that suggested that he may have begun to view himself in this light (Winans 1994: 232–33). Given the assumption in some societies in Africa, and elsewhere, that the body of the king or chief represents the chiefdom or state (Huntington and Metcalf 1979), it is possible that some among the Wahehe understood that by having Mkwawa killed and taking his skull, von Prince had also acquired something of Mkwawa's identity and become a new incarnation of the dead chief. An officer who came into possession of the skull of a king or chief might discover that this powerful relic had – in the eyes of his colonial subjects at least – come into possession of him.[6]

Skulls and the Rise of Scientific Naturalism

There seems to be no evidence of British soldiers in Africa taking skulls as souvenirs on a significant scale before the 1820s. In fact, one must probably go back to the thirteenth century to find, in the western European military tradition, norms making it acceptable for combatants to treat enemy heads or skulls as personal war souvenirs.[7] An important question is why such practices of individualized trophy-taking emerged, or rather re-emerged after an apparent gap of some six hundred years, in the context of nineteenth-century colonial warfare. So far, I have suggested that they emerged in the context of the encounter with non-European peoples who themselves had cultural practices capable of being interpreted – through the lens of Victorian historical consciousness – as primitive customs of trophy-taking.[8] It is unlikely that the sense of civilized superiority many soldiers shared would have allowed them simply to copy their enemies' practices. Rather, they needed to be able to copy them, at least as they imagined them, in such a way as to allow themselves also to disclaim the imitation. As I will try to show, the key factor which enabled them to do so was a set of important developments in Victorian science.

In 1879, during the Anglo-Zulu War, the Zulu king detained at his homestead a Dutch trader named Cornelius Vijn. After the battle of Kambula, the Zulu army's first defeat by the British, the survivors came to Vijn and asked him the meaning of some puzzling behaviour they had observed among the enemy. One of the questions they put to Vijn was: 'Why did the Whites cut off the heads of those who had fallen, and put them in their wagons? What did they do with these heads? Or was it to let the Queen see how they had fought?' (Vijn 1988: 38).

Bishop Colenso, who translated and edited Vijn's memoirs, suggests in a footnote that the 'heads' the Zulu referred to may have been skulls, 'which (it is well known) were carried off by some Whites from the battle-field' (Vijn 1988: 38). Such souvenir-hunting took place after other similar defeats of indigenous armies in nineteenth-century southern Africa, as we have seen. However, it always occurred after battles when all that remained of the African dead were bones. The Zulu, on the other hand, appear to have witnessed decapitations of bodies immediately following the fighting.

One possibility is that these acts were carried out by army physicians or medical officers, or at their behest. African battlefield dead had sometimes been treated in this way during the Eighth Frontier War. One English settler, who led a militia in which a local apothecary served as surgeon, recalled one night during the war when

> we were surprised by a dreadful stench. I sent men round the camp to find out the cause of it. They went on the scent and found Taylor the apothecary, who had volunteered to join me had brought one of the Caffers heads we had shot the first day, and had taken another man's pot. [Taylor] was boiling it to get the meat off. The old fellow had the skull in his shop until he died. (Stubbs 1978: 176, footnote omitted, brackets in the original)

There were cases of soldiers killing Africans specifically to obtain medical specimens in this way. A wealthy adventurer, who raised a private corps of volunteers in the same war, remembers one of his men who kept a broken sickle under his coat, for cutting the throats of Xhosa women and children they took prisoner (Mostert 1992: 1153; Peires 1989: 51). When a surgeon of the 60th Regiment requested some scientific specimens, his men were all too ready to comply.

> Doctor A – of the 60th had asked my men to procure for him a few native skulls of both sexes. This was a task easily accomplished. One morning they brought back to camp about two dozen heads of various ages. As these were not supposed to be in a presentable state for the doctor's acceptance, the next night they turned my vat into a caldron for the removal of superfluous flesh. And there these men sat, gravely smoking their pipes during the livelong night, and stirring round and round the heads in that seething boiler, as though they were cooking black-apple dumplings. (Quoted in Peires 1989: 49; see also Morris 1996: 75; Mostert 1992: 1153)

The military procurement of heads or skulls in this way in southern Africa for medical or scientific study seems to date back at least to the 1820s, in warfare against the Khoisan or 'Bushman' peoples (Morris 1996: 73–75). The colonial military, and military physicians in particular, became important sources of skulls and other human remains for scientific study. When Kitchener considered sending the Mahdi's skull to the Royal College of Surgeons, he was following a well established practice: army surgeons had sent skulls of African dead to the College from the siege of Shiloh and other military actions in 1851 (Bank 1996: 402; Griffiths 1996: 44; Morris 1996: 73; Skotnes 1996: 18–20).[9]

It was not only in Britain that science and the colonial military were closely linked in this way. Roque (2010) has recently explored their complex connections within the Portuguese empire in the nineteenth and early twentieth centuries. As we will see in the following chapter, a similar relationship developed in the United States. The influential Société d'Anthropologie de Paris, founded in 1859 by Paul Broca, solicited material on the races of Algeria, Sudan, the Sahara and Senegal. One of the first specimens it acquired was the head of an Algerian killed by a French soldier and preserved in salt. Initially said to be that of an Arab, the Society concluded, after careful examination of its shape, that it was probably Kabyle (Lorcin 1995: 153–55).

During the Herero uprising which began in 1904 in German southwest Africa, the military authorities there ran internment camps which seem to have functioned as skull production centres for the German scientific establishment. When inmates died, or were executed, women were made to remove the flesh from the heads with broken glass, the skulls then being packed into crates and shipped to the Berlin Pathological Institute (Madley 2005: 437, 454, 456).

As Franey (2001: 220) points out, many Victorians were ambivalent towards these collecting practices, viewing them on the one hand as legitimate contributions to knowledge, and on the other as unpleasantly similar to 'primitive' headhunting customs. The similarities were by no means illusory. 'Fundamentally speaking, then, the specimens so critical to physical anthropology are no different from trophies collected in primitive warfare: both specimen and trophy operate as legible signs of the power possessed by the man who displays them' (Franey 2001: 225–26).

Indeed, it was probably for precisely this reason that soldiers were often more than willing to assist with the collection and preparation of specimens. The emergence of a scientific fascination with skulls in Europe and North America seems to have provided an alibi for the sorts of trophy-hunting some soldiers had their own reasons for wanting to carry out. So, for example, during the official enquiry into the mutilation of the body of Luka Jantje, the officer who had had the chief's skull exhumed and boiled gave the excuse that he had intended to offer the skull to a museum 'for the benefit of students of Physiology' (Shillington 1985: 240), as if his actions had been meant as a disinterested contribution to science.

Furthermore, some nineteenth-century British soldiers were also themselves amateur naturalists, anthropologists or psychologists, and collected human remains in the name of such disciplines. One participant in the final fighting of the Eighth Frontier War, when phrenology was at the height of its popularity, recalls:

> As we ascended the evidences of the fight became more frequent; rolling skulls, dislodged by those in front, came bounding down between our legs; the bones lay thick among

the loose stones in the sluits and gulleys, and the bush on either side showed many a bleaching skeleton. A fine specimen of a [Xhosa] head I took the liberty of putting into my saddle-bag, and afterwards brought it home with me to Scotland, where it has been much admired by phrenologists for its fine development. (Quoted in Peires 1989: 52)

Grenfell, who took the induna's skull from the battlefield at Ulundi, was another such professional soldier and recreational craniologist. He was a keen amateur antiquarian, a collector and connoisseur of ancient Egyptian and other artefacts, equipped by his class background with the cultivation, refinement and knowledge properly to appreciate such objects (Weaver 1937: 362–64; for another example, see Hastings 1890).

We saw in the previous chapter how the discursive world of nineteenth-century museum collecting was pervaded by the language of the hunt or chase. Hunting, so evocative of vigorous masculinity to the Victorians, was the arch-metaphor for their scientific, as well as military, encounters with the non-European world (Ritvo 1987). I would suggest therefore that Victorian colonial soldiers could readily adopt the museological collecting practices of the time and transmute these into the appropriation of body parts as war trophies, because of the powerful pre-existing affinity between scientific collecting in the colonies and colonial warfare, both of which tended to be conceptualized as varieties of the archetypally male pursuit of hunting. In both of these activities, Europeans equated African people with their continent's often dangerous fauna, specimens of which were difficult and challenging to obtain, testing the manhood of those who sought to collect them.

Thus the question of whether the skulls of African battlefield dead were collected and displayed as scientific specimens, as hunting trophies or as war mementos may be somewhat moot, given that these distinctions may not always have been meaningful to the Victorians, for whom the similarities between these modalities of appropriating bodies or body parts seem often to have been deeper than the differences. The important point is that these remains were appropriated as a demonstration of power and conquest, the quality, value or significance attributed to them reflecting the prowess of their collectors and possessors, whether these individuals had acquired them as soldiers, natural scientists or game hunters.

Conclusion

The use of skulls as war mementos appears to have been a recurring pattern in the British military in southern Africa throughout much of the nineteenth century. As we will see in a later chapter, it continued into the mid twentieth century. My argument is that these practices were local manifestations of certain transnational advances in science. British soldiers collected the skulls of Africans, or became involved in their collection, as one of a wide range of educated and often cosmopolitan Europeans and North Americans with amateur or professional scientific interests in collecting the skulls of colonized peoples.

These developments in Western science had a special significance for soldiers in the colonies, offering them a means of resolving a fundamental dilemma of colonial warfare: namely, how to be both like and unlike their indigenous opponents at the same time. Though they were far from being the only Victorians to appropriate African skulls, they had distinctive reasons for doing so: these practices enabled them to reciprocate the perceived savagery of their opponents, and simultaneously maintain a distinction between themselves and savages. They could imitate their adversaries and claim at the same time that they were not doing so.

On the one hand, they could appear to support the cause of universal scientific progress and, in the same breath, show they could out-savage the particular and very tangible savages whom they were fighting on the frontiers, outdoing them at their own primitive customs and beating them on their own terms. The skull in the retired officer's cabinet of curiosities thereby attested to a truly comprehensive defeat of the chief whose skull it once was. It confirmed its collector's superiority in intellect and culture, while proving him to have been, in his time, the more successful savage as well.

Notes

1. See Skotnes (1996: 18) for a photograph of a probable example of such a preserved head from nineteenth-century southern Africa.
2. Recent archaeological excavation of Sandile's grave has confirmed that his body was not decapitated (Feni 2005).
3. Compare the similar disinterment and appropriation of the remains of the Zulu king Mpande by the British after their victory over the Zulu at the battle of Ulundi in 1879 (Vijn 1988: 86–88).
4. For the public reaction in Britain and elsewhere to the killing and mutilation of Hintsa, see Lehmann (1977: 196–202) and Mostert (1992: 759ff). For discussions of an attempt to repatriate his supposed 'skull' from Scotland in 1996 see Mkhize (2009).
5. See also the passage from the amateur phrenologist in the Eighth Frontier War, quoted below. On the history of collections (or 'cabinets') of curiosities see Impey and MacGregor (1985). It was not uncommon at the time for these private museums of exotica and rarities to include human body parts, as described in Chapter Three.
6. For the subsequent complex history of Mkwawa's skull, see Baer and Schröter (2001) and Winans (1994). The Treaty of Versailles included a demand that Germany return the skull to the Wahehe. In 1954, a skull believed to be that of Mkwawa was found in a German museum and finally repatriated.
7. See, for example, the treatment of the body of Simon de Montfort after his death at the battle of Evesham in 1265, discussed in Chapter Two. For a much later example, see the treatment of the skull of the American Indian chief 'King Phillip' by the seventeenth-century English Puritan Cotton Mather (Lepore 1998: 174–75).
8. For instance, educated Victorians would have been familiar with classical descriptions of the headhunting practices of the ancient Gauls (Diodorus of Sicily 1939: 173–75), and with Gibbon's account of the Lombard king Alboin, who wore an enemy king's skull on his belt and compelled his wife (the enemy's daughter) to drink from it (Gibbon 1910: 449–50, 454–55).

9. In Australia, skulls or preserved heads of Aborigines killed in action by British forces were also sent to this museum, or to its predecessor the Hunterian Museum. See, for instance, Connor (2003: 39, 134).

Chapter 8

From Hero to Specimen: Phrenology, Craniology and the American Indian Skull

Indian Celebrities

By the early nineteenth century, the human skull had long been associated in European culture with moral qualities and could signify attributes such as nobility, honour, virtue and loyalty, as well as their opposites. In medieval Europe, the dead had defined a moral spectrum whose boundaries were represented by the preserved skull and other bodily relics of the saint at one extreme, and those of the executed rebel or traitor at the other. Even after death, bones could continue to speak of good and evil, and other human qualities. The biologized understandings of human diversity which emerged in nineteenth-century science continued this moral discourse. The degeneracy of the felon was assumed to be inscribed in the anatomical features of his skull for all to see. So too was the superior nature of the artistic genius inscribed in his. To their disciples, it seemed that the gracility of Schubert's skull and the robustness of Beethoven's were emblematic of the character of their music. The physical remains of the two composers testified in this way to their inner being. Such relics were understood to be embodiments of human qualities; and to acquire a memorial object of this sort, or to form a possessive relationship with it, could therefore be understood as a claim to a certain position in society. The skull of an anatomized murderer kept by a physician, the skull of an African chief brought home by a colonial officer or a celebrated composer's skull treasured by a lover of music expressed the social identities, tastes and aspirations of their owners.

In 1832 a chief of the Sauk nation, Black Hawk, led a war against the United States authorities in Illinois and Wisconsin. After his defeat and capture, he was taken on a tour of the east. In New York and other cities, sympathetic crowds welcomed him, and he was celebrated as a romantic hero and even patriot. His autobiography, based on an account of his life given to his interpreter while in custody, was published within a year of the end of the war and was an immediate bestseller (Slotkin 1973: 359).

On his release he returned to his home in Iowa Territory, where he died in 1838. Shortly afterwards, a local physician, Dr James Turner, took his head or skull from his grave. Later, Turner and his associates seem to have returned to his grave and taken the rest of his remains. At the request of Black Hawk's kin, the Iowa Territory authorities pursued the grave robbers and managed to retrieve the bones. These were then left for safekeeping at the Geological and Historical Society in Burlington, until the building burned down in 1855 and the bones were destroyed (Jung 2008: 200–201).

A settler in Iowa who was in her teens at the time of Black Hawk's death recalls a slightly different sequence of events in a memoir written towards the end of her life.

> One of our neighbors, Dr. James Turner, thought if he could only steal Black Hawk's head he could make a fortune out of it by taking it east and putting it on exhibition. After two weeks' watching he succeeded in getting it. Black Hawk's burial place was near old Iowaville, on the north side of the Des Moines River, under a big sugar tree. It was there Dr. Turner severed the head from the body. At the time it was done I was taking care of his sick sister-in-law, Mrs. William Turner. The doctor made his home with his brother. We knew the evening he went to steal the head and sat up to await his coming. He got in with it at four o'clock in the morning and hid it till the afternoon of the same day, when he cooked the flesh off the skull. So I can say that I am the only one now living that witnessed that sight, for it was surely a sight for me. If the rest of Black Hawk's bones were ever removed it was a good many years after his head was stolen. The second morning after their ruler's head was stolen ten of the best Indian warriors came to William Turner's and asked for his brother, the Doctor. They were painted war style. He told them he did not know where his brother was. They told him they would give him ten days to find his brother, and if he did not find him in that time he would pay the penalty for his brother's crime. But he knew where his brother was. He was at the home of a neighbor named Robb .... But he did not want to find his brother and sent a boy to tell him to fly for Missouri, which he did. The Indians returned to Iowaville to hold council and conclude what to do, and while they were holding council William Turner and his wife made their escape in a canoe down the river ....
>
> But the Indians demanded their ruler's head, and for three weeks we expected an outbreak every day, but through the influence of their agent and the citizens together they gave up hostilities for a time. The whites told them they would bring Turner to justice if he could be found. The sheriff chased Turner around for awhile, which only gave him the more time to get out of the way. The Turner family finally all went to St. Louis where the Doctor was found again, and to keep the Indians quiet the sheriff went to St. Louis in search of him, but he did not find him. He did not want to find him. But Turner got frightened and took Black Hawk's skull to Quincy, Illinois, and put it in the care of a doctor there for safe-keeping (I forget the doctor's name) till the Indians would get settled down, and then he intended to take it east. But when he got ready to go east with it the doctor in Quincy refused to give it up, and he did not dare to go to law about it, so after all his trouble and excitement he lost Black Hawk's skull, and not only made Turner endless trouble, but put the lives of all settlers in jeopardy for months. We lived principally on excitement and that was a poor living. But they finally got over it till all was peace and then we were happy. The doctor that had the head took it to Burlington and sold it to a museum and the museum was burned down, so Black Hawk's skull is not now in existence. The Turner family ... died with the cholera. So I am left alone to tell the story. (Nossaman 1922: 444–45)

The theft of Black Hawk's remains seems to have been an act of celebrity body-snatching or grave robbery entirely in keeping with the early nineteenth-century romantic cult of the genius and heroic individual. In other words, the motives of Dr Turner and his accomplices probably had as much to do with Black Hawk's celebrity as with perceptions of his race. As in the case of other contemporary luminaries in Europe, such as the Swedish mystic Swedenborg or the artist Goya, whose remains suffered a similar fate (Dickey 2009), his skull was a cultural icon of his individuality and uniqueness as a man. Like any other souvenirs (S. Stewart 1993), such relics had value because of the narratives attached to them – in this case, the exemplary and highly publicized life stories which they signified.

Osceola

A contemporary of Black Hawk was Osceola, a leader of the Seminoles during the Second Seminole War of 1835–42 in Florida. He was taken prisoner and died in custody in 1838. After his death, Dr Weedon, the army surgeon who treated him during his final illness, removed his head and embalmed it in some way. Weedon had earlier collected the skull of another Seminole prisoner, Uchee Billy, who had died the previous year (Wickman 2006: 137, 182). Weedon also kept some of Osceola's personal possessions, including his pipe, earrings, bangle, garter and sheath knife, as well as a long lock of Osceola's hair, which was later plaited and woven, probably by Weedon's daughter, into a memento in the manner of nineteenth-century hair jewellery.

The rest of Osceola's personal effects were taken by a Captain Morrison, the officer in charge of the Seminole prisoners, who also ordered Weedon to make a plaster cast of Osceola's head and torso. Morrison then sent these items as personal gifts to a Major Hook, an influential figure in the War Department in Washington, and a private collector of Indiana (Wickman 2006: 257–64).

A few months after Osceola's death, Weedon obtained written statements from three army officers attesting to the authenticity of the head, and put the head on display in the window of his drug store (Wickman 2006: 187–88). It appears that Weedon may also have exhibited the head, or at least tried to exhibit it, at Peale's Museum on Broadway in New York. But he seems to have misjudged the public mood there. Like Black Hawk, Osceola had become something of a romantic hero in the northeastern United States, where there was widespread public indignation at the circumstances of his capture. There seems to have been an outcry over the maltreatment of his body, and Weedon was forced to remove the head and return with it to his home in St. Augustine in Florida (Wickman 2006: 179–80). To many New Yorkers, Weedon's behaviour would have seemed an example of the all-too-familiar and much hated practice of body-snatching (see Sappol 2002: 108–109).

In 1839, Lorenzo Fowler, who ran a thriving phrenological business enterprise in New York together with his brother Orson, wrote to Weedon offering to buy the head of Osceola and the skull of Uchee Billy (Wickman 2006: 188). The offer seems not to have been accepted, because, in 1843 Weedon's son-in-law made a present of Osceola's head to a famous and wealthy New York surgeon and collector, and at this point the head passed out of the Weedon family (Wickman 2006: 189–96). The other items taken by Weedon, however, have remained in the possession of his descendants (Wickman 2006: 177, 212, 223–28).

In this way Osceola was, as it were, deconstituted into many parts, and then distributed among a variety of recipients having sentimental, commercial, medical, scientific or some other interests in his relics. Some of the personal effects and body parts were taken in order to sell or to exhibit them for money. Some were retained as personal or family memorabilia, and others were presented as gifts to superiors or influential patrons with an interest in ethnology and natural history. In this respect, the treatment of his remains recalls the death of Hintsa, the Xhosa leader killed in 1835 in southern Africa. As the reader will recall from the previous chapter, Hintsa's weapons, ornaments, teeth, ears and 'emblems of manhood' were alleged to have been taken by military and medical personnel, and some of these items kept as souvenirs, some given away as personal gifts, and others offered for sale. It is striking how little significance seems to have been attached in either case to the distinction between the dead man's body parts and his personal possessions. The dead body and its accoutrements were treated as a single ensemble, all of whose elements seemed equally to signify the man.

Soldiers and Phrenologists

The Second Seminole War took place at the height of the popularity of phrenology in the United States. Like some British soldiers in Africa at the time, some United States Army personnel, too, had strong amateur interests in phrenology and, like their British counterparts, they particularly sought the skulls of indigenous notables and leading figures for phrenological study.

Myer Cohen, a lawyer who served as an officer with the South Carolina volunteers in the Second Seminole War, kept a journal in which he detailed the military actions in which he took part, interspersed with observations on the ethnology and natural history of Florida and the phrenological characteristics of the indigenous people. His journal mentions two occasions, separated by a week, when the bodies of Seminole leaders killed in action were brought into camp, and craniometric measurements and phrenological examinations made of their skulls. The author's day-to-day record of military actions and engagements is interrupted by two pages of discussion of the facial angles and other racial characteristics of the two skulls, speculations on the racial origins of Indians, and unflattering character portraits of the two chiefs based on the relative sizes of their cranial protuberances. On one of the skulls, evidence was discerned of an over-enlargement of the phrenological regions associated with greed and vanity. On the other, the mental organs of reflection were deduced to be small. Both skulls were found to exhibit the signs of highly developed faculties of cruelty and cunning (Cohen 1836: 162–63, 169–71).

Cohen's journal makes no mention of the process by which the flesh must presumably have been removed from the skulls to prepare them for this examination. But clearly, for him, science and warfare, the violent acquisition of territory and of knowledge, were closely related activities. The collection of enemy skulls for phrenological study became routine in the Florida wars and reoccurred in the final Seminole War of 1855–58 (Wickman 2006: 181, 184).

Many of the specimens collected in such circumstances found their way into the growing scientific collections of the time, including that of Samuel Morton, the author of the seminal *Crania Americana* of 1839. Morton assembled his collection using his large network of contacts with other collectors and dealers in specimens in the United States and overseas.

A. Fabian observes that '[i]n the marketplace where Morton traded for skulls ... a man's head was better than a woman's; a warrior's better than a farmer's; and a chief's better than a commoner's' (2003: 124). In other words, for collectors such as Morton, human skulls were ranked on a scale of social value or prestige. It is striking how similar this was to the ranking of animal hunting trophies. For here, too, it has always been the heads and horns of males, and especially the largest, dominant males of aggressive and potentially dangerous game species, that have carried the most prestige among sports hunters. While Morton's primary interests lay, at least in principle, in the objectively quantified measurement of crania, his interpretations of the skulls in practice drew on much broader social judgements. If a skull came into his collection with a story attached to it, the narrative and the craniometric specimen seem to have been, for him, inseparable. Plate 22 of *Crania Americana* is an engraving of one of Morton's specimens, the skull of a 'Seminole warrior', with a bullet-hole in the temple,

> slain at the battle of St. Joseph's, thirty miles below St Augustine, in June 1836, by Captain Justin Dimmick of the first regiment United States Artillery. At the commencement of the action Captain Dimmick rode forward, and received the fire of the Indians at a distance of about thirty yards. The Captain's horse being struck in the neck and the flank, he dismounted, and the Indians supposing him to be badly wounded, rushed towards him to scalp him. At that moment Captain D. raised his gun, (a double-barrel fowling piece,) and shot both Indians in succession. (Morton 1839: 167–68; quoted in A. Fabian 2003: 124)

The warrior shown in Plate 22 had tried to take Captain Dimmick's scalp as a war trophy, only to have his skull taken and used to illustrate the pages of *Crania Americana*. Although Dimmick himself seems to have had no wish to keep the skull as a memento of his bravery, Morton memorialized it for him in his book, commemorating the soldier's act of battlefield heroism on his behalf.

The Military and Indian Skulls

In the United States, then, the military became closely involved in the collection of craniological and phrenological specimens in the early nineteenth century, just as happened in the colonies of European nations such as Britain (Harrison 2008a). The collection of 'Indian crania', for example, became what Bieder (2003: 67) calls a cottage industry among soldiers and military physicians serving on the American frontier.

An early example is recorded in a deposition by the Indian agent Henry Schoolcraft in September 1826 in Michigan. It concerns a soldier accused of robbing an Indian grave and delivering the head, wrapped in a handkerchief, to the hospital at Fort Brady. According to Schoolcraft,

> Robert McKain has long had the reputation among his companions, of digging up dead bodies of Indians for pay. That sometime in the month of August last, between the 1st & 18th of that month, said McKain informed this deponent that he had been offered a good price by [the army surgeon at Fort Brady] for bringing him three Indian heads, and

proposed to this deponent to assist in digging them up, which (this deponent) promptly declined. This deponent further says, that on the night of the 2nd of September instant, a light was seen in the Hospital during the night, as was reported among the soldiers at the guard house on the following morning. It was further added, that some of the guards went to the Hospital windows, suspecting that the heads of the Indians were in preparation, and saw kettles on the fire. And the guards who were stationed near the Hospital that night complained that a most abominable stench was experienced by them during the night arising from the Hospital, and suppose to be the effects of boiling the Indian skulls. (Bieder 2003: 66–67; see also Thomas 2000)

A more violent instance of such behaviour is described by Daniel Conner, an eyewitness to the killing of the Apache leader Mangas Coloradas in 1863. At the time, Conner was a member of an exploring party camping in a derelict fort in New Mexico together with a company of soldiers who had taken Mangas Coloradas into custody. While on guard duty one night, he observed two guards apparently amuse themselves, when they thought he was not looking, by heating their bayonets in the camp fire and burning the prisoner on the feet and legs as he tried to sleep. When the prisoner complained, they both shot him (Conner 1956: 38–39). In the morning, Conner lifted up the head of the dead man (whom he calls Mangus) and took some amulets and 'curious trinkets' from around his neck.

> Quite a number of soldiers came to where I was standing near the corpse, and amongst them there was one who called himself John T. Wright of California, who asked the loan of my butcher knife with which to scalp the Chief. I declined upon the ground that my knife was the only cutlery that I possessed with which to prepare my food &c. He then applied to the soldier's cook, Wm. Lallier, who furnished a large bowie knife, with which the soldier took off the scalp of Mangus. He wrapped the long hair around the scalp and put it in his pocket. I thought that I had never seen the skin about the head of a buffalo much thicker than the scalp of Mangus.
>
> It was ... very cold and therefore the operation of taking this scalp was a bloodless one, leaving the inner skin as white as the skull from which it was taken. The body was left where it lay till noon, when it was carried on a blanket and dumped into a gulley, blanket and all, and covered up.
>
> A few nights after this, some soldiers dug Mangus' body out again, and took his head and boiled it during the night, and prepared the skull to send to the museum in New York. I afterward saw the skull frequently before the soldiers departed with it. Thus ended the career of the most notorious chief which the Apaches ever boasted of since the United States has owned Arizona and New Mexico. (Conner 1956: 40–41)

A day or two afterwards, some of the soldiers attacked a group of Apaches and killed ten of them. They returned to camp with scalps hanging from their saddles, and wearing their victims' boots, buckskin shirts, and headdresses. Later, the soldiers reported to their superiors that Mangas Coloradas had been killed while trying to escape. An assistant surgeon, who resigned a little over a year later, took the skull to Ohio, where he opened a private medical practice. Besides being a notorious figure in the public imagination, Mangas Coloradas was an unusually tall, powerfully built man with a large head, and for all these reasons he seems to have attracted the attention of phrenologists. At some stage, the skull seems to have come into the possession of the New York phrenologist Orson

Fowler, who published a phrenological examination and analysis of it in one of his later books (Fowler 1873: 1195–97; Conner 1956: 41; Sweeney 1998: 457, 460, 534).

A Division of the Spoils

Since at least the eighteenth century, a notable feature of frontier warfare in North America had been the considerable lengths to which fighters on both sides often went to keep their dead from falling into enemy hands. They would bury their bodies in carefully hidden graves, or conceal them in undergrowth if they could not bury them, and often risked their own lives to remove them from the battlefield, in order to prevent their dead from being scalped or otherwise mutilated (Cohen 1836: 220; Kanon 1999: 10; Mann 2005: 127). The desecration of the enemy dead seems to have been routine, completely reciprocal and expected on both sides. The Apache, for instance, later killed an army officer and beheaded his body in reprisal for the death of Mangas Coloradas (Sweeney 1998: 463).

Such behaviour was part of what I called in the previous chapter a negotiated culture of combat, common to all participants in the Indian wars of the nineteenth century. Another part of this negotiated culture was the use of similar tactics of raiding and surprise attacks. An integral part of this pattern of essentially retaliatory and reciprocal raiding was the taking of scalps and other trophies, including items of clothing and other personal effects (Axtell 1981; Calloway 1997: 103). For many men on both sides, it was a pattern of warfare that seems to have evoked the hunting and killing of game animals. Soldiers and militiamen who took scalps did so primarily for the often very substantial prices offered for them, bounties themselves modelled on long-standing practices of offering rewards for the heads or scalps of wolves (Coleman 2003). For Daniel Conner, as we saw, the sight of the body of Mangas Coloradas being scalped brought to mind the skinning of a buffalo.

The typical pattern among soldiers and militiamen, then, was to take scalps, usually in order to redeem them for a reward, rather than to retain them as keepsakes; and to retain certain items of enemy clothing, ornaments and other possessions as personal trophies. Unlike some of their British counterparts in Africa at the time, few seem to have shown an interest in retaining enemy skulls as war mementos in this way. On the other hand, some were clearly willing to procure such objects for sale to dealers and collectors, and to assist military physicians in collecting them. As we saw in the case of Osceola, the enemy body with its accoutrements seems to have been viewed as an assemblage to be undone after death, and its parts distributed for different purposes, according to certain conventions.

Executions of Indians were accompanied by similar practices, as happened in the case of the mass hanging of thirty-eight Dakota men at Mankato, Minnesota, after the six-week Dakota War of 1862 (Derounian-Stodola 2009: 72; Nudelman 2004: 42; Schultz 1992). Afterwards, at least some the bodies were looted by souvenir hunters, and later exhumed by local doctors and dissected. On the twenty-fifth anniversary of the hangings, a citizen wrote to the Minnesota Historical Society enclosing a watch-chain he had had made from the hair of Chaska, one of the hanged men who had taken part in killing a clerk called George Gleason.

> We all felt keenly the injury he [Chaska] had don [*sic*] in murdering our old friend Gleason, in cold blood. I cut off the Rope that bound his hands and feet, and cut off one Brade of his hair .... I had the hair made into a Watch chain by a Lady friend in St. Paul. I wore it until it was as you see about wore out, and now I send it to you, thinking that some day it might be of interest with the other mementoes of those terrible times and that great hanging Event. (Quoted in Derounian-Stodola 2009: 73)

Little Crow, the leader of the Dakota in this war, was shot and killed in 1863 by a Minnesota farmer, who scalped the body for the reward of $75 offered by the state for the scalps of hostile Dakota. The body was taken to the nearby town of Hutchinson and left on display in the main street until evening, when a local physician, Dr John Benjamin, had the corpse moved to a refuse pit outside the town. There, it seems to have been dug up shortly afterwards and a number of parts of the body taken, including the head, which was removed by a cavalry officer, and the skull later came into the possession of Dr Benjamin (G.C. Anderson 1986: 7–8).

> Throughout the three decades following his death, Little Crow's bones fell into the hands of various individuals who kept them as souvenirs. Frank Powell donated the skull to the Minnesota Historical Society in 1896. It, along with the scalp lock, which the state already owned, and the forearms, which the society received at about the same time, were put on display in a case in the society's museum. As the frontier closed and Minnesota entered a new era, the curiosities became an embarrassment. The display was quietly dismantled in the early twentieth century. (G.C. Anderson 1986: 181)

Little Crow's remains were finally returned to his family in 1971, and buried in a private family plot.

A similar pattern recurred, on a much larger scale, in the infamous Sand Creek Massacre of 29 November 1864, when a Cheyenne and Arapaho encampment was attacked and 133 of its people killed by a force of Colorado Territory volunteers (Hoig 1961; Stannard 1992: 131–34). The soldiers and militiamen took clothing, ornaments, scalps and other body parts from the victims, and many of these were displayed afterwards in various celebratory events, while some of the heads or skulls of those killed were sent to the newly established Army Medical Museum (Juzda 2009: 159; Riding In 1992b: 19; Thomas 2000: 52–53)

Towards Institutional Collectors

When the skulls and other remains of American Indians were collected in the early nineteenth century, they were sought by, or for, private collectors, because no governmental agencies existed at the time to receive such objects. In order to have to access to the bodily remains of contemporary Indians, these private collectors usually needed either to be members of the military, or to have connections to it (Wickman 2006: 184–87).

The mid nineteenth century saw the establishment of large public institutions with an interest in comparative anatomy and the collection of human osteological specimens. The Smithsonian Institution was founded in 1846, and opened in 1855. The Army Medical Museum was established in 1862 and, after the end of the Civil War in 1865, mainly collected Indian remains (A. Fabian 2003; Juzda 2009). In 1868, the Surgeon General, the chief medical officer of the United States Army, issued a memorandum to army physicians in the field urging them to collect Indian skulls for the museum's craniological collection (Riding In 1992b: 19; Thomas 2000).

The effect of this was to encourage the systematic harvesting of American Indian skulls and other remains. Some of this activity was carried out, often clandestinely, after executions. Following the Modoc War of 1872–73 in northern California and southern Oregon, the Modoc leader Kintpuash, or Captain Jack, was hanged at Fort Klamath, Oregon, together with three other Modoc men, and their heads sent to the Army Medical Museum.

> It was probably Col. H.S. Shaw, a reporter from the *San Francisco Chronicle*, who happened to walk past a tent at Fort Klamath and saw an amazing sight. In the center of the tent stood a long table 'similar to those used in the dissecting-room of a medical college.' A black india rubber sheet was spread over the table. In one corner stood a barrel of water and in another was a case of surgical instruments. The curious reporter set out to learn what this strange ensemble was for. He soon was able to inform the Chronicle that he had learned that the heads of Captain Jack and Schonchin John had been cut off for shipment to Washington. The Chronicle was aghast. But the *Army and Navy Journal* countered that if the story was true, it was not a case of barbarism, but the need to do a medical dissection …. On October 25 Colonel Wheaton wrote the Surgeon General notifying him of the shipment of not two but of the four heads of the executed for the Army Medical Museum. (E.N. Thompson 1971: 125–26, footnotes omitted; see also Riding In 1992b: 20)

In contrast to earlier practices of anatomizing executed criminals, which were public dramas of punishment and deterrence, the procedure was carried out purely to procure body parts, and the authorities by this time clearly sought to avoid publicity.

Nor were the personal or individual identities of such donors usually significant by this stage. In 1869 an army surgeon in northern Kansas organized a search for the bodies of a party of Pawnees who had been killed by soldiers and settlers. Six of the bodies were found, despite the survivors' attempts to hide them, and their skulls sent to the museum (Riding In 1992a, 1992b: 20). From the collectors' point of view, these victims were nameless, and their skulls were simply representatives of a racial stock.

At this point, with the shift away from private collectors towards institutional ones, we see a shift also towards the collection of the body parts of unidentified people, significant not for their biographies but primarily as illustrations of racial types or as medical specimens. These more depersonalized and routinized forms of collecting merely formalized or institutionalized practices that had been already been taking place for some decades. The structure of the market in these relics also remained the same. Indian skulls and other specimens tended to originate on the frontier and to be shipped to the cities of the east, where their consumers were mainly located: the audiences who would pay to view them, and the institutions which sought to study them.

The early nineteenth-century private collectors were interested in the individuality of their specimens, because their own preoccupations were predominantly phrenological and characterological. They sought the skulls of outstanding personalities such as Osceola and Black Hawk, objects with rich layers of life-history narrative and established public meaning attached to them. In the United States, as in Europe, the collection and display of such objects was part of the hagiography of the superior man. In the eastern United States particularly, a large reading public sentimentalized and romanticized Indians as an heroic, but vanishing, people.

The collection of skulls and other osteological specimens was therefore at first embedded in, and inseparable from, the collection of other parts and attributes of such eminent, if tragic, figures: their clothing, hair, weaponry, personal ornaments and other relics which could powerfully evoke their charismatic life stories in the minds of an audience.

During the century a noticeable change in overall emphasis occurred, away from collecting the skulls of Indian notables and celebrities, to the routinized mass collection of anonymous Indian skulls. It reflected the shift away from the almost cultic use of skulls in phrenological character portraits of leading men, towards the more modern concerns of comparative anatomy and physical anthropology, which attached particular value to the statistical analysis of large samples. Skulls were increasingly understood as a means of discovering quantitative evidence of 'racial' differences between populations, rather than as outward signs of qualitative differences between individual men.

Nonetheless, it is clear that the collection and study of the skulls of American Indians were already firmly established social practices in American settler society by the time they started to acquire a recognizably modern technical or scientific character. The Indian skull was a moral and symbolic object before it was an object of rational enquiry.

Chapter 9

Ethnology, Race and Trophy-hunting in the American Civil War

Introduction

In the 1980s and 1990s, an important change of consciousness took place in the world of museology in regard to the retention and display of human skeletal material. This change occurred largely in response to growing demands by American Indians and other indigenous peoples for the repatriation of ancestral remains held by museums. Some of these acquisitions, as we saw, originated as battlefield trophies collected by nineteenth-century colonial soldiers. The new understandings of the role of the museum were evidenced by legislation such as the Native American Graves Protection and Repatriation Act (NAGPRA) passed by the United States Government in 1990, which recognized the rights of indigenous groups to the remains of their ancestors (Fforde, Hubert and Turnbull 2002; Mihesuah 2000; Peers 2009; Thomas 2000; Turnbull 2007).

However, indigenous peoples have by no means been the only victims of these sorts of appropriations. In 1998, the newly appointed director of the Oakland County Pioneer and Historical Society in Pontiac, Michigan, discovered that the society's museum collection included the mandible of a Confederate soldier killed in the battle of South Mountain in 1862 during the American Civil War. It had been acquired as a memento by a Union infantryman, David S. Howard, who had been severely wounded in the battle. In the 1890s, Howard was a distinguished veteran and a high-ranking officer in the Grand Army of the Republic, a Union veterans' organization, and also served three terms as mayor of Pontiac. In 1968 his descendants donated the mandible and Howard's other Civil War memorabilia to the museum, where the mandible remained for the next thirty years in a cardboard box on a shelf. Among the family memorabilia, the museum director also found evidence, such as labels bearing the words 'rebel jawbone', suggesting that Howard may have displayed the mandible at veterans' reunions in commemoration of his war service. In 1998, the society decided that the bone ought to be given burial, and presented it, in a bronze urn, to the Sons of Confederate Veterans, an organization of descendants of Confederate servicemen, whose members gave it a military funeral in the cemetery for Confederate soldiers at Hagerstown, Maryland. 'This represents a human being', the director told a journalist. 'He may have fought and died for a cause we don't believe in, but he deserves a better fate than sitting on the second floor of a carriage house in Pontiac. He should join his buddies' (Thurtell 1998a; see also 1998b, 1998c).

In a similar case in 1996, the curator of the Henry County Historical Society Museum in New Castle, Indiana, was making an inventory of American Indian remains in the museum's collection in order to comply with NAGPRA legislation. Among the American Indian skulls, she came across a skull labelled 'Rebel Butler'. According to the museum's records, an assistant surgeon serving with a Pennsylvania regiment during the Civil War had obtained the skull in 1865 from the site of the battle of Spotsylvania, a year after the battle had taken place, and had been able to discover the dead soldier's surname from evidence found with his remains. The skull stayed in the surgeon's family until 1923, when his descendants gave it to the museum, where it remained on display until the early 1990s. The curator arranged with the Sons of Confederate Veterans for the skull to be buried with military honours in August 1996 at the Confederate cemetery in Fredericksburg, Virginia. An historian of the Civil War observed to a journalist: 'I don't know of another case where a skull was carried home as a souvenir …. It sounds like Vietnam, not the Civil War' (Associated Press 1996; see also Goldfield 2002: 304).

Historically, museums have been almost the only institutions which could acceptably retain and display the remains of the battlefield dead. Evidently, families have sometimes sought to dispose of unwanted war mementos of this sort by donating them to museum collections, and the museum thereby served them as a final resting place for some uncomfortable reminders of their own pasts. In this respect, museums have played an important role in erasing history as well as preserving it. By the same token, relics of old wars, material residues of conflicts from which many unpalatable memories have been expunged, can sometimes resurface in museums from time to time as strange, disturbing evidence of lost regions of social memory.

The use of enemy skulls and other bones as souvenirs or trophies during the American Civil War, though a highly contentious issue at the time, is one of these largely forgotten histories. The recovery of victims' remains has become an important political and moral issue in the aftermath of many civil conflicts (see, for instance, Fontein 2010; Petrović-Šteger 2009; Renshaw 2010), but the collection of enemy body parts as private mementos is an unusual feature of the American Civil War and calls for explanation. During the Civil War, most contemporaries strongly condemned such abuses of the battlefield dead, likening them to the savage headhunting customs of primitive tribes. But these practices seem in fact to have reflected some important developments taking place in the fields of medicine, comparative anatomy and racial science in the middle of the nineteenth century. The Civil War, a conflict in which race was a fundamental issue, occurred at a time when the human skull had acquired a central importance in scientific understandings of individual and racial differences. The emergence of this preoccupation with the skull represented a departure from Enlightenment understandings of race, and marked a shift in which significant human differences were increasingly assumed to be measurable objectively in the bones, and above all in variations in the size, shape and supposed degree of development of the skull. The collection and use of enemy skulls and bones as commemorative objects in the Civil War were local symptoms of the new significance given to these parts of the body as material evidence of the naturalness of racial hierarchy and the permanence of differences. The battlefield practices which seemed so aberrant and atavistic to many contemporaries were, to the contrary, manifestations of the growing authority and prestige of scientific rationality.

Northern Accusations

The opening land battle of the American Civil War took place in July 1861 near the town of Manassas in Virginia. This engagement, which supporters of the Union would later call the First Battle of Bull Run, was a chaotic rout of the Union Army, leaving Confederate forces occupying the battlefield until the following January. Once they had gone, relatives of the Union dead came in search of their kinsmen's remains. From these visitors' conversations with local residents, and their own observations, as well as from other evidence, a disturbing picture began to emerge of 'rebel atrocities' in the aftermath of the battle. There were claims that the Confederates had maltreated or murdered prisoners. Other allegations were of 'barbarities' perpetrated upon the dead. These charges were included in the matters investigated by a congressional Joint Committee on the Conduct of the War (United States Congress 1863).

One of the witnesses who gave evidence to this enquiry was Senator Sprague, the Governor of Rhode Island, who visited the battlefield in March 1862 to retrieve the bodies of officers of the Rhode Island infantry. He found graves in which Union soldiers had been buried by the Confederates face downwards, a disgrace which seems at the time to have been reserved for soldiers executed for desertion (Nudelman 2004: 141). Local women also told Sprague that one of the Georgia regiments had dug up the body of a Rhode Island officer, cut off his head, and burned the body, apparently in revenge for his having led an attack in which many of the Georgia men had been killed.

Other witnesses spoke of Confederate soldiers disinterring the Union dead to obtain their bones as trophies. A Union Army surgeon, captured in the battle, recalled seeing graves which had been opened during the subsequent weeks. Local slaves who had helped bury the Union dead told him that Confederate soldiers used fence-railings to pry bodies out of their graves in order to make rings from the bones and drinking cups from the tops of the skulls. Another witness, a New Yorker called Frederick Scholes, visited Manassas in April 1862 in search of the remains of his brother. A local black storekeeper told him

> that the rebel soldiers would come into his store with bones in their hands, which they showed to him, and said they were bones of Yankees which they had dug up. He said it was a common thing for the soldiers to exhibit the bones of 'the Yankees' ....
>
> I went over to the house of a free negro named Hampton, as I understood that he assisted in burying some of our dead .... I spoke to him about the manner in which these bodies had been dug up. He said he knew it had been done, and said it was most shameful. He said the rebels commenced digging up the bodies two or three days after they were buried, for the purpose at first of obtaining the buttons on their uniforms; afterwards they dug them up, as they decayed, to get their bones .... He said they had taken rails and pushed the ends down in the centre under the middle of the bodies and then pried them up in that way ....

I went over where some of [a local landowner's] negro men were, and inquired of them. Their information corroborated fully the statement of this man Hampton. They also stated that a great many of the bodies had been stripped naked on the field before they were buried, and some were buried naked; others were buried with their clothes on. They said that numbers of them had been dug up through the winter, and even shortly after they had been buried ....

[A] party of soldiers came up, and showed us part of a shin-bone, five or six inches long, which had the end sawed off. They said they had found it among many other pieces in one of the cabins the rebels had deserted. From the appearance of it, pieces had been sawed off, out of which to make finger-rings. As soon as the negroes noticed this, they said that the rebels had had rings made of the bones of our dead that they had dug up; that they had them for sale in their camps. The soldiers said that there were lots of these bones scattered all through the rebel huts sawed into rings, &c. (United States Congress 1863: 466–48)

A witness from Washington, D.C., Daniel Bixby, told the committee of having accompanied a friend to the battlefield in search of the grave of the friend's brother. They located the grave, but discovered on opening it that it contained nothing but clothes and pieces of flesh; the head and all the bones were missing. They found the remains of several other Union soldiers in a similar condition. A local woman told them she had seen Confederates, too impatient to wait for the bodies to decay, boiling parts of them in order to remove the flesh and obtain the bones 'as relics'. She said she had seen drumsticks made of what the Confederate soldiers had called 'Yankee shin-bones'. She also claimed to have seen a member of the New Orleans artillery with a human skull 'which he said he was going to send home and have mounted, and was going to drink a brandy punch out of it the day he was married' (United States Congress 1863: 477).

Lurid stories of the conversion of Union soldiers' skulls into Confederate drinking bowls persisted throughout the war. One Union soldier claimed to have found a cranium 'used by the Rebs for a soap dish' (Wiley 1952: 347; see also McWhiney and Jamieson 1982: 182). After the battle of Gaines Mill in June 1862, a war correspondent for the New York Times reported that Union soldiers had found a Confederate soldier's knapsack, 'hung to which was half a skull, used evidently as a drinking vessel. An inscription upon it stated that it came from Bull Run' (quoted in Laderman 1996: 100). The committee's report itself referred to a skull converted into a drinking cup, which had been found on a Confederate prisoner and put on display in the office of the Sergeant-at-Arms of the House of Representatives (United States Congress 1863: 456). One of the exhibits at the Metropolitan Fair held in New York in April 1864 was described in the fair's catalogue as: '766. Skull of an Union Soldier. Taken near Blufton, S.C. Used by the rebels for a drinking cup' (Department of Arms and Trophies 1864: 79).

In their private letters, too, Union soldiers sometimes referred to making gruesome discoveries of this sort in abandoned Confederate camps. Some of them came across skulls bearing commemorative inscriptions. A soldier from Massachusetts claimed to have discovered in a deserted enemy camp in May 1862 five skulls bearing the inscription 'Five Zouaves' Coconuts killed at Bull Run by Southern lead' (Wiley 1952: 347; see also McWhiney and Jamieson 1982: 182).[1] Edwin Burbank, a corporal in the Union Army, writing to his family on 11 April 1863, describes entering an abandoned Confederate camp with some companions and finding a human skull inscribed with the words: 'Bull

Run, 5th Massachusetts'. This was Burbank's own regiment, and had fought at Bull Run. He and his friends concluded from the inscription that they had found the skull of one of their comrades (Burbank 1863).

Another recurring theme in Union accusations against the Confederate army was the selling of the bones of Union soldiers as souvenirs, and the carving of bones into trinkets for their wives and families. A Union soldier wrote to his family from Winchester, Virginia, on 14 March 1862: 'We heard to-day, from a citizen, that after the battle of "Bull Run," some Northern skulls were sold here at $10 apiece; also that many officers had spurs made of our men's bones. I don't know whether to believe these things or not' (Shaw 1999: 182).

The same price is mentioned by Sarah Edmonds, a Union Army nurse who visited some of the battlefields in late 1862:

> The few families who still live in that vicinity tell horrid stories of the brutal conduct of the rebels after those battles.
> A Southern clergyman declares that in the town where he now resides he saw rebel soldiers selling 'Yankee skulls' at ten dollars apiece. And it is a common thing to see rebel women wear rings and ornaments made of our soldiers' bones – in fact they boast of it, even to the Union soldiers, that they have 'Yankee bone ornaments'. (Edmonds 1865: 299)

Southern Women and Northern Propaganda

The findings of the Joint Committee were widely publicised in the Northern press. Especially emphasized were the committee's remarks comparing the behaviour of the Confederates after their victory at Bull Run to the 'cruelties' of 'savage tribes' (see, for instance, Harper's Weekly 1862). By mutilating or maltreating the dead bodies of their enemies, making trophies of their body parts and committing other atrocities, they had shown themselves to be not a civilized army, but similar in nature to 'Indians' such as the Sioux, or to the natives of 'Feejee' – the epitome, at the time, of primitive headhunters and cannibals (Blair 2000: 167–70; Frost 2005: 18–22; McWhiney and Jamieson 1982: 182). Nathaniel Hawthorne, writing in a wartime journal, contrasted the chivalrous and 'manly' Union soldiers whom he encountered with the Confederates, whose

> peculiar taste inclines them to prefer the immediate and personal memorials of their slain foemen, such, for instance, as ornaments neatly carved out of a brave man's bones, to hang a lady's watch-chain, or a skull to hold their whiskey and water, and to be passed from lip to lip of man and maiden at their social and family gatherings. (1985: 1–2; see also Gollin 2005: 171)

One of the main Northern newspapers, *Frank Leslie's Illustrated*, published on 17 May 1862 a satirical cartoon entitled 'The Rebel Lady's Boudoir', attacking Southerners, or at least the Southern aristocracy. The cartoon referred specifically to the reports that Confederate soldiers made ornaments such as earrings and finger-rings from the remains of Union soldiers and sent them home to their families as souvenirs. It showed a woman of the Southern slave-owning class in her boudoir, reading a letter from her husband who is away fighting in the war.

My dearest wife, I hope you have received all the little relics I have sent you from time to time. I am about to add something to your collection which I feel sure will please you - a baby rattle for our little pet, made out of the ribs of a Yankee drummer boy.

She is shown surrounded by war trophies that her husband has been sending her: the bones, scalps and other remains of Union soldiers, hung on the walls as if they were hunting trophies. Parts of skeletons have been turned into a variety of household objects: table legs, teapots, footstools and so forth. At her feet, a small child plays with the skull of a Union soldier. What the cartoon is implying is that the Southern slave-owning class are savages, for all their pretensions to cultivation and gentility.

Another cartoon, published in *Harper's Weekly* on 7 June 1862, linked the 'savagery' of the South with its low level of industrial development. It purported to show a collection of 'Specimens of "Secesh" Industry', and suggested satirically that Southerners had tried to showcase them at the 'London Exhibition of 1862' as examples of their technical ingenuity. The illustrations included a 'Goblet, made from a Yankee's skull', a 'Necklace of Yankee teeth', a 'Cake Basket made of Mudsill's ribs', and a 'Paper-Weight – Ingenious application of a Yankee's Jawbone' (see Frost 2005: 21).[2]

In the same month, an article in a Northern literary magazine returned to the theme of a contradiction, supposedly exposed by the war, between the savage backwardness of Southerners and their affectations of refinement:

> In short, from the grand inception of this war by FLOYD and DAVIS, with their thievery and compulsory confederating, to the conduct of their representatives abroad, with their plain, wholesale lying, down to the spitting women and bone-stealing boors of the present day, there hardly seems to have been an individual in the South who has, so far as the war is concerned, behaved like a really civilised being in any respect. TALLEYRAND said that if you scratch or peel a Russian, you find a Tartar; it would seem that if one scratch the thin varnish of outside polish and chivalry which covers a Southron, he will find a Choctaw. We are paying a high price for the information, but it is perhaps fortunate that the country is at last finding out what constitutes the true basis of that 'Southern gentility' and 'high-toned culture' which in by-gone days was wont to impose so heavily on our own society. (The Knickerbocker 1862: 581; see also p. 566)

Stereotypes of Southern slave owners as primitive savages who pretend aristocratic manners focussed particularly on the behaviour of their womenfolk. Northern soldiers seem often to have been shocked by the animosity they encountered from Southern women, shown by behaviour such as spitting at Union officers (Leonard 2002: 304; Rable 1991: 155–56), or by reported incidents such as the following:

> **Skull-Bone Memento Kept by a Lady**
> Information was one day communicated to the Provost-Marshal of St. Louis, Missouri, that the wife of a well known Confederate officer, Warrack Hugh, – Captain and Assistant-Inspector-General on General Leonidas Polk's staff, was in that city and preparing to go to Jefferson City. Orders were immediately issued for her arrest, and carried out. In her possession were found a number of secession articles, a pack of letters, and a piece of the skull of a Union soldier, about two inches square, and so thick that it must have been a portion of the occipital bone, on which was the inscription, 'Wilson's Creek, Dec. 21st, 1861,' and then some obscure chirography, half rubbed out, that looked like 'found on the

spot.' In answer to a question where she obtained it, she replied by telling when she got it. In answer to another, as to whether she knew what it was, she answered in the affirmative, – that she knew it to be a portion of the skull of a Union soldier. When inquired of why she kept it, she replied, '*For a memento,*' – an unaccountable and perverted taste for a lady. She was committed to the female department of the prison, after an examination, and the pleasant souvenirs were retained by the officials. (Kirkland 1867: 619–20)[3]

Southern women were not only accused of visiting the sites of battles to collect the bones of Union soldiers as ghoulish souvenirs, and wearing ornaments made from their bones.[4] The Northern press even often suggested that Southern women specifically bore much of the blame for starting the war, accusing them of having goaded their menfolk into rebellion. The implication was that Southern white women were even more reprehensible in their strident militancy than their men, because they were rebels or traitors twice over: to the Union, and to their gender (Leonard 2002: 304; Massey 1994: 259).

The Soldiers' Evidence

The Southern press dismissed the atrocities reported in Northern newspapers as 'hobgoblin stories' concocted by the North to divert attention from its own cruelties – such as deliberately starving the population of the South, and fomenting war between slaves and their owners (Frost 2005: 203). However, there is strong evidence that many of these abuses did take place, albeit among a small minority of men, and that most Confederate soldiers roundly condemned them in much the same terms as did Northerners. A letter from a Georgia private describes having witnessed desecrations of the enemy dead after Bull Run:

> I am sorry to say that I saw Confederate soldiers digging them up[,] taking their skulls and other bones .... [A friend told him of a cavalryman who pried apart] the chin of a Yankee and was wearing the lower jaw bone as a spur .... I know you agree with me that this is a degree of barbarism more worthy of savages in the dark ages than our nation at this enlightened period .... I am glad to say such proceedings are discountenanced by a vast majority of us. (Glatthaar 2008: 61–62)

The immediate context of this behaviour was the widespread practice of looting the enemy for practical necessities such as food, blankets and clothes, as well as money and valuables such as rings.[5] Such items might taken from prisoners and the dead, or found in captured enemy positions. This behaviour occurred on both sides (see, for instance, Bellard 1975: 86), but it was often more of a necessity among Confederate soldiers because they were in general less well provisioned (Colby 2003: 57; Glatthaar 2008: 60–61; J.R. Neff 2005: 58–59; D. Simpson 1994: 64; Wiley 1943: 76). Personal belongings were taken from enemy knapsacks: letters, diaries, watches, pocket knives and photographs. Items of this sort might be sold, or sent to relatives as keepsakes. A Confederate soldier wrote to his sister:

> I am going to send you a trophie that come off the battle field at Gettysburg .... I got three pictures out of a dead Yankees knapsack and I am going to send you one .... The pictures are wrapped up in a letter from the person whose image they are .... She signed her name A.D. Spears and she lived in Main somewhere, but I could not make out where she lived. (Wiley 1943: 75)

A popular souvenir on both sides were buttons from enemy uniforms (Mitchell 2002: 359). Those of high-ranking officers seem to have been particularly eagerly sought after. When the Union Army general Nathaniel Lyon was killed and his body taken by the Confederates, an eyewitness reported: 'In less than a minute's time a hundred men or more got around him and his horse, cutting souvenir buttons off Lyon's coat and hairs from his horse's tail' (D. Smith 2005: 12).

The taking of body parts seems to have been largely an extension of the practice of looting the dead, and the two often occurred together. A few weeks after Bull Run, a Confederate soldier wrote to his sister, enclosing a poem left behind by the Union forces, and adding:

> We have had no opportunity to collect the trophies from the battlefield, for as long as we were about the battlefield we [were] on the march, and now we are removed far from it so there is no chance of us getting anything whatever. But Dick Lewis was here yesterday and promised to get some things from the Fourth Regt such as sword, bayonet, pistol, balls, and if you want it we can send you some yankee bones. (D. Simpson 1994: 64; see also McPherson 1997: 151)

At one level, enemy bones were simply variants of the usual battlefield trophies such as enemy weapons, and could be offered to family members in the same way as these more usual souvenirs. But they were also far more aberrant in most people's eyes, and I will try later to suggest why the accepted practices of souvenir seeking were extended in these directions in the Civil War. After Bull Run, a Confederate private called Thomas Wragg wrote to his father, a doctor, that he wanted to send him a 'Yankee skull' (Hain 2005: 54–55). A planter's son wrote to his parents after the Battle of Antietam: 'Tell Miss Anna [his sister] that I thought of collecting her a peck of Yankee finger nails to make her a sewing basket of as she is ingenious at such things but I feared I could not get them to her'. Ten weeks after the cavalry battle at Brandy Station, a Virginia cavalryman wrote to his wife that his brother, in the same regiment, 'is now making a ring of some portion of the leg bone of the dead yankee' they had found on the battlefield (McPherson 1997: 151).

The manufacture of rings and earrings from animal bones seems to have been a well established practice at the time. Confederate prisoners of war in Minnesota, for instance, occupied their time by carving rings and other trinkets from cattle bones (Carley 2000: 75). Such pastimes may have been related to the tradition of carving scrimshaws among sailors, and an early form of what later came to be known as trench art (Saunders 2003).

Women and other civilians sometimes requested such keepsakes from friends or family members in the army (Glatthaar 2008: 61). Phoebe Pember was a Confederate army nurse, and a member of the Jewish community in the city of Richmond. On 25 June 1863, she wrote to her sister describing an evening she had recently spent with a group of devout Christians.

> The feeling here against Yankees exceeds anything I could imagine, particularly among the good Christians. I spent an evening among a particularly pious sett [sic]. One lady said she had a pile of Yankee bones lying around her pump so that the first glance on opening her eyes would rest upon them. Another begged me to get her a Yankee Skull to keep her toilette trinkets in. All had something of the kind to say. (Pember 2002: xv; see also Massey 1994: 259; Rosen 1994: 89)

Her dinner companions would have assumed that she, as an army nurse, had access to the remains of Union soldiers. She suggested jokingly to her companions that they should convert to Judaism because, unlike Christianity, it does not enjoin forgiveness of one's enemies.

Although skulls seem to have been particularly valued, it was not always convenient for soldiers to collect these and send them home because of their size. Less bulky items such as hair, teeth and bone rings seem to have been understood as substitutes for them. A Virginian soldier wrote to a woman after Bull Run: 'I send you Some hair off the head of a New York Zouave .... I could have sent a skull just dug up but it was too large' (Glatthaar 2008: 61).[6] Such letters were sometimes at pains to testify to the genuineness of these relics. One soldier described how, after he and his comrades rummaged through the personal effects of the Union dead, 'We got a great many things from the Yankees. I had a tooth that I got out of one of their heads. I will send it to you in the next letter .... It is a Yankee tooth, that I know, for I got it myself' (Carmichael 1995: 90).

This behaviour in the Civil War does not seem to have been entirely limited to the Confederate army. Some Union soldiers engaged in similar practices. Alfred Bellard, a Union Army private, mentions in his memoirs an occasion when

> [t]he body of a rebel was found .... Some thoughtless man had taken the skull from the body and stuck it on the stump of a pine sapling that was directly in the rear of our picket line .... I went over to it, when I saw what it was. There was nothing on it but a small tuft of hair like a scalp lock. (Bellard 1975: 97)

Another soldier wrote to his mother describing a visit to the battlefield at Maryland Heights, where he and his companions had come across the body of a Confederate soldier, loosely covered with stones. Some of the men took clippings of hair from the corpse, and two others knocked out some of the dead man's teeth as souvenirs. The soldier told his mother, 'the way they acted with him was enough to make a dog sick let alone a man' (Mitchell 2002: 360). An article by the editor of the Pontiac Weekly Gazette on 11 July 1862 mentions a similar incident. 'After the Battle of Seven Pines ... we stumbled upon a dead rebel, over whose body no earth had been thrown. It was a sickening sight. A [Union] soldier pulled off his lower jaw and asked me if I didn't want a rebel relic of the purist [sic] water?' (quoted in Thurtell 1998a).

Most Union soldiers who referred to such behaviour in their letters to their families seem to have done so with disapproval. There is little evidence of Union soldiers sending gifts of enemy remains to their relatives, or evidence of their families requesting such items from them. There were incidents such as that described by Bellard above, in which enemy remains were displayed in army camps, but these too were strongly condemned by most soldiers. So, for instance, a Union private, Clarke Oyer, describes how during the Atlanta campaign his regiment came across the hiding place of a group of malingerers, or 'skulkers', men who had been avoiding battle. They had set a Confederate soldier's skull on a pole, and beneath it a placard which read, 'Thus we serve all rebels that fall into our hands'. The sight of this shocked Oyer and his friends. He describes how it 'created much indignation among the soldierly portion of the regiment', who tore it down (Dunkelman 2006: 178).

In the only cases I know of in which Union soldiers gave enemy body parts to women, they gave them to Southern women, and did so as an act of reprisal. A Union soldier describes in a letter an occasion in Louisiana when a woman had taunted his regiment that 'real southern men would scalp them, that she would not believe union soldiers were anything but cowards and braggards unless she should see scalps they had taken'. Later, one of the Union men sent her the ears of a dead Confederate, gift-wrapped in a box (Fellman 1990: 153, 204). On another occasion, a Union soldier, passing a group of Southern women, tossed them a skull he had picked up on a nearby battlefield, telling them it was the head of their 'brother' (Strong 1961: 205). Perhaps this was his way of retaliating against Southern women for their alleged habit of collecting the remains of Northern soldiers.

Bodies in Nineteenth-century North America

At the beginning of the Civil War, there was little notion in American or European society that the battlefield dead deserved reverence from society at large. The remains of soldiers killed in action were meaningful to their friends and relatives, to the people who had known them, and this implied that the dead could receive respectful treatment only if they were identifiable as individuals. But the war dead in general – as an abstract category including the anonymous dead – were not yet sacred to a larger entity, such as the nation (Grant 2004).

Nor was taking and retaining mementos of the dead body as such an atrocity. It was a normal part of the process of Victorian grieving to keep mementos of loved ones, such as pieces of clothing or clippings of hair, or post-mortem photographs that can seem morbid to modern sensibilities (Nudelman 2004: 4). Sarah Edmonds, the Union Army nurse who visited battlefields in late 1862, recalls coming across the remains of a cavalryman.

> [H]e and his horse both lay together, nothing but the bones and clothing remained; but one of his arms stood straight up, or rather the bones and the coatsleeve, his hand had dropped off at the wrist and lay on the ground; not a finger or joint was separated, but the hand was perfect. I dismounted twice for the purpose of bringing away that hand, but did not do so after all. I would have done so if it had been possible to find a clue to his name or regiment. (1865: 299)

If the soldier had been identifiable, she would have taken his hand and tried to return it to his family or comrades. A few Civil War soldiers seem to have kept parts of their own dead comrades as souvenirs. One Confederate army colonel claimed in his memoirs to have kept a fragment of the skull of a friend who had been killed by shellfire, as a memento of the friend's gallantry (Gilmor 1866: 74). Some Civil War soldiers left clippings of their hair with their families, to be made into hair jewellery in the event of their death (Derounian-Stodola 2009: 73).

What was an offence against the dead and their families was the separation of the remains from the circle of the dead person's kin and friends; that is, their removal from the context of mourning. An atrocity occurred when the remains of a dead soldier were taken and kept by people unconnected to them by sentiment, strangers intending to expose and display the remains for malicious purposes.

Most people who encountered such abuses during the Civil War seem to have regarded them as disgusting affronts to decency and family feeling, redolent of 'savagery' or the 'dark ages'. However, these practices were in a number of respects quite novel, and among the most important influences that shaped them were developments taking place at the time, in North America and internationally, in science and medicine.

They need to be understood, first, against the background of the rapid growth of the medical profession in mid nineteenth-century North America. Ever since the earliest days of English colonization, the bodies of people executed for murder had sometimes been given to the surgeons for anatomizing, in accordance with English legal practice (Egerton 2003).

By the late eighteenth century, the supply of bodies of executed felons was unable to meet the growing demand and, in both Britain and North America, a thriving black market in cadavers had developed. In mid nineteenth-century North America, a cadaver sold to a medical school was worth the equivalent of a skilled worker's weekly wage (Sappol 2002: 320).

One consequence, as Sappol (2002) has shown, was that the treatment of the bodies of the dead became one of the fundamental ways in which class, social status and gender were expressed and negotiated in nineteenth-century North America (see also Nudelman 2004). At one end of the scale, the wealthy kept the bodies of their dead in family tombs built almost as securely as bank vaults, with heavy doors and locks. At the other, Blacks, Indians, immigrant groups such as the Irish, prostitutes, paupers and criminals were far less able to protect their dead, and were more often than the affluent the victims of grave robbery and dissection. They resorted to measures such as burying their dead under a layer of straw to deter digging, or posting armed guards in the cemetery for several nights after a funeral.

There seems to have been little notion, certainly among grave robbers and medical students, that the middle-class dead were entitled to more respect or better treatment than the poor. There were several notorious cases in which wealthy and powerful families fell victim to body-snatching (see, for instance, Sappol 2002: 316, 322). It was simply that middle-class families typically had the resources to protect their dead, and their social inferiors did not. The racial and class hierarchies of the time were expressed powerfully in the organization of the traffic of bodies and their use in the teaching of anatomy.

The honour of a family depended to a large extent, then, upon its capacity to protect the integrity of its dead and keep them from theft, sale and dissection. For a mid nineteenth-century North American man of respectable background, the dead of his family possessed a significance very similar to that of the women of his family. Their bodies were symbols of family honour, yet at the same time perceived as defenceless, needing vigilance and protection. An important measure of a man was his capacity to protect his womenfolk and his dead from being dishonoured by other men. Dead bodies in nineteenth-century North America were implicitly gendered as female, whether they were the bodies of men or of women, because the female body and the dead body were understood to share a passivity and vulnerability to dishonour and a need for protection by their kinsmen. Body-snatching for dissection, then, was understood as gendered violence, a kind of rape of the grave (Sappol 2002: 212–37).

The behaviour of those Civil War soldiers who sought to degrade their enemies by disinterring their corpses and taking their bones for souvenirs had parallels with the practice of body-snatching, especially as it served as a rite of passage for young men into the medical profession. Indeed, battlefields had sometimes been a source of cadavers for medical training in North America and this remained the case in the Civil War (Cox 2004: 163–98; Shultz 1992: 26, 29). The soldier seems to have borrowed from the medical student a notorious convention for violating the honour of other men and their kin, adapting a medical rite of passage and turning it into a military one. Hence also the tendency of soldiers to transform enemy remains into objects with feminine associations, trinkets for their sisters and mothers, as if asserting that the appropriate resting place for the remains of their defeated enemies was among women. Indeed, it would seem to follow from the symbolic gendering of the dead body as female that a soldier, in killing an enemy, thereby feminized him, transforming his active male body into a defenceless female one, and by feminizing him subordinated or demeaned him.

Crania and the Emergence of Racial Science

Although the foregoing may shed light on the trophy-taking that occurred in the Civil War, it does not explain why these practices seem to have been more prevalent among Confederate soldiers and their supporters than on the Union side. To try to answer this, we must turn to the early history of ethnology and racial science.

As we saw earlier, army personnel had been involved in collecting American Indian bones and skulls as medical and scientific specimens for almost forty years, before any took trophies in the battles of the Civil War.

The relevance of this to the Civil War is that at least some Confederate soldiers viewed white Southerners and white Northerners as two distinct racial stocks, separate branches of the white or Anglo-Saxon 'race', differing from each other in ancestry, physical appearance and inherent character. These views of the composition of the Union were commonplace at the time, both in Europe and North America (see, for instance, Douai 1864), but for Confederates they formed the basis of a claim to separate nationhood. Such soldiers spoke of themselves as fighting, not a civil war, but an invasion by a foreign people (Carmichael 1995: 3, 35; Fellman 1990: 14–16, 160; Frost 2005: 115; McPherson 1997: 151; Wyatt-Brown 2001: 180, 188). Clearly, they were not operating with twentieth- or twenty-first-century ideas of race, in which the fundamental marker of racial difference is skin colour. In mid nineteenth-century North America, colour was, very obviously, the most important signifier of racial difference. But it was not the only one: it was still possible then for different regional populations of whites to contrast themselves racially with each other.

When white Southerners did acknowledge common racial identity with white Northerners, they often represented them as race traitors; a common taunt by supporters of slavery against white abolitionists was that they were motivated by lust for black women (Grimsted 1998: 114). Confederate soldiers sometimes sought to degrade the dead bodies of white Union soldiers by burying them in what were called 'negro' cemeteries, or among the bodies of black Union soldiers (J.R. Neff 2005: 57, 62). These were acts which most white people on both sides of the war would have considered shameful and dishonouring. From the viewpoint of many Confederates, such white soldiers had chosen to side with another race against their own, and deserved to be treated accordingly.

In short, I suggest that the Confederate soldiers and their supporters who collected Northern skulls did so because their political interests were predicated on representing Southerners and Northerners as two different peoples. In exhuming and displaying the skulls and other bones of their enemies as material evidence of this difference, they drew upon the strongly race-oriented practices and concepts of contemporary natural science, enlisting its authority on behalf of their goals.

During the Civil War, the newly established Army Medical Museum collected several thousand specimens of 'morbid anatomy' from dead or injured soldiers. These included amputated limbs, and organs removed during autopsies, exemplifying battlefield injuries and diseases (Juzda 2009: 159, 163; Laderman 1996: 145–48; M.G. Simpson 2001: 175). However, the museum did not collect craniological specimens of the battlefield dead, as it did later with American Indians (Thomas 2000).[7] To have done so would certainly have risked offending public sensibilities. Removing skulls from graves for osteological study seemed legitimate to amateur and professional craniologists in Europe and North America, but much of the broader public, and particularly the religious, viewed it as sacrilegious violation of the peace of the dead (see, for example, Hagner 2003: 204).

Hence the congressional enquiry compared Confederate abuses of the dead to the 'cruelties' of 'savages'. However, I have suggested that these actions were, in part, local symptoms of deep shifts taking place after the Enlightenment in the ways in which human diversity was conceptualized. Such changes were felt and expressed in scientific or academic circles and, sometimes in unexpected forms, elsewhere in North American and European society - including, it appears, in the behaviour of soldiers on the battlefield (Harrison 2008a, 2010).

In this sense, Civil War soldiers who collected and displayed body parts did so for some of the same reasons that ethnologists had begun to collect, display and study such objects at the time (and would continue to do so into the twentieth century). They, too, assumed that the fundamental material evidence of human differences lay under the skin, in the bones and, above all, in the skull.

Notes

1. Zouave regiments wore uniforms based on those of French North African soldiers with a particular reputation at the time for fierceness.
2. A mudsill was a manual labourer.
3. Wilson's Creek, on 10 August 1861, was another early Confederate victory.
4. Most of the battles were fought in the South, and civilians from the nearby towns seem sometimes to have visited battle sites to collect souvenirs of the Union Army dead (Massey 1994: 259; J.R. Neff 2005: 43).
5. Some body parts were themselves valuable. In a letter to a local newspaper in 1865, the Union soldier William Landon describes removing gold teeth from a Confederate corpse (Landon 1939).
6. In addition, the collection and display of scalps and severed ears seems to have been common practices among the irregular forces fighting in the Kansas-Missouri Border War, a guerrilla conflict waged in parallel with the Civil War proper (Fellman 1990: 123, 135, 186–89).
7. This is in contrast to the situation in Europe some half a century earlier, where the University of Utrecht had collected a hundred skulls as phrenological specimens from the site of the Battle of Waterloo in 1815 (Luyendijk-Elshout 1997: 573).

Chapter 10

Museums and Lynchings: Bodies and the Exhibition of Order

Lynchings

During the Civil War, Confederate soldiers tended to show a particular animosity towards black Union soldiers (Urwin 2004; Wyatt-Brown 2001: 218), and there is evidence that some of them singled out the remains of black soldiers for degrading treatment. This seems to have happened with the Fifty-fifth Massachusetts, a so-called 'coloured' regiment, after a battle in North Carolina in 1864. When members of the regiment returned to the scene eight months later, they found that the Confederates had given the bodies of white Union troops decent burial, but the black soldiers had been left unburied and all their skulls were missing (J.R. Neff 2005: 64).

This behaviour seems not to have ended with the end of the war. After the collapse of the Confederacy in April 1865 a New York magazine sent a special correspondent to travel through the South and report on conditions there. In one of his reports, he described staying overnight in South Carolina with a planter, and noticing two human skulls in a corner of the man's courtyard. His host told him that he and his neighbours had some months earlier pursued a band of black troops, or their camp followers, who were roaming the countryside looting the property of local landowners. He had shot two of them, left their bodies to decay, and then returned a few months later to retrieve their skulls as trophies (Dennett 1986: 195–96, 357). The significance of this case is that it points to a continuity between trophy-taking during the Civil War and the practices of racist lynching which developed after the war in the southern states.

Before the Civil War, lynching was mostly a frontier practice, with the typical victim being a white man accused of murder or stealing livestock. These western frontier lynchings were usually summary hangings, with an emphasis on swift retribution, and little ceremony (J.W. Clarke 1998b: 271, 274; but cf. Pfeifer 2004: 47). In the southern states, the main public spectacles in which the white population demonstrated power over the bodies of blacks were floggings. The lynching of blacks was uncommon because slaves were valuable property. But after emancipation, lynching came to replace flogging as the central public demonstration of racial power by Southern whites (J.W. Clarke 1998a: 141, 143).

In certain respects, the behaviour of some Confederate troops after battles such as Bull Run can be seen, in hindsight, as post-mortem lynchings of a sort, or at least as having some of the same features as these public spectacles would later come to have – in particular, the taking and keeping of souvenir body parts and, sometimes, the sale of victims' bones or other remains as mementos. The forms of violence which came after the Civil War to be directed in the southern states primarily at black victims may, then, have had their first large-scale rehearsal in the Civil War, with their initial victims being, predominantly, Northern white soldiers. In some respects, lynchings drew on practices that emerged in the wartime military, as though prolonging these afterwards in denial that the war had ended. They also foreshadow the treatment of the remains of Japanese soldiers by some members of the Allied forces in the Pacific War, which I discuss later in this book (Harrison 2006).

Some of the lynchings of black victims carried out between the 1880s and 1930s were elaborately ritualized spectacles performed in front of large crowds. The usual pretext was an accusation of rape of a white female. In contrast to the frontier lynchings of whites, the racial spectacle lynching often featured prolonged public torture, mutilation and dismemberment, followed by the keeping or selling of body parts as souvenirs (J.W. Clarke 1998b: 281). The atmosphere could be festive and carnivalesque (Apel 2004; Markovitz 2004).

These events usually followed a pattern. First, a hunt took place for the accused person, followed by his identification by the white victim or victim's family. The time and place of the lynching were announced. The victim was killed, mutilated before and after death, and the remains finally put on display and photographed (Markowitz 2004: xxviii; McGovern 1982: 140).

The spectacle lynching arose in a cultural milieu in which hunting played a central role in local conceptions of masculinity and bonding between men (S.A. Marks 1991; N.W. Proctor 2002). In Jackson County, Florida, where Claude Neal was lynched in 1934, hunting expeditions into the woods for quail, deer and other game

> belonged exclusively to the men and the boys, who teamed with close friends in a kind of fraternal foray, the game being carried home and given to the women for dressing and cooking. The hunt, which was basic to the experience of rural males in Jackson County, contributed to the psychology of stalking prey and doing so in the company of trusted friends, vital conditioning for the preparation of lynch parties. (McGovern 1982: 28–29)

Essentially, a lynching here seems to have been a ritualized game hunt, with the victim cast in the role of a dangerous rogue animal. An Alabama newspaper implied as much when it warned the local black population: 'when the wolf comes and carries off our lambs we must hunt him with dog and gun and shoot him down in his tracks' (Watts 1992: 8). The hunt culminated in the public killing of the prey, the dismemberment of the victim and a celebratory distribution of body parts. Hunting imagery was often reflected in lynching photographs in which lynchers – sometimes in hunting costume – would pose with their victim's body as if it were a safari trophy (J. Allen et al. 2007: 171).

As H. Young (2005) points out, one feature of lynching that has received relatively little attention in the extensive literature on the subject is the dismemberment of the victim's body for souvenirs. The possession of such objects was a source of considerable pride.

To own [fingers and toes from Claude Neal's body] conferred genuine status. One store owner [interviewed in 1977] recalled the pride with which a man came into his store that morning and declared, 'See what I have here.' It was one of Neal's fingers. (McGovern 1982: 85)

An investigator sent to gather details of Neal's lynching shortly after it occurred reported:

Fingers and toes from Neal's body have been exhibited as souvenirs in [a local town] where one man offered to divide the finger which he had with a friend as a 'special favor'. Another man had 'one of the fingers preserved in alcohol'; photographs of Neal's body were difficult to get because 'those who had them would not part with them. I offered from 50c to $5.00 for one'. (McGovern 1982: 129)

In Linden, Virginia, in 1932, Shadrick Thompson, a black man accused of rape, was found hanged. The authorities gave his body over to the crowd, who burnt and dismembered it. They distributed his teeth as souvenirs and put the burnt skull on display in a nearby town (Edsforth 2000: 113). After some lynchings, parts of the victim's body were auctioned (H. Young 2005: 640). After the burning of Sam Hose in 1899, in Georgia, fragments of bone and slices of his heart and liver were sold as souvenirs (J.W. Clarke 1998a: 140). His knuckles were put on display in the window of a local grocery store. Pieces of his body were still circulating in the locality more than seventy years later (Arnold 2009: 2, 171–72).

Sometimes, lynchers attached notices to the body requesting souvenir-hunters to let it hang undisturbed for as long as possible, so that it could serve as a warning. Although the most highly prized souvenirs were the victim's body parts, it was common for the entire lynching site to be stripped bare by souvenir-seekers. Pieces would be chopped off the hanging tree, and the ground could be stripped of grass (H. Young 2005: 646; cf. Pfeifer 2004: 194). Photographs and postcards were another important form in which lynchings were commemorated (J. Allen et al. 2007; Rushdy 2000; M. Simpson 2004). With the invention of the phonograph, visitors at county fairs in the late nineteenth century could pay to hear sound recordings of lynchings (J.W. Clarke 1998a: 154–55).

As we saw with the royal executions of Charles I and Louis XIV, it was not only the body parts of the victim that were sought as execution souvenirs but anything with which the body had come into contact. In other words, we need to understand all the keepsakes of such a killing as parts of what one might call the extended or inclusive body of the victim. In violent death, such as death by burning or beheading, the boundaries of the body do, of course, very graphically and obviously break down. Hence the fallacy of S. Stewart's (1993: 140) assertion that human body parts taken as trophies, unlike other sorts of objects, cannot function as normal souvenirs because they are appropriated and kept in order to obliterate the identity of the victim, and are therefore anti-souvenirs. Her claim rests on the unwarranted assumption that the body is a discrete entity separable from its accoutrements and from the environment of its death (see Hallam and Hockey 2001; Hallam, Hockey and Howarth 1999). In a lynching, not only was the victim's body dismembered but the entire site of the lynching was taken to pieces, and all these precious fragments dispersed. It was as if the victim's body, in being dismembered and distributed, grew to encompass everything it had touched. It thereafter pervaded everything connected with the lynching and everything capable of memorializing it, including photographs and sound recordings of the event. All these were valued as mementos because they were understood as extensions, ultimately, of the victim's body.

Body-snatching and Dissection

Some of the elements from which the spectacle lynching developed had existed in Southern society before the Civil War. For example, slave owners consciously adopted medieval English punishments for rebellion, such as quartering, burning at the stake, and the public display of decapitated heads (Banner 2002: 71–75, 137; Egerton 2003; M.M. Smith 2005; Wyatt-Brown 2001: 52, 284). Hunts for runaway slaves, using specially trained dogs, sometimes had a sporting, recreational quality which seems to have been patterned after the English upper-class pastime of hunting with hounds (Franklin and Schweninger 1999: 160-61). And, of course, the sale or auction of lynching victims' body parts echoed the way living bodies had been commodities during the era of slavery.

Body-snatching and dissection for medical training were also part of the repertoire of practices through which Southern whites sought to control blacks, both before and after the abolition of slavery. In the folklore of urban and rural Southern blacks in the nineteenth and early twentieth centuries, a much feared figure was the 'night doctor', who was said to be a white medical student, or a man employed by these students to abduct black people and take them to hospitals, where they were used in medical experiments and then killed. 'Fear of the night doctor was so pervasive in black communities in the South that throughout much of the nineteenth and early twentieth centuries people would avoid being out at night alone in the vicinity of a hospital' (Jackson 1997: 194). According to Fry (1975), threats of hospitalization were a common way of intimidating blacks. Before the Civil War, dead slaves had also been used as an alternative to body-snatching as a source of cadavers.

> Medical school personnel often asked slave owners to donate the bodies of dead slaves to practice autopsy and dissection. Because slaves were the property of the slave owner, it was within the owner's power to grant or deny the request without seeking permission of the family of the deceased slave. The request was usually, but not always, honored .... [T]he threat of dissection was another weapon in the arsenal of the slaveholder that helped him maintain psychological control over his chattel. (Jackson 1997: 196; see also Savitt 1982)

In the United States, dissections of executed criminals continued until the end of the nineteenth century, and were reported in graphic detail in the press (Banner 2002: 234; Sappol 2002: 91). United States courts seem to have had more discretion in imposing this penalty than those in Britain, and do not seem to have applied it as often as British courts. But one effect of this greater discretion seems to have been that blacks were more likely to be anatomized than whites who had been executed for the same crimes. After the abolitionist John Brown and his companions were hanged in 1859 following their failed raid on the armoury at Harpers Ferry, Brown's body was returned to his family, while the bodies of his black co-conspirators were claimed by a medical college and anatomized (Nudelman 2004: 7).

After the dissection of particularly notorious felons, their skeletons and other body parts were often kept in the anatomical museums attached to universities and medical schools (Sappol 2002: 91). These museums laid particular emphasis on collecting and exhibiting examples of abnormality and pathology, both moral and medical. Throughout much of the nineteenth century and the early twentieth, criminality was widely understood in the United States as a disease, an hereditary one or environmentally caused (Banner 2002: 103–104, 118–121). Phrenology, of course, attached a particular importance to the skulls of criminals, and the authorities sometimes gave the heads of executed criminals to phrenologists to exhibit and study (Banner 2002: 120). This happened, for instance, with Nat Turner, a slave executed and anatomized for leading a revolt in 1831 (Egerton 2003: 160; French 2004; Greenberg 2003). The medical museum was just as fitting a repository for the skull of an infanticide or a rebel slave as it was for a sample of diseased tissue, or a malformed foetus: all were aberrations of nature, specimens of biomedical abnormality.

As we have seen, such practices were by no means restricted to the United States, but part of a transnational scientific and criminological culture common to North America, European nations and their colonies. In this culture, the museum was understood to play an important role in public morality and law enforcement. The heads, skulls and other remains of infamous malefactors, placed on public display there, were didactic illustrations of human evil and its consequences. In other words, from a certain perspective museums were ancillaries to the penal system. They certainly seem often to have been viewed in this light by condemned persons. When John Ten Eyck of Pittsfield, Massachusetts, was condemned to death in 1878, he expressed great concern 'lest his body should be dissected and his skeleton grace some museum' (Banner 2002: 80). His fears were allayed by his father-in-law, who assured him he would take proper care of his corpse.

> The father-in-law did carefully remove Ten Eyck after the execution to another part of Pittsfield, where he began charging admission to see him. When the town government shut down the show, the father-in-law moved to a nearby town and netted fifteen dollars at ten cents a head. (Ibid.)

Ten Eyck did escape the anatomical museum, then, only to become an exhibit in an impromptu museum curated by his own father-in-law.

Judicial Museology

Lynchers seem often to have been concerned to give their actions an appearance of legitimacy, and consciously imitated certain aspects of legal executions – by using the method of hanging, for instance, or by allowing the condemned person an opportunity to repent, confess or pray before they were killed (McGovern 1982: 76; Pfeifer 2004: 45).

The dismemberment of the victim and the keeping of body parts as souvenirs can also be understood in this light. By the early twentieth century, middle-class opinion had come to regard lynchings as reversions to the 'barbarism of the dark ages' (Pfeifer 2004: 146), a 'cruelty which might well shock the sensibilities of the most benighted savages' (Simpson 2004: 17). But dismembering the victim for souvenirs may actually have appeared, to the perpetrators themselves, to model the practices of their own legal system and give legitimacy to their actions.

For instance, local physicians were part of the social elite of rural communities and small towns and, as important intermediaries between the worlds of formal and informal justice, they sometimes played a significant role in lynchings both in the southern states and elsewhere. In 1908, a white man called Joe Simpson was lynched for murder in the isolated Californian mining town of Skidoo, by being hanged from a telegraph pole. Afterwards, the town doctor retrieved Simpson's body, removed the head, and apparently gave it some sort of medical examination. Later, he set it on an anthill to remove the flesh, boiled it until it was clean, and then kept it in his office as a memento until he and the other residents abandoned the town some years later (Lingenfelter 1986: 298–99; Pfeifer 2004: 54).

Although Simpson was lynched by a mob and afterwards dismembered, the dismemberment was carried out not by the mob (presumably because his killing had no racial dimension) but by a local doctor. At one level, the doctor's actions could have been construed as an autopsy. But they could also have been understood as part of the lynching, an informal, extralegal anatomization as used in the formal legal system as an enhancement of the death penalty. It was not uncommon at the time for a doctor to display in his surgery, as an icon of his professional status, a skull or skeleton derived from some autopsy he had carried out (Sappol 2002: 94). But when the skull was that of a lynching victim, the professional medical specimen and the personal lynching souvenir could merge inextricably together.

A similar case of informal anatomization occurred in Rawlings, Wyoming, in 1881, when the outlaw George Parrott was lynched and the local physician, Dr Osborne, removed his brain in order to examine it for signs of abnormality. The top of the skull was kept by Osborne's assistant as a souvenir, and used as an ashtray. Osborne also partially skinned Parrott's body, and had the skin tanned and made into a pair of men's shoes. At the time of the lynching, Osborne was an aspiring politician. He became Governor of Wyoming a few years later, and congressman for that state, and sometimes wore these shoes to official functions (Carbon County Museum 2009; Pfeifer 2004: 47).

Keeping victims' body parts as souvenirs could therefore appear to be not some ghoulish aberration but a respectable practice modelled upon the normal procedures of what might be called judicial or forensic museology. There were cases in which these procedures were combined with features of a lynching in ways that made them difficult to separate. The U.S. social scientist John Dollard describes the killing of a black man in a gunfight with police during his research in 'Southerntown' in the 1930s. The man had shot at a police officer, and was then pursued through the woods and swamps by police and a posse or mob of some three hundred local men with bloodhounds, and killed in a gun fight when they caught up with him.

> There was one detail about this case quite horrifying to the Negroes. The cadaver of the slain Negro was given to a near-by college, the flesh was stripped from the bones, and the skeleton arranged and used as an anatomical exhibit. Apparently skeletons should be

nameless; at least the Negroes felt it was insulting and degrading to their group to have a Negro so used. (1937: 329)

Popular Museums

Besides the professional anatomical museums belonging to medical schools and the private collections of individual physicians, there were commercial businesses which Sappol (2004) calls popular anatomical museums in many U.S. cities between the 1840s and the 1930s. These catered to the tastes primarily of young, working-class men and exhibited a motley assortment of anatomical specimens, some real and some modelled in wax, wood or papier maché, concerned principally with sex, disease and murder. Middle-class opinion tended to regard these establishments as a threat to public morals, and the authorities often sought to close them down on grounds of indecency. Nevertheless, as was evident in their overriding preoccupation with oddity and the abnormal and grotesque, they were direct cultural descendants of 'cabinets of curiosities', the early private museums that had been fashionable among Renaissance aristocrats (Sappol 2002: 275–76; 2004). There seems to have been some traffic in specimens between the high-culture museums and their low-brow counterparts. In 1867, one such enterprise, the New York Museum of Anatomy, exhibited the preserved head of an executed murderer, together with his right arm, the limb with which he had committed his crime, both specimens having been purchased from the Philadelphia College of Surgeons, which had carried out the dissection (Sappol 2002: 290; 2004).

Again, there were cultural middlemen who brought these practices, or versions of them, to the rural and small-town hinterlands: professional entertainers who peddled yet lower-culture refractions of metropolitan low culture to country folk. Such were the entrepreneurs who exhibited the head of John A. Murrell, a Tennessean bandit imprisoned for trying to incite a slave revolt in 1835, and who died soon after his release in 1844. After his death, grave robbers dug up his body, severed the head from the corpse, leaving the rest of the body to be eaten by hogs, preserved the head in some way, and 'displayed their prize at Southern county fairs for ten cents a look' (Wyatt-Brown 1986: 34; see also Pennick 1981: 31).

A similar fate befell Elmer McCurdy, an outlaw whose mummified body was discovered by chance in 1976 during the making of a film in an amusement park in California, where it was being used as a funhouse mannequin, apparently without the operators realizing that it was a preserved human cadaver. A film technician, moving what he thought was a dummy, accidentally broke off one of the arms and discovered a bone protruding from it. The forensic anthropologists who examined the body found in its mouth a 1926 coin together with a ticket to the Museum of Crime in Los Angeles. These and other clues enabled the authorities to identify the body of that of McCurdy, who had been killed in a gunfight after robbing a train in Oklahoma in 1911. A local undertaker had embalmed his body and, according to some sources, then put it on display for $1 per view. Later, the operator of a travelling carnival tricked the undertaker into giving it up, on the pretence of being the outlaw's long lost brother. Over the years, the body was exhibited around the country for money, and sold to a succession of wax museums, carnival freak shows and amusement parks (Svenvold 2003).[1]

Like saints' relics in the Middle Ages, such objects were potentially lucrative assets because there was a large public eager to visit and view them. And, as with medieval saints, the body parts of deceased celebrities often multiplied. So it was with the actor John Wilkes Booth, the assassin of President Lincoln, five of whose skulls were being exhibited simultaneously in 1936, all of them accompanied by affidavits attesting to their genuineness. For many years, an object purported to be Booth's mummified body 'was an attraction at county fairs across the country, along with fat ladies and two-headed chickens' (Hanchett 1983: 241; see also C.W. Evans 2004).

Such, then, were the miniature, and largely rural, touring versions of the urban anatomical museum. Some visitors may have viewed Booth as a hero, not a villain, and perhaps paid to see his embalmed corpse, or his various purported skulls, to offer their respects (cf. Verdery 1999). But, to others who paid to view such curiosities, they must surely have meant something very similar to the display of a lynching victim's body parts. These audiences were paying to receive assurances that crime always met with punishment. The shows offered, in return, incontrovertible bodily evidence that the world was just.

Conclusion

The era of the racial spectacle lynching has often been viewed as a tragic aberration in the history of poor and backward regions of the South. My argument is that it needs to be understood as part of a much broader continuum of practices relating to crime and its punishment in the nineteenth and early twentieth centuries, practices which were largely metropolitan in origin, even cosmopolitan. These included procedures of criminal law, forms of public entertainment, and medical and scientific research practice. What all of these had as their central unifying theme was the collection, preservation and exhibition of the body parts of criminals - for the punishment and deterrence of crime; for scientific study; and for popular entertainment.

To the male population of small town and rural communities, these must have seemed to resonate powerfully with one particularly important aspect of their own lives: the stalking and killing of game animals, and the victorious display of their remains. To many of these men, hunting was more than simply a pastime. It must have seemed an allegory of the fight of good against evil, and of order against disorder. For all these practices appeared to share a common moral purpose, and to speak a single narrative of consummated justice: first, the hunt for the perpetrator – usually male – of a shocking crime; then his capture, death and dismemberment; and, finally, the commemoration of his life and well deserved death through the retention and display of parts of his body.

Evidence of these links between lynching and the medical museology of crime is that both came to an end as significant social phenomena at the same time. The popular anatomical museums disappeared in the 1930s (Sappol 2004). By the middle of the same decade, lynching had become repellent to the vast majority of U.S. public opinion, and was in rapid decline (McGovern 1982: 140).

The dismemberment of the victim, and the keeping of body parts, usually viewed as among the most backward and regressive aspects of lynching, may actually have been understood by the perpetrators themselves in quite the opposite light: as giving their actions an aura of propriety, even legal formality. In certain respects the racial spectacle lynching developed its particular forms and rituals as an attempt by the largely rural and working-class supporters of what Pfeifer (2004) calls 'rough justice' to imitate or appropriate what probably seemed to them elements of modernity, in an attempt to give legitimacy to their informal, home-grown methods of social control.

Lynching was at the bottom of a pyramid at the top of which stood law, medicine and science. These epitomes of modernity had their joint material embodiment in the museum, an institution whose fundamental role was to amass and display evidence of human mastery of nature. Lower down, somewhere around the middle of the pyramid, were the salacious museums of crime and bodily pathology that purveyed what would now probably be described as edutainment to urban working men. Still further below these in respectability were the itinerant carnival and sideshow exhibits that brought to rural folk views of the bodily remains of famous bandits and public enemies, along with shows of midgets, sword swallowers and South Sea cannibals.

These, then, were the sorts of practices which lynchers drew upon and moulded to serve their own local understandings of justice and racial order. At the very bottom of the pyramid were practices such as the display of the knuckles of a lynching victim in a small-town shop window. But these descended from the Renaissance cabinet of curiosities no less than did the rest of the pyramid, up to the most respected metropolitan museum. Each of them was, in its own way, an assertion of order and control in a world perceived as unruly and threatening.

Note

1. In another well known case in mid nineteenth-century California, the head of the Mexican outlaw Joaquin Murieta was preserved in a jar of alcohol, taken on tour and exhibited for $1 a view (Thornton 2003).

Chapter 11

Savages on the Frontiers of Europe

Native Auxiliaries

One of the forms which metaphors of hunting can assume in the context of war is the projection of hunting behaviour onto the enemy, casting one's own side in the role of quarry. These tropes appear in the complaints made by the German government during the First World War, concerning the use of 'coloured troops' (*farbiger Truppen*) in the French and British armies. These men, so the German authorities alleged, were not soldiers but more like predatory animals hunting German soldiers as their prey. In July 1915, the German Foreign Office issued the French and British governments with a memorandum protesting against their use of these African and Asian 'savages' against Germany in the European theatre of war.

> In the present war England and France have not relied solely upon the strength of their own people, but are employing large numbers of colored troops from Africa and Asia in the European arena of war against Germany's popular army. Gurkhas, Sikhs and Panthans, Sepoys, Turcos, Goums, Moroccans, and Senegalese fill the English and French lines from the North Sea to the Swiss frontier. These peoples, who grew up in countries where war is still conducted in its most savage forms, have brought to Europe the customs of their countries; and under the eyes of the highest commanders of England and France they have committed atrocities which set at defiance not only the recognized usages of warfare, but of all civilization and humanity ....
>
> [I]t is evident that the colored Allies employed by England and France upon the European arena of war have the barbarous practice of carrying with them as war-trophies the severed heads and fingers of German soldiers, and wearing as ornaments about their necks ears which they have cut off .... On the battlefields they creep up stealthily and treacherously upon the German wounded, gouge their eyes out, mutilate their faces with knives, and cut their throats. Indian troops commit these atrocities with a sharp dagger which is fastened in the sheath of their side-arms. Turcos, even when wounded themselves, creep around on the battlefield and like wild beasts murder the defenceless wounded ....
>
> It is incomprehensible that commanders of French troops, who are aware of this savagery and cruelty of the colored Senegalese, should allow German wounded prisoners to be escorted by these people and in this way give the Senegalese an opportunity to

murder German soldiers .... But every civilized man must feel the deepest indignation that the French military authorities have not scrupled to set these savages to guard innocent women who had the misfortune to be staying in France at the outbreak of the war, and so expose them to their animal passions ....

The laws of nations do not, indeed, expressly prohibit the employment of colored tribes in wars between civilized nations. The presupposition for such employment, however, is that the colored troops thus employed in war, be kept under a discipline which excludes the possibility of the violation of the customs of warfare among civilized peoples ....

Just as Lord Chatham once protested in the English House of Lords, during the American War of Independence ..., and Prince Bismarck in the Franco-Prussian war of 1870–71 ..., against the employment, contrary to International Law, of uncivilized peoples in wars against white troops, so the German Government sees itself compelled in the present war to enter a most solemn protest against England and France bringing into the field against Germany troops whose savagery and cruelty are a disgrace to the methods of warfare of the twentieth century. The Government bases its protest upon the spirit of the international agreements of the past few decades, which expressly make it a duty of civilized peoples 'to lessen the inherent evils of warfare,' and 'to serve the interests of humanity and the ever-progressing demands of civilization'.

In the interests of humanity and civilization therefore the German Government demands most emphatically that colored troops be no longer used upon the European arena of war. (Stowell and Munro 1916: 187–89)

An appendix to the memorandum contained supporting evidence in the form of photographs of disfigured bodies, testimonies of German witnesses, and extracts from letters and diaries found on French and Belgian soldiers.

In 1917 the German sociologist Max Weber criticized the British and French in similar terms, for having let loose 'a refuse of African and Asiatic savages' on the German people (Lawler 1992: 96). These 'savages' were imagined as eager to mutilate and dismember civilized soldiers and collect their body parts, though the reality in colonial frontier warfare was, as we have seen, often quite the reverse.

Colonial powers such as Britain and France incorporated colonized peoples into their armies in special auxiliary units of their own. They recruited these colonial troops from what the British called martial races and the French called *races guerrières*: ethnic groups to whom soldiering was believed to come naturally, and for whom fighting was in the blood (Killingray and Omissi 1999; Scheck 2006: 89; Street 2004). These men were often credited with inherent qualities of bravery, endurance, loyalty, tenacity or stealth beyond those of the average European soldier.

The Gurkhas in the British Army are a well known example (Caplan 1995; T. Gould 1999). Another are the Goumiers, Moroccan irregular soldiers who fought in the French army in the two world wars (Bimberg 1999). The Gurkhas and Goumiers both carry, or carried, large curved knives which they used in close combat, and these fearsome-looking weapons became a focus of much military folklore among European troops. It was said, for instance, that a Gurkha cannot draw his knife without shedding blood, and may have to cut himself with it before putting it back in its sheath. Goumiers in the Second World War promulgated the same self-exoticizing folklore about their relationship to their knives (Craft 1994: 63). Both groups had a reputation, which their European officers seem at times to have fostered, for grisly habits such as collecting their enemies' ears. The Gurkhas seem to have kept this reputation until at least the late twentieth century. Argentinian soldiers who fought them in the Falklands War of 1982 portrayed them as crazed, half-animal and half-human (T. Gould 1999: 370–71).

The use of these colonial auxiliaries developed in the context of colonial warfare, and their only legitimate use was there, typically fighting other tribal peoples like themselves on the margins of empire. Their role, in other words, was to help to guard the colonial frontiers, and they were not to be used against Europeans. The practices of trophy-taking with which they came to be associated were conceptualized as a phenomenon not simply of savagery, but specifically of the boundaries of civilization, and of conflicts in which 'our' domesticated savages were set against hostile and untamed ones.

To the nineteenth-century European, the boundaries of Europe represented the frontier between civilization and barbarism, and trophy-taking was a key racial or ethnic marker of the non-European. In the Balkans, the most vulnerable and contentious of Europe's border regions, headhunting between Christian communities in Montenegro and their ethnically Turkish neighbours had continued well into the nineteenth century. If for some reason the fighters could not take the whole head, they brought back the nose, sometimes with the upper lip and moustache attached (Boehm 1984: 80). The behaviour seems to have been the same on both sides. But European observers tended to valorize it in two quite different ways, depending on which of the two sides they were considering. Turks who took the heads of Christian Montenegrins were seen as Asiatic barbarians driven by bloodlust, like their cultural cousins the Huns and Mongols. But when Christians took Turkish heads, they were portrayed as the last surviving remnants of a simpler and more virile age in Europe's history. They were Homeric warrior figures with whom civilized Europeans could identify, almost nostalgically, as living images of their distant forefathers. The anomaly, as it seemed at the time, of modern Christian Europeans, albeit peripheral ones, apparently practising headhunting was resolved by relocating them imaginatively in the past, turning their geographical remoteness into an historical one. The peoples of the edges of Europe, so it was implied, embodied the temporal boundary between the modern and pre-modern stages of European society's development (Jezernik 2001).

The savage warrior, then, could be represented positively as well as negatively, as heroic, noble and virtuous, endowed with an admirably fierce fighting spirit, rather than as merely ignoble and vicious. Gurkhas, Goumiers and other similar colonial troops represented, like the Montenegrin Christians, the positive aspect of the savage warrior. Of course, this admiration was contingent on their fierce instincts being harnessed in the service of civilization, by being directed outward against other peoples similar to themselves, and never turned against Europeans. To protect the boundaries of civilization from the predatory savages beyond, one needed guards who were at least as ferocious as the savages themselves, and just as free of civilized inhibitions.

France and Germany at War

Germany had only a short-lived colonial empire, which it lost at the end of the First World War, and it did not establish significant colonial auxiliaries in its own army.

France, on the other hand, had a long history of using colonial troops both in its overseas conflicts and in Europe, though its use of these troops in Europe turned out to be a double-edged sword. During the Franco-Prussian War of 1870–71, according to one nineteenth-century historian,

> [t]he soldiers of both nations learned to respect each other's valour in these first combats of the war; but the Germans complained greatly of the ferocious and savage conduct of the Turcos in the French army. These men are native Algerians, and have the vices as well as the virtues of the desert. According to the testimony of their enemies, they are in the habit of maltreating the wounded, even lopping off their hands and ears as trophies .... There is but too much reason to fear that in many ways the French army has been injured by the importation of these barbarians, who, though courageous, are ignorant of the principles of scientific warfare, as they are indifferent to the restrictions of humanity and civilisation. (Ollier 1894: 56)

Throughout the nineteenth century, it seems to have been taken for granted in Europe and North America that the employment of what were called savage or barbarous races in wars between 'civilized' peoples was a violation of the laws and customs of war. Shortly after the end of the First World War, a U.S. jurist who reviewed the legal aspects of the conflict drew the following conclusions on this point.

> Prohibition of the employment of savage troops who do not respect the laws of humanity or the rules of civilized warfare or whose excesses cannot be restrained by their commanders has so long been a recognized rule of civilized warfare that it has never been deemed necessary to affirm it in express terms in the international conventions respecting the conduct of war .... [P]ublicists and statesmen of all countries have condemned the use of troops of an inferior civilization, whose savage instincts and manner of life make it improbable they will observe the rules of civilized warfare. (Garner 1920: 294)

Garner pointed in support to the 1914 edition of the *British Manual of Military Law*:

> Troops formed of coloured individuals belonging to the savage tribes and barbarous races should not be employed in a war between civilized States. The enrolling, however, of individuals belonging to civilized coloured races and the employment of whole regiments of disciplined coloured soldiers (e.g. troops of the Indian army, the African troops of the French army, and the negro regiments of the United States army) is not forbidden. (Quoted in Garner 1920: 296)

The *United States Rules of Land Warfare* (1914) employs very similar wording. The consensus, then, was that 'coloured people' were not prohibited in principle from serving in wars between civilized nations, so long as they had been civilized or could be kept under firm control by their officers. The risk of illegality was posed only by the 'uncivilized' races, whose 'instincts', 'excesses' and 'animal passions' were unlikely to be curbed even by strict discipline. However, military law did not fully specify which 'coloured races' were sufficiently civilized or tractable to participate in civilized warfare, and which were not. In addition, the use of savage or barbarian people was prohibited only in wars between civilized states, leaving open the possible legitimacy of using them in wars against other uncivilized peoples.

Colonial troops therefore often had an ambiguous and precarious legal status, inhabiting a sort of conceptual boundary region between civilization and savagery, and embodying some of the qualities of both. They could be represented equally as legitimate or illegitimate combatants, soldiers or savages, war heroes or war criminals, depending on one's perspective.

One such group – French West African soldiers – seem to have caused a considerable stir when they arrived in France at the start of the First World War. Crowds turned out to greet these exotic visitors in their strange uniforms, and encouraged them to cut the heads off the Germans (Scheck 2006: 93). African soldiers were widely believed to mutilate the dead and wounded, and French officers seem to have tried to play on German fears of them and promote an image of them as ferocious savages. An English war correspondent who travelled in France during the war recounted some of the rumours that circulated, even among the Allies, concerning the habits of Senegalese soldiers.

> There were two grim yarns told of the Senegalese black soldiers – most ferocious fighters as is well known. It had been noticed how jealously one of the men guarded his haversack, as though he had something of great value he was treasuring up. One day it was discovered that this consisted of a parcel containing twenty-three human ears, in various stages of decomposition. They were all from the left or 'heart side', which it appeared gave them more value, as it indicated that he had captured them from the enemy, and he explained he was going to take them home as 'souvenirs', to make a necklace with.
>
> The other story was still more gruesome, as in this instance it was actually a German's head that the black warrior was carrying in a cloth attached to his belt, and which he likewise proposed to take back with him as a 'war-trophy'. (Price 1919: 57–58)

A U.S. serviceman recalls a British officer telling him very similar stories of the Gurkhas. The officer claimed that while had been recuperating in hospital from a wound, a Gurkha in the next bed had been found by the medical staff to be wearing around his waist a wire with twenty-two ears strung on it (Libby 2000: 183).

What is particularly interesting is that almost identical stories circulated on both sides of the war. One of the witnesses whose testimony was cited by the German memorandum claimed to have seen a north African soldier exhibiting twenty-one ears, which he intended to take home as trophies, taken from German soldiers whom he had shot. Another testified to discovering a German soldier's head in the pocket of a captured Turco (Garner 1920: 293). The German writer Richard Grasshoff (1915), in a work of pro-German propaganda, claimed he had seen one Turco with twenty-three ears, and another exhibiting a severed head. Many of these stories are so similar, even in small details such as the precise numbers of ears the soldiers were supposed to have collected (always, it seems, twenty-one, twenty-two or twenty-three), as to suggest that we are dealing here with folklore, shared by European soldiers on both sides of the war, and transposable onto the soldiers of almost any non-European origin.

But the two opposing sides promoted and used the stories for quite different purposes. While the British and French meant to terrorize the German army, the Germans, as we have seen, invoked these stereotypes to attack the morality and legitimacy of the British and French war effort. But what neither side doubted was that it was in the nature of African troops to commit atrocities.

French army reports during the war suggest that some colonial troops may indeed have collected and displayed ears and heads of enemy soldiers, just as they had been encouraged to do by the Parisian crowds that welcomed them (Scheck 2006: 95). A London war correspondent in Paris in the first year of the war describes an Algerian soldier displaying a German helmet to a crowd of admiring Parisians, and demonstrating how he had beheaded the soldier who wore it.

> 'Coupe gorge, comme ça. Sale boche, mort. Sa tête, voyez. Tombé à terre. Sang! Mains, en bain de sang. Comme ça!'
> So the Turco spoke under the statue of Aphrodite in the gardens of the Tuileries to a crowd of smiling men and girls. He had a German officer's helmet. He described with vivid and disgusting gestures how he had cut off the man's head – he clicked his tongue to give the sound of it – and how he had bathed his hands in the blood of his enemy, before carrying this trophy to his trench. He held out his hands, staring at them, laughing at them as though they were still crimson with German blood.... A Frenchwoman shivered a little and turned pale. But another woman laughed – an old creature with toothless gums – with a shrill, harsh note.
> 'Sale race!' she said; 'a dirty race! I should be glad to cut a German throat!'. (P. Gibbs 1915: 257)

The curious detail mentioned earlier, concerning the Senegalese soldier who took only his enemies' left ears, suggests the possibility that officers may have been offering the African troops rewards for proof of each enemy they killed.[1]

In a sense, it is irrelevant whether colonial troops did or did not collect enemy ears and heads. What is important is that most European troops, of both sides, were convinced that they did and, indeed, seem to have taken it for granted that they would do so. At the same time, comparable behaviour among their own white allies and compatriots seems to have been underreported. Higonnet has described the endemic and almost frenetic nature of souvenir-hunting and pilfering among Allied military personnel. They collected enemy helmets, weapons, cigarette cases, watches, leather boots and other items of clothing, and sometimes body parts or personal items difficult to separate from body parts. For example, a U.S. canteen worker who served for a year in France from 1918 to 1919, recorded in her diary:

> two women of the canteen are taking home skulls as 'souvenirs', and some of the nurses pull belts and boots off of dead Germans. Sometimes the feet come off in the boots, but that seems to be no objection! Talk about the Germans becoming a degenerate nation because of lack of food, what have we become through our passion for 'souvenirs'. (Quoted in Higonnet 2007: 72)

Such acts tended to be viewed as distasteful, but only temporary, wartime aberrations. In contrast to the sorts of trophy-hunting attributed to the 'coloured' troops, the unsavoury collecting practices of some of the white military personnel were not understood as typical or expected of them, or in their nature. One must conclude that accounts of such behaviour, though sometimes recorded in private observations such as the one above, did not circulate widely or become part of public wartime culture. If the German authorities had learned of such incidents, they would doubtless have made use of them for propaganda purposes.[2]

Internalizing Savagery

In practice, then, European colonial powers in the early twentieth century organized themselves to fight two types of conflict – warfare proper, and a residual category of armed conflicts much less constrained by law and morality – while at the same time associating themselves exclusively with the first in the public mind. Their response was to internalize this distinction in the structure of their armies. They established ethnic divisions of labour between European soldiers, understood to fight in accordance with civilized norms, and troops drawn from non-European 'warrior races' who were expected to follow tribal customs of their own. The two types of soldier were ranked, with the auxiliaries typically under the command of European officers rather than officers of their own background.

Savagery, or a reputation for it, was thereby contracted out to special, ethnically distinct units perceived to enjoy certain exemptions from the laws and customs of war, permitting them to carry out acts which the civilized, European soldier would be unwilling or forbidden to engage in (see, for example, D. Anderson 2006). The colonial power could thus wage, or threaten to wage, primitive war by proxy, while disclaiming responsibility for it. Or, to put it differently, it could preserve a distinction between civilization and savagery, while at the same time violating it.

Having special units with a reputation for savagery seems to have been recognized as so useful that some European powers created in their armed forces military units which were modelled on colonial auxiliaries, and played a similar role, but were recruited from their own nationals. An example is the Spanish foreign legion, when it was formed in 1920 to suppress a Berber insurrection in the Rif region of Morocco. This was a military force specialized for fighting tribal enemies by their own rules, or what were imagined to be their rules. Despite its name, most of the legion's members were Spanish citizens, or came from Spanish-speaking countries. Many were veterans of the First World War who had been unable to adjust to civilian life (Balfour 2002: 211–12; Preston 1994: 27). On joining the legion they underwent a dramatic 'betrothal to death' in which they symbolically renounced their earlier lives and ritually dissociated themselves from conventional society.

> [R]itual was an important part of the Legionnaire's life on the battlefield and in the camp or garrison. The ceremony of the Legionnaire Saturday or Sábado Legionario, in which the effigy of 'Christ of the Good Death' (el Cristo de la Buena Muerte) was placed between the flags of Spain and the Legion, promoted the idea that the violence practised by the Legion was part of a sacred liturgy. Their goose-stepping and arm-swinging march (so different from the rather untidy drill of the Spanish recruit on military service), the strange uniform with its beret capped by dangling tassel, the barked orders, the chants and hymns were complemented by a fetishization of the bodily parts of killed enemies. Severed ears and noses were worn on the body hung from string, and decapitated heads were carried on the end of bayonets, all of them trophies of war characteristic of more ritualized pre-modern societies, including, and indeed influenced by, those of northern Morocco. The practice of cutting off parts of the enemy's body and wearing them or collecting them as mementos also strengthened the Legionnaires' warrior macho identity and helped to sanction the violence meted out against a diminished and objectified enemy. (Balfour 2002: 212–13)

When they were visited in 1922 by the Duquesa de la Victoria, a philanthropist who had organized a team of Red Cross nurses, the legion presented her with a basket of roses in the centre of which were the severed heads of two Moroccans (Balfour 2002: 87; Preston 1994: 29). The Spanish dictator Miguel Primo de Rivera, visiting Morocco in 1925, reprimanded the legion's members when they paraded before him with severed heads, arms and ears impaled on their bayonets (Alvarez 2001: 174, 187; Balfour 2002: 213; Woolman 1968: 201). Such acts were part of an ongoing reciprocity of terrorism with the Rifians, with similar atrocities taking place on both sides (Alvarez 2001: 174; Balfour 2002: 87).

Franco spent many years in Morocco as an officer in the foreign legion. He had helped to found the legion and eventually became its commander. Later, during the Spanish Civil War, he used both Moroccan colonial troops and the legion itself in the fighting in Spain, because he could not trust Spanish regular soldiers to fire on civilians. In other words, he brought some of the features of colonial frontier warfare into the conflict in Spain itself, and did so quite consciously, arguing that the war against communism in Spain was a frontier war – between civilization and barbarism – and needed to be fought by the same brutal methods that he had helped to develop in Morocco (Preston 1994: 104–105).

Dichotomies between civilized and savage warfare have been reflected in the structure of the armies of colonial nations since at least the eighteenth century, and these have specifically organized themselves to fight both kinds of war. The Cossacks played a similar role in the imperial Russian army, and Bashi Bazouks in the Ottoman army (Murphey 1999). In modern armies, similar dichotomies are often recognized under a distinction between conventional and unconventional warfare, or between regular and irregular forces. Conventional or regular forces are typically made up of ethnic nationals. Irregular units are drawn either from ethnic others and foreigners, or else – as in the case of units such as the Spanish foreign legion – marginal members of the nation itself, savages by choice rather than birth, who can venture into dark regions of unregulated violence off-limits to the mainstream, regular soldier.

Senegalese in the Second World War

After the end of the First World War, the French used African and other colonial troops in their occupation of the Rhineland. A consequence of this was a German press campaign which came to be known as *Die Schwarze Schande*, or 'the black shame'. German newspapers accused the black troops of raping German women, and accused the French authorities of having deliberately stationed them on German soil in order to humiliate and dishonour the German people (Echenberg 1985: 370–71).

By the outbreak of the Second World War, Germans had experienced, within the previous seventy years, two European conflicts in which their opponents had employed colonial troops against them. To many Germans, these were remembered as savage hordes which had threatened German bodies with rape and mutilation. Many thousands of Tirailleurs Sénégalais, Senegalese infantrymen, fought in France during the German invasion of May and June 1940, and some of them paid a heavy price for these historical stereotypes. Like the Gurkhas and Goumiers, they wore long knives and used them in hand-to-hand fighting, a practice which horrified German soldiers, who assumed that the knives were headhunting weapons, intended specifically for mutilating the dead and wounded and taking their body parts as trophies. In striking contrast to their own racially 'pure' army, the French army seemed to German soldiers a kind of degenerate, multiracial horde. Some German soldiers had never seen black people before, and seem to have been alarmed by the sight of them. They did not accept the Senegalese as fellow soldiers but regarded them as armed savages or 'black beasts from the jungle', and accused them of cannibalism (Scheck 2006: 68–74, 95, 106, 116, 122–23). Some refused to allow the burial of dead Senegalese, or removed the name tags from their bodies to prevent identification (Scheck 2006: 41). Some German units, when taking French soldiers prisoner in 1940, immediately separated them by skin colour and shot the black prisoners or, in some cases, killed them with their own knives (Echenberg 1985: 369–70; Scheck 2005; Scheck 2006: 27, 60).

Senegalese veterans interviewed after the war vehemently denied the charges of atrocities such as trophy-taking. They seem to have had strong cultural taboos on taking items of any sort from the bodies of the enemy dead, including money and valuables, for fear it would cause their own death (Lawler 1992: 96, 162). While it is possible that they caused mutilations to the bodies of German soldiers, intentionally or otherwise, in close fighting with their knives, it seems they did not retain body parts of the dead or use them as personal mementos.[3]

More often, they seem to have been victims of such behaviour. Some German soldiers cut off fingers of dead Senegalese soldiers to obtain their rings (Scheck 2006: 36). Because the Senegalese believed, with some justification, that they would be murdered if they were captured, a significant number of them chose to fight to the death rather than surrender. What seems to have emerged between German and Senegalese units fighting each other in May and June 1940 was a cycle of escalating brutality which led to the two sides neither giving nor expecting quarter (Scheck 2006: 143).

Nazi Medical and Anthropological Research

Official Nazi attitudes defined 'Slavs' as subhuman (Weiner 2006: 199). The German army fighting the Soviet Union committed many atrocities, such as the systematic murder of prisoners of war, but it seems that German soldiers fighting on the Eastern Front did not mutilate the enemy dead for trophies (Weingartner 1996). A Ukrainian partisan who fought them recollected: 'The Germans just hanged people .... They just killed us' (Weiner 2006: 119). The explanation perhaps lies in Germany's relatively brief colonial empire. In the United States and Britain, both the regular army and settler militias had had experience of involvement in the overlapping activities of colonial warfare and collecting human remains for medical and scientific research for a century and a half or more. In Germany, no close and historically long-standing connection of this sort had been able to develop between racial science and the military.

Of course, members of the Nazi medical and scientific establishment showed very different attitudes to the bodies of race enemies. An example was August Hirt,

Professor at the Institute for Anatomy at Strasbourg, who had inmates of concentration camps killed in order to form a collection of Jewish skulls and skeletons. Hirt's plan, explained in a memorandum to Heinrich Himmler, had originally been to obtain skulls of captured Russian prisoners.

> There exist extensive collections of skulls of almost all races and peoples. Of the Jewish race, however, only so very few specimens of skulls stand at the disposal of science that a study of them does not permit precise conclusions. The war in the East now presents us with the opportunity to remedy this shortage. By procuring the skulls of the Jewish Bolshevik Commissars, who personify a repulsive, yet characteristic subhumanity, we have the opportunity of obtaining tangible, scientific evidence.
>
> The actual obtaining and collecting of these skulls without difficulty could be best accomplished by a directive issued to the Wehrmacht in the future to immediately turn over alive all Jewish Bolshevik Commissars to the field M.P. [Military Police]. The field MP in turn is to be issued special directives to continually inform a certain office of the number and place of detention of these captured Jews and to guard them well until the arrival of a special deputy. This special deputy, commissioned with the collection of the material is to take a prescribed series of photographs and anthropological measurements, and is to ascertain, in so far as is possible, the origin, date of birth, and other personal data of the prisoner. Following the subsequently induced death of the Jew, whose head must not be damaged, he will separate the head from the torso and will forward it to its point of destination in a preservative fluid within a well-sealed tin container especially made for this purpose. On the basis of the photos, the measurements and other data on the head and, finally, the skull itself, the comparative anatomical research, research on race membership ..., the pathological features of the skull form, the form and size of the brain and any other things can begin. (Quoted in Mendelsohn 1982: 199; see also Lifton 2000: 285)

However, it was decided to collect whole skeletons rather than just skulls, and to do so from among the male and female inmates of Auschwitz. In the end, a sample of men and women of a number of different European nationalities were selected there. Most of them were brought to a small concentration camp near Strasbourg in the summer of 1943. Eighty-six of them were killed there with poison gas, and their bodies brought to Hirt's laboratory. However, Hirt was prevented from completing his museum by the circumstances of the end of the war. When the Allied military liberated Strasbourg in late 1944, they found some of the bodies in his laboratory still in storage in vats of alcohol, some partially dissected and others intact, despite the desperate efforts he and his assistants had made to destroy all evidence of the collection (Klarsfeld 1985; Lifton 2000).

Viewed in the context of the history of European and North American racial science, such practices had much in common with the standard, militarized, colonial collecting practices of the previous century. At the time they occurred, they were not so much aberrations as anachronisms. This is apparent also in the case of Max Schmid, a German medical officer in occupied France, who was tried after the war.

> Just before the D-Day landings, the body of an American aviator was brought to Schmid's dispensary by a German burial detail. Schmid 'severed the head from the body, boiled it and removed the skin and flesh and bleached the skull which he kept on his desk for several months' [according to the court records] before sending it to Germany. At his trial, the prosecution claimed he sent it to his wife as a souvenir. He claimed he used it

only for instructional purposes and sent it home so that it might be buried in a cemetery. He argued that he acted without malice and had no intention of mutilating the body. An American military commission convicted him and sentenced him to ten years in prison. Schmid had violated Articles 3 and 4 of the 1929 Geneva Convention by subjecting the body to maltreatment and failing to honorably inter it. (Elliott 1996: 13)

Such behaviour on the part of a military physician might have been tolerated in the previous century on a frontier outpost in Africa or the American West. It certainly was not novel. What was most anomalous about it was that, like the crimes of Hirt, it imported the methods of nineteenth-century colonial frontier science into twentieth-century Europe, and employed them in the construction of racial divisions at home, applying them to an enemy within, rather than to savages on the distant fringes of empire.

Notes

1. Some Goumiers fighting in the French army in the Second World War wore necklaces of enemy ears, as a U.S. Army nurse who treated some of them recalls in her memoirs. Her hospital's policy with Goumier patients was to keep their necklaces in a safe place, out of sight, so as not to alarm other patients, and return them to their owners when they were discharged (Tomblin 2003: 109).

    In some cases, white officers have taught such behaviour to Africans fighting under their command. The South African army recruited !Kung men as soldiers in the war against the guerrillas of the South West African People's Organization in the 1970s; and taught them to mutilate the bodies of the enemy - instructing them, in other words, how to act as savages (Lee and Hurlich 1982: 344).

2. In 2002 a member of the public went to a police station near Melbourne, Australia, and handed in a wooden box containing a mummified human head. He informed the police that an Australian soldier had brought it back from the Battle of Gallipoli in the First World War. He also said that he no longer wanted it in his family, nor did he want himself or his family publicly identified. The police, not knowing what else to do with it, contacted an Australian war veterans' organization, which in turn contacted a prominent member of the Turkish community in Melbourne, who then collected the head from the police. He immediately contacted the press, and began giving interviews and news conferences at which the head was prominently displayed. The head still had some skin and hair, and also entry and exit wounds from a bullet. The box in which it had been kept was made of pine, had a lid, and was lined with red velvet, suggesting perhaps that it was meant as a miniature coffin. At this point, amidst growing public consternation in both Turkey and Australia, the authorities intervened and took possession of the head in order to hold an inquest and determine what to do with it. Australian war veterans expressed their shock and disgust; although some had heard of servicemen in some conflicts such as Vietnam taking ears as trophies, none had ever heard of an Australian serviceman collecting an enemy head. After a forensic investigation the authorities concluded that the head was most likely the remains of a Turkish, or Ottoman Empire, soldier from the Gallipoli campaign of 1915, who had been shot

with a .303 calibre bullet, the standard ammunition used by British Empire forces. The inquest also concluded that the head had mummified naturally. The head was handed over in an official ceremony to representatives of the Turkish government, who returned it to Turkey, where it was buried at Gallipoli with military honours later in 2002 (Altintas 2008; Fewster, Basarin and Basarin 2003: 147–48; Victoria State Coroner's Office 2002). Although a highly abnormal case, it may nevertheless have been influenced by official Australian policy at the time. Australian soldiers in the First World War were under orders to collect 'relics' of the conflict for the proposed national war memorial, and by the end of the war they had obtained some twenty-five thousand items (Australian War Memorial 2010).

3. As we saw in Chapter Six in regard to the members of Schweinfurth's expedition to central Africa, whether or not combatants engage in acts of trophy-taking seems to reflect, not whether they are 'civilized' or 'savage' – whatever such terms might mean – but the presence or absence of cultural taboos and prohibitions relating to contact with dead bodies.

Chapter 12
Skull Trophies of the Pacific War

The Papas Case

In June 2003, detectives in the city of Pueblo, Colorado, searching a house for drugs, discovered a small trunk inscribed with the word 'Guadalcanal' and the date 'November 11 1942'. Finding a human skull inside it, they seized it. Photographs taken by the coroner's office, and published in a local newspaper, showed that the skull bore many inscriptions. Across the frontal bone, in neat capital letters, were the words:

THIS IS A GOOD JAP

GUADALCANAL S.I.

11-NOV.-42

OSCAR

M.G. J.PAPAS U.S.M.C.

The skull also bore autographs of two or three dozen servicemen up to the rank of lieutenant colonel, and had been lacquered. The lower jaw had been fixed in place by a wire staple or pin. The householder told the police that the skull was a family heirloom, and demanded its return. It was the skull, he said, of a Japanese soldier killed in the battle of Guadalcanal by his great-grandfather, Julius Papas. Papas and other members of his unit had signed their names and ranks on it and given it the nickname 'Oscar'. Forensic analysis by anthropologists at the U.S. Army Central Identification Laboratory confirmed the probability of wartime Japanese origins, and in May 2004 the skull was handed over to the Japanese authorities for interment (P. Malone 2003a, 2003b, 2003c, 2004a, 2004b).[1]

Papas apparently told his family that he had obtained the skull by killing a Japanese soldier who had killed his best friend. But the forensic tests carried out on the skull revealed signs of decomposition and of gnawing by rats and indicated that skull was old when Papas collected it (P. Malone 2004b).

In a newspaper interview after the discovery of the skull, a spokesman for the Marine Corps expressed shock at such reprehensible and unlawful treatment of the dead:

> As a God-fearing person, it violates all moral laws of everything I've been raised to know .... I don't need to look in the Uniform Code (of Military Justice) to tell you that you can't walk off the battlefield with the remains of the enemy. Has it ever happened? It has, but it's just wrong .... There are things that happen in war that you wouldn't entertain in your worst nightmare during times of peace. People do some strange things (in wartime), but it still doesn't make it right. (P. Malone 2003a)

But the relatives of Papas, who died in 1960 after a long career in the Corps, spoke of their sense of loss. For them, the passage of time had transformed the skull into a cherished possession redolent with family sentiment and affection. The niece of Papas, for instance

> has fond memories of the skull as a family heirloom. She said she was saddened that the artifact has been taken from her family and returned to the Japanese government.
> 'Anybody that knew the family or went in (Papas') house saw it .... Whenever you walked in that house, it was right there in the middle of the shelf .... It was just somebody that was dead, and this was the way my uncle felt about it. Yes, nowadays people would be outraged about it. But then, we didn't know any better, it was no big deal. It was war. Uncle Julius just thought he was doing what he was supposed to do over there'. (P. Malone 2004b)

The collection of skulls and other remains of Japanese soldiers for souvenirs by Allied servicemen is an aspect of the Pacific War that seems largely forgotten.[2] Yet several historical studies have shown that it occurred on a large enough scale to concern the Allied military authorities throughout the conflict, and was reported and commented on in the U.S. and Japanese wartime press (Dower 1986; Fussell 1988, 1989; Hoyt 1986: 277, 357–59; Lewis and Steele 2001: 99, 145, 148–49; Shillony 1981; Weingartner 1992, 1996). The problem I address in this chapter is why these practices occurred to such a significant extent throughout the course of this war. In the next chapter I consider why they disappeared from public memory so quickly after the war ended.

Race, War and Expeditionary Trophy-taking

In the eyes of many Allied servicemen and civilians in the Second World War, their enemies were ranked by degrees of humanness, with Germans and Italians acknowledged as human, as 'men just like us' (Spector 1984: 410), Italians at times slightly more so than Germans (Fussell 1989: 116–17). And attitudes to Germany tended to define the enemy in political terms – as 'Hitler' or 'the Nazis', rather than the German people. But attitudes to the humanness of the Japanese tended to be at best ambivalent. In the words of a U.S. war correspondent:

> In Europe we felt that our enemies, horrible and deadly as they were, were still people', he explained in one of his first reports from the Pacific. 'But out here I soon gathered that the Japanese were looked upon as something subhuman and repulsive; the way some people feel about cockroaches or mice. (Quoted in Dower 1986: 78)

Some Allied servicemen, in short, drew a dichotomy between near and distant enemies, coded in terms of the permissibility or impermissibility of trophy-taking. Historians have described the deep mutual racial animosities which gave the Pacific War its particular brutality (Dower 1986; Johnston 2000: 85–89; Weingartner 1996).

For some among the Allies, the Japanese were a primitive subspecies separate from the European, and these differences were widely assumed to be marked, above all, in the skull. From 1933 until the end of the war, Roosevelt corresponded with Professor Ales Hrdlicka, Curator of Physical Anthropology at the Smithsonian Institution. Hrdlicka informed him that the brutality and perfidy of the Japanese was probably due to their descent from the Ainu, whose skulls 'were some 2,000 years less developed than ours' (Thorne 1978: 168; see also pp. 158–59). Roosevelt commissioned Hrdlicka to write a report on the possibility of crossing the Japanese with other 'races' in order to create a less aggressive breed (see also Aldrich 2005: 17; Dower 1986: 108).

At the same time, a conspicuous feature of wartime representations of the Japanese was the pervasive use of animal terms: monkeys, rats, cockroaches, lice, vermin, reptiles and so forth (Dower 1986: 77–180; Fussell 1989: 116–17). Japanese soldiers were portrayed as brutish, simian, often rabid, with an affinity for jungles and jungle warfare unfathomable to civilized combatants. In short, for many U.S. Americans in particular, the conflict in the Pacific was a war (for some, a war to the death) between peoples or races – almost between species – in a way that the war in Europe was not (Dower 1986: 77; Weingartner 1996).

A particularly significant aspect of these attributions of animality and ferality to the Japanese was a recurrent imagery of hunting in U.S. depictions of the war in the Pacific.

> The evocation of the hunt appears everywhere in American writing about combat in the Pacific, sometimes with an almost lyric quality, evoking images of the Old West and physical pleasures that have always been part of the picture of the good life in the more rural American consciousness. Advertisers played up this theme. A magazine advertisement for the brewing industry, for example, depicted a hunter and his companions with a fine deer trophy, identified as one of the 'little things' (along with beer and ale) that meant a lot to a Marine on leave, and went on to note that 'he's been doing a different kind of hunting overseas.' An advertisement by a cartridge company carried a headline reading 'Now Your Ammunition Is Getting Bigger Game,' and juxtaposed a painting of a hunter sighting in on a mountain sheep with a scene of ammunition stores on Guadalcanal. An ad for telescopic sights showed a Japanese soldier crouched on his hands and knees, with the cross hairs fixed behind his shoulder. 'Rack up another one,' the heading read. Cards for display in automobile windows proclaimed 'Open Season for Japs'. (Dower 1986: 89–90)

Similarly, humorous recruiting posters for the Marine Corps offered 'Jap hunting licences', with the bonus of free weapons and ammunition (Weingartner 1992: 55). To grasp the full force of such tropes, one must understand the place of hunting in the symbolism of U.S. national identity. Herman (2001) has described how hunting became a mass pursuit among U.S. men during industrialization in the late nineteenth and early twentieth centuries. For many U.S. Americans, urban and rural, and to some extent irrespective of social class, hunting came to symbolize masculine qualities of self-reliance and hardihood associated with pioneer times (Herman 2001: 270). In the annual hunting season a wide range of men could reaffirm and relive powerful national myths of the frontier and the conquest of wilderness. Among the reasons that Herman suggests for this were the nineteenth-century stereotypes of American Indians as hunters. The European settlers imagined they could succeed the indigenous peoples as legitimate owners of the land by taking over what they understood to be the autochthonous mode of relating to the environment and its resources. So hunting came to express a type of white U.S. nationalism that rested on a symbolically appropriated indigeneity (Herman 2001: xiii, 7, 171–72). To some of the sport's most passionate advocates, such as Theodore Roosevelt, the figure of the hunter had an almost mystical significance as the quintessential expression of the U.S. male character (Herman 2001: 223). In 1945, a quarter of U.S. men hunted for sport (Herman 2001: 271), and many of these must have had personal experience of preparing animal trophy heads and skulls.

In short, at the time of the Pacific War, hunting was not simply a mass leisure pursuit, but an important symbolic affirmation of U.S. white male identity, and to some extent it still is, more perhaps among rural and working-class men. In particular, it can have some of the qualities of a rite of passage for adolescent boys.

> [H]unting is a seasonal ritual of working-class solidarity for many rural American men. When they go hunting, they feel that they are renewing their bonds with friends and kinfolk and reaffirming their ties to the land and way of life they have inherited from their ancestors .... Many male hunters believe that hunting affirms their identity as men, and feel that taking a boy hunting cements his bonds to other males and helps make a man of him. (Cartmill 1993: 232–33, footnotes omitted; see also Fine 2000; S.A. Marks 2001)

A boy's first kill, for instance, may be celebrated by the ritual of 'blooding', initiating him into the deer-hunting fraternity (Bronner 2008). Many servicemen, whether hunters themselves or not, must have shared this image of hunting, rich with associations of male camaraderie, coming-of-age, patriotism and white racial identity and brought it with them into combat with an enemy which many of them viewed as subhuman. Hence in their accounts of fighting in the Pacific, servicemen often drew on familiar experiences – familiar also to much of their audience – of shooting rabbits, quails, ducks, deer, mountain sheep and other game back home (Dower 1986: 89–90). It was perhaps inevitable that some would pursue the implications of such metaphors to the point of treating Japanese remains as hunting trophies. Even the setting of the fighting – remote islands and jungles in New Guinea and elsewhere, evocative of headhunting and cannibalism in the public imagination – may have tended to reinforce this image of a war being waged at the frontier between culture and nature, civilization and the wild.

Bodies and Souvenirs

In 1944, the U.S. poet Winfield Townley Scott worked as book editor of *The Providence Journal*, a Rhode Island newspaper. His diary records the excitement of his colleagues one day in January, when word spread through the building that a sailor, recently home from the Pacific, was in the office displaying the skull of a Japanese soldier killed at Guadalcanal. All the staff stopped work and gathered round eagerly to view the souvenir (Goldstein 2002: 61). This event became the basis of his poem *The U.S. Sailor with the*

Japanese Skull, a work which a critic has called 'one of the most revelatory and widely-reprinted poems about the savagery of World War II' (Goldstein 2002: 68). In the poem, a sailor decapitates an enemy corpse on a Guadalcanal beach. He skins the head and, on the voyage home, cleans and polishes the skull by towing it behind his ship in a net, and finally scrubs it with caustic soda. The description of the process by which the skull is cleaned takes up four of the poem's eight stanzas, and in its graphic detail seems unlikely to have sprung purely from Townley Scott's imagination.

At the time, other newspapers had reported servicemen coming home from the Pacific with similar objects. On 1 October 1943, a communiqué from the Army Chief of Staff to General MacArthur (Supreme Allied Commander of the Southwest Pacific theatre) expressed alarm over some recent items in the U.S. press. He referred to a newspaper story which told:

> how a soldier had 'made himself a string of beads from the teeth of Japanese soldiers.' Another report he cited concerned a soldier who had recently returned from the southwest Pacific theater with photos showing various steps 'in the cooking and scraping of the heads of Japanese to prepare the skulls for souvenirs'. (Spector 1984: 411; see also Weingartner 1992: 57)

A photograph of this sort appears in an essay by Fussell (1988: 47), himself a veteran of the Second World War. Taken on a beach on Guadalcanal during the war, the photograph was revealed to Fussell in the 1980s by a friend who had served there as a marine. It shows the friend and another marine tending a small metal vat in which they are boiling a clearly visible human head. Fussell makes the point that snapshots such as these 'were taken (and preserved for a lifetime) because the marines were proud of their success' (1988: 48).

> It was by no means an 'atrocity' that these photographs were recording. They were taken out of pride, like the photos of hanged partisans snapped at the same time a world away by Wehrmacht soldiers. Both kinds of pictures were taken to record proud achievements. (Fussell 1988: 46–48)

Charles Lindbergh, the pioneer aviator, went to the Pacific War area in April 1944 to serve as a civilian adviser to the U.S. Army and Navy, and refers to several of these sorts of acts in his *Wartime Journals*. On 14 August 1944 in the Marshall Islands, he records a marine officer telling him that some of his men:

> had a little sack in which they collected teeth with gold fillings. The officer said he had seen a number of Japanese bodies from which an ear or a nose had been cut off. 'Our boys cut them off to show their friends in fun, or to dry and take back to the States when they go. We found one Marine with a Japanese head. He was trying to get the ants to clean the flesh off the skull, but the odor got so bad we had to take it away from him.' It is the same story everywhere I go. (Lindbergh 1970: 919)

But skulls seem rarely to have been obtained from bodies of the newly killed (though I will mention later a case of a Japanese prisoner apparently being murdered for his skull). Most were taken from remains partially or fully skeletonized.[3] Weinstein (2000), for instance, regretfully recalls what he terms his 'primitive behaviour' when he and a companion found some decaying Japanese bodies in the New Britain jungle in 1943. Deciding that the skulls were too precious to leave, they wove makeshift baskets out of vines and twigs, and carried the skulls back to camp, where they boiled them in old fuel drums. Weinstein's own souvenir was stolen shortly afterwards, but his companion managed to ship his home. Later, a directive was issued forbidding the ownership of skulls and teeth, a practice which in Weinstein's experience was widespread.

Many of the relics that servicemen brought home seem to have been collected a considerable time after the end of fighting in an activity perhaps best described as trophy-scavenging, though these objects might be misrepresented back home as proof of fighting prowess, taken in combat. Bass (1983: 801–802) mentions the origins of one of the two Japanese trophy skulls he analyses: a serviceman, securing some Pacific island, came across a crashed Japanese fighter plane and took the pilot's skull as a memento.

On 26 June 1945, a navy lieutenant from New Orleans wrote to his wife from Corregidor in the Philippines:

> We looked all over the island and in the hospital cave where the last fighting took place. There were dead Japs all over the place and I thought of sending Pack his Jap skull, but most were still being used slightly. We got some pens and stuff out of the pockets and one of the fellows got 2 bayonets. I got a rifle and other papers. There were a lot of helmets, canteens etc lying around. The Japs were pretty ripe and one of the boys got sick. (E.L. King 1945)

Such souvenir seekers were not necessarily combat troops. An ambulance driver wrote home from India on 23 September 1944:

> Yesterday we hiked four miles into the hills to the ex-Jap headquarters .... There were no souvenirs whatsoever. However, we did take some good pictures of bomb craters and bombed out buildings. Do you want a Jap skull? Now that I'm better acquainted with mailing ways I'll try to ship home something better than I have already. A Jap canteen, insignia, flag, sword, medals, etc. Enclosed are some Jap invasion notes, a sleeve division insignia, a sketch and an Irish money order. Also a Jap instruction sheet for mosquito preventive. (American Field Service 1944)

Notable in these letters are the casual references to skulls as souvenirs along with other popular mementos of the Japanese such as sabres, pistols and battle flags. All such items were collected for much the same reasons that tourists collect souvenirs: as proof of 'having been there' (Graburn 1989: 33–34; Hitchcock 2000: 2).[4]

Some servicemen who collected enemy remains sought to personify them by giving them pet names, as a member of the Army Transportation Corps recorded in an entry in his private journal, dated 19 February 1944 in New Britain.

> We were following a small trail when Norm stepped in front of me and said that the object in front of him looked like a bone. And so it was, a leg bone, lower leg from all appearances. Then we found two ribs. We each took one. (Norm later lost his when he was helping a fellow get his truck out of deep mud.) A few feet further down the trail we were following I spied a skull .... When we returned to camp, I took the skull down to the ocean and thoroughly washed it, losing one of its teeth in the process. Now it has two teeth on each side as it sits out in the sun drying and bleaching. There are sharp, jagged edges left where

part of the skull was blown out. Am going to use it for a candle-holder. We have named him Charlie. (Kahn 1993: 82; see also pp. 83–85)

In 1943, Thomas Larson was stationed in the Solomon Islands as a radio operator in the U.S. Navy. In August that year, he paid a visit to Guadalcanal in search of souvenirs.

> An Army officer drove me way up by the Matanikau River where many Japs had been slaughtered. I had to look out for booby traps. I found dead Japs. The ants had eaten out the brains and soft parts leaving the skull clean. I scraped off the hair of several and dumped them into a gunny sack plus a nice helmet I have to this day. (Larson 2003: 112)

Larson had a strong interest in natural history, and was a keen collector of seashells and other similar objects, some of which he would give away to his friends. He seems to have viewed Japanese skulls in a very similar way as natural history specimens.

> Here I'm known as the local beetle and butterfly, snake, seashell, and lizard authority. My reputation as such has spread around through the South Pacific. Even brought a sack full of Jap skulls back from Guadalcanal. I gave some to friends, and kept one for putting my helmet on and my pipe in the mouth. The Protestant Chaplin [sic] tried to get me to give the poor thing a Christian burial. I told him that he was Shinto and I needed his skull where I put it. (Larson 2003: 113)

He filled in the eye sockets with plaster of Paris and fitted them with the opercula of turban shells to suggest eyes, and kept the decorated skull at the head of his bunk (Larson 2003: 137–38). Later that year, he was appointed liaison officer on board a New Zealand navy warship as it was being sent for repairs at the dockyards at Boston. During the voyage, some of his behaviour provoked the disapproval of the ship's officers.

> I'd circulated with the enlisted men of the ship especially some of the Petty officers who invited me to have a meal with them. This was unheard of for British officers. The biggest mistake I made was that I had a Jap skull from the battle field of Guadalcanal in my duffel bag. I was told to get rid of it. Yes, get it off the ship! With the lame excuse by them that the Maoris on board were superstitious .... That afternoon I presented my skull with the sea shell cat's eyes opercula's [sic] of the Turban shell to a curator at the Auckland Museum of Natural History. (Larson 2003: 122; see also pp. 126, 137–38)

Like other Japanese souvenir items, skulls and other remains were sometimes traded among military personnel. In January 1944 an Allied intelligence report referred to members of the Naval Construction Battalions stationed on Guadalcanal selling Japanese skulls to merchant seamen (Weingartner 1992: 57). Teeth were sometimes similarly commoditized. Weinstein (2000) recalls almost falling ill the first time he saw his sergeant wearing a necklace of teeth, an investment which the sergeant planned to sell on his return home. He had set the more valuable gold ones between every five or so of the commoner natural ones. He polished them constantly, and often concocted tales of personal heroism to explain how he had acquired them, though most of them had actually been bought or bartered from other personnel. Half a century later, Weinstein still sometimes wondered whether his sergeant's 'unsold collection decorates some bar he frequented where he traded them for beer, while recounting his tales of bravery'.[5]

One factor which veterans themselves, as well as other writers on the Pacific War, often cite in explaining such behaviour was the notoriously harsh and brutal conditions of the campaign. Sledge, in his classic first-hand account of fighting on Peleliu and Okinawa as a marine infantryman, concludes that the 'fierce struggle for survival ... eroded the veneer of civilization and made savages of us all' (1981: 121). Weinstein (2000), similarly, describes himself and his companions undergoing a 'decline of enlightened, civilized discipline' in the jungles of New Britain. Such factors may indeed explain mutilation and ill-treatment of enemy dead, though some servicemen expressed intentions to obtain Japanese body parts even before embarking for overseas; that is, before any experience of combat or exposure to its stresses (Dower 1986: 65; Tregaskis 2000 [1943]: 14; Weingartner 1996: 56).[6]

War as a Continuation of Tourism by Other Means

The collection of Japanese trophy skulls and other body parts seems to have represented the far end of a continuum, at the other end of which was a common and generally accepted military practice: namely, the taking of possessions from prisoners and enemy dead. Such pilfering or robbery is widely reported in twentieth-century wars (see, for instance, Hynes 1998: 156; Johnston 2000: 18). Sledge describes the way in which not only equipment such as helmets, swords, pistols and so forth, but all personal effects – letters, photographs, pens, watches, eyeglasses and the like – were routinely taken as souvenirs from all Japanese corpses encountered (1981: 118–20). He calls this practice 'fieldstripping', as if an enemy body with its accoutrements were an object to be disassembled like a piece of captured ordnance. Jones, who fought at Guadalcanal and wrote a novel, *The Thin Red Line*, based on his experiences, describes in the novel daily barter markets in which front-line infantry troops traded such souvenirs to other military personnel in return for whiskey, beer and other luxury items (see also Sledge 1981: 118–20). But fieldstripping was not just motivated by the economic value of enemy belongings. Sledge calls it a 'ritual' to degrade the defeated enemy and, very interestingly, compares it in this respect to scalping.[7]

The collection of skulls, teeth and other body parts seems on the whole to have been carried out as an extension of this 'normal' and widely practised looting of corpses. According to Hynes (a marine veteran of the Pacific War) the mutilation of enemy dead has been 'part of military behavior from the beginning of wars. If you kill your enemy, his body belongs to you, it's part of the loot' (1998: 191–92). On the other hand, Hynes also tells us that he has never heard of a U.S. serviceman mutilating German or Italian dead for souvenirs.

In fact, none of the Second World War trophy skulls occurring in the forensic record derive from the European theatre; all have been identified as Japanese. The reasons for this are not far to seek. As Dower remarks:

> It is virtually inconceivable ... that teeth, ears, and skulls could have been collected from German or Italian war dead and publicized in the Anglo-American countries without provoking an uproar; and in this we have yet another inkling of the racial dimensions of the [Pacific] war. (1986: 65–66, my parentheses; see also Fussell 1989: 117)

Personal effects certainly might be taken from German and Italian dead as souvenirs. But the killers, it seems, felt no sense of ownership of their bodies.[8] I suggest that the special fetishizing of Japanese remains as desirable acquisitions was permitted or encouraged by the way in which the different enemy peoples were classified racially by degrees of humanness. One consequence, among the armed forces and civilians in the United States at least, was an implicit conception of the war in the Pacific as a sort of nation-wide, collective hunting expedition, allowing the moral boundaries of normal military fieldstripping and souvenir seeking to be widened, in the case of the Japanese, to the collection of body parts. Here, for example, a U.S. sailor describes in his diary a kamikaze attack on his ship in November 1944:

> Parts of destroyed suicide planes were scattered all over the ship. During a little lull in the action the men would look around for Jap souvenirs and what souvenirs they were. I got part of the plane .... One of the Marines cut the ring off the finger of one of the dead pilots .... One of the fellows had a Jap scalp, it looked just like you skinned an animal .... One of the men on our [gun] mount got a Jap rib and cleaned it up, he said his sister wants part of a Jap body. One fellow from Texas had a knee bone and he was going to preserve it in alcohol from the sick bay. (Fahey 1963: 231, my parentheses; see also Fussell 1989: 117; Hynes 1998: 170–71)

In these respects, trophy-taking shared certain similarities with lynching. These parallels seem to have been very evident to some African American soldiers at the time (Lewis and Steele 2001: 148). Like lynching, trophy-taking was not simply an expression of racism but, to those who carried it out, a form of racialized justice or retribution. Trophy-taking was in part understood as revenge for Japanese atrocities: the attack on Pearl Harbor, the brutal mistreatment of Allied prisoners of war after the Japanese capture of the Philippines, and many other violations of which the Japanese forces were accused throughout the course of the war (Hoyt 1986).

Lindbergh, in his *Wartime Journals*, 14 August 1944, reports fighter control personnel at the air base on Noemfoor Island in New Guinea carrying out patrols to hunt the last remaining Japanese as a sort of hobby, often taking leg bones from those they killed and carving objects such as letter openers and pen holders from them (1970: 906, 997; see also Weingartner 1992: 61). Military personnel have been known to manufacture in their spare time trinkets and souvenirs of a genre usually called trench art, primarily in the context of the First World War (Saunders 2000, 2003), and Lindbergh seems to have been describing an extension of this long-established pastime. In the same way that odds and ends such as old shell casings, or pieces of aircraft wreckage, might be fashioned into cigarette cases, decorative mugs, watchstraps and so forth (see for instance, Lince 1997: 96), so, it seems, enemy bones were fashioned into desk equipment or other artefacts. Johnston (2000: 82) mentions an Australian soldier in the Aitape area of New Guinea who made a tobacco jar from a Japanese skull, probably in 1944.

What we see with the treatment of the Japanese dead is a drive to push the normal practices of military souvenir taking to an extreme, not merely by appropriating body parts, but often then by extending this appropriation further still and modifying these objects so as to impress some mark of ownership on them: writing signatures on them, giving them pet names, fashioning them into commemorative artefacts, or in some other way making bodies memorialize their own defeat and destruction.

In the same way that enemy aircraft parts and enemy pilots' body parts were alike categorized as souvenirs as they rained down together on Fahey's ship, so the Japanese dead seem sometimes to have been viewed as one type of surplus Japanese war *matériel*, raw matter on which the winners were free to stamp their will. For instance, parts of bodies might be made to circulate as objects alongside goods such as whiskey in the informal barter which flourished among military personnel (cf. Jones 1963: 309–11). Bodies can become commoditized in many contexts (see Scheper-Hughes and Wacquant 2002); here, the commoditization occurred as a ritual of retribution, degradation and power akin, as Sledge sensed, to scalping.

How far these extensions were taken seems to have depended largely on self-regulation, and thus varied considerably between military units (cf. A. Young 1995: 127–28). In Sledge's experience, the taking of teeth seems to have been largely accepted or tolerated, by both officers and enlisted men, but not other parts of the body. During the fighting on Peleliu, a member of his unit announced he had a 'unique souvenir' and produced from his pack, carefully wrapped in waxed paper, a partially dried hand. His companions were disgusted and told him to throw it away before it started to smell: it gave them 'the creeps', they told him, and the commanding officer would 'raise hell' if he saw it (Sledge 1981: 152–53).[9]

To Sledge and his companions, taking body parts other than teeth was reprehensible, indeed inconceivable. Undoubtedly, only a minority of men extended souvenir taking to body parts, and of those, fewer still went so far as to collect trophy skulls or carve bones into desk ornaments. But their behaviour reflected attitudes which were very widely shared, and such practices were a source of constant disquiet to the military authorities. Weingartner describes in detail the efforts of the authorities to curtail them throughout the course of the war. So, for example, in January 1944 a directive from the Joint Chiefs of Staff to all theatre commanders 'called upon them to adopt measures to prevent the preparation of skulls and "similar items" as war trophies, and to prevent members of the armed forces and others from removing from the theater skulls and other objects which might be represented as Japanese body parts' (Weingartner 1992: 57). Such abuses of the dead not only violated the Geneva Conventions but, perhaps more importantly, were a propaganda gift to the Japanese and might have provoked reprisals against U.S. prisoners and detainees (Weingartner 1992: 64).

Interestingly, the Commander in Chief of the Pacific Fleet had ordered 'stern disciplinary action' against the use of enemy body parts as souvenirs as early as September 1942 (Fussell 1989: 117), only a few weeks into the Battle of Guadalcanal, the first land offensive against the Japanese. Clearly, the collection of body parts on a scale large enough to concern the military authorities had started as soon as the first living or dead Japanese bodies were encountered.

The official directives may have been effective in some areas of the campaign, but they seem to have been implemented only partially and unevenly by local commanders in the field (cf. Winslow 1998). Weinstein (2000) recalls that his officers never encouraged the collection of skulls and teeth, but never tried to prevent it either, even when orders came forbidding the ownership of skulls and directing them to be handed over to Graves Registration. The officers did not want to discourage expressions of animosity towards the enemy. Skulls, as well as the sergeant's collection of teeth, were often still displayed openly. John Rowland Barker, serving in an air force fighter control squadron in the Pacific in 1943, described in a letter to his parents how '[n]early every squadron has a Jap skull outside their orderly room as an ornament and lots of trucks have them on their radiator caps. Some even illuminate the insides with an electric light to give them an eerie expression at night' (Barker 1943).

Lindbergh (1970: 897) saw a skull hung as a decoration on the blackboard in the pilots' alert tent at the airbase on Biak on 6 August 1944, and there are other accounts of the use of skulls to decorate military boats at Saipan and elsewhere, and in various other sorts of display (Daws 1994: 278; Fussell 1988: 12, 47; McCall 2000: 297–98).

Notes

1. The Battle of Guadalcanal, in the Solomon Islands, was fought from August 1942 to March 1943. A photograph of Papas in a sergeant's uniform appeared in *The Pueblo Chieftain* in 1943 (see P. Malone 2004b), and the letters before his name may stand for Master Gunnery [Sergeant]. The significance of the name Oscar is unclear, though the Allies called a certain type of Japanese fighter aircraft an Oscar (Francillon 1979: 206–14).
2. Australian, as well as U.S., servicemen sometimes collected Japanese skulls (see P. Clarke and McKinney 2004: 68–69; Johnston 2000: 82; Stanley 1997: 140).
3. Similarly, in some 'headhunting' societies of Borneo: 'Just how heads were obtained was of secondary importance. I was told that Kayan and Kenyah folk even broke into Berawan mausoleums to steal skulls' (Metcalf 1996: 273).
4. In his novel *The Thin Red Line*, based on his experiences of fighting at Guadalcanal, Jones describes Captain Stein preparing to leave for New Zealand: 'He had a bloodstained battleflag, a Luger-type pistol, two officers' collar insignia, and sundry photographs and leather articles as souvenirs to prove he had been there' (Jones 1963: 331).
5. See Lindstrom and White (1990: 142) for a photograph, taken on Guadalcanal in November 1943 (some eight months after the battle for the island), showing an enterprising corporal's makeshift market stall or souvenir shop displaying for sale human skulls, as well as helmets, canteens and other mementos of the Japanese.

    Servicemen could therefore buy souvenir Japanese skulls because there was a trade in them at the time, along with other souvenir items such as canteens and helmets. A kind of local souvenir industry could emerge after an important victory, offering enemy remains together with enemy belongings and equipment, to servicemen who had not been able to obtain these items themselves.

    Local Melanesian communities with their own indigenous practices of headhunting often had long-standing experience of supplying trophy heads and skulls as ethnographic curios to Westerners, and sometimes traded these as 'native souvenirs' to Allied servicemen (see Lindstrom and White 1990: 143). One such skull, overmodelled with clay as a 'traditional' headhunting trophy and acquired in the Solomon Islands by a U.S. servicemen, was that of a Japanese soldier (G. White

2005). Such cases suggest there may have been some complex synergies between indigenous and Allied practices of trophy-taking in the Pacific theatre.
6. In her memoirs of her time on bases in the United States as a member of the Women's Army Corps during 1944-45, Henderson recalls some friends playing a joke on her in which a 'Jap skull from Guadalcanal' was made to rise up before her in a photographic darkroom (2001: 109). Some servicemen may have learned the practice of taking Japanese trophy skulls during their training in the United States, particularly if such skulls were in evidence on military bases.
7. Sledge describes almost surreal battle scenes in which groups of rear-echelon service troops, looking for souvenirs, would saunter unwittingly up to the front line much as if they were on holiday, sometimes blundering into Japanese-held territory (1981: 133–34, 151; see also Kahn 1993: 148).
8. Johnston mentions an Australian soldier taking a gold tooth from a German soldier's body in the North Africa campaign, and states that similar behaviour occurred sometimes in the First World War (2000: 82, 166). But such behaviour seems to have been comparatively rare in the European theatre of the Second World War.
9. Japanese soldiers on Peleliu appear to have remained quite unaware of these collecting practices (Lewis and Steele 2001: 145).

Chapter 13

Transgressive Objects of Remembrance

On Boiling Heads

In the previous chapter, I referred to a photograph taken during the Battle of Guadalcanal and published by Fussell (1988: 48). It shows two U.S. marines boiling the severed head of a Japanese soldier in order to remove the flesh and obtain the skull as a trophy. Much of the difficulty of this image has to do with categorizing the incident it portrays. One is unsure whether one is observing a scene of war or of hunting. Two men are carrying out an unpleasant act upon a human body. But if they had been boiling the head of a deer in the woods at home, this could have been an entirely normal hunting scene.

What is happening in this photograph is an event which belongs to a forbidden region on the boundary between the domains of warfare and hunting. Or rather, the marines are acting to open up such a region and create it. Within this small transgressive world the borderline between the human and animal has been shifted and the Japanese soldier excluded from the human category. The concept of a species boundary has been made to serve as a model for a social or political boundary – the boundary between two human groups at war. Such scenes did not occur, and for ideological reasons could not have occurred, among Allied servicemen in Europe in the Second World War. Here too, combat could sometimes be spoken of as a sort of hunting activity. Perhaps hunting has often offered soldiers a familiar cognitive schema with which to cope with the unfamiliar, chaotic and abnormal experiences of battle. But if so, conceptions of 'trophy hunting' were acted upon in the European theatre of the war only to the extent of seeking more orthodox and acceptable war souvenirs such as enemy helmets or bayonets. Hence there are no trophy photographs of Allied servicemen in the Second World War boiling the heads of German or Italian soldiers to procure their skulls as mementos, because these particular enemies were acknowledged as human, and there was no collective will to portray them as anything other than people, if misguided and dangerous ones.

The behaviour recorded in the photograph does not seem to have been entirely new. We have seen that there were reports of soldiers boiling the remains of their enemies to obtain bones as souvenirs in the American Civil War. It may be significant in this regard that the final reunions of Civil War veterans were held in the 1930s (Fellman 1990:

256). In other words, some of these men were still active, and still meeting to share their reminiscences, on the eve of the Second World War. It is therefore entirely possible that some soldiers serving in the Pacific War had learned of such practices from veterans of the Civil War.

But it is not necessary to suppose a direct historical link of this sort. We do not, for instance, need to posit some sort of 'tradition' of boiling enemy heads. The resurgence of the behaviour can be perfectly well explained by the fact that in both wars many soldiers were also hunters. Quite apart from the fact that many of them would have had experience of preparing animal skulls, horns and so forth as hunting trophies, hunting was for some of them fundamental to their conceptions of their own masculinity.

In other words, the recurrence of this behaviour in two wars some eighty years apart may lie, not so much in the cultural transmission of the behaviour itself, as in the way that some domains of social behaviour are, so to speak, conceptually adjacent to each other and share a boundary. One must imagine that the boundaries between such neighbouring regions of social behaviour are partially permeable, but also continually reaffirmed by implicit prohibitions which serve to ensure the domains remain distinct. This is perhaps especially so with domains related, as are hunting and warmaking, by powerful metaphors and symmetries. During both the Civil War and the Pacific War, many civilians and service personnel perhaps accepted that combat could be likened in some respects to a blood sport. But few of them would have accepted that the parallel should be pursued to the point of treating enemy combatants literally as animals, as quarry to be hunted for food or sport. Even the marines boiling the Japanese soldier's head would probably have been unwilling to treat Japanese soldiers as quarry to the extent, let us say, of consuming their enemies' flesh. But while there may have been widespread consensus that there were limits beyond which such metaphors ought not to be pursued, the precise placement of these limits could be contested. During the Second World War, some people clearly disapproved of taking personal possessions from the enemy dead as souvenirs (Harrison 2008b). Others, such as the marines in the photograph from Guadalcanal, perhaps drew the line at cannibalism. Practices such as boiling enemy heads emerged in tabooed and ambiguous regions between domains of permitted social action, but there were broad regions of indeterminacy within which the limits of acceptable behaviour were uncertain and shifting. Metaphors of the hunt could acceptably be pushed further, and their implications explored more deeply, the more the enemy was represented as racially alien.[1]

It is possible, then, that recurrent patterns in the treatment of enemy remains in these two wars arose, at least in part, from the recurrent use of the idea of the hunt or chase as a cultural metaphor for war. Some servicemen generated similar behaviour because they were trying to express a similar idea: the representation of their enemies as akin to game animals or quarry.

A veteran of the Pacific War whom I shall call R., and who served as a signalman in the U.S. Navy, remembers an occasion during the war when he and some companions went ashore on the island of Saipan in search of souvenirs. Walking inland they came across a cliff face in which there were many foxholes, each one holding the skeleton of a Japanese soldier together with his rifle. R. remembers that he and his companions took some of the dead soldiers' weapons, helmets and other belongings. But he also took one of the skulls and brought it back to his ship, where he washed it and set it in the sun to bleach, telling his comrades that he intended to take it home and put it on his mantelpiece. When the ship was approaching Honolulu, an officer saw the skull and ordered him to dispose of it. After the ship anchored at Pearl Harbor, R. stood at full attention on the ship's fantail and dropped the skull overboard. He says he still has to this day mixed feelings about his actions. He regrets violating a fellow human being who was only doing his duty as he had been trained. On the other hand, he also feels a certain sense of justice in having deposited a Japanese skull at the bottom of Pearl Harbor (Balcomb 2006).

When I asked if he had seen or heard of other servicemen taking skulls as souvenirs during the war, he replied that he knew of no-one other than himself doing such a thing, and that he very much hoped that nobody ever did. To him, it seems, his actions appeared a private aberration, carried out spontaneously and by him alone. In other words, he was, and apparently still remains, unaware of the shared and social nature of his own behaviour.

Cases such as this suggest that wartime acts of this sort were not always learned. I mean that we do not have to suppose that specific details of the behaviour such as boiling enemy heads or collecting skulls were transmitted over the past century or two, but only some more general underlying cognitive schemas to do, for example, with cultural representations of masculinity or hunting. Men who shared these largely unspoken and unconscious schemas, and whom historical events had placed in similar circumstances during war, could thereby independently generate very similar patterns of behaviour.

Body Parts as Tokens of Love and Respect

During the American Civil War, soldiers who collected war trophies from the enemy dead did so in many cases not for themselves but – as is often the case also with souvenirs and holiday mementos purchased by tourists (Graburn 2000: xiv–xv; Mars and Mars 2000) – as gifts for relatives and others back home. At the root of such behaviour were the sorts of schemas to which I just referred: cultural conventions relating to hunting and gender, in which men achieve adult masculinity by supplying game to their womenfolk and other family members. Hunting, whether for subsistence or recreation, was understood as an important affirmation of kinship ties and the role of adult men in the family.

Similar behaviour was repeated during the Pacific War, with servicemen often collecting such objects at the specific request of family members. That is, a perceived demand for Japanese remains among their civilian relatives seems to have driven the behaviour of some servicemen. In April 1943, a Baltimore newspaper wrote of a local mother seeking permission from the authorities for her son to send her a Japanese ear which she wanted to nail to her front door; and a Detroit newspaper in the same month ran a story 'of an underage youth who had enlisted and "bribed" his chaplain not to disclose his age by promising him the third pair of ears he collected' (Dower 1986: 65). In other words, some servicemen set out for the Pacific with an express intention, indeed a promise, of obtaining such tokens for friends and family.

One case of a departing serviceman pledging enemy remains in this way received international publicity on 22 May 1944, when *Life Magazine* published a 'Picture of the Week', with the caption: 'Arizona war worker writes her Navy boyfriend a thank-you note for the Jap skull he sent her'. In this full-page photograph a modishly dressed young woman composes a letter, and gazes, pen in hand, at a skull on her writing desk, a love token from a navy officer in the Pacific. The following commentary accompanies the photograph:

> PICTURE OF THE WEEK
> When he said goodby [sic] two years ago to Natalie Nickerson, 20, a war worker of Phoenix, Ariz., a big, handsome Navy lieutenant promised her a Jap. Last week Natalie received a human skull, autographed by her lieutenant and 13 friends, and inscribed: 'This is a good Jap – a dead one picked up on the New Guinea beach.' Natalie, surprised at the gift, named it Tojo. The armed forces disapprove strongly of this sort of thing.[2]

Even at the 'top' of the social scale, similar attitudes sometimes revealed themselves. On 13 June 1944, the New York Times reported a Congressman Walter presenting to President Roosevelt a letter opener made from a Japanese soldier's arm bone, and apologizing ironically to the president for being unable to offer him more of the Japanese anatomy (Hoyt 1996: 357–58; Weingartner 1992: 60–61). Some weeks later, the same newspaper reported that Roosevelt had given the letter opener back, declaring himself unwilling to possess such an object and suggesting that it be given burial (Weingartner 1992: 65). At the time, the military authorities and some of the civilian population, including church groups, had condemned the desecration of Japanese dead, especially following the publication of the photograph in *Life Magazine* (the lieutenant who sent his girlfriend a skull was traced and given an official reprimand), and Roosevelt appears to have been sensitive to this public feeling (Dower 1986: 330). Such gifts were by no means always welcome. One woman recalled her shock when a former boyfriend serving in the Marines on Saipan wrote her a letter offering a necklace made from the teeth of Japanese soldiers. She did not reply (Lewis and Steele 2001: 99).[3]

There is no evidence that servicemen who collected trophies of this sort were typically suffering from what was at the time called combat fatigue, or were, psychologically, other than entirely normal men who understood such souvenirs to be tangible expressions of their loyalties to family and nation and perceived a demand for these objects back home. Certainly, some seem to have had commercial motives, like Weinstein's entrepreneurial sergeant with his plans to sell his collection of teeth on his return. But for many other men, skulls, teeth and other body parts were proper and fitting items to collect because they were understood to be symbols of attachment and moral relatedness to people in their own country. Some of the collectors were non-combatants such as ambulance drivers, happening upon a skull on some old battlefield and taking it as a curio for their relatives, never making any pretence that they acquired it in combat. Others, as we shall see, passed off such objects as personal kills after the war, and very few do appear to have killed to acquire body parts as trophies. But a common attribute many shared was that once in the combat areas they valued such items, and sought them, often as expressions of love and esteem for parents, siblings, fiancées, children, their political leaders or other figures of authority, to whom they may have promised such tokens of duty and affection before leaving for overseas.

Pacific War Trophy Skulls in the Post-war Years

On 14 September 1944, Charles Lindbergh left the Pacific theatre and passed through customs at Hawaii:

> The customs officer asked me if I had any bones in my baggage. He said that he had to ask everyone that question because they had found a large number of men taking Japanese bones home for souvenirs. He said he had found one man with two 'green' Jap skulls in his baggage. (1970: 923)

There is evidence that a substantial quantity of human remains may have been brought home, or sent home, by Allied servicemen during the Pacific War, and perhaps also in the immediate post-war years, despite the efforts of the authorities to prevent it.

Because it was unlawful to send home human remains, servicemen who wished to do so had to smuggle them. I have been told of one case in which a serviceman in the Pacific obtained permission from his commanding officer to send a coconut home as a souvenir, and then at the last minute replaced the coconut with a Japanese skull (A. Howard 2006, 2007).

In another similar case, a U.S. serviceman stationed in the Mariana Islands acquired from a local woodcarver a coconut, one side of which bore a carving representing the face of a Japanese soldier with a wide, grimacing mouth. The mouth had been inlaid with twenty-two teeth, some natural, and others gold and silver, taken from the bodies of Japanese soldiers. The carved face was visible only from the front; viewed from the back, the artefact appeared to be a perfectly normal coconut. The serviceman obtained permission to send it home by laying it face down in its packing crate, and persuading his officer that it was merely a coconut. This artefact still remains in the serviceman's family, where it is now a valued heirloom (Wavell 2007).

Sledzik and Ousley (1991: 521) report that skulls were missing from about 60 per cent of the remains of Japanese war dead repatriated from the Mariana Islands in 1984. A Japanese priest, who had visited Iwo Jima regularly since 1952 to conduct ceremonies for the dead, reported similarly in 1985 that skulls had been taken from many of the remains, presumably for souvenirs (Ross 1986: 357–59; see also Fussell 1988: 51).

Evidence of the post-war fate of remains brought back to the United States is now meagre but suggests that, unlike animal hunting trophies, they did not usually become objects of display or family heirlooms. Some families possessing trophy skulls may have grown attached to them, as did the family of Julius Papas and the owners of the inlaid coconut described above. But the passage of time seems to have had a very different effect on most veterans, or veterans' families, turning these mementos into increasingly unwanted burdens, particularly as their perceptions of the Japanese changed in the post-war years. As we will see, many veterans, or their heirs, eventually sought to rid themselves of their relics – in some cases repatriating them, or trying to repatriate them, to Japan, often despite considerable official obstacles.

Many other remains seem simply to have been discarded, since abandoned trophy skulls are sometimes discovered and brought to the attention of the authorities. Some, like the skull kept by Papas, have been found by chance during police raids. Most have come to public light only when their keepers tried to rid themselves of them.[4]

The forensic anthropologist Maples describes a probable Japanese trophy skull recovered by chance from Lake Travis in Texas. It had been weighted down, tied by fishing line to a large rock (Maples and Browning 1995: 26–29), a measure which one would not normally take if disposing, say, of a broken teapot or bicycle. It indicates a determination to ensure that the skull would not re-emerge from the lake, and thus a concern that it somehow might. In short, it suggests that the disposal of the skull may have had, to the person who carried it out, something of the quality of an exorcism.

Another skull, recovered from a lake in Illinois, had been thrown there after becoming an object of avoidance and fear to its own keeper. It had been brought home from the Pacific by a navy medic who became a high-school science teacher after the war and used it in his biology classes. Years after his death, it was discovered in a trunk in the attic by his teenage grandson, who spray-painted it gold, tied a bandana around it, and used it as a bedroom decoration until he became frightened of it and in January 2000 threw it into nearby Lake Springfield. A spell of dry weather exposed the skull on the lake bed a month later, and a passer-by reported it to the police. After examination by an Illinois State Police anthropologist, the local police working with U.S. military officials sent the skull to the U.S. Naval Hospital in Okinawa, to be handed over to the Japanese government at the Group of Eight economic summit on Okinawa later that year. In the event, the transfer was delayed for three years because the U.S. authorities deemed there was insufficient evidence that the skull was that of a Japanese soldier. On the verge of being disposed of as hospital waste, the skull was finally handed over to the Okinawan authorities in a small ceremony in 2003 (D. Allen 2004; Antonacci 2000a, 2000b, 2000c, 2003; Oliva 2002, 2003).

Some trophy skulls seem to have become a source of family conflict in the post-war years. One, analysed by the forensic anthropologist Gill-King and his colleagues, had originally been presented as a gift to one of the senior marine officers involved in planning the invasion of Saipan, and was apparently the skull of a member of the Japanese garrison there. After the war, the skull circulated in the officer's family for many years, with some wanting to return it to Japan, while others – referred to by Gill-King as the 'John Wayne' faction of the family – wanted to keep it. Eventually, the skull came into the possession of the officer's great-nephew, a young lawyer, who offered it to the Japanese Consulate in Houston. He was told that it could not be accepted without supporting evidence, which Gill-King's laboratory successfully provided (Gill-King 1992, 2005).

Veterans and Repatriation

The attempts by some veterans to repatriate their trophies are especially interesting, because these show how veterans' attitudes to the enemy could change fundamentally over the course of their lives. A change of this sort is recorded, for instance, in the memoirs of Marsden Hordern, who served in the Royal Australian Navy in coastal New Guinea.[5] When he first joined his warship, a type of small vessel called a Fairmile, he was shocked by the sight of a figurehead or mascot attached to its mast.

> Close to the White Ensign just above the bridge, a man's skull with a bullet hole near his right eye-socket was wired to the mast and cross-trees .... Fairmilers working with the army had

often been ashore in recent battlegrounds where Japanese bodies still lay about. Apparently some of *817*'s crew had found this skull, brought it back on board, called it 'Percy', stuck it up on the mast and then forgotten about it. It disconcerted me, but further questioning produced such an awkward silence that I gave up. From the distance of about sixty years, the very thought of a man's head wired to the mast of a warship wearing the White Ensign shocks me. It shocked me then too, for I had had little experience of the aftermath of land battles. And when I later saw heads stuck up on posts in Hollandia in Dutch New Guinea and photographed one outside the RAAF headquarters there, I realised that such displays were not peculiar to any nation or service. (Hordern 2005: 161–63)

Later, his ship was ordered to sail to Sydney for refitting. During the voyage, Hordern recollected lectures on Oriental History he had attended at Sydney University, and found himself wondering about the dead soldier's background, occupation and family life. He recalled also an incident in which he had come close to being killed by the Japanese, and speculated that his own skull might have ended up as some sort of trophy in the hands of the enemy (2005: 164–65). On the way to Sydney the ship docked briefly at Townsville, in Queensland, where an outraged captain in the Royal Australian Navy ordered Hordern to take the skull down from the mast. Hordern stowed it in one of the ship's lockers, and the ship then continued on to Sydney, where it was handed over to the dockyard workers for refitting (2005: 165–66). At this point, Hordern decided he had no alternative but to take the skull home with him. It was, he felt,

> [i]mpossible to leave him there. Imagine the press headlines when the workers found him. That would look bad for the navy. I wrapped him in an old flag, stuffed him in my kit bag and went home to the rectory in a tram with Percy on my knee. There I put him in a wooden box, stowed it in the garage, and for the time being forgot about him.
>
> But I had a man's head on my hands – a legacy which was to dog me for a quarter of a century.... In 1953, when I married ... and set up house in Sydney, Percy, still in his box, moved in with us and was stowed in the laundry. The problem of his disposal oppressed me. There could be no thought of burying him in the garden or consigning him to the waters of Sydney Harbour; the possible subsequent discovery by a plumber, builder or scuba diver of a human skull with a bullet wound under the eye would raise questions I would be bound to answer. Nor was there any official machinery for disposing of the heads of former enemies; ours is not a head-hunting society. I could not discuss the matter with [a former comrade] for he was dead, and although I considered taking Percy to Canberra and presenting him to the Japanese ambassador, the prospect of the complications that would flow from such action quickly put paid to that idea.
>
> For twenty-five years the problem continued to vex me while the skull remained in the laundry, disturbing my wife and children, and I felt the irony of Percy's sleeping in his box under the house more peacefully than I sometimes slept in my bed above him. But, at last, on 5 September 1970, I found my peace of mind. Three hours before dawn, while cruising along the New South Wales coast, due east of Crocodile Head, I rounded the yacht up into the wind, backed the headsail, and hove to. And there, under the glittering southern constellations, as we gently rose and fell on the long Pacific swell, I let the mortal remains of one of the Mikado's men slip from my hands, bound on his own uncharted journey to the bottom of the Pacific Ocean. (Hordern 2005: 166–67)

In the 1990s there was a noticeable cluster of cases of veterans trying to repatriate trophy skulls. This sudden upsurge seems to have coincided with the fiftieth anniversaries of important wartime milestones such as the Japanese attack on Pearl Harbor, and the public celebrations and commemorations of these events. At the same time, servicemen who had fought in the war had now reached old age, and in many cases wished to rid themselves of their war memorabilia, often because their families did not want to inherit these objects (see Harrison 2008b).

In April 1993, a Cincinnati newspaper columnist wrote of having recently been contacted by a 76-year-old man whom I will call G., who had served as an artillery gunner on Guadalcanal, where he lived for twenty-two months in a tent with eight other marines. One of the men went looking for souvenirs one day, and brought back a number of items, including the head of a Japanese soldier. The men boiled the head, breaking the bones behind the eyes to remove the brain, and kept the skull in their tent as a trophy. Later, the souvenir collector was sent to hospital in New Caledonia with malaria. When G. developed malaria a month later, and was also shipped to New Caledonia, his friends packed the skull in his seabag for him to return to its collector. In the event, the two never caught up with each other, and G. ended up with the skull at the end of the war:

> 'I put it in my basement on a shelf. My wife knew about it. Every so often, she says, "What are you going to do with that thing?" But time passed. After a while, I didn't give it a thought.'
>
> A couple years ago, [G.] starts seeing all these 50-year anniversary stories in magazines he gets from the Disabled American Veterans and the American Legion about Pearl Harbor, the U.S. Marine landing on Guadalcanal, the first raid on the Japanese mainland. This gets him thinking. He sounds like a man who's taking account of his life: 'Don't get me wrong – it's not like I'm remorseful. War is war. After the devastation the Japanese warlords ordered against our country in 1941, I can never forgive or forget Pearl Harbor.'
>
> 'On the other hand, if we're having celebrations here, maybe they're having celebrations in Japan. I'm thinking, this skull oughta go back to Japan. Anyhow, I'm at a point where I'd really like to get rid of it'. (Wecker 1993a)

G. handed the skull in a shopping bag to the columnist, who contacted various Japanese organizations, including the Japanese Consulate in Detroit, all of which declined the skull because of the lack of proof that it belonged to a Japanese soldier. A team of film makers preparing to fly to the Solomon Islands told the columnist of a group of Japanese priests who return there each year to recover remains of their war dead, and the columnist gave the skull to the film makers to take with them and return to the priests (Wecker 1993a, 1993b).

Do-it-yourself repatriation of war dead often turns out to be harder than veterans, and those who seek to help them, initially realize because the Japanese and U.S. authorities are clearly unwilling to receive these remains without strong proof of their origins. Such difficulties were encountered by a middle-aged Dallas man, M., who contacted a local newspaper columnist in 1993 for help with an unusual problem. During the Second World War, a relative of M. had served on Guadalcanal as a member of a platoon which captured a Japanese sniper. The platoon did not want the prisoner, and had nowhere to keep him, and shot him during the night:

'They cut his head off – the corpsman [medical personnel] cut it off,' [M.] said. 'I don't know, I guess they boiled it. Then the squad signed their names on it, and they put the head on a pole.' ... [M.] 's relative eventually got the skull. 'He decided he wanted it for a souvenir, and so he sent it home.'

With that introduction, [M.] took me to a back bedroom and removed from a plastic bag the skull of 'Sam,' as the squad had named him. 'Shot at Guadalcanal,' said the handlettered inscription across Sam's forehead. All over the skull were signatures, nicknames and hometowns. And just above the eyes, in letters almost faded from view: 'One Dead Jap.' ...

[M.] said his relative, who wishes to remain anonymous, is now filled with remorse. 'He's a different person now – religious and a family man.' Several years ago he asked [M.] to help him return Sam to Japan. [M.] made a few phone calls at the time and got nowhere. So Sam remained in a closet until recently, when [M.] decided to try again and called the newspaper.

'I think he's a soldier that rates a ticket back home,' [M.] said. 'He defended his country just as we defended ours. I think he deserves to be buried with Japanese honors'. (Blow 1993a; my parentheses)

The columnist posted the skull to the Japanese Consulate in Houston, which returned it a few weeks later it with a courteous but firm note of refusal. Later, on the advice of a well informed reader, he shipped it to the Tokyo address of the priest I mentioned earlier in connection with Iwo Jima, who had publicly undertaken to receive such relics if they were offered to him (Blow 1993a, 1993b).[6]

Perhaps for some veterans, returning from war with a trophy skull and putting it on show in their home had at first seemed no more aberrant than displaying a souvenir of some foreign holiday. But – for soldiers and military families of the mid twentieth century – as the years passed, and the enemy ceased to be viewed as semi-human, divisions grew within some veterans' families (and between some veterans' own older and younger selves) over whether these memorabilia belonged in the realm of things or persons. To some veterans in old age, or to their surviving relatives, their trophy eventually came to seem 'a soldier who rates a ticket home' – the 'last prisoner of World War II' as M. expressed it to the Dallas columnist (Blow 1993a) – an actual person wrongfully prevented for fifty years from returning to his own people. The skull was no longer an object which could be 'owned' as an article of display, like a sports trophy or commemorative dinner set. It had assumed the form of a reproachful human presence in the family, someone whose remains had been misappropriated for half a century, and to whom restitution was owed.

Historical Amnesia

To some of those who collected them, or to their inheritors, such objects eventually became unwanted and disturbing presences in the home. These transformations can shed light on a puzzling aspect of military trophy-taking. I have argued that powerful and compelling cultural schemas associating masculinity and hunting sometimes motivated soldiers in the Pacific War to use enemy remains as trophies. The question these practices pose, however, is not just why they occurred, but also why they seem to have disappeared so rapidly from public memory once the war ended.

In some situations we can clearly observe these processes of historical amnesia at work, especially when state institutions have become active participants in them. In 1999 a doctor in Brisbane, Australia, handed in to the local Coroner's Office a box containing some human skulls and other bones. He told the coroner that they were the remains of Japanese soldiers who had died during the Second World War in the Balikpapan region of Borneo, and that an Australian soldier had brought them home at the end of the war. In 1998, when this ex-serviceman was dying from a terminal illness as one of the doctor's patients, he asked the doctor to arrange an honourable burial for them. The coroner ordered forensic tests to be carried out on the bones, which appeared to come from at least three separate individuals, and the tests indicated that the remains were those of Asian men of the Second World War period. Following discussions with the Japanese Embassy, the bones were interred in 2000 in the Japanese military cemetery at Cowra in New South Wales, Australia's only Japanese war cemetery. According to a brief news item published on the preceding day, the ceremony was to have been a military funeral attended by the Japanese ambassador, local town officials, war veterans and Buddhist and Christian priests. The Australian and Japanese authorities seem to have regarded the affair as diplomatically sensitive and potentially embarrassing, and avoided drawing attention to it. The arrangements for the funeral were made confidentially, and the event seems to have passed off largely unnoticed by the public. Little publicity was given to it afterwards. The following day a brief notice in the local press referred to an 'interment service for the remains of unknown Japanese soldiers' at the Cowra cemetery and gave no further details. With deceptive simplicity, the grave itself is marked 'unknown Japanese soldier', and gives no hint of the highly unusual circumstances under which the remains came to be there (Adelaide Advertiser 2000; Canberra Times 2000; Miles 1999; Office of Australian War Graves 2010; Queensland State Coroner's Office 1999).

But in most cases it was not so much that there were organized efforts to censor the existence of these sorts of aberrant mementos after the war. Certainly they were distasteful, even potentially incriminating, but worse wartime atrocities are remembered and openly acknowledged. Acts of trophy-taking tended to be not just unpleasant or uncomfortable to remember but, in a certain sense, difficult to remember. To put it more precisely, they were difficult to transmit in the long term as shared memories.

This was due in part to their infrequency; some men who fought in the Pacific War never witnessed such behaviour or even heard of it (Fussell 1988: 45–46). But I suggest that this slippage from memory also reflected a lack of coherent cultural schemas for giving meaning to these objects beyond the immediate context of warmaking in which they were produced. Such processes of erasure, or partial erasure, are consistent with evidence from cognitive psychology which suggests that conceptual schemas exert a powerful influence on memory. In particular, memories tend to be altered retrospectively so as to bring them into conformity with previously established schemas. Those aspects of experience that cannot readily be made to conform in this way are likely to be recollected more poorly than those that can, and to be forgotten more rapidly (see, for instance, Brewer and Treyens 1981).

Human remains brought home from the war were objects which seemed to violate fundamental cultural distinctions between persons and things, and to have come into being through the alienation of the inalienable or the appropriation of the inappropriable. The occurrence of trophy-taking during the war diminished from public historical consciousness, I suggest, partly because this consciousness lacked categories with which it could assimilate such acts and the aberrant objects they generated.

At times, such processes of forgetting have had to overcome or circumvent some of the past's stubborn and intractable materialities. After their trophies were sent home, or brought home, many servicemen, or their families and descendants, seem eventually to have reached a point at which they felt they no longer knew what to do with these objects other than to try either to return them, or in some other way to dispose of them. Their aim was to lose the burden of remembering the dead, perhaps by passing these obligations on to someone else.

In relinquishing an object of this sort they sought to lay a part of their past to rest, in an act akin in some ways to exorcism. In most cases these families seem to have made no explicit reference to ghosts or the spirits of the dead. But there is a parallel with exorcism in the sense that in order to understand the meaning of their behaviour, we have to recognize social forgetting as an active, effortful process of erasure or expulsion of memory in certain respects, particularly when it must confront inconvenient and obstinate material residues of past actions (Forty and Küchler 1999; Harrison 2004). The disposal of an old war memento, its removal from the circle of kin, was an attempt also to let go of disquieting memories the object embodied. And each time this succeeded it was a small contributory step in the erasure of trophy-taking from collective memory.

Notes

1. There were well authenticated cases of Japanese units in the Philippines and New Guinea murdering prisoners of war, local villagers, and sometimes their own men, in order to consume the victims' flesh (Lewis and Steele 2001: 185ff; Tanaka 1996: 111–34). According to one Japanese soldier who served in New Guinea, towards the end of the war Allied soldiers were referred to as 'white pigs' and the local population as 'black pigs' (Tanaka 1996: 114). Most cases of cannibalism occurred near the end of the war when many Japanese units had been abandoned by their own high command and were starving. But not all cases were explicable in this way, as some occurred early in the war when the Japanese forces were still well supplied (Tanaka 1996: 128). In some ways, cannibalism among the Japanese forces in parts of the Pacific seems to have been the equivalent of human trophy-taking among the Allies as an extreme modality of appropriating and incorporating the enemy body. Both seem to have involved similar representations of the enemy as a game animal, and of combat as hunting (Tanaka 1996: 126).
2. Some of the autographs and part of the motto are visible in the photograph. General Hideki Tojo was the Japanese Prime Minister. For other discussions of this image, see Dower 1986: 65, 249; Fussell 1988; Lucaites and McDaniel 2004; Weingartner 1992: 57–58. The idea that enemy remains were fitting gifts for

departing soldiers to pledge to their loved ones seems to have transcended the racial and class divisions of the time. In Arkansas in 1942, the folklorist and musicologist Alan Lomax recorded a blues song in which a black soldier bids farewell to his wife and infant son, saying he has to 'fight for you, America and my boy.' He promises to send his son a 'Jap's skull' as a Christmas present and, in a later verse, a 'Jap's tooth' to ease the child's teething pains. 'Jap's skull' was until recently mistranscribed as 'Jap's girl' (O'Neal 2002). A gift of a skull to a child is puzzling, but a clue is provided by the two skulls, found in Tennessee, discussed by Bass (1983). With both, the foramen magnum had been enlarged, and one was known to have been used as a lantern at Halloween, the enlargement having been done to accommodate a light bulb. Japanese wartime press reports of U.S. children playing with the skulls of Japanese soldiers brought home by their fathers (Weingartner 1992: 61) may also have referred to the use of skulls as Halloween decorations. The Vietnamese trophy skull analysed by Willey and Leach (2003) had been used as a Halloween lantern by the family of the serviceman who collected it.

3. Soon after the publication of the *Life Magazine* photograph, and the news of Roosevelt's receipt of the letter opener, both were widely publicized in Japan (Hoyt 1986: 357–59) to portray Americans as deranged, primitive, racist and inhuman. The Japanese press also reported, in August 1944, the Japanese government requesting Spain to investigate American desecrations of Japanese dead (Weingartner 1992: 63). Weingartner points out the strong element of hypocrisy in these reactions, given the Japanese army's own atrocities (1992: 62). Hoyt (1986: 391) argues that what he calls the 'unthinking' practice of taking home bones as souvenirs was exploited so effectively by Japanese government propaganda that it contributed to a preference for death over surrender and occupation, shown, for example, in the mass civilian suicides on Saipan and Okinawa after the Allied landings.

4. In 1957, a man called Edward Gein was arrested in a small town in rural Wisconsin, on suspicion of having murdered a local woman. The police discovered in his house a large number of human body parts, including skulls. Gein appears to have murdered at least two women and, between 1947 and 1952, to have also exhumed the corpses of at least twelve women from local graveyards, including the body of his own mother.

In Gein's community, most men were keen and experienced hunters. Gein butchered the bodies of all his victims in a manner similar to the treatment of the carcasses of deer and other game, and had made masks and various other artefacts from their skin and other body parts. He had not served in the Second World War, but his behaviour may have been informed by underlying conceptual schemas related to hunting similar to those that had motivated wartime trophy-taking in the Pacific a few years earlier.

A visitor to his house once asked him why he had what appeared to be human faces hanging on his walls. Gein replied that they were shrunken heads from the 'South Seas' and had been sent to him by a cousin who had fought the Japanese in the Philippines (see Frasier 1996: 174). Though he seems to have made no claim that these were Japanese heads, the incident suggests that it would not have been thought abnormal for servicemen who fought in the Pacific to have sent human trophy objects

to their relatives, and that this could have been considered at the time a reasonable explanation for having human body parts on display in one's home.
5. I am grateful to Robin Hide (2010) for drawing this case to my attention.
6. For a trophy photograph of a Japanese skull displayed on a pole at Guadalcanal, see Fussell (1988: 47).

Chapter 14

The Colonial Manhunt and the Body Parts of Bandits: Hunting Schemas in British Counter-insurgency

The Hunter and the Colonial Soldier

In the mythology of nineteenth- and twentieth-century colonialism, the general features of which were common to both Europe and the United States, the white or European hunter was a figure of the frontier. He was imagined as inhabiting a borderland between civilization and savagery, and between humanity and the animal realm. He was a liminal figure, straddling these opposed worlds and possessing attributes of both.

On the one hand, the hunter was a harbinger of civilization, as Ritvo (1987: 254–55) puts it, the first type of European to venture into unexplored territories, an heroic pioneer at the vanguard of imperial conquest (see also Webster 2005: 119–48). On the other hand, the hunter had a deep intuitive understanding of his environment. He knew the habits of his prey and could anticipate their movements, having come to think and feel like the animals themselves (Mangan and McKenzie 2003: 106). He had empathy with them, a capacity even to become their double (Slotkin 1973). This convergence of identity between hunter and quarry, human and animal, was especially apparent in the hunting of man-eating predators such as the tiger. When two such closely matched antagonists pitted themselves against one another, the roles of hunter and prey could become indistinguishable.

In some respects, then, hunting appears in colonialism as a civilizing activity requiring distinctively human capacities of skill, enterprise, stratagem and intelligence. One of the most fundamental ways in which human beings can mark themselves off symbolically from animals is to formulate and carry out plans to kill them. But in other respects, hunting can also be viewed as a 'natural' activity, a mode of existence which humans share with many other creatures and which connects them to the rest of nature. From this perspective, the hunter is just another predator among predators, an animal among other wild animals.

His relationship with untamed nature is one of mastery gained through courage and superior intelligence. But it is also one of understanding, intimacy and partnership. He is required to be both like and unlike the animals he hunts, the equal and superior of his prey, living completely and immanently in their world and transcending it at the same time. In growing more experienced and successful, the hunter becomes increasingly similar to an animal, and increasingly distinct from one. He can survive in both worlds, and in colonialism his special role was to mediate between them on the ever-advancing frontiers of empire.

The Malaya Emergency

I suggested in the preceding chapter that trophy-taking practices may sometimes have emerged spontaneously among military personnel subscribing to these imageries of hunting. We can see further evidence of this in what appears to be the independent development of such practices in a number of the colonial powers, one of which was the U.K.

During the Malaya Emergency of 1948–60, a counter-insurgency war against the guerrilla army of the Malayan Communist Party (MCP), the British security forces seem to have drawn implicitly on conceptual imagery of this sort in developing their responses to the conflict. They attached paramount importance to intelligence in defeating the guerrillas, who were mostly ethnic Chinese. The Special Branch of the Malayan Police had the role of gathering and analysing this intelligence, and its overriding priority was to build up a picture of the structure and organization of the guerrilla forces. This involved identifying the guerrilla fighters, the villages they came from, and their kin and other social contacts. When a patrol killed an enemy, it was required to bring the body in for what were called 'identification purposes'. Once back at headquarters, the body would be photographed, fingerprinted and shown to informants who could identify it. Killing guerrillas, in other words, quite apart from any other military benefits it yielded, was understood as a vital method of gathering intelligence (Comber 2008).

Initially, the guerrilla fighters were called 'bandits', but it was felt that this term could tend to glamorize them, and they were henceforth officially designated as Communist Terrorists, or CTs. They were accused of mutilating the dead bodies of British soldiers, and there is evidence that they did sometimes carry out such acts (Carruthers 1995: 110–11; Gamble 2009: 157). They were also said to take no prisoners, and to torture and kill any British soldiers who fell into their hands. A police lieutenant newly arrived in Malaya recalls how he and the other new recruits were advised during their introductory pep talks always to save their last bullet for themselves. They were also told to cut off the heads and fingers of dead CTs for identification purposes if they were unable to carry their bodies out of the jungle (Andrew 1995: 46, 101). In the early stages of the campaign, patrols routinely brought in severed heads, hands and fingers if they found it too difficult to carry back the bodies whole.

Webster (2005) shows how Britain's colonial wars of the late nineteenth and early twentieth centuries tended to be represented in terms of extended metaphors of safari. This observation certainly applies to the Malaya emergency. In his study of the memoirs of military personnel who served there, Newsinger observes:

> Inevitably, a number of these accounts explicitly portray the conflict as a hunt for a particularly dangerous kind of game. For Richard Miers, the guerrillas definitely deserved

'the classification of Dangerous Game. They had lived for so long like hunted animals ... [they] had acquired an instinct for danger and a speed of reaction to it which were little short of uncanny'. While, according to M.C.A. Henniker, the methods used in hunting down the guerrillas were similar to those used when 'hunting man-eating tigers'. He observes somewhat nostalgically that young officers no longer go off hunting big game in Africa on leave because today they can take patrols out into the jungle 'and hunt the biggest game of all – man'. (1994: 58)

Patrolling in the jungle was accompanied by much of the paraphernalia of big game hunting, such as the use of 'native' trackers and Alsatian and mastiff tracker dogs (Scurr 1982: 38). The human trackers were usually Dyaks, from Borneo, men with a tradition of headhunting themselves, who would sometimes ask permission to behead the bodies with their long knives after a successful ambush (Andrew 1995: 119; Carruthers 1995: 115–16). When whole bodies were brought back to base, they were carried trussed up on poles, very much like big game killed on safari (Scurr 1982: 5).

A patrol might bring back captured enemy prisoners. It might also return with hands, fingers, heads or whole bodies. The official purpose of these tactics was not simply to kill or capture the enemy, or terrorize them with the spectacle of dismembered remains. Above all, it was to transform them, whether they happened to be alive or dead, into named persons with kin, friends, and other social connections. This was the real prize brought back from the jungle by the hunting party: not the captured enemy prisoner, or the dead enemy body, or body part, but the understandings that could be gleaned from these hard-won prizes. In this respect, soldiers were rather like naturalists collecting specimens in order to catalogue and label them and extend the frontiers of science. Or, given that the information they were seeking was essentially sociological, it was as if they were carrying out a violent form of ethnographic data collection. These practices reflect a conception of power as connected inextricably with knowledge. Control over something mysterious, secretive and unknown is gained only after it has been brought, perhaps violently, into the realm of the knowable – to be studied, categorized and at last displayed.

The practice of removing enemy heads 'for identification purposes' – either to confirm the identity of the dead person or, in the case of an unidentified body, to discover its identity – had a long history in British colonial warfare, as we saw earlier in the case of Bambata, the rebel Zulu leader killed by British forces in 1907. The military had always defended the practice as a crucial source of information and evidence. Of course, the display of a severed head does indeed at least confirm that a person is dead. But there was an equally long history of official embarrassment whenever such colonial practices came to public light in Britain. One such incident had occurred in Burma in 1931, during the Saya San rebellion, a peasant revolt against the British authorities, and was reported shortly afterwards in *The Times*.

> An official *communiqué* issued this afternoon states that after the Wetto engagement in Prome District early this month 22 rebel corpses were found, a number which the 27 Punjabis and three civil police, who composed the Government forces, found it impossible to bring in. The police inspector insisted that it was most important that the identity of the dead rebels should be established, and the officer in command allowed the civil police to cut off the heads of the corpses and take them to Prome. Identification of these heads

proved most valuable, for it was established that among the dead rebels were residents of six villages not previously suspected of being disaffected.

When the Commissioner of Prome District heard of this affair, the *communiqué* states, he issued an immediate order prohibiting the cutting off of heads for identification or any other purpose whatever. The Government of Burma has confirmed this order and an inquiry is now being held to fix the responsibility for what happened. (The Times 1931)

After the detachment returned to the police station, they displayed the heads publicly on a table, perhaps as a warning to the local population, and a number of unauthorized souvenir photographs were taken of these remains. One appeared soon afterwards in the British press, and another was later published in a rebel pamphlet. Although the enquiry cleared the officers concerned, the police were ordered in future either to bring in dead bodies whole, or photograph them on the spot where they were killed. If neither was possible, the evidence had to be abandoned (Mockaitis 1990: 39; see also Aung-Thwin 2003: 419; Ba Maw 1968: xv; Cady 1958: 316).

A very similar chain of events occurred a little over twenty years later in Malaya, when a series of photographs showing British servicemen posing with the severed heads of MCP guerrillas was published in *The Daily Worker*, a British communist newspaper, in April and May 1952. One showed a Royal Marine holding the heads of two guerrillas by the hair. One head is clearly that of a woman and the other is male. 'Other photos reproduced in British papers showed severed hands propped next to severed heads in mock salute and dead guerrillas stretched out like tiger skins in front of the units that had "bagged" them' (Mockaitis 1990: 53). In the ensuing controversy, the military again vigorously defended the practice of removing heads and hands in circumstances where it was the only means of identifying dead enemy fighters. But despite their protests, the government decided that the risks of handing the enemy a propaganda advantage outweighed the benefits, and had the practice banned later that year. Henceforth police and soldiers serving in Malaya were required to bring back enemy bodies entire (C. Allen 1990: 29; Carruthers 1995: 110, 126; Mockaitis 1990: 52–53).

Like soldiers in many conflicts before and since, British soldiers in Malaya sometimes took trophy photographs of themselves posing in groups with items such as flags and caps which they had captured from the enemy (Scurr 1982: 17). But since the late nineteenth century, British colonial police and army personnel had also sometimes taken commemorative group photographs of this sort in which they posed with the bodies of rebels and outlaws after successful military actions or, in some cases, after executions (for examples, see Morris 1996: 76, 77; Shillington 1985: plate following p. 238; Woodcock 1969: 29).

The photographs of marines posing with severed heads belonged to this well established genre. Such images were intended to commemorate not just the prowess of the servicemen who appeared in them, but rather the accomplishment of a certain kind of justice. Historically, the roots of such imagery probably lie in the figure of the public executioner holding up to the watching crowd the severed head of a rebel, or a king.[1] This act, a formal part of the British execution ritual, was not meant to demonstrate the martial valour of the executioner, of course, but the successful conclusion of a legal process. So it was too with these disturbing images from the jungles of Malaya. They were not meant simply to affirm the prowess of the soldiers who appeared in them but, much more importantly, the power of the state which they served.

Taking such personal trophy photographs was forbidden, but it recurred because it grew organically from official military policies and routines, and shared many of the same fundamental premises or, rather, was driven by the same underlying metaphors. Fundamental to the conception of the counter-insurgency operations in Malaya and, as we will shortly see, in Kenya, was the archetypal image of the hunt. The enemy was envisaged, implicitly or explicitly, as a sort of dangerous rogue animal that could be caught and killed only by means of stratagem based on careful and thorough study of its nature and habits.

In Malaya, the use of enemy remains as personal trophy objects was not restricted to security forces personnel. A military pilot who served in the mid 1950s recalls how at the end of a day's flying he would sometimes land at remote plantations and stay overnight with the managers.

> These hardy men lived a lonely life behind barbed wire, a gun always within reach, and were invariably pleased to see friendly faces. Isolation bred eccentricities and one evening, after supper with the manager of a particularly isolated plantation, I noticed an extraordinary ornament on an aspidistra stand in the corner of the room. There, highly polished and gleaming white, with a light inside so it shone like a halloween lantern, was a skull. It had a bullet hole in the centre of the forehead. I asked about it, unsure whether the brandy had affected my vision, and was told it was the skull of a terrorist who had been killed outside the manager's house, buried and later exhumed for display. (Perkins 1988: 57)

Some objects of this sort were brought back to Britain. One of the British regiments that fought in Malaya has a museum, in which it displays mementos of its history and of the many campaigns in which it has served. One of the display cases is concerned with mementos of the Malaya campaign. It contains a human cranium along with many other objects – a rifle, examples of jungle uniform, and captured objects such as MCP flags. The cranium was brought back as a souvenir of that campaign. The display caption describes it as: 'Skull, found in a Communist terrorist camp'. It is a cranium without a lower jaw, lacks most of the teeth and is heavily stained brown, indicating that it had probably been exposed to the elements for a considerable time before it was found. Perhaps it was taken from a shallow grave or found lying on the surface. In the middle of the frontal bone a five-pointed star has been engraved through the layer of staining, exposing the white bone below, and this exposed bone has then been stained with a red pigment. The caps worn by MCP guerrillas had a communist red star design on the front, and these caps were themselves popular trophies among British servicemen in Malaya. The red star design incised on the skull is very obviously meant to represent this badge. Engraved into the bone just where the badge would be, the star is intended to signify that this was the skull of a MCP fighter.[2]

Museums, it seems, are settings which continue to be able to make the exhibition of human remains seem normal and acceptable no matter what the purpose of the display, or how questionable the origins of the remains. To keep a human skull in a museum collection is to frame it as a contribution to knowledge, just as displays of severed heads on tables were contributions to the gathering of vital intelligence. Both cases suggest an assumption that the collection and display of human body parts are justifiable if they can be made to appear to have been carried out in the service of reason.

The Kenya Emergency

During much of the period of the Malaya Emergency, the British also fought a counter-insurgency war in Kenya, against an anti-colonial movement they called Mau Mau. This movement drew its members mostly from among the Kikuyu people. The Kenya Emergency, as the British called it, lasted from 1952 to 1960.

As a political ideology, Mau Mau was viewed by white settlers in Kenya as a sort of transmissible mental illness that caused young Africans to revert to savagery. It was said to turn them into brutal animals driven by blood lust, 'sub-human creatures without hope and with death as their only deliverance' (D. Anderson 2005: 177, 281; see also Edgerton 1990: 142–43).

Many of the tactics employed against the Mau Mau reminded British soldiers of hunting. One soldier recalled large-scale sweeps through open country that were 'rather like a pheasant shoot' (C. Allen 1990: 131). When they were successful, operations such as these were described as resulting in a 'bag' of rebels (Edgerton 1990: 99). The forest camps of Mau Mau fighters were spoken of as secret 'lairs' to which these elusive enemies had to be 'tracked' (Blaxland 1971: 276).

White settlers sometimes engaged professional game hunters to stalk and kill Mau Mau (Edgerton 1990: 151). George Adamson, a noted white hunter and game-park warden in Kenya, was recruited by the police and army to use his hunting and tracking skills to help in the campaign. In 1953 he recorded in his diary one such hunting foray in pursuit of a Mau Mau 'gang'.

> Started off this morning with full safari. Found the gang had headed SE. Followed up. Off saddled and away again about 3.00 pm. Found another boma recently vacated, part of freshly killed ox and a little posho (maize flour). Hard ground, difficult spooring .... Sent 5 men along the west side of the stream to look for tracks, while the main safari took the eastern side .... After about 2 miles Kikango killed a Mau Mau. (Quoted in Webster 2005: 125–26)

To many army officers, too, fighting the Mau Mau seemed like a superior, exciting form of hunting. A military intelligence officer in Kenya recalled: 'one cannot savour the full thrill of the chase until one hunts something which is capable of retaliation' (quoted in Webster 2005: 126).

It was perhaps attitudes such as this that gave rise to one of the most remarkable tactical innovations of the counter-insurgency in Kenya: namely, the use of what were called pseudo-gangs by the Special Branch of the Kenya Police. These were units made up of Kikuyu loyalists and ex-Mau Mau disguised as insurgents and led by white officers with blackened faces. Their role was to penetrate the Mau Mau organization, gather intelligence and, in the later stages of the campaign, also to kill or capture guerrillas.

> When operating with the pseudos, the European officers used potassium permanganate solution to give their skin the right colour. Eventually, as the Mau Mau learned of the existence of these pseudo gangs, it was often necessary for European officers to paint

their entire bodies, in case a shirt was suddenly jerked up to look for white skin. A weaker potassium permanganate solution was also used to give their eyes the proper yellow coloration. The hair was normally the most obvious giveaway for white pseudos and though they tried using floppy hats, eventually many used wigs, often obtained from the hair of dead terrorists. So they would not give away their group, Europeans had to learn to squat, eat, take snuff, and in general act as genuine Mau Mau. To get the proper look and smell they wore captured Mau Mau clothing, and did not wash. Even so, each white in a pseudo group had a cover man or bodyguard, whose primary job was to draw attention away from him. (L. Thompson 1988: 99)

Perhaps surprisingly, this deadly mimesis of hunter and quarry turned out to be highly effective, and resulted in many successes, including the capture of the Mau Mau leader Dedan Kimathi in 1956 (Edgerton 1990: 102). It is perhaps an indication of the power of the mythology of the white hunter at the time that some colonial officers were willing to volunteer for operations of this sort, and indeed that such a strategy was deemed practicable in the first place.

The use of sporting and hunting imagery by the Kenyan authorities to report operations against the Mau Mau was so pervasive that it led to many criticisms both in Britain and internationally. A constant problem for the Colonial Office in London was the need to eliminate such language from the press releases emanating from Kenyan officialdom (Carruthers 1995: 152). A Labour Party Member of Parliament complained in 1954 that the Devonshire regiment's accounts of its role in Kenya read 'as though it were a hunt for game' rather than a conflict between human opponents (Carruthers 1995: 152; Webster 2005: 126). As an example, he pointed to the way the regiment's commanding officer had offered his men a reward of £5 for the first kill during some operations, so as to encourage rivalry between units when they were 'Mau Mau hunting' (Blaxland 1971: 276, 279).

Evidence such as this seemed to confirm allegations made during the trial in 1953 of Captain Gerald Griffiths, a local farmer and officer in the King's African Rifles, who had been court-martialled for murdering Africans. He had testified that his company kept in its headquarters a scoreboard of kills and captures, and that soldiers received a reward of £5 for each insurgent they killed (Carruthers 1995: 174; Clayton 1984: 41; Edgerton 1990: 169; Webster 2005: 121).

The resulting headlines in the British press provoked a parliamentary enquiry. Though the enquiry exonerated the British troops, the 'league tables', scoreboards, cash prizes and other overt evidence of 'kill competitions' disappeared (Blaxland 1971: 281; Edgerton 1990: 170–71; Mockaitis 1990: 50).

Another practice which came to light early in the insurgency was the collection of the hands of dead insurgents (Bennett 2006: 62–63). This was done ostensibly for identification purposes, as the Criminal Records Office in Nairobi held fingerprint records of nearly half a million Kenyans by the end of 1953 (Bennett 2006: 63). But another purpose – in some cases perhaps the only purpose – seems to have been to confirm kills and claim the bounty (D. Anderson 2005: 258). In effect, the practice of amputating the hands of dead guerrillas in order to fingerprint them, and of offering rewards for kills, though perhaps often unconnected, when taken together could make it appear that monetary payments had sometimes been paid to soldiers for bringing severed limbs back from military operations. Directives were issued forbidding the practice of removing hands, and orders given for the general issue of fingerprinting equipment (Bennett 2006: 68; Carruthers 1995: 174; Clayton 1984: 42; Edgerton 1990: 160, 166). But the removal of hands still continued, at least among units recruited from local whites, and the authorities could not always impose their own regulations on their personnel in the field (Bennett 2006: 74). The rank and file of the security forces had developed their own unofficial practices and strongly resisted abandoning them. These routines, deeply rooted in the conceptual imagery of hunting, were presumably fundamental to the ways in which these men understood their own role in the conflict.

The Kenya security forces were not alone in engaging in such behaviour towards Africans. In 1961 in the Congo, following the murder in custody of the Prime Minister, Patrice Lumumba, a Belgian police chief was given the task of disposing of the body by destroying it with acid. During an interview in 1999, this officer, by then retired and living in Belgium, showed journalists what he claimed were two of Lumumba's teeth and hinted that he had also kept a finger-bone (De Witte 2001: xviii, 140–43, 201).

During the Mau Mau rebellion, the British often sought to portray their approach to dealing with the insurgents as relatively humane and civilized, by contrast to the brutal methods, including the removal of hands, widely alleged at the time to be employed by the Belgians in the Congo (Bennett 2006: 74). But the recurring problem the British authorities faced lay in the way that their own counter-insurgency strategies were deeply embedded in conceptual metaphors of hunting. The rank and file of the security forces, particularly those from the local white settler community in Kenya, tended to pursue the implications of this imagery much further than their superiors in London found tolerable. In particular, they tended to take the implication that their enemies were animals to extremes that flouted the law and risked the loss of public support in Britain and overseas. Personnel at all levels of the counter-insurgency operation tended to understand the conflict broadly in terms of the same fundamental, conceptual schemas, but the higher and lower levels often disputed the limits and applications of these ideas in practice.

Conclusion

Britain was involved in a number of wars of decolonization in the middle of the twentieth century, in Palestine, Cyprus, Aden and Northern Ireland among others. But there is evidence of trophy-taking only in the Kenya and Malayan Emergencies.

These were the only two of these conflicts fought in remote locations in jungle and forest, and these conditions perhaps inevitably gave rise to military tactics with some overt resemblances to big game hunting. Certainly, the semi-official practice of removing heads and hands for identification purposes would have been impossible to justify in any other circumstances than these.

However, trophy-taking was only one of the abuses that appear to have occurred only in these two conflicts.

> When Mau Mau were killed in the reserves, their bodies were lined up for public display. Sometimes they were photographed with their dead eyes staring into the lens of the camera. Afterwards the dead were often kicked, spat at, urinated on, and mutilated. When

a prominent Mau Mau officer was killed, his body might be left on public display for days. White Kenya Police Reserve brought the body of General Nyoro back to the reserve and displayed it to the inhabitants. The police, who wanted to leave no doubt that his death was ignominious, kept his body on display for 48 hours as it swelled in the heat and dogs nibbled at it. (Edgerton 1990: 170)

Another factor contributing to behaviour of this sort was undoubtedly race. In the racial orderings current in British society at the time, Africans and Malay Chinese appeared more different and distant than Arabs, Greeks or Irish. It was as if these perceptions of increasing racial distance were accompanied by an increasing preoccupation with the sheer physicality or corporeality of other peoples. On the one hand, it seems sometimes to have been felt to be allowable in conflicts against racially distant enemies to take exemplary measures intended to reduce them, as it were, to pure body. At the same time, such measures were assumed to be unnecessary with more civilized opponents. One colonial officer said of the Mau Mau that they were 'hard men and need hard methods' (Edgerton 1990: 202). To him, these enemies were, like animals, essentially corporeal in their nature and would therefore respond only to harsh and brutal tactics.

Notes

1. See, for instance, the anonymous engraving, dated c.1649, of the execution of Charles I, currently held in the National Portrait Gallery, London (NPG D1306).
2. I am grateful to Erik Lyman (2008) for bringing this museum display to my attention.

Chapter 15

Kinship and the Enemy Body in the Vietnam War

> A gook skull was not a human skull but a tool with which to laugh at death.
> (Dougherty 1992: 58)

Trophies

During their countries' military involvement in Vietnam from 1960 to 1975, servicemen in the forces of the United States and their allies were sometimes alleged to have mutilated the enemy dead for 'trophies' such as ears and fingers. General Westmoreland, the commander of the United States forces in Vietnam, sent a memorandum to his officers in 1967 describing such behaviour as 'subhuman' and ordering stern measures to prevent it. Some servicemen were later court-martialled for offences of this sort (MacPherson 2002: 505).

Many ordinary servicemen shared Westmoreland's views. David Christian describes how he and his platoon rejected a soldier who had applied to join them, because he was reputed to have cut off the head of a North Vietnamese soldier, cleaned and polished the skull, and kept it as a souvenir. When the soldier was killed a few days after his unsuccessful attempt to join the platoon, Christian felt that his death may perhaps have been divine retribution (Christian and Hoffer 1990: 54).

Another U.S. soldier, Robert Gates, describes how he once entered a hamlet in South Vietnam and found the skeleton of someone, perhaps a minor government official, whose body appeared to have been impaled on a stake by the Viet Cong and then left to decay. The villagers had been too frightened to remove the remains. To show that he was not intimated, Gates took the skull, saying to himself, 'It is mine now'. He painted it red and kept it as a souvenir. Later, he was wounded and hospitalized. When he returned to his quarters to collect his belongings before leaving for the United States, his sergeant came to see him and told him: 'You're not taking it home with you'. Gates took the skull out of his bag and handed it over. They both recognized that it would have been unacceptable to return from Vietnam with such an object in his possession (Sauro 2006: 142, 193, 198, 202).

A former military lawyer in Vietnam, interviewed in 2000, described a case in which he had defended a sergeant accused of ordering one of his men to remove the head from the corpse of an enemy soldier. The sergeant was further accused of having then boiled the head in a pot of water in order to use the skull as an ornament on his armoured vehicle. This had occurred three weeks after the Tet offensive of January and February 1968 in which the North Vietnamese army and Viet Cong had suffered heavy casualties. There were

> NVA [North Vietnamese army] and VC [Viet Cong] bodies all over the place, you know, a lot of kills. My client is accused of telling an enlisted guy to go out in the field, chop off the head of a dead body, because he wants to clean up the head and put the skull on his track. So, the enlisted guy cuts off the head of a dead body. The body's been out there 3 weeks, its decomposing. He brings the head back. The head is then boiled in a pot of water. There are pictures of my client standing next to the pot of water, and he boils the head and he cleans off the skull. So, my guy is a sergeant E7 with 20 years of service and he's charged with violating MACV [Military Assistance Command, Vietnam] directives by ordering the soldier to chop off the head and by boiling the head in a pot of water, and the government has, well, from a defense stand point the evidence is awful. Apparently, there was a soldier who was going home, so the soldier's out in the field taking motion pictures and in the beginning of the picture he takes a picture of this body with the face up and at the end of this reel of film, you have this head in this pot of water with my client stewing, so obviously an alibi is no defense. He was there, and we had to figure out how to defend that case.... The government had all these pictures and I had to get these pictures, I mean, I had to keep these pictures out of evidence because that would inflame the jury, so the theory was that what we do is we pleaded guilty to the boiling the head part, and not guilty to the part about the ordering the soldier to do it, and fortunately because of the way we pleaded the pictures weren't necessary, so we kept the pictures out. He got convicted of the whole thing and he got ... a one grade bust and a fine of not much money, and he was very pleased and so was I because he was facing the loss of a 20 year career. That was one of those unique Vietnam type cases. (Maxner 2000)

Such behaviour towards the enemy dead had its roots in strongly racialized attitudes towards the Vietnamese. In their more extreme forms, these attitudes could give rise to representations of the enemy as a sort of animal (see, for instance, Knightley 2004: 409–41). One symptom of this denial of full humanness to the enemy was the pervasiveness of hunting imagery to describe the fighting, and portrayals of the enemy as a type of quarry, whose remains could be kept for display like the trophy heads or skulls of game animals after they had been killed (Christian and Heffer 1990: 56; Grossman 2009: 238; Sallah and Weiss 2006; D.L. Smith 2007: 201).

Sociable Skulls

However, men who acquired a reputation for collecting body parts such as ears and fingers merely as private fetishes or keepsakes seem often to have been viewed as misfits and liabilities to their own side (see, for examples, MacPherson 2002: 481–85, 504–509). Nevertheless, these were clearly social practices rather than symptoms of individual pathology, because they were partly a product of the military's own emphasis upon 'body count' as its key metric of success throughout the war (MacPherson 2002: 505).

On the other hand, many servicemen seem to have drawn a distinction between the appropriation of enemy body parts for motives such as personal ostentation, or private bitterness towards the enemy, and other, more positively social uses of the enemy body. In fact, some parts of the enemy body seem to have been viewed as more acceptable to take than others, specifically because they appeared more amenable and appropriate to these social uses. This seems to have been the case with skulls in some circumstances. These were, for instance, sometimes bestowed as gifts. George Smith Patton, the son of the famous Second World War general of the same name, commanded the 11th Armored Cavalry Regiment in Vietnam. During his farewell party in April 1969, the men who had served under his command presented him with a number of farewell gifts, one of which was the skull of a Viet Cong insurgent. It had been mounted on a base and had a bullet hole above one eye. In a letter to his commanding officer following criticism of this incident in the press, Patton explained:

> The skull, an old one, obviously retrieved from the jungle, was presented to me on the same evening…. On a base beneath it was inscribed, 'We found this bastard and piled on.' The slogan, 'Find the Bastards and Pile On,' was the regiment's motto prior to my arrival at the unit in July of 1968. (Quoted in Sobel 1997: 131)

The skull was an acceptable gift, so he implied, because it was just an 'old' one, and had been offered to him not to dishonour the enemy but to affirm ties of sentiment and loyalty between his men and himself.

Another socially approved use to which soldiers could put enemy remains was to assimilate them into their units in such a way as to affirm or enhance the group's identity. In 1970, a war correspondent interviewed a marine reconnaissance patrolman who had dug up the skull of a Viet Cong fighter. He had had his companions autograph the skull, and then sent it home to his family.

> It was last Christmas that Denny got his skull. For a while, before that, the ears of enemy soldiers were trophies, but commanders ordered an end to that. Then gold teeth became war prizes but, Denny recalls, 'they were pretty hard to come by.'
> His patrol had come across a large patch of freshly dug dirt. A command post, contacted by radio, gave instructions to dig – and several caskets holding Viet Cong dead were bared. That's where the skull came from. And Denny's patrol had matched competing U.S. patrol teams that had brought back skulls from the bush. (Gammack 1979: 96)

The serviceman expressed some regret at having sent the skull home. But he also seemed to feel that the other members of his unit had given him their authorization or approval. By signing their names on it, he and his companions had used the skull to commemorate their ties with one another and so, as it were, had socialized the skull. To keep an object of this sort could be excused or tolerated because it signified fidelity and commitment among the members of a team, rather than some merely private antipathy towards the enemy.

When skulls were used in this way by small, relatively intimate and low-level groups such as platoons or the crews of tanks or other vehicles, these groups usually referred to them as 'mascots' (see, for instance, Dougherty 1992: 58). The crew of one armoured personnel carrier in the 5th Infantry Division in 1970 christened their vehicle 'Easy Rider' and painted this name on its side. They also possessed a skull which they referred to as their vehicle's mascot. They named it 'Easy', as if it were the vehicle's human personification (Kethcart n.d.).

In such units, men often seem to have regarded their ties with one another as highly exclusive ones. To them, the possession of a skull mascot was a symbolic means of excluding outsiders, just as much as an affirmation of their unit's internal cohesion. Skull mascots were often displayed as territorial markers, to warn other units to stay away. A member of the Air Cavalry stationed at the large military base at Chu Lai in the late 1960s recalls how his platoon

> made it clear to passing rear echelon types that our tents were off limits to them. Someone placed a skull with a Viet Cong bush hat at the entrance to our tent street. That seemed to frighten them a bit. The Marine MPs [military police] complained that the skull wasn't sanitary, but it stayed in place. (Brennan 1985: 156)

The purpose of exhibiting the skull was not to intimidate the enemy. Indeed, the display was not directed at the enemy at all. Its purpose was to define the platoon's area of the base as private and warn outsiders among their own armed forces to keep out.

A skull used in this way by a small, closely knit group might acquire an affectionate personal name. It might be made to wear a cap or helmet belonging to the enemy, or to the soldiers' own side. In this way, an anonymous dead enemy was turned into a sort of person. He became an individual, of a humorous kind, to whom mock solicitude and friendship could be shown – for instance, by placing a cigar or cigarette in his mouth.[1]

Units sometimes used skull mascots in commemorating their 'kills' and other military successes. Early in their tour of duty in Vietnam, the members of one Australian platoon erected a scoreboard at the entrance to their quarters, giving a tally of the kills they had achieved. Above the sign they placed a skull wearing an enemy helmet. When their own casualties started to mount, the sign was torn down and the skull buried (Hall 2000: 200).

A U.S. serviceman recalls revisiting in September 1969 a reconnaissance platoon which he had seen on an earlier visit keeping a skull as a sort of decoration on its radio. The skull had ribbons attached to it, each commemorating an action in which the platoon had served.

> At that time the platoon leader's radio had been adorned with a gleaming white skull which had many colored ribbons attached to the forehead. Each piece of cloth had a date and a number, chronicling the date and body count of each contact over the past year.
>
> When I asked about the skull, [the Company Commander] told me it had 'been found in the paddies' long before we came north. He said the platoon no longer carried the trophy after a picture of it had appeared in *Stars and Stripes*. It seemed that several of the high ranking folk in Saigon had objected to the platoon's method of maintaining historical records. [He] added that the skull 'may have been buried in the jungle or sent home by one of the troops.' He laughed, saying he did not want to know the method of disposition. (Lanning 2007: 244)

Most skulls used in this way had simply been found, and were rarely the remains of people the unit had killed. To pick up an old skull and use it as a mascot was undoubtedly a more acceptable practice than severing body parts from the corpse of someone newly killed. Such views seem to have been shared by much of the general public at the time. In December 1966, the magazine *Jet*, a publication aimed at an African American readership, published a photograph showing a black U.S. soldier in Vietnam holding a human skull on a stick. The skull, which appears to have a hole below one eye, wears a cap and has a cigar in its jaws.

> **War mascot**: In South Vietnam, Cpl. Shirly Crain, 24, of Waco, Tex., dug up this Viet Cong skull, stuck an old Army cap on it, a cigar in its mouth, christened it 'George,' and takes the grim companion everywhere he goes. Crain is in the 25th Infantry Division. (Jet Magazine 1966)

Of course, the motif of a human skull or death's head is also a common military emblem, and the possession of an actual skull as a mascot could be taken to signify successful kills, or aggression against the enemy, in some abstract sense. But it also symbolized the taming or domestication of a particular enemy, his incorporation into the group in a dependent capacity. Although he may not have been killed by the soldiers who came into possession of his skull, he had been in a sense reborn or revivified by them, taking on a second life in an appropriated form. To display an enemy skull as a mascot demonstrated a power not so much to destroy the enemy as to bring him back to life again afterwards in a sociable and harmless form.

Animals and Children as Military Mascots

In some armed forces it is traditional for regiments or other units to keep an animal such as a goat or dog as a mascot. The animal mascot plays an important ceremonial role, and is treated as an honorary member of the unit. It has a uniform and an official rank, and when it dies it is buried with military honours (see, for instance, Jobson 2009: 96–98).

In the Vietnam War many U.S. and allied military units had official or unofficial animal mascots. One, for example, kept a tame monkey called Mac Na Hong, with a uniform and the rank of second lieutenant (Rast 2000: 48). In addition to these official mascots, soldiers also often adopted animals such stray dogs as pets.

A military doctor who served in Vietnam describes how the base at which he was stationed was at times almost overrun with animals, and the number of pets often become a serious problem. Besides the two dogs which were official mascots, the base 'was literally crawling with pet pythons, monkeys, dogs' and other creatures. At one stage, these had included a tiger (eventually removed after it injured someone) and an 'ocelot', which turned out to be a domestic cat on which spots had been painted by the market trader from whom it had been bought (Bartecchi 2006: 165).

In addition to animals, some units also unofficially adopted Vietnamese children. Local children, in some cases disabled or orphaned, attached themselves to a group of soldiers, carrying out errands and odd jobs for them in return for food and cigarettes. Some acquired a semi-official position in the unit, a role often described as that of mascot (Burcham and Burcham 2007: 153–54; Hunt 1967; R. West 1995: 65).

Again, such practices seem to have a long history. A famous case occurred in the First World War, when a squadron of the Australian Flying Corps serving in France adopted an eight-year-old local orphan as their mascot. They gave him the rank of acting corporal and had a special uniform made for him. At the end of the war, they smuggled him, at one stage hidden in a sack, back to Australia where one of the servicemen later formally adopted him (Hill 2002).

Often in such cases the animal or child is described as having attached itself to a particular soldier, or to a group of soldiers, of its own accord (see, for instance, F.M. Bell 1917: 139). In other words, the orphan or animal appears to choose its benefactors, rather than the converse. In some cases, soldiers have regarded the stray that attaches itself to them unexpectedly and unbidden in this way as in some sense 'lucky', or a good omen.

In civilian life, the social groups that possess children and pets are, of course, families. By incorporating a pet animal or a child, the members of a military unit thereby assimilate themselves conceptually to a familial group. A marked feature of military organizations is strong cohesion within small, 'primary', face-to-face groups (Janowitz and Shils 1975; A. King 2006; Siebold 2007). In seeking to give expression to this intense sense of interdependence, men of the same unit may draw upon cultural images of the family, and represent their relations with each other as kin-like.

Their relationship with the child or animal mascot is modelled, at least partially, on parenthood. It is a reciprocity in which soldiers, in adopting a dependent animal or child to whom they give nurture and care, connect themselves together as a group of fictive co-parents, while the child or animal mascot may in return be understood as bringing them some diffuse benefit such as good luck.

The appropriation of enemy skulls for use as mascots by some military units in the Vietnam War was, I suggest, modelled on the adoption of animals and local children, and was an extension of these more orthodox and socially acceptable practices. In being appropriated, the enemy skull was equated in some respects with a child or pet. Children, pet animals and enemy skulls, when attached to a military unit, had the common feature that they were attached as partial or incomplete persons, subordinate and dependent on the unit for their existence, like a child within a family. In establishing social relationships with a skull, or a pet or child, the members of the unit were attempting to represent their relations with each other as like those of kinship.

Familiarizing Predation

United States and Australian soldiers serving in Vietnam were by no means the only social groups to have equated animals, foreign children and the bodily remains of their enemies with each other. Amazonian Indians, for instance, hunted animals for food, and also captured and tamed them to keep as pets, and these were the two complementary modes in which they assimilated wild animals into their society (Erikson 2005).

Fausto (1999) has described this relationship of Amazonian communities to their environment as one of familiarizing predation. Hunting and killing wild animals and catching them to tame as pets both ultimately had the same purpose: to harness the powers these wild creatures were understood to embody and channel them into the regeneration of the kin group. Warfare, too, was another mode of familiarizing predation. Enemy body parts taken as war trophies, captive and abducted children, and wild animals caught and domesticated as pets, all belonged to a single, named, cultural category. They were equated with each other in this way because they were understood to represent different forms in which the kinship community could appropriate the potentially or actually hostile forces of the wild into its own reproduction. This took place through a process Fausto calls 'adoptive filiation', a relationship modelled on that of a parent to an adopted child, or of a pet owner to an animal he has captured in the forest, brought home and tamed.

The explanation for these ethnographic parallels between soldiers serving in Vietnam, and Amazonian societies, is not hard to find. Both groups conceived of their warfare activities as closely related to hunting and, indeed, as modelled on it. To represent an enemy as, metaphorically speaking, a creature of the jungle or forest, a sort of denizen of the wild, implies two alternative modes of behaviour towards him. One can try either to kill or to domesticate him. He can be considered either as prey or as a potential pet. In collecting and displaying an enemy skull, a group of soldiers suggested that they had succeeded at both simultaneously. Certainly, at one level, the skull represented an enemy who had been killed. But at another it represented an enemy whom they had made companionable and tame, adopting him into their group in a semi-infantilized form.

The Assault Helicopter Company and Mother Missile

An animal, a foreign child or an enemy skull might be incorporated into a military unit as a mascot, a quasi-member whose role was to signify the group or symbolize its identity. The animal, child or skull could serve in this way precisely because it came from outside the group itself. It belonged to the category of the remote other, and could provide a shared reference point for the members of the unit because its origins were equally distant from all of them.

The use of skulls as mascots suggests that the relationship with the enemy body was sometimes conceptualized in terms of metaphors of parenthood or adoptive filiation. In treating an enemy body part as if it were similar in some respects to a child, men framed their own relations with each other as similar to those of adoptive co-parenthood.

There was another, related way in which kin-like relations could be established within a military unit through the medium of the enemy body and this, for reasons I explore later, seems distinctive to the Vietnam War. In this pattern, the metaphorical parent-child relationship between a group and its mascot was reversed. The enemy body part was represented as a sort of collective parent figure, with the group as its children. The members of a military unit represented themselves as having come to share with each other the bodily substance of the enemy, with this acquired consubstantiality connecting them in a kin-like bond modelled on siblingship.

My first example of this pattern concerns an assault helicopter company stationed at the military base at Chu Lai in the late 1960s and early 1970s. The company was divided into several platoons with different functions. Some, known as the lift platoons, carried cargo and personnel. But one platoon flew helicopter gunships, and was the elite group within the company because its role was considered to require higher levels of skill and motivation. The members of the gunship platoon called themselves the Missiles.[2] Their helicopters were painted with a distinctive emblem, a stylized skull resembling a frontal view of a helicopter gunship.

In the autumn of 1969 they came into possession of an actual human skull when one of their pilots landed at a remote military outpost. The garrison there had left the body of an enemy soldier to decay on the perimeter wire to intimidate (or as one informant put it, to 'dare') the North Vietnamese. The pilot took the skull, which had a bullet hole in the top, and some remaining skin, brought it back to his base and boiled it to clean it.

The platoon gave the skull the name Mother Missile, and it became their mascot. They had placed a sign bearing the platoon's emblem on the outside of the building which served as their quarters, and they displayed the skull there too, on a shelf. In late 1970, the skull was banned by their commanding officer, and thereafter they kept it hidden, at least when senior officers were around.

On one occasion some members of the platoon were drinking on the porch of their quarters when one of them had the idea of using the skull as a drinking vessel, and this soon became part of an initiation ceremony for new members. Whenever the gunship platoon needed a new member, they would recruit him from the company's lift platoons. They would meet informally and choose someone from the transport platoons whom they felt had the necessary qualities to be promoted in this way. As part of his initiation, the recruit would have to drink an alcoholic concoction through the bullet-hole in the top of the skull. The skull had to be held in a special way, upside-down over the initiate's head, with the forefingers blocking the eye sockets to prevent it from leaking, and the little fingers covering the bullet-hole. Later, the eye sockets seem to have been filled in and black diamonds painted to suggest eyes. One member of the lift platoons who examined the skull when it was hidden in a friend's refrigerator recalls that it was green inside and had a foul smell. But no-one was ever known to have refused to drink from it, though one former member of the gunship platoon remembers having an unpleasant taste in his mouth the next day (Wells 2010; Zipperer 2010).[3]

Although the skull was that of a man, it was called Mother Missile, and represented as female, because the way in which the men drank from it – through the bullet hole in the top – was clearly meant to suggest the idea of the breastfeeding of an infant. This symbolism of aggressive nurture, or of male appropriation of the maternal or reproductive capacities of women, seems to occur widely in male initiation ceremonies, including those of Melanesia. In all these cases, men appear to be trying to create a universe of kinship and reproduction that is independent of women and exclusively male (M.R. Allen 1967; Dundes 1976). The Missiles, too, spoke of themselves as an exclusive and elite 'brotherhood'. And what made them brothers was that they, in contrast to the other members of their company and all other outsiders, were, in a sense, sons of a skull mother, or had become so by accepting nurture from this skull of a male enemy transfigured into a maternal symbol.

One of the platoon members used to wear a tooth from the skull as an amulet on a string around his neck. Currently, some forty years later, he still has this tooth, and wears it on a gold chain to his unit's reunions. It is not a 'trophy' in the normal sense of a symbol of some personal achievement or military prowess. He makes no pretence to have killed the soldier whose tooth it was. Rather, it is an expression of his kinship with the other men in his platoon, the Missiles Brotherhood. Evidently this relationship, like siblingship proper, is for him a permanent and unalterable one.

Grayhorse Cavalry Troop

The Missiles did not acquire the skull with the intention of using it as a drinking vessel or creating an initiation ceremony. The ritual developed later and, it seems, quite spontaneously. A similar process of ritualization occurred in another helicopter unit, an air cavalry troop which I will call Grayhorse.

At some point during 1968, the troop had started to suspect that the local Vietnamese maids who cleaned their quarters were stealing soft drinks and other small items from their lockers and refrigerators. One of the pilots decided to take drastic measures. The Tet offensive earlier in the year had left many dead Viet Cong and North Vietnamese soldiers unburied. The pilot landed at the site of a battle where remains of enemy soldiers lay exposed on the surface, and he brought one of the skulls back to his quarters and put it in his refrigerator. Shortly afterwards a maid opened the refrigerator, screamed and ran away. The men then started putting the skull in various locations around their quarters to deter any further thefts (J.B. West 1999).

On one occasion, some members of the troop were drinking in their quarters. The skull, which was being used as a candlestick at the time, was on a table in front of them. As an experiment, one of them decided to see how much beer the skull could hold, and found that it could hold two twelve-ounce bottles of Budweiser. From that point, drinking from the skull became a troop ritual, and a part of the initiation for new members.

The members of this troop had adopted the practice of wearing distinctive triangular yellow scarves as a badge of unit identity. From 1968 to 1971 a new troop member had to earn the right to wear the scarf by imbibing from the skull an unpleasant concoction of different alcoholic drinks, mixed with leftover scraps of food and cigarette butts. After their initiation, troop members were rarely seen without their scarf (Callison 1996, 1998). The troop did not give the skull a personal name, but simply called it the Skull, the Troop Cup or the Skull Cup (Little 1998).

It mysteriously disappeared in 1971, and one member of the troop was suspected of having taken it home with him at the end of his tour of duty that year. But he denies this rumour, claiming that he left the skull in Vietnam for fear of being caught with it and charged with a war crime. However, at the annual troop reunion in 1998, he produced what he described as an 'anatomically correct plastic model' of a human skull he had purchased shortly after returning home. Using this replica skull, the drinking ceremony was performed again for the first time in some twenty-seven years. Known now as the Troop Cup or Ceremonial Cup, it has continued to be used in this way at the group's annual reunions to toast the memory of fallen members with beer or champagne. Some of the members' wives and children, too, now sometimes take part (Callison 1998).

Of course, there have been some changes in the meaning of this ritual. It has much less of the character of a traumatic drinking ordeal entitling a new member to wear the scarf, and has more to do now with honouring the memory of the dead and renewing ties between old comrades, ties which have evidently come to include some of their wives and children. The current custodian of the 'replica' skull says that his son has agreed to care for it after he dies. Like a clan, the group seems to be understood now as an enduring one that includes its dead, and its future members or posterity. At this point, a generation after the end of the war, the skull has started to take on some of the significance that an ancestor, or the bodily remains of an ancestor, can have in the world of kinship proper in some societies (see, for instance, Bloch and Parry 1982).

Conclusion

The bodily remains of the enemy seem to have been put to a variety of uses during the Vietnam War. They could serve to terrorize, for instance, or to provide evidence of kills. But they were sometimes also a medium through which men sought to establish social relationships with each other; and these practices were grounded in conceptual schemas to do with kinship. Of course, relations mediated in this way through the enemy body were not understood as kinship ties per se. For one thing, they were, at least during the war itself, connections only between men and did not include women. Nor, it seems, did they overtly reference ideas of sexuality or sexual reproduction. But they certainly seem to have drawn upon some of the features of the cultural domain of kinship. In particular, they employed notions of consubstantiality, the sharing of bodily substance, and of nurture as a means of creating relatedness. Men drew upon their understandings of kinship because, for them, this domain offered the most powerful and compelling conceptual imagery with which to express their own sense of intense mutual dependence and cohesion. The men of the same unit, usually a face-to-face group such as a platoon, could use the enemy body to create among themselves relations modelled on some of the attributes of a family. In some cases these relationships have continued to endure long after the war has ended.

In a manner reminiscent of the 'familiarizing predation' described by Fausto among Amazonian hunters, the act of appropriating the body part of an enemy represented the symbolic socialization of the enemy. He was captured from the wild, tamed and incorporated into the group in such a way as to contribute to its reproduction or perpetuation. In some military units in Vietnam, the enemy body part was appropriated in order to give it a role in the group modelled on the role of a child, or sometimes that of a parent, in the world of kinship. Because they all drew upon similar conceptual schemas, different military units seem sometimes to have generated, quite independently and spontaneously, strikingly similar rites of passage in which the enemy body was used to represent the bonds between their members as a familial one.

Notes

1. For other similar photographs, see Brennan (1985: 180–81), Jury (1986: 20), and Heynowski and Scheumann (1968). For an example from the Second World War, see Aldrich (2005: plate following p. 468).
2. To protect this group's identity I have given it a pseudonym similar in meaning and spelling to its original name.
3. Rasimus, a fighter pilot, describes a visit in 1973 to a pilots' club on the military base at Ben Hoa, whose décor included 'an array of combat trophies such as AK-47s, deactivated Soviet grenades, a VC bamboo coolie hat, and a human skull mounted on a carved wooden base that was occasionally used for the drinking of toasts to fallen comrades, sexual conquests, and almost anything else that might strike the fancy of the moment' (2006: 262).

Chapter 16

Returning Memories

Trophy Skulls as Artefacts

The preceding chapters have documented instances in which military personnel, mostly from the early nineteenth century onwards, collected as war souvenirs objects which forensic anthropologists usually refer to as trophy skulls. Considered as material objects, these remains seem to have reflected some consistent patterns of use over this period. Forensic anthropologists have noted that a common indicator of military 'trophy' use is that the remains have been defaced in some manner, or have undergone what might be described as aggressive modification at or after the time of death (Bass 1983; Willey and Leach 2003). Some of the objects of this sort we have encountered so far in this book have displayed signs of battlefield injuries such as bullet holes. Some carried mocking inscriptions or graffiti, and some showed damage or alteration as a result of having been used as lanterns or candle holders. Besides signs of violence or aggression, many of these objects also showed signs of tending and care, such as attempts to conserve or repair them. Some were kept in specially made containers, were mounted for display purposes, bore commemorative labels or were ornamented in some way. Taken together, all these taphonomic practices suggest an uneasy tension between strong but contrary impulses to destroy on the one hand, and to preserve or even enhance on the other. They indicate that such objects could have an enduring value to their possessors and were intended to last, perhaps as family heirlooms, even beyond the individual possessor's own lifetime.

These patterns are apparent in a collection of six human crania analysed by the forensic anthropologists Sledzik and Ousley (1991). The bones had recently been acquired, along with a human tooth and some finger-bones, by the National Museum of Health and Medicine of the United States Armed Forces Institute of Pathology. All the remains had been confiscated in the early 1970s by the military authorities from United States servicemen during the Vietnam War. Most of them were seized in Vietnam itself, when the servicemen concerned had attempted to take them home, or ship them home. The forensic analysis of the skulls indicated that they were those of Asian men of military age, with one of the six identified as possibly female.

The first two specimens were seized from a pair of servicemen who had contacted customs officials in Vietnam to ask about the procedures for shipping human skulls home to the United States. The orbits of one of these skulls were filled with red candle wax. The name 'LITTLE AL' was written on the frontal bone, and eyebrows and a moustache were painted in black. The second was more elaborately decorated. On the frontal bone two names were written: 'BiG ART' and, above that, 'CHUCKY'. In U.S. military parlance at the time, the Viet Cong were variously called VC, Victor Charlie, Charlie or Chuck (Dalzell 2009: 201). It is possible that the skull had been given the nickname Chucky to indicate that it was the skull of a member of the Viet Cong. Just above the orbits of the eyes were the words 'Chu Lai trip skull', indicating that the skull was obtained during a visit to the large military base of that name.

Much of the surface of the skull was covered in graffiti. These included a date ('1971') and the names Frank, John, Pat and Prince. The most noticeable feature was the words 'My PRAYeR DeCK' written in large letters across the top of the skull. The serviceman who labelled the skull his prayer deck (a collection of cards with prayers printed on them) presumably meant to suggest ironically that the skull was his religious talisman or icon, the good luck charm that he himself used for prayer. In short, the background circumstance that the graffiti on the skull evokes is a journey to Chu Lai in 1971 by a group of servicemen, members of a relatively small, low-level military unit, perhaps a platoon or section of a platoon. At some stage on this visit, some of them acquired this skull and decorated it with their names and other graffiti to commemorate this shared experience. Later, one of the men tried to send the skull home, perhaps at the end of his tour of duty.

Japanese and Vietnamese Skulls Compared

Several of the skulls analysed by Sledzik and Ousley seem more extensively decorated or modified than those described earlier originating in the Pacific War. One, found in 1971 in a locker at a military base in the United States during a customs inspection of personal belongings returning from Vietnam, bore a large amount of graffiti, including eyebrows, two Hispanic names, a date and references to drug use. Another specimen, seized from a serviceman in Vietnam attempting to post it to his wife, had a sequence of digits (possibly a serial number) written across the forehead. The palate and teeth were painted black, and the skull bore evidence of use as a candle holder. The sixth skull in Sledzik and Ousley's series bore the most elaborate modifications. The front of the skull was painted in vertical stripes, apparently in imitation of the U.S. flag. The orbits and the nasal cavity were painted orange, and the top of the skull painted blue. A multicoloured five-pointed star was visible on top of the skull, largely hidden by the residue of a large black candle whose drippings cover much of the skull. An internal inspection revealed a hole drilled in the top of the skull, perhaps for suspending it.

Overall, then, most of these skulls carried more graffiti than the Japanese trophy skulls and had other traits which the latter did not, such as coloured decorations made with paint or crayons, or facial features such as eyebrows and moustaches drawn or painted on them.[1] These differences may reflect the social conditions under which they were created and used. In the Pacific War, as we saw, servicemen who collected enemy skulls did so primarily as gifts and souvenirs for family members back home. In many cases, they collected these objects at the request of relatives, or had pledged them to their families as they left for war. The primary moral and affective orientation of these men seems to have been towards their own relations at home. Although military units sometimes used Japanese skulls as mascots, I have not come across accounts of servicemen in the Second World War performing initiation ceremonies involving the use of Japanese skulls as drinking vessels. The sorts of uses to which some servicemen in Vietnam put enemy remains, on the other hand, suggest that these individuals were oriented more towards the other members of their own military unit than to their civilian kin. This may have been related to the fundamental differences between the political backgrounds of the two wars: namely, that there was overwhelming public support at home for the war against Japan, and a lack of such unequivocal support in the case of the Vietnam War. It may have been this greater moral ambiguity of the military in Vietnam, its greater isolation from the wider society at home, that sometimes led to an elaboration of the use of skulls as unit mascots, symbols of unit cohesion and identity, a use reflected in the extensive ornamentation seen on some of these objects. As we have seen, in some military units such uses took the extreme form of covert and transgressive initiation ceremonies focussed upon the skull, marking themselves off radically from the civilian population and other outsiders. Some of the alterations to the Vietnamese skulls, such as filling in the orbits with wax, may have been made specifically to facilitate the use of the skulls as drinking vessels.

There are, however, also some striking underlying continuities or similarities between skulls collected in these two wars. For instance, if we compare the first of Sledzik and Ousely's specimens with the skull collected by Julius Papas in the battle of Guadalcanal (see Chapter Twelve), it is clear that they share four basic decorative features in common. They both bear a date and the name of the place where they were acquired; they have a pet name or nickname written on the frontal bones; they both carry an ironic motto; and they bear the names or autographs of a group of servicemen.

I would suggest that these similarities are too close to be coincidental and need to be explained. One possible explanation is that the inscriptions on the Vietnamese skull, and on other similar trophy skulls from the Vietnam War, were modelled after those on trophy skulls from the Pacific War. That is, servicemen who inscribed enemy skulls in Vietnam had seen inscribed Japanese skulls similar to the one brought home by Papas and had copied them. It may be significant here that some veterans of the Pacific War also served later in Vietnam. One serviceman collected a Japanese skull in New Guinea in 1943, and took it with him in the 1960s to Vietnam, where it was stolen (Bergerud 2001: 123).

Another pathway for the transmission of these practices may have been within the family. The reader will recall that Julius Papas displayed his trophy skull in a prominent position on a shelf in his home for many years after the war and that some Japanese skulls brought home by servicemen were used as Halloween decorations by their families. It is therefore possible that some men who fought in Vietnam had seen trophy skulls in the homes of veterans when they were growing up. Some of them had fathers and uncles who had served in the Pacific War. In other words, it is possible that we are dealing with evidence of a submerged and highly deviant cultural tradition of decorating skulls in certain ways, perhaps being passed down by members of military families, or families with a tradition of military service.

As we saw, there are even earlier examples of skulls and other bones being inscribed with dates and locations of military victories in the American Civil War, and kept as commemorative objects, primarily among Confederate troops and their supporters. I mentioned earlier that reunions of Civil War veterans took place until the 1930s, and it is possible that some of the soldiers who fought the Japanese in the Pacific had encountered oral traditions concerning inscribed skulls in the Civil War, or had even perhaps seen examples of such objects. At any rate, as far as the United States military is concerned, these particular practices seem to begin in the American Civil War, and I have not been able to find earlier examples. A practice of keeping inscribed enemy remains does not seem to occur again until it reappears in the Second World War in the Pacific, and then recurs for a third time during the Vietnam War.[2]

Unwanted Legacies in the Family

As Sledzik and Ousley indicated in their discussion of the Vietnamese skulls, some servicemen tried to bring or send such objects home to their families. Skulls originating in the Vietnam War have come to light in the United States from time to time. One was discovered by police in a box in the basement of the house of a homicide suspect in New York State. He had returned several years earlier from service in Vietnam, where he had found the skull and brought it home as a souvenir. It was a female skull, with a bullet hole in the temple, and on the underside bore indications of having been used as an ashtray. Glue had been used to stabilize some of the bones of the nose and other loose bones, and Taylor and his colleagues suggested that these sorts of repairs were a strong forensic indicator of 'trophy' use (Taylor, Roh and Goldman 1984).

Some servicemen brought enemy remains home as souvenirs during the Pacific War and, earlier still, in the American Civil War. Again, it is possible that these patterns formed part of a learned tradition that persisted for some generations at least up to the period of the Vietnam War. The fact that such remains sometimes became valued family heirlooms offers a clue to how these practices may have been transmitted in this way: they may have been passed down within families, or through kinship ties, along with the objects themselves.

Clearly, some very similar practices relating to the collection and use of enemy remains seem to have emerged, primarily among U.S. servicemen, in certain wars of the nineteenth and twentieth centuries. These practices include decorating these objects with specific sorts of graffiti and utilizing them as gifts for family and friends. I suggest there are two possible ways of explaining the recurrence of these patterns of behaviour, though I should stress that these explanations are not mutually exclusive.

I have already outlined one explanation: namely, that these practices are evidence of a cultural tradition apparently stretching back to the mid nineteenth century. But another possibility is that these practices themselves were not passed down in the intervals between these three wars. Rather, something else was transmitted: namely, a sort of formula capable of generating, or regenerating, these practices whenever appropriate conditions arose. This formula was a set of cultural conventions concerned, principally, with hunting and with the display of animal remains as hunting trophies.

Since the emergence of hunting as a leisure pursuit in the nineteenth century, European and North American hunters have mounted animals' heads and skulls as trophies, and the most important or valuable trophies have often carried a plaque or nameplate below the animal's head or skull, describing the trophy's provenance. The nameplate bears the date and place of the kill; sometimes, too, the name of the hunter who killed the animal; and sometimes the name of the species. Occasionally, in the case of skull trophies, these details are written directly on the skull itself. It is possible, then, that the inscriptions on human skulls from all three of these wars may have been modelled – at least partly – on hunting trophies. And this could well have occurred quite independently in each of the wars.

We may be seeing evidence, then, not of a tradition of inscribing enemy skulls, or not only of such a tradition, but rather of recurrent attempts among military personnel in wartime to equate the enemy with animals, using conventional practices borrowed from the domain of hunting. In other words, these collecting practices may have had their roots in the cultural domain of hunting, an important part of which is, of course, the convention that a man's success or prowess as a hunter must be demonstrated by bringing home tangible evidence of the hunt to his family or household. From this point of view, we appear to be dealing with the cultural transmission, not so much of specific ways of using the bodily remains of the enemy in wartime, but of much broader cultural schemas relating to gender and to the ideological role of hunting and war in cultural images of masculinity. Warriors returning from combat and hunters returning from the hunt were both conceived, stereotypically, to bring home the kill, or parts of it, to their wives and families. It was perhaps such notions that led some men, like Julius Papas in the 1940s, to return home with skulls, in most cases already old when they acquired them, and to misrepresent themselves to their families as having carried out acts akin to headhunting during their war service.

For them, the skull brought from war was a sort of theatrical prop with which to perform elements of their own culture's standard fantasies of savage warriorhood to audiences back home. A case of this sort during the Vietnam War concerned a man whom I will call D., a builder from the midwestern United States, who served as a soldier in Vietnam. Shortly after his death in middle age, his daughter published a biography (Trussoni 2006) in which she describes how he brought home from Vietnam certain mementos which shocked and disturbed his family. One was a photograph of a dead enemy soldier. Another was a human cranium. His daughter remembers the skull, as the family called it, being usually kept on top of the television when she was a child. Her uncles recalled how D. used to invite them to his house to watch football, where they would endure the uncomfortable ordeal of watching television with the skull apparently watching them.

A family photograph taken in D.'s home at Christmas in 1973 shows him seated by the fireplace, holding his infant daughter. To one side, there is a decorated Christmas tree with presents arranged around it. Behind him, and strikingly at odds with this conventional image of festive warmth and domesticity, the cranium sits on the mantelpiece, among the family photographs and other ornaments. It is without a lower jaw, has no teeth, and appears to be heavily stained and discoloured, suggesting that it had been in contact with the ground for a significant time before it had been collected. In other words, it is unlikely that D. had had any personal involvement in this person's death. More likely, he found it, already old, and took it home at the end of his tour of duty.[3]

There were no inscriptions on the skull, and D. never explained to his family how he came to acquire it. Nor do his family seem to have enquired. But they suspected that it was the skull of a person he had killed, and D. perhaps encouraged them to draw this implication by his silence. What disturbed his family was not that he had killed during the war, but that he had brought human remains back with him – a body part, as it seemed to them, of someone whose life he had taken – and placed it in the heart of the family home. His daughter and other family members were never able to comprehend why he should have wanted to bring this evidence of the violence of war into his home and continually confront them with it. They found him more aggressive and disturbed in his behaviour after his return from Vietnam, and the skull seemed to them emblematic of some unknown emotional and physical injury he had suffered there. His daughter does not know what became of the skull, but believes that her mother eventually threw it out. It is not clear whether the skull was a factor in the decision D.'s wife eventually made to leave him, but she clearly felt that the family home was in a sense violated by this reminder of violent death placed conspicuously on display within it (Trussoni 2006, 2007).

Historically, a major part of the meaning of the human skull in the Western cultural tradition has been that of a *memento mori*, an icon of mortality and life-threatening danger. As symbols of death, the skull, the skull and crossbones and the *totenkopf* or death's head have all been used as military emblems for several centuries. These associations of death and danger are presumably felt to be appropriate in the context of war, but they are entirely dissonant with the Western cultural symbolism of the family as a site of reproduction in a context of love and security (Schneider 1968). The ambivalence and distaste which servicemen's wives often express towards trophy skulls is notable, and contrasts markedly with the unreservedly enthusiastic reception accorded such trophies by women among the Dayaks or Shuar (Geddes 1954: 21; Harner 1972; McKinley 1976: 114). One of the Japanese trophy skulls forensically analysed by Bass was given to his museum by a veteran's widow who told Bass she had never liked it and wanted to be rid of it now that her husband had died (1983: 803).

The forensic anthropologists Willey and Leach (2003) report a case in which the attachment of a Vietnam War veteran to his trophy skull appears to have contributed to the breakdown of his marriage. In 1992, a woman in northern California found her grandchildren playing with a human skull and mandible and called the police. The forensic examination of the bones found, among other modifications, holes drilled in the bones so as to allow the jaw to be hinged to the skull, and evidence of burning consistent with its having been used as a candle holder or lantern. When the police questioned the children's mother,

> She said that when her husband returned from a tour of duty in Vietnam, he brought mementos home with him. Among his souvenirs were a human skull and jaw. He kept the skull in their garage, displaying it at Halloween and other such times. She demanded that he rid their home of the bones. When he failed to do that – and presumably for other

transgressions and incompatibilities as well – she divorced him. As part of their separation, he moved to Southern California. Although he vacated the house, some legacies remained – among them the bones. (Willey and Leach 2003: 186–87)

As happened after the Pacific War, it seems that most families who received such objects could not assimilate them in the long term. And this would appear to argue against the existence of a continuous tradition of the sort I referred to above.

The families of some Vietnam veterans eventually discarded such objects. Others have tried to return them to Vietnam in the hope that they could receive funeral rites there or be restored to their next of kin. A furniture maker whom I will call P. was raised by a stepfather who had served as a helicopter pilot in the Vietnam War. In 1967, nearing the end of his tour of duty, the stepfather had mailed home to a relative the cranium and both femurs of a North Vietnamese soldier. When P. was growing up, these were kept in the garage and his family had a pet name for the soldier, whom they called String Bean. P. remembers how his stepfather, over drinks with his friends, would sometimes tell the story of String Bean's bones and how he came to acquire them. During the war, the stepfather used to fly each day over a rice paddy in one corner of which lay the body of an enemy soldier. As time went by the body decayed, and when only bones remained he landed and took the cranium and the two femurs. Presumably, he took these particular bones in order to construct a representation of a skull and crossbones, and perhaps he used them in this way as a mascot of his military unit.

As a child, P. used to enjoy the story of String Bean's bones but when he became a teenager he started to find the story increasingly disturbing, and began avoiding the garage. Later, as an adult, he moved the remains to his business premises following his stepfather's death in 2002, and he still keeps them there. Since then, he has written to the Vietnamese authorities, and more recently to his own government, in an attempt to have them returned to Vietnam. He has given radio and newspaper interviews to publicize his efforts and gain support for them. His argument is that the United States government expends a great deal of resources on locating and repatriating the remains of its own servicemen killed in action overseas, and he feels that the remains of this Vietnamese soldier ought to be treated in the same way. So far, he has had no success. Neither the Vietnamese nor the U.S. authorities are willing to become involved, without evidence confirming P.'s account of the bones' origins, and P. remains their unwilling custodian (Brown 2003; Lorie 2004; Patterson 2007).

There is a marked contrast here with the treatment of trophy objects in some indigenous societies in which practices such as headhunting were publicly accepted. These were societies which elaborated the parallels between hunting and war, and utilized cultural schemas relating to hunting quite explicitly in the context of war and in behaviour towards the enemy body. Many of these societies had elaborate rituals in which enemy heads or other body parts were incorporated into the world of kinship and family, and into the processes of social reproduction, as if they had been transformed into persons or parts of persons. In other words, taking heads was understood as a male contribution – in some societies, an essential one – to reproduction and fertility, and in the context of kinship relations these objects were symbols of life, not of death (Harner 1972: 147, 193; Hoskins 1996b: 18–23; McKinley 1976). Hence, in the celebrations following a successful raid, women might dance with the head to welcome it, offer it food as if it were an honoured guest, or treat it as an infant to nurse and coddle. These were rituals of adoption, in other words, in which the potentially hostile and dangerous life-force of a distant stranger was made friendly and tractable. The purpose of the celebratory rituals was not only to commemorate the killer's achievement but, in effect, to socialize the body part he had brought home. A power gained from the remote wild was thereby domesticated and incorporated into his social relationships, like a wild bird or animal captured in the forest, taken home and rendered tame (Fausto 1999; McKinley 1976: 114–15).

In the case of men such as D. and the stepfather of P., their cultural backgrounds seem to have given them the means and motivation to collect enemy remains during their war service. As we saw, some military units in Vietnam were also able to assimilate enemy body parts in such a way as to create kin-like homosocial ties among their members. And some men were motivated to bring these remains home to their families at the end of their tour of duty, as if such objects were the mementos of a hunting expedition. But just as we saw in the aftermath of the Pacific War, there were no publicly accepted cultural schemas by means of which veterans and their descendants could incorporate such objects into their actual kin relationships.

In some societies, former enemies might return headhunting trophies to one another as part of the rituals of peace making (see, for instance, Hoskins 1996c: 230). However, the primary and immediate aim of many veterans' families seems to have been not so much to make peace with old adversaries, but to remove such objects from their homes, an aim which they could in principle achieve by either repatriating or simply discarding them. Not only were there no institutionalized means of incorporating such objects into the family, there were no formal conventions for expelling them either, and there were certainly no formal channels for repatriating them to their countries of origin – a point made by the Australian veteran Hordern (see Chapter Thirteen).

Unlike some indigenous societies that had comparable patterns of trophy-taking, and similar conceptions linking hunting with male identity, there were no culturally established roles for such objects within a family or community. More often, the objects came to appear to violate their own keepers' distinctions between persons and things, or between persons and property, in such a way as to resist assimilation into their social relations and perhaps, in the long term, into collective memory as well.

Notes

1. But compare the case of Larson (see Chapter Twelve), who decorated a Japanese skull with artificial eyes made from seashell opercula. By contrast, only one of the skulls in Sledzik and Ousley's series was without markings or graffiti. Its principal feature was a circular fracture of the frontal bone, which Sledzik and Ousley concluded was caused by a blow from the muzzle of an M16A1 rifle.
2. An early case of a skull being used in a manner similar to a military unit's mascot occurred in Texas during the Civil War. At the time, ethnic German Texans were widely suspected of Unionist sympathies by Confederates and were persecuted by

them. A Confederate soldier visiting the camp of a frontier regiment early in the war recalls seeing the skull of a German on display.

> One thing I mustn't forget, as it shows what sort of men these were. High up on a pole, on the top of their commissary store-hut, grinned a human skull. I was told it had belonged to an unfortunate German, who with other of his countrymen had been killed by these valiant warriors, when attempting to cross the Rio Grandé some months before. They were quite indignant when I suggested it would be more seemly to bury the poor remnant of humanity, evidently regarding it as a trophy to be proud of. (Williams 1908: 267; see also Marten 1990: 115)

A German observer of the Philippine-American War (1899–1902) saw evidence of desecration of the enemy dead by U.S. military personnel (Rinne 1901: 47). A photograph taken during that war, entitled 'Private Toolman and his collection of curios', shows a serviceman posing with a collection of captured weapons and other items, one of which is a human skull in use as a candle holder (Fralin 1985: 75). There is also evidence of such behaviour among U.S. servicemen in the Korean War (1950–53). Two ex-marines describe in their memoirs their shock on seeing an enemy skull on a pole at the entrance to one of their tents shortly after their arrival in Korea (Ravino and Carty 2003: 204). Michael Harris, a soldier who served in the mid 1950s on Eniwetok at the Pacific Proving Ground, remembers one of his comrades, a veteran of the Korean War, who kept on his bunk a skull which he said was that of a North Korean soldier (Harris 2005: 17). He told Harris he had killed the soldier in battle, removed his head and buried it for a week to clean it. Neither of these two skulls appears to have carried inscriptions or graffiti.

3. I am grateful to Danielle Trussoni for allowing me to see this photograph.

Conclusion

Cultural Learning and Improvisation

In this book I have sought to trace the history of certain wartime collecting practices among Euro-American military personnel. On the one hand, these forms of behaviour have occurred only rarely. They have involved only a very small minority of military personnel, and appear pathological in the context of the prevailing social values of Euro-American cultures. On the other hand, they have exhibited a high degree of consistency at least since the early part of the nineteenth century. There are pronounced regularities in the ways in which human remains were collected and used in military contexts over this period, and these patterns of behaviour seem to be predictable in certain respects, as I shall suggest below.

It is this combination of abnormality and regularity that has posed the central problem of this book. My task has been to explain how some highly aberrant social practices, occurring only sporadically, nevertheless recurred in a markedly consistent form for some two centuries.

One of the very few axioms of social anthropology is that culture is transmitted by learning. It is possible that these practices were conserved in this conventional way at least in part, by being passed on from one generation to the next through processes of socialization. They may, for instance, be evidence of the existence of some subterranean, deviant traditions within the military forces of some nations.

We can date the start of any such traditions to the late eighteenth and early nineteenth centuries. As we saw in the case of scalping among settler militias in North America, and trophy-hunting among nineteenth-century British soldiers in Africa, such practices originated in the encounters of military personnel with colonized peoples, many of whom themselves put the body parts of their enemies to ritual uses. That is, these practices developed in the negotiated cultures of combat that were synthesized in violent colonial encounters between opponents who both transformed and accommodated to each other's behaviour. The cultural assumptions and expectations which they brought to these encounters included, of course, some concerned with the collection and display of bodily remains. Euro-American military personnel came from backgrounds which gave meaning to the collection and display of animal remains in the context of hunting, and to the collection and display of human remains particularly in judicial and medico-scientific contexts. Moreover, these contexts were themselves richly interconnected. The game-hunting trophy, the natural-history specimen and the remains of the executed felon were, as we have seen, sometimes equated with each other so closely at the time as not to form entirely distinct categories. Ultimately, they all signified the same idea: domination over the order of 'nature'.

It could therefore seem natural and unproblematic to some colonial soldiers that the remains of their indigenous opponents might also become objects of such forms of collecting. This was particularly so when indigenous practice towards the enemy body lent itself to being likened to the behaviour of predatory wildlife such as tigers or wolves, relegating these peoples to nature.

However, there must have been many obstacles to the transmission of military trophy-taking over the following two centuries. Wars occurred only episodically, military authorities punished dishonourable treatment of the enemy dead and, perhaps most importantly, the majority of servicemen and military families during this period undoubtedly had no motivations to engage in any such behaviour in the first place and would have strongly condemned it. If submerged 'traditions' of collecting and displaying enemy remains persisted in some military organizations, they must have been very tenuous and discontinuous. Indeed, the history of these practices would be a case study in cultural persistence under the most adverse conditions.

Of course, there are well known cases of cultures or subcultures proving highly resilient under highly unfavourable circumstances (see, for example, M. Stewart 1997). But the material I have discussed in this book suggests the possibility that processes other than those of conventional cultural learning may have contributed to the historical recurrence of military trophy-taking.

In particular, these patterns of behaviour may have been repeatedly improvised independently from the very beginning, using conceptual schemas borrowed from the domain of hunting. I have assumed that the routine practices and conventions of sports hunting in Europe and North America, such as preserving and displaying animal trophy heads and skulls, were themselves reproduced during this period by cultural learning. They were, quite simply, a tradition within hunting communities. This is not to suggest that they were static, but that most of those relevant to military trophy-taking were established by the time military trophy-taking emerged and remained relatively stable subsequently. But military trophy-taking, on the other hand, may not have been reproduced in entirely the same way. It may have occurred, for the most part, as an adaptation or extension of these hunting practices. In other words, military trophy-taking may have had a history parasitic on another, and in this case continuous, stream of cultural transmission to do with the display of animal trophies among hunters.

Some servicemen may, then, have adapted schemas familiar to them - concerned, for example, with the preservation and display of animal remains - and applied them, or rather misapplied them, in the context of warfare. Their actions were, in other words, observable or surface expressions of underlying metaphorical associations of war with hunting. The use of an enemy skull as a mascot, let us say, may often have arisen as an extemporization on this long-standing cultural metaphor. It proclaimed: 'Our enemies are animals, and we are hunting and killing them for sport.' Of course, such behaviour was certainly not a normal or acceptable part either of soldiering or of hunting. It was a transgressive and, in a sense, creative hybrid of elements of both of these domains.

In other words, it was what I have called an interstitial practice – a deviant or transgressive activity produced by transposing schemas from one domain of social interaction into another. A characteristic of transgressive patterns of behaviour of this sort is that they are not necessarily learned; or, to put it more precisely, they do not in themselves require learning in order to recur. Aberrant military practices of trophy-taking may have been reinvented repeatedly, though they could not of course have been invented out of thin air. Men possessing similar conceptual schemas to do with hunting, finding themselves similarly situated in the highly abnormal conditions of war, could have produced similar aberrant behaviours without necessarily having explicitly learnt them from others.

As we saw, some servicemen do seem to have engaged in at least some of these forms of misconduct, such as collecting enemy skulls as souvenirs from old battle sites, without having explicitly learnt them. They were quite unaware that other members of their own forces had engaged in similar activities in the past, or were engaged in them at that very time. In other words, they appeared – *to themselves* – to have generated their misconduct independently.

Of course, such patterns of behaviour may also have been part of some deviant, oppositional culture within certain military forces, and some servicemen may have learned these patterns in this way. But I would argue that behaviour of this sort would have continued to recur even without being transmitted through this route, so long as certain conditions held: in particular, that armed conflicts occurred which some serving personnel framed in imagery of hunting or predation. These practices were reproduced across time in identifiably the same forms, perhaps partly through direct learning, but more fundamentally through processes of recurring improvisation, and these were often subjectively experienced as spontaneous by the men concerned.

Interstitial Practices

It is said that in the Middle Ages a certain musical chord, the tritone, was prohibited because its discordant sound seemed to evoke evil. It was called the *diabolus in musica*, and its use was strictly forbidden. In the context of Euro-American cultural history over the past two hundred years, the practices I have discussed in this book seem to have represented a sort of *diabolus in cultura* – a forbidden conjunction of cultural themes, each unexceptionable in itself, but highly disturbing when brought together. Emerging, as it were, from the margins between the domains of hunting and of war, they disturb us because they confound – indeed, intentionally confound – our normal conceptual distinctions between humans and animals.

Although military trophy-taking is certainly not normative behaviour, neither is it the disordered behaviour of disturbed individuals such as Edward Gein, the serial killer and grave-robber who kept parts of his victims' bodies as trophies (see Chapter Thirteen). Interstitial practices are generated not by individuals acting alone, but typically by small, face-to-face social groups. The schemas by means of which they are produced are typifications of social interaction, mental models with which to interpret and generate social behaviour. It follows that the creative misapplication of these schemas, opening up marginal and transgressive regions of behaviour, is an inherently social or group enterprise. It usually occurs in small, cohesive groups within some larger, and perhaps more impersonal, collectivity.

> In October 2006, the German newspaper *Bild* provoked a nationwide scandal by publishing a series of photographs which a small unit of German soldiers in the NATO peacekeeping force in Afghanistan had taken of themselves in 2003. The soldiers had come across what seems to have been an old burial ground, where human skulls and other bones were lying on the surface. The soldiers collected some of the bones and photographed themselves pointing their weapons at them and in various other poses. In one of the photographs, a soldier had exposed his penis and was miming oral sex with one of the skulls. In another, one of the skulls was mounted on the end of a winch on the front of their vehicle, with the soldiers posing around it as if it were a vehicle mascot.

This case illustrates a number of points. Some soldiers have kept such photographs of human remains – or kept the remains themselves – in order to convey to others the impression that the remains were of enemies they had killed, as if they were seeking to adopt the role of hunters displaying proof of a kill. But few such objects seem really to have been 'kill trophies' in this sense. As in many of the other cases I have discussed in this book, the skulls and other bones in this case were old – perhaps not even the remains of an enemy – and the way they were obtained was more similar to grave-robbery than headhunting.

But perhaps more to the point, the case illustrates how the appropriation and use of human remains have usually occurred in a group context. We are dealing with social behaviour, carried out by a group or in a group setting, and not with the behaviour of disordered individuals acting in isolation. The great majority of incidents of trophy-taking among military personnel discussed in this book have been carried out not by individuals but by small groups, and in many cases these acts were unplanned. In the case just described, they emerged spontaneously when a group of soldiers came across some old skeletal remains, apparently quite by chance, and proceeded unbidden to recapitulate the broad outlines of a pattern of aberrant behaviour that has recurred in some Western militaries for two centuries.

Trophy-taking and Race

At the start of this book I outlined the currently prevailing view of military trophy-taking: namely, that such occurrences are a type of behavioural disorder related to combat stress. The evidence I have reviewed in this book suggests that this sort of misconduct has been carried out most often, not by servicemen experiencing unusual stress in combat, but by those who have perceived the enemy as different racially from themselves.

So, for instance, all the known military trophy skulls deriving from the Second World War appear to be those of Japanese individuals, with none of them originating from the European theatre of the war. More recently, similar behaviour occurred among some NATO servicemen in Afghanistan, as described above. But there are no reports of such misconduct in the NATO forces during their interventions in the former Republic of Yugoslavia, where the population is European.

On the relatively rare occasions when human trophy-taking has occurred in the U.S. and European militaries, it seems to have been carried out almost exclusively across 'racial' lines, by soldiers who sought to racialize their enemies. Here, we must remember, of course, that 'races' are social constructs and not facts of human biology. We have seen that racial classifications in Europe and North America changed over the course of time and were often contested. During the American Civil War, for example, some Confederate soldiers sought to portray Southerners and Northerners as two distinct subvarieties of a white or Anglo-Saxon 'race'. It was these representations of racial difference, largely unremembered now but current at the time, that motivated some men, or permitted them, to treat the remains of their enemies as battle trophies.

We also saw that patterns of military trophy-taking were influenced by changes in beliefs concerning the bodily basis of race. In the early nineteenth century, the physical locus of racial difference shifted from surface features of skin and hair, to the inner structures of anatomy and the skeleton. The collection specifically of skulls dates back to that time, and to the emergence of scientific racism with its preoccupation with the skull as the critical signifier of racial categories. Different parts of the enemy body have been collected as trophies depending on the particular bodily sites at which the embodiment of racial difference was imagined to be most pronounced or concentrated.

Trophy-taking has tended to occur, then, in conflicts in which military personnel were strongly motivated to classify their enemies as racially different from themselves. It is as if the conceptual domain of war in Euro-American cultures was, for some two centuries, periodically colonized by cultural representations originating in the domain of game hunting. These episodes did not occur randomly but were triggered in a relatively predictable way by the social and political conditions under which certain wars were fought. Historically, wars with the most highly pronounced racial character have been the most susceptible to this penetration by the cultural imagery of predation.

In short, military trophy-taking first emerged somewhat over two centuries ago because ideologies of 'race' emerged at that time – social classifications according to which some human populations are closer to animals in their inherent nature than others. If some peoples are animal-like in their nature, then wars with such peoples must, quite literally, be more like hunting forays than conflicts between human opponents. This notion proved an enduring one, and it was due to its strong persistence over the past two hundred years that metaphorical associations of war and hunting continued to generate acts of trophy-taking.

It was above all in colonial wars that the ostensibly 'natural' distinctions between humans and wild animals were projected onto social boundaries between human groups. Hence the majority of the trophy skulls collected by European and U.S. military personnel have been those of individuals identified as Asian, African, American Indian and Aboriginal Australian, and many of these were collected in the context of colonial frontier warfare. Here, trophy-taking did not merely reflect ideologies of colonialism and race. It was one of many social practices through which these ideologies were perpetuated and reproduced, a point to which I shall return shortly.

Spontaneous Disappearance

In Chapter One, I defined interstitial practices as patterns of transgressive behaviour that express cultural metaphors in prohibited or unconventional ways. They are forms of behaviour that explore the outer margins and forbidden regions of metaphors of this kind. I have suggested that metaphors of war as hunting have tended to be more fully realized in these ways the more closely the enemy has been identified with nature or with the world of animals. I have also suggested that such practices tend to emerge in small, primary social groups, and may seem to the actors themselves to arise spontaneously. Many such groups, placed in similar circumstances, can produce in this way very similar patterns independently or in parallel.

A further characteristic of an interstitial practice is that it tends also just as suddenly to disappear once the conditions that give rise to it no longer hold. When I say that it disappears, I mean not only that it stops occurring, but that it also tends to disappear from social memory, and may be problematical to assimilate into social memory in the first place. For example, we saw how practices of making gifts or offerings of enemy remains to family and friends emerged among some U.S. servicemen in certain wars during the nineteenth and twentieth centuries. After each of these wars, the practices then seem to have disappeared from public consciousness for a significant period (a process in which museums sometimes served as burial sites for disquieting and unwanted memory objects) until reappearing in later wars in much the same form. These cycles of episodic recurrence followed by historical amnesia suggest, again, that these practices did not themselves require learning in order to persist but were secondary phenomena, effects originating in some other historically more stable and enduring cultural representations and practices. I have suggested that these included, in particular, long-standing conventions relating to hunting in which kills, or parts of kills, were brought home as gifts or offerings to womenfolk or family. In combination with a cultural predisposition to conceptualize war in terms of metaphors of hunting, these were a prescription for repeatedly generating wartime behaviour in which enemy bodies could be equated in certain respects with those of game animals or quarry, behaviour which would subsequently come to appear too disturbing and anomalous to be publicly recollected or commemorated. It was not so much these patterns of misconduct themselves, then, that were passed from one generation to the next. Rather, other cultural representations in combination could act to reconstitute them, almost predictably, under certain conditions. Even after long periods in abeyance, the same aberrant patterns of gift giving and other transgressive forms of behaviour could therefore recur, continue for a time, and then be forgotten again until their next reappearance.

So, as we saw, trophy-taking seemed to vanish from public memory after the Pacific War, only for the same schemas of predation to re-emerge intact a generation later in Vietnam, with the same transgressive practices resurfacing in relation to another people.

The principle of racialized trophy-hunting endured, while different peoples could be made to take on and resign the role of victims as political circumstances changed.

Such processes indicate that trophy-taking does not merely reflect racialized imagery of the enemy as subhuman, but is one of the symbolic practices by which these wartime concepts can be vividly reproduced and sustained – in opposition to a contrasting default recognition of the enemy as human. That these attributions of animality are counter-representations (they explicitly transgress, negate and deny others more fundamental and enduring) is shown by the way they have been resisted and disputed even in wartime, and by the rapidity with which they have fallen apart afterwards. They disintegrate as the enemy, as it were, lapses back into humanness once a war has ended, with the former enemy's souvenir-remains reverting from the category of things to their default location in the world of persons.

Predation as Desocialization

A conceptual imagery of hunting has played a comparable role in some other cultures too. For example, imageries of this sort have a very similar significance in the belief systems of the indigenous peoples of Amazonia (Viveiros de Castro 1998; see also Descola 1992). In these American Indian cosmologies, all sentient beings are imagined to perceive themselves and their kind as human, with human bodies, human social institutions and so forth. But they are assumed to see other beings quite differently – especially, it seems, those creatures they either hunt or are hunted by (Viveiros de Castro 1998: 471). Those they hunt appear to them as game animals, while the beings that in turn hunt them appear either as predatory animals or as spirits. So, for instance, jaguars see other jaguars as people, but they see people as tapirs and peccaries. It is above all through hunting and being hunted that beings differentiate themselves as subjects from others who become their objects. In this way, every kind of creature distinguishes, from its own perspective, culture from nature, a collective 'I' from a collective 'it'. The implication of these cosmologies seems to be that a world without predation would be one of undifferentiated and unbounded sociality between sentient beings. Indeed, Amazonian mythology seems to portray a world of precisely this sort, an original state in which beings once still appeared to each other in their human forms (Viveiros de Castro 1998: 471–72). So humans and animals, for instance, are all people but are no longer normally visible to each other as such, as they were primordially in the time of myth. They are, as it were, former fellow human beings who have grown estranged, and have become so principally by establishing relations of predation with one another.

In a similar way, the sorts of racism manifested in military trophy-taking are not so much failures to recognize the humanness of an enemy, as active misperceptions or denials of a humanness tacitly acknowledged. Someone recognized as a human being is purposefully objectified as a sort of animal through a real or metaphorical act of predation. In this respect, the trophy-taker resembles the Amazonian hunter. He understands that the beings he hunts perceive themselves as human subjects, and that his own perceptions of them as non-human, objectifying them as animal bodies, are integral to the stance of predation which he adopts towards them. In other words, he assumes that a special mode of perception in which prey appear dehumanized is inherent in the subject position of the hunter (just as it is inherent in the subject position of the prey to perceive itself as human). In the sorts of racialized trophy-taking I have examined in this book, as in the hunting of animals among Amazonian peoples, the relationship of predator and prey needs to be understood as a specially reduced and attenuated form of sociality.

Military trophy-taking seeks to accomplish in human-to-human relations the sorts of mutual dissociation which these Amerindian Indians imagine hunting produces in their relations with animals. In both cases, predation is a means by which human groups subjectively dehumanize or depersonalize selected parts of their cognized social world. Encompassed within a universe of human relations, the creation of violent partnerships of hunter and prey introduces relationships of distance and disconnection that appear natural and belie their own social character. In this respect, the racial boundaries which acts of military trophy-taking seek to project are, in fact, occluded forms of sociality like those that Amazonian hunters imagine between themselves and other species.

Recurring Metaphors

I have suggested that interstitial practices can be reproduced over long periods without appearing to be continuously or explicitly transmitted, exhibiting instead a pattern of episodic, seemingly spontaneous, recurrence. So, for example, in 2005 the members of a U.S. platoon in the city of Mosul in Iraq ambushed a group of insurgents.

> After the ambush, the Americans scooped up a piece of skull and took it back to their base as evidence of the successful mission.
> [The platoon leader] said the decision to pick up the skull fragment and take it back to the base was a 'sarcastic' gesture to confirm the kill to the battalion. [His company commander], who was not present during the attack, said the soldiers picked up the fragment not as a trophy, which is prohibited under military regulations, but to confirm 'that we had the remains of a terrorist'. (Fainaru 2005)

In another case in 2010, members of a U.S. Army platoon in Afghanistan went on trial accused of the premeditated murder of several Afghan civilians. Some of the soldiers were also charged with taking 'trophy' photographs of themselves posing with the victims' bodies, cutting off fingers from some of the victims and keeping them as trophies. Some faced charges of possessing other human body parts, including a skull, a tooth and a leg bone (Bates and Duell 2011; McGreal 2010).

As such incidents suggest, aberrant or marginal behaviour of this sort may resemble the mainstream cultural practices of other societies or the normal conventions of other historical periods. Such resemblances arise because the same or similar cultural metaphors can occur in different times and places although the boundaries beyond which they can be acceptably expressed in social action may be placed differently.

A given social practice can therefore be interstitial in one society or epoch in history, and mainstream in another and, indeed, its status may be contested. Mainstream practices are encoded in schemas transmitted as part of the socialization process. An interstitial practice is potentially mainstream, and becomes mainstream to the extent that it gains social acceptance and starts to be reproduced through learning. What may principally differ between one time or place and another is not so much the social practices in which people engage, nor even perhaps the frequency with which particular practices occur, but rather the respects in which these acts are permitted or proscribed, acknowledged or denied – in short, the ways in which they are valorized positively or negatively.

So for instance, some societies, though historically unrelated to each other, have nevertheless drawn a marked and very similar distinction between close and distant enemies, encoded in a distinction between fighting and hunting. A group of men fight their close enemies, but they *hunt* their distant ones. In other words, warfare against distant enemies is understood as taking the prototypical form of long-distance raiding, ritualized expeditions to faraway hunting grounds whose inhabitants are likened to game or quarry. Such expeditions are a rite of passage for men, an initiatory quest whose goal is to return home with material proof of prowess as a hunter.

The basic features of this military cosmology are evident across a broad spectrum of societies, ranging from some small-scale indigenous communities to some of the nation states involved in the major wars of the twentieth century and in some more recent conflicts. As the incidents just described suggests, the metaphor of soldier-as-hunter appears still to remain very much in evidence in some armed forces in the early twenty-first century, playing a prominent role in military training, in media representations of the military and in soldiers' own self-concepts (Wills and Steuter 2009).

I said earlier that military trophy-taking is a social or group activity of small units such as the platoon. The same seems to be true of expeditionary trophy-hunting in some indigenous societies as well. The Amazonian Shuar war party recorded by Harner, for instance, was similar in size to a platoon, consisting typically of thirty or forty men (Harner 1972: 184). Such parallels raise the question whether there may be another, entirely different explanation for the historical recurrence of trophy-taking: namely, that the roots of this behaviour lie in human evolution (see, for instance, Ardrey 1976; Burkert 1983). It could be argued that small, highly cohesive, face-to-face groups of men in wartime will tend to generate trophy-taking behaviour because evolved mental schemas connected with hunting are likely to be strongly activated in such situations. In short, if war has often been likened to a blood sport, or experienced as one, the reason may be that this particular conceptual metaphor is powerfully motivated intrinsically. Humans, males in particular, may be strongly predisposed to equate hunting and war by the evolutionary history of their species.

But ethnographic studies of hunting societies, at least those that have persisted into modern times, show that hunting is a far from uniform phenomenon. Rather, it encompasses a loose-knit family of practices conceptualized in very diverse ways by the societies that engage in them. Some peoples who depend on hunting represent it in imagery of seduction and charming of the prey and systematically de-emphasize any accompanying violence or bloodshed (Bird-David 1993; Kwon 1998; Willerslev 2004). At the other extreme, some hunting societies represent hunting as an aggressive and bloody contest or power struggle between men and animals. In other cases, the relation of hunter to prey lies somewhere in between: it is an ambivalent mixture of intimacy and distance, friendship and animosity, often represented as a tie of affinity – that similarly ambivalent bond between people related through marriage (see, for example, Brightman 1993; Descola 1994).

Furthermore, some hunting or foraging peoples do not practice organized warfare in any case, quite apart from human trophy-taking (see, for example, Howell 1989). Human trophy-taking seems to occur in social milieus in which the killing of game can appear an act of deadly force and such acts are important in the validation of male identity. It is likely, then, that neither trophy-taking nor the conceptual schemas that give rise to it are in some sense innate, because they appear to be culturally specific and limited in their distribution rather than universal.

But for men from backgrounds in which the relationship of the hunter to the quarry is conceptualized in a certain way, the relationship can offer powerful and compelling models with which to represent their opponents in war as animal-like, or rank them lower than themselves in some putatively natural order. In such circumstances, I suggest, practices of human trophy-taking will at least sometimes occur quite spontaneously, without having to be taught or learned. In the context of war, men in different times and places have sometimes generated similar social practices because, in seeking to give meaning to their experiences of war, they have drawn upon similar understandings of the activity of hunting.

In this respect, human trophy-taking is closely connected with the ways in which people relate to animals. It is a pattern of behaviour that emerges when hunting is conceptualized and practised in a manner that enables it to serve as a symbol of adult masculinity and as a model for warmaking. This is the key similarity between the military trophy-taking practices I have discussed in this book and the trophy-hunting of peoples in Amazonia, Melanesia and Southeast Asia. The taking of heads or other body parts was a socially prescribed practice among these indigenous peoples, a part of their culture transmitted from one generation to the next through the socialization of the young. It was a mainstream social practice, in other words, not an interstitial one. But the argument of this book suggests that incidents of human trophy-taking of some sort will probably occur whenever war, hunting and masculinity are conceptually linked in these ways, even if the behaviour is not explicitly taught or learned, and indeed even if it is prohibited. This is the case with the forms of trophy-taking that have emerged intermittently among Euro-American military personnel over the past two centuries. These were interstitial social practices, forbidden improvisations on a widespread and enduring cultural theme.

Bibliography

Adelaide Advertiser. 2000. 'Funeral for War Bones', 15 April, p. 29.
Aldrich, R.J. 2005. *The Faraway War: Personal Diaries of the Second World War in Asia and the Pacific*. London: Doubleday.
Allen, C. 1990. *The Savage Wars of Peace: Soldiers' Voices 1945–1989*. London: Futura.
Allen, D. 2004. 'Skull from WWII Casualty to be Buried in Grave for Japanese Unknown Soldiers', *Stars and Stripes (Pacific Edition)*, 13 May. Retrieved 5 October 2005 from http://www.stripes.com/article.asp?section=104&article=21322&archive=true
Allen, J., H. Als, J. Lewis and L.F. Litwack. 2007. *Without Sanctuary: Lynching Photography in America*. Santa Fe, NM: Twin Palms Publishers.
Allen, M.R. 1967. *Male Cults and Secret Initiations in Melanesia*. Carlton: Melbourne University Press.
Almond, R. 2003. *Medieval Hunting*. Stroud: Sutton.
Al-Shetawi, M. 1987. 'The Arab-West Conflict as Represented in Arabic Drama', *World Literature Today* 61(1): 46–49.
Altintas, R. 2008. Personal communications, 23–24 September.
Alvarez, J.E. 2001. *The Betrothed of Death: The Spanish Foreign Legion during the Rif Rebellion, 1920–1927*. Westport: Greenwood Press.
American Field Service. 1944. American Field Service Letters. Retrieved 5 October 2005 from http://www.ku.edu/carrie/specoll/AFS/library/4-ww2/AFSletters/31.html
Anderson, C. 2004. *Legible Bodies: Race, Criminality and Colonialism in South Africa*. Oxford: Berg.
Anderson, D. 2005. *Histories of the Hanged: Britain's Dirty War in Kenya and the End of Empire*. London: Weidenfeld and Nicolson.
_____. 2006. 'Surrogates of the State: Collaboration and Atrocity in Kenya's Mau Mau War', in G. Kassimeris (ed.), *The Barbarization of Warfare*. New York: New York University Press, pp. 159–74.
Anderson, G.C. 1986. *Little Crow, Spokesman for the Sioux*. Saint Paul: Minnesota Historical Society Press.

Anderson, K. and C. Perrin. 2009. 'Thinking with the Head: Race, Craniometry, Humanism'. *Journal of Cultural Economy* 2(1–2): 83–98.
Anderson, T., S. O'Connor and A.R. Ogden. 2004. 'An Early Eighteenth-Century Denture from Rochester, Kent, England'. *Antiquity* 78: 858–64.
Andrew, H. 1995. *Who Won the Malayan Emergency?* Singapore: Graham Brash.
Antonacci, S. 2000a. 'Skull Found at Lake from World War II Passed Down in Family until Discarded by Teen'. *The [Springfield, IL] State Journal-Register*, 16 February, p. 1.
―――. 2000b. 'Officials Trying to Return WWII Skull'. *The [Springfield, IL] State Journal-Register*, 10 June, p. 7.
―――. 2000c. 'WWII-Era Skull to be Buried in Hiroshima'. *The [Springfield, IL] State Journal-Register*, 24 June, p. 1.
―――. 2003. 'Japanese Skull Unburied Three Years after Discovery'. *The [Springfield, IL] State Journal-Register*, 27 May, p. 1.
Apel, D. 2004. *Imagery of Lynching: Black Men, White Women, and the Mob*. New Brunswick: Rutgers University Press.
Appadurai, A. (ed.). 1986. *The Social Life of Things: Commodities in Cultural Perspective*. Cambridge: Cambridge University Press.
Ardener, E. 1975. 'Belief and the Problem of Women', in S. Ardener (ed.), *Perceiving Women*. London: Malaby Press, pp. 1–17.
Ardrey, R. 1976. *The Hunting Hypothesis: A Personal Conclusion Concerning the Evolutionary Nature of Man*. London: Macmillan.
Arens, W. 1979. *The Man-Eating Myth: Anthropology and Anthropophagy*. Oxford: Oxford University Press.
Ariès, P. 1977. *The Hour of Our Death*. Trans. H. Weaver. Harmondsworth: Penguin.
Arnold, E.T. 2009. *What Virtue There Is in Fire: Cultural Memory and the Lynching of Sam Hose*. Athens, GA: University of Georgia Press.
Aron, É. 1996. *Descartes et la Médecine*. Cambrai: C.L.D.
Associated Press. 1996. 'Skull of Rebel Finally to Be Buried: Soldier Was Slain at Spotsylvania'. *The Washington Times*, 17 August, A3.
Aung-Thwin, M. 2003. 'Genealogy of a Rebellion Narrative: Law, Ethnology and Culture in Colonial Burma'. *Journal of Southeast Asian Studies* 34(3): 393–419.
Australian War Memorial. 2010. 'Origins of the Australian War Memorial'. Retrieved 1 June 2010 from http://www.awm.gov.au/about/origins.asp
Axtell, J. 1981. *The European and the Indian: Essays in the Ethnohistory of Colonial North America*. Oxford: Oxford University Press.
Baer, M. and O. Schröter. 2001. *Eine Kopfjagd: Deutsche in Ostafrika*. Berlin: Ch. Links Verlag.
Balcomb, R. 2006. Personal communications, 14–16 November.
Balfour, S. 2002. *Deadly Embrace: Morocco and the Road to the Spanish Civil War*. Oxford: Oxford University Press.
Ballard, C. 2001. 'A.F.R. Wollaston and the "Utakwa River Mountain Papuan" Skulls'. *Journal of Pacific History* 36(1): 117–26.
Ba Maw, U. 1968. *Breakthrough in Burma: Memoirs of a Revolution*. New Haven: Yale University Press.

Bank, A. 1996. 'Of "Native Skulls" and "Noble Caucasians": Phrenology in Colonial South Africa'. *Journal of Southern African Studies* 22(3): 387–403.
Banner, S. 2002. *The Death Penalty: An American History*. Cambridge, MA and London: Harvard University Press.
Barker, J.R. 1943. 'Letter of 3 November to Parents'. Rhode Island History Society, Manuscripts Division, MSS 1099.
Barnes, B., D. Bloor and J. Henry. 1996. *Scientific Knowledge: A Sociological Analysis*. London: Athlone.
Bartecchi, C.E. 2006. *A Doctor's Vietnam Journal*. Bennington, VT: Merriam.
Bass, W.M. 1983. 'The Occurrence of Japanese Trophy Skulls in the United States'. *Journal of Forensic Sciences* 28(3): 800–803.
Bates, D. and M. Duell. 2011. '"Death Squad": Full Horror Emerges of How Rogue U.S. Brigade Murdered and Mutilated Afghan Civilians and Kept their Body Parts as Trophies'. *Daily Mail*, 29 March. Retrieved 12 April 2011 from http://www.dailymail.co.uk/news/article-1370758/Shocking-video-shows-U-S-troops-cheering-airstrike-blows-Afghan-civilians.html
Beckett, I.F.W. 2001. *Modern Insurgencies and Counter-Insurgencies: Guerrillas and Their Opponents since 1750*. London: Routledge.
Bell, D.A. 2007. *The First Total War: Napoleon's Europe and the Birth of Warfare as We Know It*. New York: Houghton Mifflin.
Bell, F.M. 1917. *The First Canadians in France: The Chronicle of a Military Hospital in the War Zone*. Toronto: McClelland, Goodchild and Stewart.
Bellard, A. 1975. *Gone for a Soldier: The Civil War Memoirs of Private Alfred Bellard*. Ed. D.H. Donald. Boston: Little, Brown.
Benn, C. 1998. *The Iroquois in the War of 1812*. Toronto: Toronto University Press.
Bennett, H.C. 2006. 'The British Army and Controlling Barbarization during the Kenya Emergency', in G. Kassimeris (ed.), *Warrior's Dishonour: Barbarity, Morality and Torture in Modern Warfare*. Aldershot: Ashgate, pp. 59–80.
Bennett Ross, J. 1984. 'Effects of Contact on Revenge Hostilities among the Achuara Jivaro', in R.B. Ferguson (ed.), *Warfare, Culture, and Environment*, pp. 83–124. Orlando, FL: Academic Press.
Bergerud, E.M. 2001. *Fire in the Sky: The Air War in the South Pacific*. New York: Basic Books.
Bieder, R.E. 2000. 'The Representations of Indian Bodies in Nineteenth-Century American Anthropology', in D.A. Mihesuah (ed.), *Repatriation Reader: Who Owns American Indian Remains?* Lincoln: University of Nebraska Press, pp. 19–36.
_____. 2003. *Science Encounters the Indian, 1820–1880: The Early Years of American Ethnology*. Norman: University of Oklahoma Press.
Bimberg, E.L. 1999. *The Moroccan Goums: Tribal Warriors in a Modern War*. Westport and London: Greenwood.
Bird-David, N. 1993. 'Tribal Metaphorization of Human-Nature Relatedness: A Comparative Analysis', in K. Milton (ed.), *Environmentalism: The View from Anthropology*. London: Routledge, pp. 111–24.
Blair, W.A. 2000. 'The Seven Days and the Radical Persuasion: Convincing Moderates in the North of the Need for a Hard War', in G.W. Gallagher (ed.), *The*

Richmond Campaign of 1862. Chapel Hill and London: University of North Carolina Press, pp. 153–80.

Blaxland, G. 1971. *The Regiments Depart: A History of the British Army, 1945–1970*. London: William Kimber.

Bloch, M. 1989. *Ritual, History and Power: Selected Papers in Anthropology*. London: Athlone.

———. and J. Parry (eds). 1982. *Death and the Regeneration of Life*. Cambridge: Cambridge University Press.

Blow, S. 1993a. 'War Atrocity Proves Tough to Put to Rest', *The Dallas Morning News*, 14 March, A35.

———. 1993b. 'Can't This Episode Just Be Buried?', *The Dallas Morning News*, 4 April, A37.

Blumenthal, W.H. 1955. *Bookman's Bedlam: An Olio of Literary Oddities*. New Brunswick, NJ: Rutgers University Press.

Boehm, C. 1984. *Blood Revenge: The Enactment and Management of Conflict in Montenegro and Other Tribal Societies*. Lawrence: University Press of Kansas.

Boon, J.A. 1982. *Other Tribes, Other Scribes: Symbolic Anthropology in the Comparative Study of Cultures, Histories, Religions, and Texts*. Cambridge: Cambridge University Press.

Bourdieu, P. 1977. *Outline of a Theory of Practice*. Trans. R. Nice. Cambridge: Cambridge University Press.

Bourke, J. 1999. *An Intimate History of Killing: Face-to-Face Killing in Twentieth-Century Warfare*. London: Granta.

Brandao, J.A. 2000. *Your Fyre Shall Burn No More: Iroquois Policy toward New France and Its Native Allies to 1701*. Lincoln: University of Nebraska Press.

Brennan, M. 1985. *Brennan's War: Vietnam 1965–69*. Novato, CA: Presidio Press.

Brewer, W.F. and J.C. Treyens. 1981. 'Role of Schemata in Memory for Places', *Cognitive Psychology* 13: 207–30.

Brightman, R.A. 1993. *Grateful Prey: Rock Cree Human-Animal Relationships*. Berkeley: University of California Press.

Bronner, S.J. 2008. *Killing Tradition: Inside Hunting and Animal Rights Controversies*. Lexington: University Press of Kentucky.

Brown, K. 2003. 'Interview with Dereyk Patterson'. WFCR Public Radio, New Hampshire, broadcast 7 October.

Brumwell, S. 2002. *Redcoats: The British Soldier and War in the Americas, 1755–1763*. Cambridge: Cambridge University Press.

Bryant, C.D. 1979. *Khaki-Collar Crime: Deviant Behavior in the Military Context*. New York and London: The Free Press.

Burbank, E. 1863. 'Letter of April 11'. Schoff Civil War Collection, Soldiers' Letters 47, The Burbank Brothers Papers. University of Michigan.

Burcham, R. and G. Burcham. 2007. *Vietnam: Triumphs and Tragedies*. Longwood, FL: Xulon Press.

Burke, E. 2001 [1790]. *Reflections on the Revolution in France*. Ed. J.C.D. Clark. Stanford: Stanford University Press.

Burkert, W. 1983. *Homo Necans: The Anthropology of Ancient Greek Sacrificial Ritual and Myth*. Trans. P. Bing. Berkeley: University of California Press.

Cady, J.F. 1958. *A History of Modern Burma*. Ithaca: Cornell University Press.

Callison, D. 1996. 'The Order of the Scarf'. Retrieved 1 June 2010 from http://www.lighthorseaircav.com/s-order-of-the-scarf.html

——————. 1998. 'Origin of the Skull'. Retrieved 1 June 2010 from http://www.lighthorseaircav.com/s-origin-of-the-skull.html

Calloway, C.G. 1997. *New Worlds for Old: Indians, Europeans, and the Remaking of Early America*. Baltimore and London: The Johns Hopkins University Press.

——————. 2008. *White People, Indians, and Highlanders: Tribal Peoples and Colonial Encounters in Scotland and America*. Oxford: Oxford University Press.

Canberra Times. 2000. 'Cowra Service Remembers Japanese Soldiers', 16 April, p. 7.

Canny, N.P. 1973. 'The Ideology of English Colonization: From Ireland to America', *William and Mary Quarterly* 30(4): 575–98.

Caplan, L. 1995. *Warrior Gentlemen: 'Gurkhas' in the Western Imagination*. Oxford: Berghahn.

Carbon County Museum. 2009. 'Carbon County Museum: Preserving Our Heritage'. Retrieved 1 June 2010 from http://www.carboncountymuseum.org

Carley, K. 2000. *Minnesota in the Civil War: An Illustrated History*. Minneapolis: Minnesota Historical Society Press.

Carlyle, T. 1837. *The French Revolution: A History: Vol. 3, The Guillotine*. London: James Fraser.

Carmichael, P.S. 1995. *Lee's Young Artillerist*. Charlottesville and London: University Press of Virginia.

Carruthers, S.L. 1995. *Winning Hearts and Minds: British Governments, the Media and Colonial Counter-Insurgency 1944–1960*. London and New York: Leicester University Press.

Cartmill, M. 1993. *A View to a Death in the Morning: Hunting and Nature through History*. Cambridge, MA: Harvard University Press.

Chacon, R.J. and D.H. Dye (eds). 2008. *The Taking and Displaying of Human Body Parts as Trophies by Amerindians*. New York: Springer.

Chilvers, H.A. 1933. *The Yellow Man Looks On: Being the Story of the Anglo-Dutch Conflict in Southern Africa and Its Interests for the Peoples of Asia*. London, Toronto, Melbourne and Sydney: Cassell and Company.

Christian, D. and W. Hoffer. 1990. *Victor Six: The Saga of America's Youngest, Most Decorated Officer in Vietnam*. New York: McGraw-Hill.

Churchill, W.L.S. 1899. *The River War: An Historical Account of the Reconquest of the Soudan, Vol. 2*. London: Longmans, Green and Co.

Clarke, J.W. 1998a. *The Lineaments of Wrath: Race, Violent Crime and American Culture*. New Brunswick: Transaction Publishers.

——————. 1998b. 'Without Fear or Shame: Lynching, Capital Punishment and the Subculture of Violence in the American South', *British Journal of Political Science* 28: 269–89.

Clarke, P. and M. McKinney. 2004. *The Equal Heart and Mind: Letters between Judith Wright and Jack McKinney*. Saint Lucia: University of Queensland Press.

Clarke, P.D. 1870. *Origin and Traditional History of the Wyandotts and Sketches of Other Indian Tribes of North America, True Traditional Stories of Tecumseh and His League, in the Years 1811 and 1812.* Toronto: Hunter, Rose & Co.

Clayton, A. 1984. *Counterinsurgency in Kenya: A Study of Military Operations Against the Mau Mau, 1952–1960.* Manhattan, KS: Sunflower University Press.

Clymer, L. 1999. 'Cromwell's Head and Milton's Hair: Corpse Theory in Spectacular Bodies of the Interregnum', *The Eighteenth Century* 40(2): 90–112.

Cohen, M.M. 1836. *Notices of Florida and the Campaigns.* Charleston, SC: Burgess and Honour; and New York: B.B. Hussey.

Cohn, N. 1970. *The Pursuit of the Millennium: Revolutionary Millenarians and Mystical Anarchists of the Middle Ages.* Oxford: Oxford University Press.

Colby, N.T. 2003. *The Civil War Papers of Lt. Colonel Newton T. Colby, New York Infantry.* Ed. W.E. Hughes. Jefferson, NC: McFarland.

Coleman, J.T. 2003. 'Terms of Dismemberment', Common-place 4(1). Retrieved 1 June 2010 from http://www.historycooperative.org/journals/cp/vol-04/no-01/coleman/

Collier, J.F. and M.Z. Rosaldo. 1981. 'Politics and Gender in Simple Societies', in S.B. Ortner and H. Whitehead (eds), *Sexual Meanings: The Cultural Construction of Gender and Sexuality.* Cambridge: Cambridge University Press, pp. 275–329.

Comber, L. 2008. *Malaya's Secret Police, 1945–60: The Role of the Special Branch in the Malayan Emergency.* Clayton, Victoria: Monash Asia Institute.

Conner, D.E. 1956. *Joseph Reddeford Walker and the Arizona Adventure.* Ed. D.J. Berthrong and O. Davenport. Norman: University of Oklahoma Press.

Connor, J. 2003. *The Australian Frontier Wars 1788–1838.* Sydney: University of New South Wales Press.

Contamine, P. 1980. *War in the Middle Ages.* Trans. M. Jones. Oxford: Basil Blackwell.

Costain, T.B. 1951. *The Magnificent Century.* London: Tandem.

Cox, C. 2004. *A Proper Sense of Honor: Service and Sacrifice in George Washington's Army.* Chapel Hill: University of North Carolina Press.

Craft, W.B. 1994. *Agony of Hell.* Nashville, TN: Turner.

Crawford, D. 1912. *Thinking Black: 22 Years Without a Break in the Long Grass of Central Africa.* London: Morgan and Scott.

Crawley, E. 2004. *Doing Prison Work: The Public and Private Lives of Prison Officers.* Portland, OR: Willan Publishing.

Dalzell, T. 2009. *The Routledge Dictionary of Modern American Slang and Unconventional English.* New York: Routledge.

Davison, J. and V. Sutlive, Jr. 1991. 'The Children of Nising: Images of Headhunting and Male Sexuality in Iban Ritual and Oral Literature', in V. Sutlive (ed.), *Female and Male in Borneo: Contributions and Challenges to Gender Studies.* Williamsburg: Borneo Research Council, pp. 153–230.

Daws, G. 1994. *Prisoners of the Japanese: POW's of World War II in the Pacific.* New York: Morrow.

Dennett, J.R. 1986. *The South as It Is.* Ed. and introd. H.M. Christman. Athens and London: University of Georgia Press.

Dennis, J.B.P. 1867. *Catalogue of Valuable Specimens in Natural History, Antiquities, Fossils, etc.* Ripon: W. Clowes and Sons. Retrieved 1 June 2010 from http://www.bl.uk/learning/langlit/texts/tourists/cat/tongue/witch.html

Department of Arms and Trophies. 1864. *Catalogue of the Museum of Flags, Trophies and Relics Relating to the Revolution, the War of 1812, the Mexican War, and the Present Rebellion.* New York: Charles O. Jones.

Derounian-Stodola, K.Z. 2009. *The War in Words: Reading the Dakota Conflict through the Captivity Literature.* Lincoln: University of Nebraska Press.

Descola, P. 1992. 'Societies of Nature and the Nature of Society', in A. Kuper (ed.), *Conceptualizing Society.* London: Routledge, pp. 107–26.

_____. 1994. *In the Society of Nature: A Native Ecology in Amazonia.* Cambridge: Cambridge University Press.

_____. 1996. *The Spears of Twilight: Life and Death in the Amazon Jungle.* Trans. J. Lloyd. New York: The New Press.

De Witte, L. 2001. *The Assassination of Lumumba.* Trans. A. Wright and R. Fenby. London, New York: Verso.

Dick, L. 1993. 'The Skull of Charlotte Corday', in B. Massumi (ed.), *The Politics of Everyday Fear.* Minneapolis: University of Minnesota Press, pp. 187–210.

Dickey, C. 2009. *Cranioklepty: Grave Robbing and the Search for Genius.* Cave Creek, AZ: Unbridled Books.

Diodorus of Sicily. 1939. *Diodorus of Sicily.* With an English translation by C.H. Oldfather, Vol. 3. London: William Heinman.

Dollard, J. 1937. *Caste and Class in a Southern Town.* New Haven: Yale University Press.

Douai, A. 1864. *Land und Leute in der Union.* Berlin: Janke.

Dougherty, P. 1992. 'The Sanctity of Life', in A. Signorelli and P. MacAdam (eds), *Rooster Crows at Light from the Bombing: Echoes from the Gulf War.* Minneapolis: Inroads Press, pp. 58–59.

Douglas, B. 2008. 'Climate to Crania: Science and the Racialization of Human Difference', in B. Douglas and C. Ballard (eds), *Foreign Bodies: Oceania and the Science of Race, 1750–1940.* Canberra: Australian National University Press, pp. 33–98.

Douglas, M. 1966. *Purity and Danger: An Analysis of Concepts of Pollution and Taboo.* London: Routledge.

_____. 1996. *Natural Symbols: Explorations in Cosmology.* London: Routledge.

Dower, J.W. 1986. *War Without Mercy: Race and Power in the Pacific War.* New York: Pantheon Books.

Dundes, A. 1976. 'A Psychoanalytic Study of the Bullroarer', *Man* 11: 220–38.

Dunkelman, M.H. 2006. *War's Relentless Hand: Twelve Tales of Civil War Soldiers.* Baton Rouge: Louisiana State University Press.

Easson, A. 1993. 'From Terror to Terror: Dickens, Carlyle and Cannibalism', in A. Yarrington and K. Everest (eds), *Reflections of Revolution: Images of Romanticism.* London: Routledge, pp. 96–111.

Echenberg, M. 1985. '"Morts Pour la France": The African Soldier in France during the Second World War', *Journal of African History* 26: 363–80.

Eden, T. 2001. 'Food, Assimilation, and the Malleability of the Human Body in Early Virginia', in J.M. Lindman and M.L. Tarter (eds), *A Centre of Wonders: The Body in Early America*. Ithaca and London: Cornell University Press, pp. 29–42.

Edgerton, R.B. 1990. *Mau Mau: An African Crucible*. London: I.B. Tauris.

Edmonds, S.E.E. 1865. *Nurse and Spy in the Union Army: Comprising the Adventures and Experiences of a Woman in Hospitals, Camps and Battle-Fields*. Hartford, Philadelphia : W.S. Williams & Co., Jones bros. & Co.

Edsforth, R. 2000. *The New Deal: America's Response to the Great Depression*. Oxford: Blackwell.

Egerton, D.R. 2003. 'A Peculiar Mark of Infamy: Dismemberment, Burial and Rebelliousness in Slave Societies', in N. Isenberg and A. Burstein (eds), *Mortal Remains: Death in Early America*. Philadelphia: University of Pennsylvania Press, pp. 149–60.

Egmond, F. and R. Zwijnenberg (eds). 2003. *Bodily Extremities: Preoccupations with the Human Body in Early Modern European Culture*. Aldershot: Ashgate.

Eliade, M. 1958. *Birth and Rebirth: The Religious Meanings of Initiation in Human Culture*. Trans. W.R. Trask. London: Havrill Press.

Elias, N. 1969. *The Civilizing Process, Vol. I: The History of Manners*. Oxford: Blackwell.

Elliott, Lt Col. H.W. 1996. 'The Third Priority: The Battlefield Dead', *The Army Lawyer*, July, pp. 3–20.

Erikson, P. 2005. 'The Social Significance of Pet-Keeping among Amazonian Indians', in A.L. Podberscek, E.S. Paul and J.A. Serpell (eds), *Companion Animals and Us: Exploring the Relationships between People and Pets*. Cambridge: Cambridge University Press, pp. 7–26.

Evans, C.W. 2004. *The Legend of John Wilkes Booth: Myth, Memory, and a Mummy*. Lawrence: University Press of Kansas.

Evans, R.J. 1996. *Rituals of Retribution: Capital Punishment in Germany 1600–1987*. Oxford: Oxford University Press.

'F.S.' of Churchdown. 1856. 'Human Skin Tanned, Etc.', *Notes and Queries* 39: 250–51.

Fabian, A. 2003. 'The Curious Cabinet of Dr Morton', in L. Dilworth (ed.), *Acts of Possession: Collecting in America*. New Brunswick: Rutgers University Press, pp. 112–37.

Fabian, J. 2002. *Time and the Other: How Anthropology Makes Its Object*. New York: Columbia University Press.

Fahey, J.J. 1963. *Pacific War Diary, 1942–1945*. Boston: Houghton Mifflin.

Fainaru, S. 2005. 'In Mosul, a Battle "Beyond Ruthless"', *Washington Post*, 13 April, A1.

Fauconnier, G. and M. Turner. 2002. *The Way We Think: Conceptual Blending and the Mind's Hidden Complexities*. New York: Basic Books.

Fausto, C. 1999. 'Of Enemies and Pets: Warfare and Shamanism in Amazonia', *American Ethnologist* 26(4): 933–56.

Fellman, M. 1990. *Inside War: The Guerrilla Conflict in Missouri during the American Civil War*. Oxford: Oxford University Press.

Feni, L. 2005. 'King Sandile's Full Remains Found with Skull Intact', Daily Dispatch Online. Retrieved 15 September 2006 from http://www.dispatch.co.za/2005/06/02/Easterncape/bdig.html

Fernandez, J. 1977. 'The Performance of Ritual Metaphor', in J.D. Sapir and J.C. Crocker (eds), *The Social Use of Metaphor: Essays on the Anthropology of Rhetoric.* Philadelphia: University of Pennsylvania Press, pp. 100–131.
Fewster, K., V. Basarin and H.H. Basarin. 2003. *Gallipoli: The Turkish Story.* Crows Nest, NSW: Allen and Unwin.
Ffolliot, P. and R. Liversidge. 1971. *Ludwig Krebs: Cape Naturalist to the King of Prussia.* Cape Town: A.A. Balkema.
Fforde, C., J. Hubert and P. Turnbull (eds). 2002. *The Dead and Their Possessions: Repatriation in Principle, Policy, and Practice.* London: Routledge.
Finch, M.L. 2001. '"Civilized" Bodies and the "Savage" Environment of Early New Plymouth', in J.M. Lindman and M.L. Tarter (eds), *A Centre of Wonders: The Body in Early America.* Ithaca and London: Cornell University Press, pp. 43–60.
Fine, L.M. 2000. 'Rights of Men, Rites of Passage: Hunting and Masculinity at Reo Motors of Lansing, Michigan, 1945–1975', *Journal of Social History* 33(4): 805–82.
Fissell, M.E. 2002. *Patients, Power and the Poor in Eighteenth-Century Bristol.* Cambridge: Cambridge University Press.
Fontein, J. 2010. 'Between Tortured Bodies and Resurfacing Bones: The Politics of the Dead in Zimbabwe', in K. Krmpotich, J. Fontein and J. Harries (eds), *The Substance of Bones: The Emotive Materiality and Affective Prescence of Human Remains.* Special Issue, *Journal of Material Culture* 15(4), pp. 423–48.
Forty, A. and S. Küchler (eds). 1999. *The Art of Forgetting.* Oxford, New York: Berg.
Foucault, M. 1995. *Discipline and Punish: The Birth of the Prison.* Trans. A. Sheridan. New York: Vintage Books.
Fowler, O.S. 1852. *Hereditary Descent: Its Laws and Facts Applied to Human Improvement.* New York: Fowlers and Wells.
———. 1873. *Human Sciences or Phrenology.* Philadelphia: National Publishing Company.
Fox, J.J. 1971. 'Sister's Son as Plant: Metaphors in an Idiom of Consanguinity', in R. Needham (ed.), *Rethinking Kinship and Marriage.* London: Tavistock, pp. 219–52.
Fralin, F. 1985. *The Indelible Image: Photographs of War – 1846 to the Present.* New York: Harry N. Abrams.
Francillon, R.J. 1979. *Japanese Aircraft of the Pacific War.* New York: Putnam.
Franey, L. 2001. 'Ethnographic Collecting and Travel: Blurring Boundaries, Forming a Discipline', *Victorian Literature and Culture* 29(1): 219–31.
Franklin, J.H. and L. Schweninger. 1999. *Runaway Slaves: Rebels on the Plantation.* New York and Oxford: Oxford University Press.
Frasier, D.K. 1996. *Murder Cases of the Twentieth Century.* Jefferson, NC and London: McFarland.
French, S. 2004. *The Rebellious Slave: Nat Turner in American Memory.* Boston and New York: Houghton Mifflin.
Frost, L. 2005. *Never One Nation: Freaks, Savages, and Whiteness in U.S. Popular Culture, 1850–1877.* Minneapolis, London: University of Minnesota Press.

Fry, G.-M. 1975. *Night Riders in Black Folk History*. Knoxville: University of Tennessee Press.

Fumerton, P. 1991. *Cultural Aesthetics: Renaissance Literature and the Practice of Social Ornament*. Chicago: University of Chicago Press.

Fürer-Haimendorf, C. von. 1968 [1939]. *The Naked Nagas*. Calcutta: Thacker, Spink and Co.

Fussell, P. 1988. *Thank God for the Atom Bomb*. New York: Summit.

———. 1989. *Wartime: Understanding and Behavior in the Second World War*. New York, Oxford: Oxford University Press.

Gamble, R. 2009. *My Service Life, 1939–1979: Bill Balmer*. Coleraine: Causeway Museum Service.

Gammack, G. 1979. *Gordon Gammack: Columns from Three Wars*. Ames: Iowa State University Press.

Gannon, M. 2001. *Understanding Global Cultures: Metaphorical Journeys through 23 Nations*. Thousand Oaks, CA: Sage.

Garner, J.W. 1920. *International Law and the World War, Vol.1*. London and New York: Longmans, Green and Co.

Gatrell, V.A.C. 1996. *The Hanging Tree: Execution and the English People, 1770–1868*. Oxford: Oxford University Press.

Gaukroger, S. 1995. *Descartes: An Intellectual Biography*. Oxford: Oxford University Press.

Geary, P. 1986. 'Sacred Commodities: The Circulation of Medieval Relics', in A. Appadurai (ed.), *The Social Life of Things: Commodities in Cultural Perspective*. Cambridge: Cambridge University Press, pp. 169–91.

Geddes, W.R. 1954. *The Land Dayaks of Sarawak*. London: HMSO.

Geertz, C. 1973. 'Deep Play: Notes on the Balinese Cockfight', in *The Interpretation of Cultures*. New York: Basic Books, pp. 412–54.

Geiringer, P. 1982. *Haydn: A Creative Life in Music*. Berkeley: University of California Press.

Gibbon, E. 1910. *The History of the Decline and Fall of the Roman Empire, Vol. 5*. London: J.M. Dent.

Gibbons, L. 2003. *Edmund Burke and Ireland: Aesthetics, Politics and the Colonial Sublime*. Cambridge: Cambridge University Press.

Gibbs, P. 1915. *The Soul of the War*. London: W. Heinemann.

Gibbs, R.W. 1994. *The Poetics of Mind: Figurative Thought, Language and Understanding*. Cambridge: Cambridge University Press.

Giddens, A. 1979. *Central Problems in Social Theory: Action, Structure and Contradiction in Social Analysis*. London: Macmillan.

Gilet, P. 1998. *Vladimir Propp and the Universal Folktale: Recommissioning an Old Paradigm – Story as Initiation* (Middlebury Studies in Russian Language and Literature, Vol. 17). Bern: Peter Lang.

Gillingham, J. 1999. 'Killing and Mutilating Political Enemies in the British Isles from the Late Twelfth to the Early Fourteenth Century: A Comparative Study', in B. Smith (ed.), *Britain and Ireland 900–1300*. Cambridge: Cambridge University Press, pp. 114–34.

Gillings, K.G. 1989. 'The Bambata Rebellion of 1906: Nkandla Operations and the Battle of Mome Gorge, 10th June 1906', *South African Military History Society Military History Journal* 8(1): 21–31.

———. 2002. 'The "Death" of Bambata Zondi: A Recent Discovery', *South African Military History Society Military History Journal* 12(4): 133–37.

Gill-King, H. 1992. 'A Japanese "Trophy Skull" from the Battle of Saipan', *Program and Abstracts of the American Academy of Forensic Sciences Annual Meeting, February 1992, New Orleans*. Colorado Springs, CO: American Academy of Forensic Sciences, p. 162.

———. 2005. Personal communications, 1, 13 and 22 April.

Gilmor, H. 1866. *Four Years in the Saddle*. New York: Harper.

Given, J.B. 1997. *Inquisition and Medieval Society: Power, Discipline, and Resistance in Languedoc*. Ithaca: Cornell University Press.

Glatthaar, J.T. 2008. *General Lee's Army: From Victory to Collapse*. New York: Free Press.

Goldfield, D.R. 2002. *Still Fighting the Civil War: The American South and Southern History*. Baton Rouge, LA: LSU Press.

Goldstein, L. 2002. '"The Imagination Problem": Winfield Townley Scott and the American Wars', *War, Literature and the Arts* 14: 59–77.

Gollin, R.K. 2005. 'Estranged Allegiances in Hawthorne's Unfinished Romances', in M. Bell (ed.), *Hawthorne and the Real: Bicentennial Essays*. Columbus: Ohio State University Press, pp. 159–80.

Gon, P. 1984. *Send Carrington! The Story of an Imperial Frontiersman*. Craighall: Ad. Donker.

Goody, J. (ed.). 1973. *The Character of Kinship*. Cambridge: Cambridge University Press.

Gordon, D. 2001. 'Owners of the Land and Lunda Lords: Colonial Chiefs in the Borderlands of Northern Rhodesia and the Belgian Congo', *International Journal of African Historical Studies* 34(2): 315–38.

Gorton, J. 1851. *A General Biographical Dictionary*. London: Henry G. Bohn.

Gould, S.J. 1996. *The Mismeasure of Man*. New York: W.W. Norton.

Gould, T. 1999. *Imperial Warriors: Britain and the Gurkhas*. London: Granta.

Graburn, N.H. 1989. 'Tourism: The Sacred Journey', in V.L. Smith (ed.), *Hosts and Guests: The Anthropology of Tourism*. Philadelphia: University of Pennsylvania Press, pp. 21–36.

———. 2000. 'Foreword', in M. Hitchcock and K. Teague (eds), *Souvenirs: The Material Culture of Tourism*. Aldershot: Ashgate, pp. i–xvii.

Grant, S.-M. 2004. 'Patriot Graves: American National Identity and the Civil War Dead', *American Nineteenth Century History* 5(3): 74–100.

Grasshoff, R. 1915. *The Tragedy of Belgium: An Answer to Professor Waxweiler*. New York: Dillingham.

Graymont, B. 1972. *The Iroquois in the American Revolution*. New York: Syracuse University Press.

Greenberg, K.S. 2003. 'Name, Face, Body', in K.S. Greenberg (ed.), *Nat Turner: A Slave Rebellion in History and Memory*. Oxford: Oxford University Press, pp. 3–23.

Grenfell, F.W. 1925. *Memoirs of Field-Marshall Lord Grenfell, P.C., G.C.B., G.C.M.G. With a Preface by Maj.Gen. Sir Ronald Lane, K.C.B., K.C.V.O. With Four Illustrations in Colour by Lord Grenfell*. London: Hodder and Stoughton.

Grenier, J. 2005. *The First Way of War: American War Making on the Frontier, 1607–1814*. Cambridge: Cambridge University Press.

Griffin, E. 2007. *Blood Sport: Hunting in Britain Since 1066*. New Haven and London: Yale University Press.

Griffiths, T. 1996. *Hunters and Collectors: The Antiquarian Imagination in Australia*. Cambridge: Cambridge University Press.

Grimsted, D. 1998. *American Mobbing, 1828–1861: Toward Civil War*. New York and Oxford: Oxford University Press.

Grossman, Lieutenant Colonel D. 2009. *On Killing: The Psychological Cost of Learning to Kill in War and Society*. New York, Boston and London: Little, Brown.

Gruber, H.E. and K. Bödeker (eds). 2005. *Creativity, Psychology and the History of Science*. Dordrecht: Springer.

Hagner, M. 1999. 'Prolegomena to a History of Radical Brains in the Nineteenth Century: Physiognomics, Phrenology, Brain Anatomy', *Physis* 36(2): 321–38.

———. 2003. 'Skulls, Brains and Memorial Culture: On Cerebral Biographies of Scientists in the Nineteenth Century', *Science in Context* 16(1/2): 195–218.

Hain, P.C. 2005. *A Confederate Chronicle: The Life of a Civil War Survivor*. Columbia: University of Missouri Press.

Hall, R. 2000. *Combat Battalion: The Eighth Battalion in Vietnam*. Crows Nest, NSW: Allen and Unwin.

Hallam, E. and J. Hockey. 2001. *Death, Memory and Material Culture*. Oxford and New York: Berg.

Hallam, E., J. Hockey and G. Howarth. 1999. *Beyond the Body: Death and Social Identity*. London and New York: Routledge.

Hallowell, I. 1960. 'Ojibwa Ontology and World View', in S. Diamond (ed.), *Culture in History: Essays in Honor of Paul Radin*. New York: Columbia University Press, pp. 19–52.

Hampshire Chronicle. 1782. 'Home News', Monday 2 September. Retrieved 1 June 2010 from http://freepages.genealogy.rootsweb.ancestry.com/~dutillieul/ZOtherPapers/HCSep21782.html

Hanchett, W. 1983. *The Lincoln Murder Conspiracies*. Urbana and Chicago: University of Illinois Press.

Hanlon, C. 2003. 'O.S. Fowler and "Hereditary Descent"', in M.I. Lowance Jr. (ed.), *A House Divided: The Antebellum Slavery Debates in America, 1776–1865*. Princeton and Oxford: Princeton University Press, pp. 284–91.

Harner, M.J. 1972. *Jivaro: People of the Sacred Waterfalls*. London: Robert Hale.

Harper's Weekly. 1862. 'Barbarities at Manassas', 7 February, p. 87.

Harris, M.D. 2005. *The Atomic Times: My H-Bomb Year at the Pacific Proving Ground: A Memoir*. Novato, CA: Presidio Press.

Harrison, S. 1982. 'Yams and the Symbolic Representation of Time in a Sepik River Village', *Oceania* 52(3): 141–62.

———. 1985. 'Ritual Hierarchy and Secular Equality in a Sepik River Village', *American Ethnologist* 12(3): 413–26.

———. 1989. 'The Symbolic Construction of Aggression and War in a Sepik River Society', *Man* (n.s.) 24(4): 583–99.

———. 1993. *The Mask of War: Violence, Ritual and the Self in Melanesia*. Manchester: Manchester University Press.

———. 2004. 'Forgetful and Memorious Landscapes', *Social Anthropology* 12(2): 135–52.

———. 2005. *Fracturing Resemblances: Identity and Mimetic Conflict in Melanesia and the West*. Oxford and New York: Berghahn.

———. 2006. 'Skull Trophies of the Pacific War: Transgressive Objects of Remembrance', *Journal of the Royal Anthropological Institute* 12(4): 817–36.

———. 2008a. 'Skulls and Scientific Collecting in the Victorian Military: Keeping the Enemy Dead in British Frontier Warfare', *Comparative Studies in Society and History* 50(1): 285–303.

———. 2008b. 'War Mementos and the Souls of Missing Soldiers: Returning Effects of the Battlefield Dead', *Journal of the Royal Anthropological Institute* 14(4): 774–90.

———. 2010. 'Bones in the Rebel Lady's Boudoir: Race, Ethnology and Trophy-Hunting in the American Civil War', *Journal of Material Culture* 15(4): 385–402.

Harvey, P.D. 2002. *The Tokens of Esteem: An Essay in Ritual Inhumanity*. Lincoln, NE: iUniverse.

Hastings, E.S. 1890. 'Exhibition of the Skulls of a Burmese Dacoit and of a Rebel Chinese Mandarin', *Journal of the Anthropological Institute of Great Britain and Ireland* 19: 94–96.

Hawthorne, N. 1985. 'Northern Volunteers: From a Journal', *The Hawthorne Society Newsletter* 11(1): 1–2.

Hay, D., P. Linebaugh, J.G. Rule, E.P. Thompson and C. Winslow (eds). 1975. *Albion's Fatal Tree: Crime and Society in Eighteenth-Century England*. London: Allen Lane.

Henare, A.J.M. 2005. *Museums, Anthropology and Imperial Exchange*. Cambridge: Cambridge University Press.

Henderson, A.K. 2001. *Stateside Soldier: Life in the Women's Army Corps, 1944–45*. Columbia, SC: University of South Carolina Press.

Henschen, F. 1966. *The Human Skull: A Cultural History*. Trans. S. Thomas. New York and Washington: Frederick A. Praeger.

Herman, D.J. 2001. *Hunting and the American Imagination*. Washington and London: Smithsonian Institution Press.

Hertz, R. 1960. *Death and the Right Hand*. Trans. R. Needham and C. Needham. Introd. E.E. Evans-Pritchard. London: Cohen and West.

Heynowski, W. and G. Scheumann (dirs). 1968. *Piloten im Pyjama* (film). Berlin: DEFA.

Hide, R. 2010. Personal communications, 3–5 April.

Highet, M.J. 2005. 'Body Snatching and Grave Robbing: Bodies for Science', *History and Anthropology* 16(4): 415–40.

Higonnet, M.R. 2007. 'Souvenirs of Death', *Journal of War and Culture Studies* 1(1): 65–78.

Hiley-Young, B., D.D. Blake, F.R. Abueg, V. Rozynko and F.D. Gusman. 1995. 'War Zone Violence in Vietnam: An Examination of Premilitary, Military and Post-military Factors in PTSD In-patients', *Journal of Traumatic Stress* 8(1): 125–41.

Hill, A. 2002. *Young Digger*. Melbourne: Penguin.

Hitchcock, M. 2000. 'Introduction', in M. Hitchcock and K. Teague (eds), *Souvenirs: The Material Culture of Tourism*. Aldershot: Ashgate, pp. 1–17.

Hoig, S. 1961. *The Sand Creek Massacre*. Norman: University of Oklahoma Press.

Holliday, R. and G. Letherby. 1993. 'Happy Families or Poor Relations? An Exploration of Family Analogies in the Small Firm', *International Small Business Journal* 11(2): 54–63.

Hordern, M.C. 2005. *A Merciful Journey: Recollections of a World War II Patrol Boat Man*. Carlton, Vic.: Miegunyah Press.

Horn, D.G. 2003. *The Criminal Body: Lombroso and the Anatomy of Deviance*. London and New York: Routledge.

Hoskins, J. (ed.). 1996a. *Headhunting and the Social Imagination in Southeast Asia*. Stanford: Stanford University Press.

_____. 1996b. 'Introduction: Headhunting as Practice and as Trope', in J. Hoskins (ed.), *Headhunting and the Social Imagination in Southeast Asia*. Stanford: Stanford University Press, pp. 1–49.

_____. 1996c. 'The Heritage of Headhunting: History, Ideology and Violence on Sumba, 1890-1990', in J. Hoskins (ed.), *Headhunting and the Social Imagination in Southeast Asia*. Stanford: Stanford University Press, pp. 216–48.

Howard, A. 2006. Personal communication, 31 December 2006.

_____. 2007. Personal communication, 5 January 2007.

Howard, M.J., G.J. Andreopoulos and M.R. Shulman (eds). 1984. *The Laws of War: Constraints on Warfare in the Western World*. New Haven and London: Yale University Press.

Howe, N. 1988. 'Metaphor in Contemporary American Political Discourse', *Metaphor and Symbol* 3(2): 87–104.

Howell, S. 1989. '"To Be Angry Is Not to Be Human, but to Be Fearful Is": Chewong Concepts of Human Nature', in S. Howell and R. Willis (eds), *Societies at Peace: Anthropological Perspectives*. London: Routledge, pp. 45–59.

Hoyt, E.P. 1986. *Japan's War: The Great Pacific Conflict*. New York: McGraw-Hill.

Huggan, G. 2001. *The Post-colonial Exotic: Marketing the Margins*. London: Routledge.

Hummel, C. 1989. 'Appendix A: The Controversy and Legends Surrounding Sandile', in C. Hummel (ed.), *The Frontier War Journal of Major John Crealock: A Narrative of the Ninth Frontier War by the Assistant Military Secretary to Lieutenant General Thesiger*. Cape Town: Van Riebeeck Society, pp. 163–67.

Hunt, G.P. 1967. 'Louie, the Boy on the Cover', *Life Magazine* 63(8), 5 August, p. 1.

Huntington, R. and P. Metcalf. 1979. *Celebrations of Death: The Anthropology of Mortuary Ritual*. Cambridge: Cambridge University Press.
Hutton, J.H. 1921. *The Sema Nagas*. London: Macmillan.
Hynes, S. 1998. *The Soldiers' Tale: Bearing Witness to Modern War*. London: Pimlico.
Ignatieff, M. 1998. *The Warrior's Honor: Ethnic War and the Modern Conscience*. London: Vintage.
Impey, O. and A. MacGregor. 1985. *The Origins of Museums: The Cabinet of Curiosities in Sixteenth and Seventeenth Century Europe*. Oxford: Clarendon.
Jackson, H. 1997. 'Race and the Politics of Medicine in Nineteenth Century Georgia', in R.L. Blakely and J.M. Harrington (eds), *Bones in the Basement: Postmortem Racism in Nineteenth-Century Medical Training*. Washington and London: Smithsonian Institution Press, pp. 184–205.
Jahoda, G. 1999. *Images of Savages: Ancient Roots of Modern Prejudice in Western Culture*. London and New York: Routledge.
Janowitz, M. and E. Shils. 1975. 'Cohesion and Disintegration in the Wehrmacht in World War II', in M. Janowitz (ed.), *Military Conflict*. London: Sage, pp. 177–220.
Jennings, F. 1975. *The Invasion of America: Indians, Colonialism and the Cant of Conquest*. Chapel Hill: University of North Carolina Press.
Jet Magazine. 1966. 'War Mascot'. Vol. 31(10), 15 December, p. 32.
Jezernik, B. 2001. 'Head-Hunting in Europe: Montenegrin Heroes, Turkish Barbarians and Western Observers', *Ethnologia Europaea* 31(1): 21–36.
Jobson, C. 2009. *Looking Forward, Looking Back: Customs and Traditions of the Australian Army*. Wavell Heights, Qld.: Big Sky Publishing.
Johnston, M. 2000. *Fighting the Enemy: Australian Soldiers and their Adversaries in World War II*. Cambridge: Cambridge University Press.
Jones, J. 1963. *The Thin Red Line*. London: Collins.
Jung, P.J. 2008. *The Black Hawk War of 1832*. Norman: University of Oklahoma Press.
Jury, M. 1986. *The Vietnam Photo Book*. New York: Vintage.
Juzda, E. 2009. 'Skulls, Science, and the Spoils of War: Craniological Studies at the United States Army Medical Museum, 1868-1900', *Studies in History and Philosophy of Biological and Biomedical Sciences* 40: 156–67.
Kahn, S.M. 1993. *Between Tedium and Terror: A Soldier's World War II Diary*. Urbana and Chicago: University of Illinois Press.
Kanon, T. 1999. '"A Slow, Laborious Slaughter": The Battle of Horseshoe Bend', Tennessee *Historical Quarterly* 58(1): 3–15.
Kaye, J.W. 1857. *History of the War in Afghanistan, Vol 1*. London: Richard Bentley.
Keeley, L.H. 1997. *War Before Civilisation: The Myth of the Peaceful Savage*. Oxford: Oxford University Press.
Keener, C.S. 1999. 'An Ethnohistorical Analysis of Iroquois Assault Tactics Used against Fortified Settlements of the Northeast in the Seventeenth Century', *Ethnohistory* 46: 777–807.
Kelsay, I.T. 1986. *Joseph Brant, 1743–1807*. Syracuse: Syracuse University Press.
Kethcart, R. n.d. 'Clyde Wesley Lawrence Jr'. Retrieved 1 June 2010 from http://www.bobcat.ws/lawrencetrib.htm

Kidd, C. 2004. 'Ethnicity in the British Atlantic World, 1688-1830', in K. Wilson (ed.), *A New Imperial History: Culture, Identity and Modernity in Britain and the Empire, 1660–1840*. Cambridge: Cambridge University Press, pp. 260–80.

Killingray, D. and D. Omissi (eds). 1999. *Guardians of Empire: The Armed Forces of the Colonial Powers, c. 1700–1964*. Manchester: Manchester University Press.

King, A. 2006. 'The Word of Command: Communication and Cohesion in the Military', *Armed Forces and Society* 32(4): 493–512.

King, E.L. 1945. 'The Edward Lacy King Collection'. Retrieved 17 September 2007 from http://www.war-experience.org/collections/sea/alliedusa/king/pagetwo.htm

Kirkland, F. 1867. *The Pictorial Book of Anecdotes and Incidents of the War of the Rebellion, Civil, Military, Naval and Domestic*. Hartford: Hartford Publishing Co.

Klarsfeld, S. (ed.). 1985. *The Struthof Album: Study of the Gassing at Natzweiler-Struthof of 86 Jews Whose Bodies Were to Constitute a Collection of Skeletons*. New York: The Beate Klarsfeld Foundation.

Knickerbocker, The. 1862. 'Editor's Table', *The Knickerbocker, or New-York Monthly Magazine* 59(6): 578–90.

Knightley, P. 2004. *The First Casualty: The War Correspondent as Hero and Myth-Maker from the Crimea to Iraq*. 3rd edition. Baltimore: The Johns Hopkins University Press.

Kolig, E. 1986. 'Andreas Reischek and the Maori: Villainy or the Nineteenth-Century Scientific Ethos?', *Pacific Studies* 10(1): 55–78.

Koller, V. 2004. *Metaphor and Gender in Business Media Discourse: A Critical Cognitive Study*. Basingstoke: Palgrave Macmillan.

Krmpotich, C., J. Fontein and J. Harries (eds). 2010. 'The Substance of Bones: The Emotive Materiality and Affective Presence of Human Remains'. Special Issue, *Journal of Material Culture* 15(4).

Kuper, A. 1988. *The Invention of Primitive Society: Transformations of an Illusion*. London: Routledge.

Kwon, H. 1998. 'The Saddle and the Sledge: Hunting as Comparative Narrative in Siberia and Beyond', *Journal of the Royal Anthropological Institute* (n.s.) 4: 115–27.

Labordier, O. de, J.R. Maddicott and D.A. Carpenter. 2000. 'The Last Hours of Simon de Montfort: A New Account', *English Historical Review*, April, pp. 378–412.

Laderman, G. 1996. *The Sacred Remains: American Attitudes toward Death, 1799–1883*. New Haven and London: Yale University Press.

Lakoff, G. 1989. *Women, Fire, and Dangerous Things: What Categories Reveal about the Mind*. Chicago: University of Chicago Press.

———. 1993. 'The Contemporary Theory of Metaphor', in A. Ortony (ed.), *Metaphor and Thought*. Cambridge: Cambridge University Press, pp. 202–51.

———. 2002. *Moral Politics: How Liberals and Conservatives Think*. Chicago: University of Chicago Press.

Lakoff, G. and M. Johnson. 1980. *Metaphors We Live By*. Chicago: University of Chicago Press.

Landau, P.S. 1996. 'With Camera and Gun in Southern Africa: Inventing the Image of Bushmen, c.1880 to 1935', in P. Skotnes (ed.), *Miscast: Negotiating the Presence of the Bushmen*. Cape Town: University of Cape Town Press, pp. 129–41.

Landon, W. 1939. 'Last Letters to the Vincennes Sun', *Indiana Magazine of History* 35(1): 76–94.

Lanning, M.L. 2007. *The Only War We Had: A Platoon Leader's Journal of Vietnam*. College Station: Texas A & M University Press.

Larson, T.J. 2003. *Hell's Kitchen Tulagi 1942–1943*. New York: iUniverse.

Lawler, N.E. 1992. *Soldiers of Misfortune: Ivoirien Tirailleurs of World War II*. Athens: Ohio University Press.

Leach, E. 2001 [1964]. 'Anthropological Aspects of Language: Animal Categories and Verbal Abuse', in S. Hugh-Jones and J. Laidlaw (eds), *The Essential Edmund Leach: Culture and Human Nature, Vol I*. New Haven: Yale University Press, pp. 322–43.

Lee, R. and S. Hurlich. 1982. 'From Foragers to Fighters: South Africa's Militarization of the Namibian San', in E. Laycock and R. Lee (eds), *Politics and History in Band Societies*. Cambridge: Cambridge University Press, pp. 327–46.

Lehmann, J.H. 1977. *Remember You Are an Englishman: A Biography of Sir Harry Smith, 1787–1860*. London: Jonathan Cape.

Lennon, J. and M. Foley. 2004. *Dark Tourism: The Attraction of Death and Disaster*. London: Thompson Learning.

Leonard, E.D. 2002. 'Mary Surratt and the Plot to Assassinate Abraham Lincoln', in J.E. Cashin (ed.), *The War Was You and Me: Civilians in the American Civil War*. Princeton: Princeton University Press, pp. 286–312.

Lepore, J. 1998. *The Name of War: King Philip's War and the Origins of American Identity*. New York: Knopf.

Lewis, J. and B. Steele. 2001. *Hell in the Pacific: From Pearl Harbor to Hiroshima and Beyond*. London: Channel 4 Books.

Libby, F. 2000. *Horses Don't Fly: A Memoir of World War I*. New York: Arcade Publishers.

Lifton, R.J. 2000. *The Nazi Doctors: Medical Killing and the Psychology of Genocide*. New York: Basic Books.

Lince, G. 1997. *Too Young the Heroes: A World War II Marine's Account of Facing a Veteran Enemy at Guadalcanal, the Solomons and Okinawa*. Jefferson, NC, and London: McFarland.

Lindbergh, C.A. 1970. *The Wartime Journals of Charles A. Lindbergh*. New York: Harcourt Brace Jovanovich.

Lindenbaum, S. 2004. 'Thinking about Cannibalism', *Annual Review of Anthropology* 33: 475–98.

Lindstrom, L. and G. White. 1990. *Island Encounters: Black and White Memories of the Pacific War*. Washington, DC: Smithsonian Institution Press.

Linebaugh, P. 1975. 'The Tyburn Riot against the Surgeons', in D. Hay, P. Linebaugh, J.G. Rule, E.P. Thompson and C. Winslow (eds), *Albion's Fatal Tree: Crime and Society in Eighteenth-Century England*. London: Allen Lane, pp. 65–118.

Lingenfelter, R.E. 1986. *Death Valley and the Amargosa: A Land of Illusion*. Berkeley: University of California Press.

Lipman, A. 2008. '"A Meanes to Knitt Them Togeather": The Exchange of Body Parts in the Pequot War', *William and Mary Quarterly* 65(1): 3–28.
Little, L. 1998. 'The Troop Cup'. Retrieved 1 June 2010 from http://www.lighthorseaircav.com/s-little-c-cup.html
Locke, R. 2004. Personal communication, 25 September.
Locke, R., and P. Quantrill. 2002. *Zulu Victory: The Epic of Isandlwana and the Cover-up*. London: Greenhill Books/Lionel Leventhal.
Lorcin, P.M.E. 1995. *Imperial Identities: Stereotyping, Prejudice and Race in Colonial Algeria*. London: I.B. Tauris.
Lorie, C. 2004. 'The Ghosts of Vietnam: An Unsettling Legacy for the Children of Some Veterans', *Daily Hampshire Gazette*, 9 January, p. 23.
Lucaites, J.L. and J.P. McDaniel. 2004. 'Telescopic Mourning/Warring in the Global Village: Decomposing (Japanese) Authority Figures', *Communication and Critical/Cultural Studies* 1(1): 1–28.
Luyendijk-Elshout, A.M. 1997. 'Opening Address: The Magic of the Skull. "Commercium Craniorum" in the Nineteenth Century', *International Journal of Osteoarchaeology* 7: 571–74.
Lyman, E. 2008. Personal communications, 12–13 February.
MacDonald, H. 2005. 'Reading the "Foreign Skull": An Episode in Nineteenth-Century Colonial Human Dissection', *Australian Historical Studies* 37(125): 81–96.
_____. 2006. *Human Remains: Dissection and Its Histories*. New Haven: Yale University Press.
MacKenzie, J.M. 1987. 'The Imperial Pioneer and Hunter and the British Masculine Stereotype in Late Victorian and Edwardian Times', in J.A. Mangan and J. Walvin (eds), *Manliness and Morality: Middle-Class Masculinity in Britain and America, 1800–1940*. Manchester: Manchester University Press, pp. 176–98.
_____. 1988. *The Empire of Nature: Hunting, Conservation and British Imperialism*. Manchester: Manchester University Press.
MacPherson, M. 2002. *Long Time Passing: Vietnam and the Haunted Generation*. Bloomington: Indiana University Press.
Maddicott, J.R. 1996. *Simon de Montfort*. Cambridge: Cambridge University Press.
Madley, B. 2005. 'From Africa to Auschwitz: How German South West Africa Incubated Ideas and Methods Adopted and Developed by the Nazis in Eastern Europe', *European History Quarterly* 35(3): 429–64.
Malchow, H.L. 1996. *Gothic Images of Race in Nineteenth Century Britain*. Stanford: Stanford University Press.
Malone, P. 2003a. 'Macabre Mystery: Coroner Tries to Find Origin of Skull Found during Raid by Deputies', *Pueblo Chieftain*, 25 August, p. A5.
_____. 2003b. 'Pueblo Soldier a Product of His Times', *Pueblo Chieftain*, 2 November, p. B1.
_____. 2003c. 'Skull Likely Is WWII Trophy', *Pueblo Chieftain*, 3 November, p. B1.
_____. 2004a. 'Skull Found in Pueblo to be Returned to Japan', *Pueblo Chieftain*, 5 February, p. B3.
_____. 2004b. 'Unknown Soldier's Remains Home at Last', *Pueblo Chieftain*, 17 May, p. A10.

Malone, P.M. 2000. *The Skulking Way of War: Technology and Tactics among the New England Indians*. Lanham, MD: Madison Books.

Manchester, W. 1983. *The Last Lion: Winston Spencer Churchill: Visions of Glory 1874–1932*. Boston, Toronto: Little, Brown.

Mandell, N. 2002. *The Corporation as Family: The Gendering of Corporate Welfare, 1890–1930*. Durham, NC: University of North Carolina Press.

Mangan, J.A. and C. McKenzie. 2003. '"Pig-Sticking Is the Greatest Fun": Martial Conditioning on the Hunting Fields of Empire', in J.A. Mangan (ed.), *Militarism, Sport, Europe: War Without Weapons*. London: Frank Cass, pp. 97–119.

_____. 2009. *Militarism, Hunting, Imperialism: 'Blooding' the Martial Male*. London: Routledge.

Mann, B.A. 2005. *George Washington's War on Native America*. Westport and London: Praeger.

Maples, W.R. and M. Browning. 1995. *Dead Men Do Tell Tales: The Strange and Fascinating Cases of a Forensic Anthropologist*. London: Random House.

Markovitz, J. 2004. *Legacies of Lynching: Racial Violence and Memory*. Minneapolis and London: University of Minnesota Press.

Marks, S. 1970. *Reluctant Rebellion: The 1906–8 Disturbances in Natal*. Oxford: Clarendon Press.

_____. 1986. 'Class, Ideology and the Bambatha Rebellion', in D. Crummey (ed.), *Banditry, Rebellion and Social Protest in Africa*. London: James Curry, pp. 351–73.

Marks, S.A. 1991. *Southern Hunting in Black and White: Nature, History, and Ritual in a Carolina Community*. Princeton: Princeton University Press.

Mars, G. and V. Mars. 2000. '"Souvenir-Gifts" as Tokens of Filial Esteem: The Meanings of Blackpool Souvenirs', in M. Hitchcock and K. Teague (eds), *Souvenirs: The Material Culture of Tourism*. Aldershot: Ashgate, pp. 91–111.

Marten, J. 1990. *Texas Divided: Loyalty and Dissent in the Lone Star State*. Lexington: University Press of Kentucky.

Marvin, W.P. 2006. *Hunting Law and Ritual in Medieval English Literature*. Cambridge: D.S. Brewer.

Massey, M.E. 1994. *Women in the Civil War*. Lincoln: University of Nebraska Press.

Masson, S. 2004. 'The Tanned Human Skin of Nantes', *Quadrant Magazine* 48(12): 36–38.

Maxner, S. 2000. 'Interview with Herbert Green. Transcribed by Tammi Mikel'. Unpublished manuscript. Texas Tech University, Vietnam Archive. Retrieved 1 June 2010 from http://www.vietnam.ttu.edu/star/images/oh/oh0103/OH0103.pdf

McCall, J.H., Jnr. 2000. *Pogiebait's War: A Son's Quest for His Father's Wartime Life*. Bloomington, IN: Xlibris Corporation.

McCaskie, T.C. 2003. *State and Society in Pre-colonial Asante*. Cambridge: Cambridge University Press.

McGovern, J.R. 1982. *Anatomy of a Lynching: The Killing of Claude Neal*. Baton Rouge and London: Louisiana State University Press.

McGreal, C. 2010. 'US Soldiers "Killed Afghan Civilians for Sport and Collected Fingers as Trophies": Soldiers Face Charges Over Secret "Kill Team" Which Allegedly Murdered at Random and Collected Fingers as Trophies of War'. *The Guardian*, 9 September. Retrieved 12 April 2011 from http://www.guardian.co.uk/world/2010/sep/09/us-soldiers-afghan-civilians-fingers

McKinley, R. 1976. 'Human and Proud of It! A Structural Treatment of Headhunting Rites and the Social Definition of Enemies', in G.N. Appell (ed.), *Studies in Borneo Societies: Social Process and Anthropological Explanation*. Special Report Number 12. De Kalb: Center for Southeast Asian Studies, Northern Illinois University, pp. 92–126.

McLynn, F. 1989. *Crime and Punishment in Eighteenth-Century England*. London and New York: Routledge.

McMains, H.F. 2000. *The Death of Cromwell*. Lexington: University Press of Kentucky.

McPherson, J.M. 1997. *For Cause and Comrades: Why Men Fought in the Civil War*. New York and Oxford: Oxford University Press.

McWhiney, G. and P.D. Jamieson. 1982. *Attack and Die: Civil War Military Tactics and the Southern Heritage*. Tuscaloosa: University of Alabama Press.

Melish, J.P. 2001. 'Emancipation and the Em-bodiment of "Race"', in J.M. Lindman and M.L. Tarter (eds), *A Centre of Wonders: The Body in Early America*. Ithaca and London: Cornell University Press, pp. 223–36.

Meller, W.C. 1924. *A Knight's Life in the Days of Chivalry*. London: T.W. Laurie.

Mendelsohn, J. (ed.). 1982. *Medical Experiments on Jewish Inmates of Concentration Camps*. New York, London: Garland.

Meredith, W. 2005. 'The History of Beethoven's Skull Fragments: Part One', *The Beethoven Journal* 20: 1–25.

Metcalf, P. 1996. 'Images of Headhunting', in J. Hoskins (ed.), *Headhunting and the Social Imagination in Southeast Asia*. Stanford: Stanford University Press, pp. 249-92.

Mihesuah, D.A. (ed.). 2000. *Repatriation Reader: Who Owns American Indian Remains?* Lincoln: University of Nebraska Press.

Miles, J. 1999. *QLD – Old Bones Believed to Be Those of Japanese Soldiers*. Australian Associated Press Information Services, 17 June.

Mitchell, R. 2002. 'From Volunteer to Soldier: The Psychology of Service', in M. Barton and L. M. Logue (eds), *The Civil War Soldier: A Historical Reader*. New York and London: New York University Press, pp. 354–85.

Mkhize, N. 2009. 'Nicholas Gcaleka and the Search for Hintsa's Skull', *Journal of Southern African Studies* 35: 211–21.

Mockaitis, T.R. 1990. *British Counterinsurgency, 1919–60*. London: Macmillan.

Molina, M. 2002. 'More Notes on the Verreaux Brothers', *Pula: Botswana Journal of African Studies* 16(1): 30–35.

Monaghan, D. 1991. 'The Body-Snatchers', *The Bulletin*, 12 November, pp. 30–38.

Moorehead, A. 1971. *The White Nile*. London: Hamish Hamilton.

Morgan, P.D. 1999. 'Encounters between British and "Indigenous" Peoples, c.1500–c.1800', in M. Daunton and R. Halpern (eds), *Empire and Others:*

British Encounters with Indigenous Peoples, 1600–1850. Philadelphia: University of Philadelphia Press, pp. 42–78.

Morris, A.G. 1996. 'Trophy Skulls, Museums and the San', in P. Scott (ed.), *Miscast: Negotiating the Presence of the Bushmen*. Cape Town: University of Cape Town Press, pp. 67–79.

Morton, S.G. 1839. *Crania Americana: Or, a Comparative View of the Skulls of Various Aboriginal Nations of North and South America*. Philadelphia: J. Dobson.

Mostert, N. 1992. *Frontiers: The Epic of South Africa's Creation and the Tragedy of the Xhosa People*. London: Jonathan Cape.

Murphey, R. 1999. *Ottoman Warfare 1500–1700*. London: Routledge.

Murphy, R.F. 1957. 'Intergroup Hostility and Social Cohesion', *American Anthropologist* 59(6): 1018–35.

Namias, J. 1993. *White Captives: Gender and Ethnicity on the American Frontier*. Durham, NC: University of North Carolina Press.

Nash, D. 1989. 'Tourism as a Form of Imperialism', in V.L. Smith (ed.), *Hosts and Guests: The Anthropology of Tourism*. Philadelphia: University of Pennsylvania Press, pp. 37–52.

Neff, J.R. 2005. *Honoring the Civil War Dead: Commemoration and the Problem of Reconciliation*. Lawrence: University Press of Kansas.

Neff, S.C. 2005. *War and the Law of Nations: A General History*. Cambridge: Cambridge University Press.

Nester, W.R. 2000. *'Haughty Conquerors': Amherst and the Great Indian Uprising of 1763*. Westport: Praeger.

Newsinger, J. 1994. 'The Military Memoir in British Imperial Culture: The Case of Malaya', *Race and Class* 35(3): 47–62.

Nossaman, S.W. 1922. 'Pioneering at Bonaparte and Near Pella', *Annals of Iowa* 13: 444–45.

Nott, J.C. 1866. 'The Negro Race', *The Popular Magazine of Anthropology* 1(3): 102–118.

Nudelman, F. 2004. *John Brown's Body: Slavery, Violence and the Culture of War*. Chapel Hill and London: University of North Carolina Press.

Nunn, H.M. 2005. *Staging Anatomies: Dissection and Spectacle in Early Stuart Tragedy*. Aldershot: Ashgate.

Obeyesekere, G. 2005. *Cannibal Talk: The Man-Eating Myth and Human Sacrifice in the South Seas*. Berkeley: University of California Press.

Office of Australian War Graves. 2010. Personal communication, 6 July.

Oliva, M. 2002. 'Forensic Efforts Fail to Shed Light on Mystery of Skull', *Stars and Stripes (Pacific Edition)*, 31 July. Retrieved 5 September 2005 from http://www.stripes.com/article.asp?section=104&article=9239&archive=true

———. 2003. 'WWII "Souvenir" Turned Over to Okinawa Officials', *Stars and Stripes (Pacific Edition)*, 17 June. Retrieved 5 September 2005 from http://www.stripes.com/article.asp?section=104&article=15460&archive=true

Ollier, E. 1894. *Cassell's History of the War between France and Germany, 1870–1871. Vol. 1*. London, Paris and New York: Cassell, Petter and Galpin.

O'Neal, J. 2002. 'Bluesoterica Research Forum'. Retrieved 5 September 2005 from http://bluesoterica.com/jimoneal/p3.html

Pannell, S. 1992. 'Travelling to Other Worlds: Narratives of Headhunting, Appropriation and the Other in the "Eastern Archipelago"', *Oceania* 62(3): 162–78.

Park, K. 1994. 'The Criminal and the Saintly Body: Autopsy and Dissection in Renaissance Italy', *Renaissance Quarterly* 47: 1–33.

Parsons, N. and A.K. Segobye. 2002. 'Missing Persons and Stolen Bodies: The Repatriation of "El Negro" to Botswana', in C. Fforde, J. Hubert and P. Turnbull (eds), *The Dead and Their Possessions: Repatriation in Principle, Policy, and Practice*. London: Routledge, pp. 245–55.

Patterson, D. 2007. Personal communication, 9 March.

Pearce, S. 1995. *On Collecting: An Investigation into Collecting in the European Tradition*. London and New York: Routledge.

Peckham, H.H. 1947. *Pontiac and the Indian Uprising*. Princeton: Princeton University Press.

Peers, L. 2009. 'On the Treatment of Dead Enemies: Indigenous Human Remains in Britain in the Early Twenty-First Century', in H. Lambert and M. McDonald (eds), *Social Bodies*. New York and Oxford: Berghahn Books, pp. 77–99.

Peires, J. 1989. *The Dead Will Arise: Nongqawuse and the Great Xhosa Cattle-Killing of 1856–7*. Johannesburg and Capetown: Jonathan Ball.

Pember, P.Y. 2002. *A Southern Woman's Story*. Introd. G.C. Rabie. Columbia, SC: University of South Carolina Press.

Pennick, J.L. 1981. *The Great Western Land Pirate: John A. Murrell in Legend and History*. Columbia and London: University of Missouri Press.

Perkins, K. 1988. *A Fortunate Soldier*. London: Brassey's.

Petrović-Šteger, M. 2009. 'Anatomizing Conflict – Accommodating Human Remains', in H. Lambert and M. McDonald (eds), *Social Bodies*. New York and Oxford: Berghahn Books, pp. 47–76.

Pfeifer, M.J. 2004. *Rough Justice: Lynching and American Society, 1874–1947*. Urbana and Chicago: University of Illinois Press.

Poole, S. 2000. *The Politics of Regicide in England, 1760–1850: Troublesome Subjects*. Manchester: Manchester University Press.

Potter, H. 1993. *Hanging in Judgement: Religion and the Death Penalty in England from the Bloody Code to Abolition*. London: SCM Press.

Pramling, N. 2009. 'The Role of Metaphor in Darwin and the Implications of Teaching Evolution', *Science Education* 93(3): 535–47.

Preston, P. 1994. *Franco: A Biography*. London: Harper-Collins.

Prestwich, M. 1988. *Edward I*. London: Methuen.

Price, J.M. 1919. *On the Path of Adventure*. London and New York: John Lane.

Proctor, N.W. 2002. *Bathed in Blood: Hunting and Mastery in the Old South*. Charlottesville: University of Virginia Press.

Proctor, T.M. 2003. *Female Intelligence: Women and Espionage in the First World War*. New York: New York University Press.

Propp, V. 1958. *Morphology of the Folktale*. Ed. and introd. S. Pirkova-Jakobson; trans. L. Scott. Bloomington: Indiana University Research Center in Anthropology, Folklore and Linguistics.

Queensland State Coroner's Office. 1999. 'Coroner's Decision and Notification that the Holding of an Inquest is Unnecessary'. File COR 223/99, 30 July 1999.
Quiggin, A.H. 1942. *Haddon the Headhunter: A Short Sketch of the Life of A.C. Haddon*. Cambridge: Cambridge University Press.
Rable, G.C. 1991. *Civil Wars: Women and the Crisis of Southern Nationalism*. Urbana: University of Illinois Press.
Rasimus, E. 2006. *Palace Cobra: A Fighter Pilot in the Vietnam Air War*. New York: Saint Martin's Press.
Rast, F.D. 2000. *Ghosts in the Wire*. Boca Raton, FL: Universal Publishers.
Ravino, J. and J. Carty. 2003. *Flame Dragons of the Korean War*. Paducah, KY: Turner Publishing.
Rede, L.T. 1831. *York Castle in the Nineteenth Century*. London: John Bennett.
Remini, R.V. 2001. *Andrew Jackson and His Indian Wars*. New York: Viking.
Renshaw, L. 2010. 'The Scientific and Affective Identification of Republican Civilian Victims from the Spanish Civil War', in K. Krmpotich, J. Fontein and J. Harries (eds), *The Substance of Bones: The Emotive Materiality and Affective Presence of Human Remains*. Special Issue, *Journal of Material Culture* 15(4), pp. 449–64.
Richardson, R. 1987. *Death, Dissection and the Destitute*. London and New York: Routledge.
Richter, D.K. 1983. 'War and Culture: The Iroquois Experience', *The William and Mary Quarterly* 40: 528–59.
_____. 2001. *Facing East from Indian Country: A Native History of Early America*. Cambridge: Cambridge University Press.
Riding In, J. 1992a. 'Six Pawnee Crania: Historical and Contemporary Issues Associated with the Massacre and Decapitation of Pawnee Indians in 1869', *American Indian Culture and Research Journal* 16(2): 101–19.
_____. 1992b. 'Without Ethics and Morality: A Historical Overview of Imperial Archaeology and American Indians', *Arizona State Law Journal* 24: 11–34.
Rinne, F. 1901. *Zwischen Filipinos und Amerikanern Auf Luzon*. Hanover: Gebrüder Jänecke.
Ritchie, E.C, B. Schneider, J. Bradley and R.D. Forsten. 2008. 'Resilience and Military Psychology', in B.J. Lukey and V. Tepe (eds), *Biobehavioural Resilience to Stress*. Boca Raton: Taylor and Francis, pp. 25–42.
Ritvo, H. 1987. *The Animal Estate: The English and Other Creatures in the Victorian Age*. Cambridge, MA: Harvard University Press.
Robins, R. 1996. 'Paradox and Paradigms: The Changing Role of Museums in Aboriginal Cultural Heritage Management', *Ngulaig* 16: 1–30.
Robley, H.G. 1896. *Moko, or Maori Tattooing*. London: Chapman and Hall.
Roque, R. 2010. *Headhunting and Colonialism: Anthropology and the Circulation of Human Skulls in the Portuguese Empire, 1870–1930*. Houndmills: Palgrave Macmillan.
Rosen, R.N. 1994. *Confederate Charleston: An Illustrated History of the City and the People During the Civil War*. Columbia, SC: University of South Carolina Press.

Ross, B.D. 1986. *Iwo Jima: Legacy of Valor*. New York: Vintage Books.
Roughead, W. 1921. *Burke and Hare*. Edinburgh: Hodge.
_____. 1941. *The Murderer's Companion*. New York: Readers Club Press.
Royal College of Surgeons of Edinburgh. 2007. 'French Officer's Skin from the Battle of Breda, 1793'. Retrieved 1 February 2011 from http://www.anatomyacts. co.uk/exhibition/object.asp?objectnum=52&search=breda&pageNum=1
Rubenstein, S.L. 2004. 'Shuar Migrants and Shrunken Heads Face to Face in a New York Museum', *Anthropology Today* 20(3): 15–18.
_____. 2007. 'Circulation, Accumulation, and the Power of Shuar Shrunken Heads', *Cultural Anthropology* 22(3): 357–99.
Rushdy, A. 2000. 'Exquisite Corpse', *Transition* 9(3): 70–77.
Sallah, M. and M. Weiss. 2006. *Tiger Force: A True Story of Men and War*. New York, Boston: Little, Brown.
Sappol, M. 2002. *A Traffic of Dead Bodies: Anatomy and Embodied Social Identity in Nineteenth-Century America*. Princeton and Oxford: Princeton University Press.
_____. 2004. '"Morbid Curiosity": The Decline and Fall of the Popular Anatomical Museum', *Common-place* 4(2). Retrieved 1 June 2010 from http://www.common-place.org/vol-04/no-02/sappol/
Saunders, N.J. 2000. 'Bodies of Metal, Shells of Memory: "Trench Art", and the Great War Re-cycled', *Journal of Material Culture* 5(1): 43–67.
_____. 2003. *Trench Art: Materialities and Memories of War*. Oxford: Berg.
Sauro, C.W. 2006. *The Twins Platoon: An Epic Story of Young Marines at War in Vietnam*. Saint Paul, MN: Zenith Press.
Savitt, T.L. 1982. 'The Use of Blacks in Medical Experimentation and Demonstration in the Old South', *Journal of Southern History* 48: 331–48.
Schank, R.C. and R.P. Abelson. 1977. *Scripts, Plans, Goals and Understanding: An Inquiry into Human Knowledge Structures*. New York: Erlbaum.
Scheck, R. 2005. '"They Are Just Savages": German Massacres of Black Soldiers from the French Army in 1940', *The Journal of Modern History* 77(2): 325–44.
_____. 2006. *Hitler's African Victims: The German Army Massacres of Black French Soldiers in 1940*. Cambridge: Cambridge University Press.
Scheper-Hughes, N. and L. Wacquant. 2002. *Commodifying Bodies*. London: Sage.
Schneider, D.M. 1968. *American Kinship: A Cultural Account*. Englewood Cliffs, NJ: Prentice-Hall.
Schultz, D.P. 1992. *Over the Earth I Come: The Great Sioux Uprising of 1862*. New York: Saint Martin's Press.
Schweinfurth, G. 1874. *The Heart of Africa: Three Years' Travels and Adventures in the Unexplored Regions of Central Africa, from 1868 to 1871. Vol. 2*. Trans. E.E. Frewer. Introd. W. Reade. New York: Harper and Brothers.
Scurr, J. 1982. *The Malayan Campaign 1948–60*. London: Osprey.
Secher, R. 1986. *A French Genocide: The Vendée*. Trans. G. Holoch. Notre Dame, Indiana: University of Notre Dame Press.
Sewell, W.H. 1992. 'A Theory of Structure: Duality, Agency, and Transformation', *The American Journal of Sociology* 98(1): 1–29.

———. 2005. *Logics of History: Social Theory and Social Transformation*. Chicago: University of Chicago Press.
Sharpley, R. and P.R. Stone (eds). 2009. *The Darker Side of Travel: The Theory and Practice of Dark Tourism*. Bristol: Channel View Publications.
Shaw, R.G. 1999. *Blue-Eyed Child of Fortune: The Civil War Letters of Robert Gould Shaw*. Athens and London: University of Georgia Press.
Shillington, K. 1985. *The Colonisation of the Southern Tswana 1870–1900*. Braamfontein: Ravan Press.
Shillony, B.-A. 1981. *Politics and Culture in Wartime Japan*. Oxford: Clarendon Press.
Shoemaker, N. 2001. 'Body Language', in J.M. Lindman and M.L. Tarter (eds), *A Centre of Wonders: The Body in Early America*. Ithaca and London: Cornell University Press, pp. 211–22.
Shultz, S.M. 1992. *Body Snatching: The Robbing of Graves for the Education of Physicians in Early Nineteenth Century America*. Jefferson, NC and London: McFarland.
Siebold, G.L. 2007. 'The Essence of Military Group Cohesion', *Armed Forces and Society* 33(2): 286–95.
Simpson, D. 1994. *Far, Far From Home: The Wartime Letters of Dick and Tally Simpson, Third South Carolina Volunteers*. Ed. G.R. Everson and E.H. Simpson, Jr. New York and Oxford: Oxford University Press.
Simpson, M. 2004. 'Archiving Hate: Lynching Postcards at the Limit of Social Circulation', *English Studies in Canada* 30(1): 17–38.
Simpson, M.G. 2001. *Making Representations: Museums in the Post-colonial Era*. London: Routledge.
Skotnes, P. 1996. 'Introduction', in P. Skotnes (ed.), *Miscast: Negotiating the Presence of the Bushmen*. Cape Town: University of Cape Town Press, pp. 15–23.
Sledge, E.B. 1981. *With the Old Breed: At Peleliu and Okinawa*. New York: Presidio Press.
Sledzik, P.S. and S. Ousley. 1991. 'Analysis of 6 Vietnamese Trophy Skulls', *Journal of Forensic Sciences* 36(2): 520–30.
Slotkin, R. 1973. *Regeneration through Violence: The Mythology of the American Frontier, 1600–1860*. Norman: University of Oklahoma Press.
———. 1979. 'Massacre', *The Berkshire Review* 14: 112–32.
———. 1985. *The Fatal Environment: The Myth of the Frontier in the Age of Industrialization, 1800–1890*. New York: Atheneum.
Smith, D. 2005. *The Gallant Dead: Union and Confederate Generals Killed in the Civil War*. Mechanicsburg, PA: Stackpole Books.
Smith, D.L. 2007. *The Most Dangerous Animal: Human Nature and the Origins of War*. New York: Saint Martin's Press.
Smith, M.M. 2005. *Stono: Documenting and Interpreting a Southern Slave Revolt*. Columbia, SC: University of South Carolina Press.
Sobel, B.M. 1997. *The Fighting Pattons*. With a foreword by Major General George S. Patton (retired). Westport, CT: Praeger.
Spector, R.H. 1984. *Eagle against the Sun: The American War with Japan*. Harmondsworth: Penguin.

Stacey, R.C. 1984. 'The Age of Chivalry', in M.J. Howard, G.J. Andreopoulos and M.R. Shulman (eds), *The Laws of War: Constraints on Warfare in the Western World*. New Haven and London: Yale University Press, pp. 27–39.

Stairs, W.G. and R. MacLaren. 1997. *African Exploits: The Diaries of William Stairs, 1887–1892*. Montreal: McGill-Queen's Press.

Stammers, T. 2008. 'The Bric-a-brac of the Old Regime: Collecting and Cultural History in Post-revolutionary France', *French History* 22(3): 295–315.

Stanley, P. 1997. *Tarakan: An Australian Tragedy*. Sydney: Allen and Unwin.

Stannard, D.E. 1992. *American Holocaust: The Conquest of the New World*. Oxford: Oxford University Press.

Starkey, A. 1998. *European and Native American Warfare, 1675–1815*. Norman: University of Oklahoma Press.

Steel, D. 1999. 'Trade Goods and Jivaro Warfare: The Shuar, 1850–1957, and the Achuar, 1940-1978', *Ethnohistory* 46(4): 745–76.

Stepan, N.L. 1993. 'Race and Gender: The Role of Analogy in Science', in S. Harding (ed.), *The 'Racial Economy' of Science: Toward a Democratic Future*. Bloomington: Indiana University Press, pp. 359–76.

Stern, M.B. 1971. *Heads and Headlines: The Phrenological Fowlers*. Norman: University of Oklahoma Press.

Stewart, M. 1997. 'The Puzzle of Roma Persistence: Group Identity without a Nation', in T. Acton and G. Mundy (eds), *Romani Culture and Gypsy Identity*. Hatfield: University of Hertfordshire Press, pp. 82–96.

Stewart, S. 1993. *On Longing: Narratives of the Miniature, the Gigantic, the Souvenir, the Collection*. Durham, NC: Duke University Press.

Stockwell, P. 1999. 'The Inflexibility of Invariance', *Language and Literature* 8(2): 125–42.

Stowell, E.C. and H.F. Munro. 1916. *International Cases: Arbitrations and Incidents Illustrative of International Law as Practised by Independent States. Vol. 2: War and Neutrality*. Boston: Houghton Mifflin.

Street, H. 2004. *Martial Races: The Military, Race and Masculinity in British Imperial Culture*. Manchester: Manchester University Press.

Strickland, M. 1996. *War and Chivalry: The Conduct and Perception of War in England and Normandy, 1066–1217*. Cambridge: Cambridge University Press.

Strong, R.H. 1961. *A Yankee Private's Civil War*. Ed. A. Halsey. Chicago: Henry Regnery.

Stuart, K. 1999. *Defiled Trades and Social Outcasts: Honor and Ritual Pollution in Early Modern Germany*. Cambridge: Cambridge University Press.

Stubbs, T. 1978. *The Reminiscences of Thomas Stubbs, Including Men I Have Known*. Ed. W.A. Maxwell and R.T. McGough. Cape Town: A.A. Balkema.

Sugden, J. 1985. *Tecumseh's Last Stand*. Norman and London: University of Oklahoma Press.

———. 1997. *Tecumseh: A Life*. New York: Henry Holt.

Suppe, F.C. 1989. 'The Cultural Significance of Decapitation in High Medieval Wales and the Marches', *Bulletin of the Board of Celtic Studies* 36: 146–60.

Sutherland, D.M.G. 2003. *The French Revolution and Empire: The Quest for a Civic Order*. Oxford: Blackwell.

Svenvold, M. 2003. *Elmer McCurdy: The Misadventures in Life and Death of an American Outlaw*. New York: Basic Books.
Sweeney, E.R. 1998. *Mangas Coloradas: Chief of the Chiricahua Apaches*. Norman: University of Oklahoma Press.
Sweet, J.W. 2003. *Bodies Politic: Negotiating Race in the American North, 1730–1830*. Baltimore and London: The Johns Hopkins University Press.
Tanaka, Y. 1996. *Hidden Horrors: Japanese War Crimes in World War II*. Oxford and Boulder, CO: Westview Press.
Tanner, A. 1979. *Bringing Home Animals: Religious Ideology and Mode of Production of the Mistassini Cree Hunters*. New York: Saint Martin Press.
Taussig, M. 1987. *Shamanism, Colonialism and the Wild Man: A Study in Terror and Healing*. Chicago and London: University of Chicago Press.
Taylor, J.V., L. Roh and A.D. Goldman. 1984. 'Metropolitan Forensic Anthropology Team (MFAT) Case Studies in Identification 2: Identification of a Vietnamese Trophy Skull', *Journal of Forensic Sciences* 29(4): 1253–59.
The Times. 1931. 'Dead Burmese Rebels Decapitated: Inquiry into Police Action'. 16 June, p. 13.
Thiébaux, M. 1967. 'The Medieval Chase', *Speculum* 42(2): 260–74.
Thomas, D.H. 2000. *Skull Wars: Kennewick Man, Archaeology, and the Battle for Native American Identity*. New York: Basic Books.
Thompson, E.N. 1971. *Modoc War: Its Military History and Topography*. With a preface by K.A. Murray. Sacramento: Argus Books.
Thompson, L. 1988. *Dirty Wars: Elite Forces vs. the Guerrillas*. Newton Abbot: David and Charles.
Thompson, L.S. 1946. 'Tanned Human Skin', *Bulletin of the Medical Library Association* 34(2): 93–102.
Thorne, C. 1978. *Allies of a Kind: The United States, Britain and the War against Japan, 1941–1945*. London: Hamish Hamilton.
Thornton, B. 2003. *Searching for Joaquin: Myth, Murieta and History in California*. San Francisco: Encounter Books.
Thurtell, J. 1998a. '"Confederate Mandible" Speaks of History: A Plundered Rebel Soldier's Jawbone May Rest With Buddies', *Detroit Free Press*, 3 March, B3.
———. 1998b. 'Confederate Soldier's Jawbone to Head Home: Civil War Relic to Get Southern Burial', *Detroit Free Press*, 22 April, B6.
———. 1998c. 'Unknown Confederate Soldier Laid to Rest: His Jawbone Was Found in Museum Artifacts', *Detroit Free Press*, 11 May, B5.
Tomblin, B.B. 2003. *G.I. Nightingales: The Army Nurse Corps in World War Two*. Lexington: University Press of Kentucky.
Townsend, W.H. 1955. *Lincoln and the Bluegrass: Slavery and Civil War in Kentucky*. Lexington: University Press of Kentucky.
Tregaskis, R. 2000 [1943]. *Guadalcanal Diary*. New York: Random House.
Trigger, B.G. 1990. *The Huron: Farmers of the North*. Chicago: Holt, Rinehart and Winston.
Trussoni, D. 2006. *Falling through the Earth: A Memoir*. New York: Henry Holt.
———. 2007. Personal communication, 3 March.

Turnbull, P. 1991. *Science, National Identity and Aboriginal Body Snatching in Nineteenth Century Australia.* Working Papers in Australian Studies, No. 65. Institute of Commonwealth Studies, University of London.
———. 1997. 'The Body and Soul Snatchers', *Eureka Street* 7(7): 34–38.
———. 1999. 'Enlightenment Anthropology and the Ancestral Remains of Australian Aboriginal People', in A. Calder, J. Lamb and B. Orr (eds), *Voyages and Beaches: Pacific Encounters, 1769–1840.* Honolulu: University of Hawai'i Press, pp. 202–25.
———. 2001. '"Rare Work among the Professors": The Capture of Indigenous Skulls within Phrenological Knowledge in Early Colonial Australia', in B. Creed and J. Hoorn (eds), *Body Trade: Captivity, Cannibalism and Colonialism in the Pacific.* New York: Routledge, pp. 3–23.
———. 2007. 'Scientific Theft of Remains in Colonial Australia', *Australian Indigenous Law Review* 11(1): 92–102.
Turner, V. 1967. *The Forest of Symbols: Aspects of Ndembu Ritual.* Ithaca and London: Cornell University Press.
Turner, W. (ed.). 1868. *The Anatomical Memoirs of the Late John Goodsir.* Edinburgh: Adam and Charles Black.
United States Congress. 1863. *Report of the Joint Committee on the Conduct of the War.* Washington: Government Printing Office.
United States Department of the Army. 1994. *Field Manual 22-51: Leaders' Manual for Combat Stress Control.* Washington, DC: Department of the Army.
———. 2003. *U.S. Army Combat Stress Control Handbook.* Guilford, CT: The Lyons Press.
Urry, J. 1989. 'Headhunters and Body-Snatchers', *Anthropology Today* 5(5): 11–13.
Urwin, G.J.W. (ed.). 2004. *Black Flag over Dixie: Racial Atrocities and Reprisals in the Civil War.* Carbondale: Southern Illinois University Press.
Valentin, S. and E. Miller. 2004. 'Analysis of Four Contemporary Trophy Skulls in Los Angeles County, California'. Presentation, American Association of Physical Anthropologists 73rd Annual Meeting, Tampa, Florida, April 14–17.
Van Baal, J. 1966. *Dema: Description and Analysis of Marind-Anim Culture (South New Guinea).* The Hague: Martinus Nijhoff.
Vanden Bossche, C.R. 1991. *Carlyle and the Search for Authority.* Columbus: Ohio State University Press.
van Gennep, A. 1909. *Les Rites de Passage.* Paris: Emile Nourry.
van Wyhe, J. 2004. *Phrenology and the Origins of Victorian Scientific Naturalism.* Aldershot: Ashgate.
Verdery, K. 1999. *The Political Lives of Dead Bodies: Reburial and Postsocialist Change.* New York: Columbia University Press.
Victoria State Coroner's Office. 2002. 'Record of Investigation into Death'. Case no.1427/02, 15 November.
Vijn, C. 1988 [1880]. *Cetshwayo's Dutchman: Being the Private Journal of a White Trader in Zululand during the British Invasion.* London: Greenhill.
Visser, M. 1982. 'Worship Your Enemy: Aspects of the Cult of Heroes in Ancient Greece', *The Harvard Theological Review* 75(4): 403–28.

Viveiros de Castro, E. 1998. 'Cosmological Deixis and Amerindian Perspectivism', *Journal of the Royal Anthropological Institute* 4(3): 469–88.
Wakefield, W.E. 1997. *Playing to Win: Sports and the American Military, 1898–1945*. New York: SUNY Press.
Ward, H.M. 2003. *The War for Independence and the Transformation of American Society*. London: Routledge.
Washington, E.K. 1860. *Echoes of Europe: Or, Word Pictures of Travel*. Philadelphia: James Challen and Son.
Watts, J. 1992. *God, Harlem U.S.A.: The Father Divine Story*. Berkeley and Los Angeles: University of California Press.
Wavell, B. 2007. Personal communications, 20–23 March.
Way, P. 1999. 'The Cutting Edge of Culture: British Soldiers Encounter Native Americans in the French and Indian War', in M. Daunton and R. Halpern (eds), *Empire and Others: British Encounters with Indigenous Peoples, 1600–1850*. Philadelphia: University of Philadelphia Press, pp. 123–48.
Weaver, J.R.H. (ed.). 1937. *Dictionary of National Biography, 1922–30*. Oxford: Oxford University Press.
Webb, D. 2000. *Pilgrimage in Medieval England*. London: Hambledon and London.
Webster, W. 2005. *Englishness and Empire 1939–65*. Oxford: Oxford University Press.
Wecker, D. 1993a. 'What Would You Do With a Skull?', *The Cincinnati Post*, 13 April, B1.
⎯⎯⎯⎯. 1993b. 'Skull Goes Home 50 Years Later', *The Cincinnati Post*, 22 April, C1.
Weiner, A. 2006. 'Something to Die For, a Lot to Kill For: The Soviet System and the Barbarisation of Warfare, 1939–45', in G. Kassimeris (ed.), *The Barbarization of Warfare*. New York: New York University Press, pp. 101–25.
Weingartner, J.J. 1992. 'Trophies of War: U.S. Troops and the Mutilation of Japanese War Dead, 1941–1945', *Pacific Historical Review* 61(1): 53–67.
⎯⎯⎯⎯. 1996. 'War against Subhumans: Comparisons between the German War against the Soviet Union and the American War against Japan, 1941–1945', *The Historian* 58(3): 555–73.
Weinstein, S. 2000. 'Tanka: Lost Thoughts of War Return'. Retrieved 5 September 2005 from http://haiku.cc.ehime-u.ac.jp/~shiki/shiki-tanka.archive/html/0012/0004.html
Wells, M. 2010. Personal communication, 10 March.
West, J.B. 1999. 'J.B. West: From Interview in April 1999'. Retrieved 1 June 2010 from http://www.lighthorseaircav.com/intv-jb-west.html
West, R. 1995. *War and Peace in Vietnam*. London: Sinclair-Stevenson.
Westerhof, D. 2007. 'Deconstructing Identities on the Scaffold: The Execution of Hugh Despenser the Younger, 1326', *Journal of Medieval History* 33: 87–106.
Wheeler, R. 2000. *The Complexion of Race: Categories of Difference in Eighteenth-Century British Culture*. Philadelphia: University of Pennsylvania Press.
White, G. 2005. Personal communication, 25 September.
White, R. 1991. *The Middle Ground: Indians, Empires and Republics in the Great Lakes Region, 1650–1815*. Cambridge: Cambridge: University Press.

Whittaker, D.K. 1993. 'Oral Health', in T. Molleson, M. Cox, A.H. Waldron and D.K. Whittaker, *The Spitalfields Project Volume 2, The Anthropology of the Middling Sort*. Council for British Archaeology Research Report 86, pp. 49–65.

Wickman, P.W. 2006. *Osceola's Legacy*. Tuscaloosa: University of Alabama Press.

Wiley, B.I. 1943. *The Life of Johnny Reb: The Common Soldier of the Confederacy*. Indianapolis and New York: Bobbs-Merrill.

———. 1952. *The Life of Billy Yank: The Common Soldier of the Union*. Baton Rouge and London: Louisiana State University Press.

Willerslev, R. 2004. 'Not Animal, Not *Not*-Animal: Hunting, Imitation and Empathetic Knowledge among the Siberian Yukaghirs', *Journal of the Royal Anthropological Institute* (n.s.) 10(3): 629–52.

Willey, P. and P. Leach. 2003. 'The Skull on the Lawn: Trophies, Taphonomy, and Forensic Anthropology', in D.W. Steadman (ed.), *Hard Evidence: Case Studies in Forensic Anthropology*. Upper Saddle River, NJ: Prentice Hall, pp. 176–88.

Williams, R.H. 1908. *With the Border Ruffians: Memories of the Far West, 1852–1868*. London: John Murray.

Wills, D. and E. Steuter. 2009. 'The Soldier as Hunter: Pursuit, Prey and Display in the War on Terror', *Journal of War and Culture Studies* 2(2): 195–210.

Winans, E.V. 1994. 'The Head of the King: Museums and the Path to Resistance', *Comparative Studies in Society and History* 36(2): 221–41.

Winslow, D. 1998. 'Misplaced Loyalties: The Role of Military Culture in the Breakdown of Discipline in Peace Operations', *Canadian Review of Anthropology and Sociology* 35(3): 345–67.

Woodcock, G. 1969. *The British in the Far East*. London: Weidenfeld and Nicolson.

Woodthorpe, Lt. R.G. 1978 [1873]. *The Lushai Expedition, 1871–72*. Aizawl: Tribal Research Institute.

Woolman, D.S. 1968. *Rebels in the Rif: Abd el Krim and the Rif Rebellion*. Stanford, CA: Stanford University Press.

Wright, R. 1864. *The Life of Major-General James Wolfe*. London: Chapman and Hall.

Wyatt-Brown, B. 1986. *Honor and Violence in the Old South*. Oxford: Oxford University Press.

———. 2001. *The Shaping of Southern Culture*. Chapel Hill and London: University of North Carolina Press.

Yamamoto, D. 2000. *The Boundaries of the Human in Medieval English Literature*. Oxford: Oxford University Press.

Young, A. 1995. *The Harmony of Illusions: Inventing Post-traumatic Stress Disorder*. Princeton, NJ: Princeton University Press.

Young, H. 2005. 'The Black Body as Souvenir in American Lynching', *Theatre Journal* 57(4): 639–57.

Zipperer, C. 2010. Personal communications, 10–11 March.

Zou, D.V. 2005. 'Raiding the Dreaded Past: Representation of Headhunting and Human Sacrifice in North-East India', *Contributions to Indian Sociology* (n.s.) 39(1): 75–105.

Zubrinich, K.M. 1999. 'Asmat Cosmology and the Practice of Cannibalism', in L.R. Goldman (ed.), *The Anthropology of Cannibalism*. Westport, CT: Bergin and Garvey, pp. 123–42.

Index

adoptive filiation, 171
Amaya, 60–61
American Civil War, 9, 93–108, 141, 143, 180, 184n2, 191
American Indians, 40, 41–42, 43, 45, 84, 86–89, 132, 170, 194
    Apache, 88–89
    Dakota, 89–90
    Iroquois, 46
    Pawnee, 91
    representations of, 46, 55
    romanticization of, 92
    Shawnee, 44
    Woodland, 39, 41
    See also Sand Creek Massacre
American War of Independence, 43, 46, 118
Amungme. *See* Wollaston Expedition
Anatomy Act of 1832, 35, 50, 57
Anglo-Zulu War, 70, 76, 78
animals
    enemies viewed as, 71, 117, 142, 151n1, 157, 159, 162–63, 166, 181, 188–89, 192–93, 196
    See also mascots
anthropology, 8, 14, 79, 187
    criminal, 54
    forensic, 3, 182
    physical, 79, 92
Ashanti, 72, 76
Asmat, 6, 66

Bambata, (Zulu leader), 71–72. *See also* Zulus

Bateman, Mary, 44-5
Battle of Bull Run, 95-97, 99, 100, 101, 108
Battle of Guadalcanal, 129, 131–34, 135, 138, 139n1, 139nn4–6, 141, 142, 148–49, 153n6
Beethoven, Ludvig, van, 52
behaviour
    social, 142–43, 180, 187, 190, 195–96
    transgressive, 190, 192, 194
beheading, 22, 33, 78
Black Hawk (Sauk leader), 83–85
blooding (hunting ritual), 70, 132
bodily remains, 33, 90, 115, 170, 174, 181, 187
body parts, 118, 122, 125, 136–38
    and dissection, 110–11
    and legitimacy, 111, 114
    trade in, 40, 62–65, 87, 135–36, 139n5
    and Vietnam War, 165, 174
    See also ears; fingers; genitalia; gifts; heads; noses; scalps; skin; skulls
body snatching, 34, 49–51, 59, 84–85, 103–4, 110
bounties, 40–41, 64, 89, 161
Bourdieu, P., 12–14
Brown, John, 110
Burbank, Edwin, 96–97
burial, 24, 36, 52, 71, 84, 93, 107, 125, 135, 144, 150
Burke, Edmund, 32, 38, 40, 47
Burke, William, 34–36, 45
Burton, Richard, 76

cabinets of curiosities, 34, 81n5, 113. *See also* collections, private
cannibalism
    accusations of, 125
    as desecration, 31–32
    prohibition of, 17, 18, 142. *See also* behaviour, transgressive
    Western view of, 25–26, 63, 65
    in World War II, 151n1
Cape Frontier Wars, 69–70, 71, 73, 78–80
Carlyle, Thomas, 31–32, 35, 38, 47
Carrington, Lieutenant Frederick, 71–72, 76
Charles l (Charles the Martyr), 33, 63, 109, 163n1
Christians, 21, 25, 36, 101, 119
classifications, 14
    hierarchical, 38, 55–56, 76, 94–95
    racial, 191
    of skulls, 8, 74
    social, 6, 7, 191
Cohen, Myer, 86, 89
collections, private, 37, 53, 81n5, 86, 185n2. *See also* museums
colonialism, 47, 74, 77–78, 81, 118, 123, 155–56, 191
    and collecting, 73, 125-26
    colonial troops, 118–22, 124
    and hunting, 8, 70
Combe, George, 51, 53
commoditization, 34, 37, 51, 72, 110, 138
Congo, 63, 70, 162
Corday, Charlotte, 54
counter-insurgency, 9, 155–63
Crania Americana, 55, 86–87
criminals, 22, 36–37, 50, 54, 56, 91, 103, 110–11, 114
Cromwell, Oliver, 33, 76
Crowther, William, 57
cultural schemas, 12, 13
    of kinship, 174
    and memory, 150
    misapplications of, 14, 17–19
    See also hunting and masculinity, metaphors
Cuvier, Georges, 53, 56

Darwin, Charles, 11
de Montfort, Simon, 23, 81n7
Descartes, Rene, 53, 56

de Vos, Charles, 56–57
Dimmick, Captain Justin, 87, 97
disinterment, 51, 52, 81n3, 84, 103, 113
dissection, 33–4, 36–37, 57, 91, 104, 110, 111
    of body of Mata Hari, 54
Dollard, John, 112

ears, 24, 27, 69, 102, 106n6, 117, 119–24, 127n1, 136, 143, 165–67
Edward l, 23–24
Edward ll, 23–24
European Enlightenment, 27, 42, 55, 94, 105
execution, 23, 28, 33–36, 89, 109, 111, 158
    and dismemberment, 37, 53, 91

familiarizing predation, 170–71, 174
family
    conflict, 146, 149, 181–83
    honour of, 104
    as recipient of trophies, 6, 100, 101, 143, 145, 151n2, 167, 179, 180, 192
    symbolism of, 13, 174, 182
Fausto, C., 170–71, 174, 184
fieldstripping, 136–37. *See also* looting
fingers, 33, 34, 109, 117, 125, 156, 157, 165–6
France, 117–22, 125–26
Franco. *See* Spanish Foreign Legion
French Revolution, 31, 35, 47
Fussell, P., 130, 131, 133, 136–39, 141, 145, 150, 151n2, 153n6

Gall, Franz, 51, 56, 64
game animals, 39–41, 70, 75, 87, 89, 108, 132, 162, 191. *See also* hunting
Gates, Robert, 165
Gein, Edward, 152n4, 189
gender
    of dead bodies, 104
    and hunting, 143, 181
Geneva Conventions, 1, 25, 138
genitalia, 23, 69, 86
Giddens, A., 12–14
gifts, 9, 40, 54, 85–86, 143–44, 151n2, 167, 179, 180
Gill-King, H., 3, 146
Gleason, George, 89–90

Gordon, Major-General Charles George, 73
Goumiers, 118–19, 125, 127n1
grave robbing. *See* body snatching, disinterment
Grenfell, Field Marshall Lord Alfred, 75, 80
Guadacanal. *See* World War, 2
Gurkhas, 117–19, 121

Haddon, A.C., 59
hair
    as evidence of racial differences, 42–43, 55, 161, 191
    as jewellery, 89–90, 103
    as souvenir, 33, 52, 72, 85, 100, 101, 102
    as wig, 29, 31–32, 47, 161
hands, 23, 33, 40, 120, 156, 157, 158, 161, 162
Haydn, Joseph, 51–52
headhunting, 1, 5, 6, 7, 8–9, 26, 62, 65, 74, 82, 119, 132, 157, 183
    and collecting, 67, 79
    expeditions, 5, 60, 66, 108, 195
heads
    animal, 70, 72, 87, 181, 188
    boiling, 64, 65, 88, 133, 141–43
    display of, 33, 35, 110, 122, 147
    and phrenology, 51, 53, 54, 111, 121
    trade in, 62–63, 64, 87, 89, 139n5
    See also scalps
Hintsa (Xhosa leader), 69, 81n4, 86. *See also* Xhosa
Hirt, August, 125–27
holy relics, 24, 33, 53–54, 83, 92, 114
hospitals, 33, 45, 60, 110
Hrdlicka, Ales, 131
Hugh Despenser the Younger, 23
humanness, 6, 26, 130, 137, 166, 193, 195
hunting
    and identity, 114, 131, 132
    imagery, 131, 156, 166, 189, 193
    and masculinity, 9, 70, 80, 108, 131, 142, 143, 149, 181, 196
    and warfare, 137, 141, 142, 151n1, 152n4, 157, 160–62, 171, 181, 183, 191, 192, 195, 196

identity
    disguised, 41–42
    group, 10, 123, 167, 173, 179
    male, 184, 196
    and race, 27, 42, 72, 104–105
Ilongot, 70
Induna (Zulu leader), 75, 76, 80. *See also* Zulus
initiation ceremonies, 49, 50, 172–73, 179. *See also* rites of passage
interstitial practices, 17–19, 189, 192, 194

Jacobins, 32, 38
Jews, 126
Jivaro. *See* Shuar
Johnson, M., 11–14, 16
justice, 33, 36, 46, 64, 112, 114, 158
    and medical science, 47
    retributive, 38, 45, 137
    rough, 115

Kenya Emergency, 160–3
kills, scorekeeping of, 161, 168
kinship, 7, 12, 72, 143, 170–4, 183
Kintpuash (Captain Jack). *See* Modoc War
Kitchener, Lieutenant-General Sir Frederick Walter, 73, 76, 79
Korean War, 185n2
Krebs, Ludwig, 60
!Kung, 127n1

Lakoff, G., 7, 11–14, 16
Lanney, William, 57
Larson, Thomas, 135, 184
Lindbergh, Charles, 133, 137, 139, 145
Lombroso, Cesare, 54
looting, 1, 2, 69, 72, 89, 99–100, 107, 136
Lumumba, Patrice, 162
Lushai, 67
lynching, 9, 107–12, 114–15, 137

McCarthy, Sir Charles, 72, 76
McCurdy, Elmer, 113
Mahdi (religious leader), 73, 76, 79
Malaya Emergency, 156–59
Maori, 56–7, 59, 62–3
mascots, 167
    animals as, 169, 170
    children as, 170

skulls as, 168–71, 179
Mau Mau rebellion. *See* Kenya Emergency
medical personnel, 33, 34, 42, 45, 49, 50, 54, 57, 67, 78, 86, 103, 104–5, 110–11, 125–26, 149
medical study, 47, 59, 62, 79, 91, 114
medieval Europe, 21, 75, 83
Melanesia, 5, 7, 139n5
mementos. *See* souvenirs
memory, 94, 130, 150–51, 184, 192
metaphors, 117, 142, 156, 159, 162, 171, 192, 194
Mkwawa (Wahehe leader), 77, 81n6
Modoc War, 91
mokomokai (Maori preserved heads), 62
Monbutto (Mangbetu), 63-65
Moroccans, 117, 124
Morton, Samuel, 86-7, 97
Mpande (Zulu King), 81n3. *See also* Zulus
Murder Act of 1752, 36
murderers, treatment of, 33–38, 45, 53–54
museology, 3, 4, 93, 112, 114
museums, 34, 56, 81, 93–94, 111, 159

Nagas, 67
native auxiliaries. *See* colonial troops
naturalists, 60, 79, 157
Nazi medical research, 9, 125. *See also* Jews
Neal, Claude, 108-9
New Guinea, 5, 6, 66, 132, 137, 144, 146–47, 151n1, 179
non-combatants, 25, 144
noses, 24, 123

Osceola (Seminole leader), 85, 89. *See also* Seminoles

Papas, Julius, 129–30, 139n1, 179, 181
Parrott, George, 112
Pearl Harbor, 137, 143, 148
Pember, Phoebe, 100–101
Philippine-American War, 185n2
photographs,
    lynching, 108–10
    as souvenirs, 100, 136, 139n4, 158
    trophy, 158–59, 190, 194
phrenology, 51, 53–6, 64, 80, 83–86, 111

possessions, 22, 53, 77, 108, 130, 168–9
    burden of, 145, 151. *See also* repatriation of skulls and other remains
predation, familiarizing, 170–71
prey. *See* game animals
Prince, Tom (von Prince), 77
prisoners of war, 25, 28, 41, 100, 125, 137, 151n1
pseudo-gangs, 160–61

quartering, 23, 110

race, concepts of, 42, 55, 56, 57, 126, 131, 191
    in the American Civil War, 94, 104–5
rape, 108, 109, 124
rebels, 24, 28, 157, 158, 160
remorse, 143, 149
repatriation of skulls and other remains, 81n4, 81n6, 93, 146, 148, 183–84
revenge, 45, 65, 76, 95, 137
rites of passage, 6, 49–50, 132, 174, 195
Roosevelt, Franklin D., 131, 144, 152n3
Royal College of Surgeons, 57, 73, 79

Sand Creek massacre, 47, 90
Sandile (Xhosa leader), 71, 72, 81n2. *See also* Xhosa
Sappol, M., 50, 103–4, 113
savagery
    and civilization, 32, 35, 119, 121, 155
    and the southern states of USA, 98, 103
    Western imagery of, 1, 8, 26-9, 41, 45, 63, 81n8
scalping, 1, 26, 29, 39–45, 136, 138, 187. *See also* scalps
scalps, 2, 26, 29, 32, 40, 41, 88–90, 106n6. *See also* scalping
schemas. *See* cultural schemas
Schubert, Franz, 52, 83
Schweinfurth Expedition, 63–65, 128
Schweinfurth, Georg. *See* Schweinfurth Expedition
science,
    developments in nineteenth century, 9, 80–81, 103
    and expeditions, 59, 60, 65
    and law, 38, 47

racial, 9, 25, 94, 104, 105, 115, 125–27
Seminoles, 85, 87. *See also* Seminole Wars
Seminole Wars, 85–86, 88
Senegalese, 117, 121–22, 124–5
Seven Years' War, 41–2
Shuar (Jivaro), 5–6, 62–3, 182, 195
Simpson, Joe, 112
skin, 43–47
    colour, 42, 55, 104, 125, 191. *See also* race
    of criminals, 34, 36, 37–8, 57, 112
    slippers from, 35
skulls
    inscriptions on, 96, 129, 177, 179, 181
    naming of, 168, 178, 183
    uses (abuses) of, 95, 96, 139, 152n2, 178–79, 184–85n2
    See also phrenology
slavery, 98, 99, 105, 110
Sledge, E.B., 2, 136, 138, 140n7
Smith, Richard, 37–8, 49–50
social class, 31–32, 35–38, 40, 47, 70, 103–4, 113, 115, 132, 152n2
souvenirs, 94, 122. *See also* trophies; body parts
Spanish Civil War, 124
Spanish Foreign Legion, 123–24
Stokell, George, 57
symbolic boundaries, 10, 14, 17, 19, 27, 42, 121, 141, 146, 191, 194
    moral, 72, 83, 137

taboos, 14–18, 128. *See also* metaphors
Tecumseh (Shawnee leader), 44–46
teeth, 69, 86, 101, 109, 133, 136
    as amulet, 172
    gold, 2, 106n5, 133, 167

necklaces from, 98, 135, 144
'Waterloo', 37
Topinard, Paul, 54
torture, 2, 32, 39, 73, 108, 156
Townley Scott, Winfield, 132–33
trench art, 100, 137
trophy-taking
    expeditions, 5–6, 10, 195
    of Japanese body parts, 130, 133–34, 136–37, 139n2, 139n5, 140n6, 141, 143–48, 152n6, 182, 184n1, 190–1
    military, 3–4, 7, 9, 188
    and race, 5, 190–94
tsantsa (shrunken heads), 62–63

US Sailor with the Japanese Skull, The. *See* Townley Scott, Winfield

Verreaux brothers, 60
veterans, 2, 3, 44, 141–42, 147–49, 179–80, 183–84
    organizations of, 93, 94, 127n2
Vietnam War, 165–75, 177, 179–83
Vijn, Cornelius, 78

war magic, 7, 72
Weingartner, J.J., 125, 130–131, 133, 135–38, 144, 151n2, 151n3
Wollaston, A.F.R. *See* Wollaston Expedition
Wollaston Expedition, 66
World War I, 117, 120–21, 127n2, 128, 140n8, 170,
World War II, 2, 3, 124–25, 129, 130, 133, 142, 148–52
    Pacific War, 3, 129–39, 178–79. *See also* Battle of Guadalcanal

Xhosa, 69–70, 72–74, 78, 80

Zulus, 71, 72, 75–76, 78, 81n3